MITHRAS TO MORMON

MITHRAS
— TO —
MORMON

A RELIGIOUS HISTORY
OF LONDON

PHILIPPA BERNARD

SHEPHEARD-WALWYN (PUBLISHERS) LTD

First published in 2018 by
Shepheard-Walwyn (Publishers) Ltd
107 Parkway House, Sheen Lane,
London SW14 8LS
www.shepheard-walwyn.co.uk

British Library Cataloguing in Publication Data
A catalogue record of this book
is available from the British Library

ISBN: 978-0-85683-524-7

Typeset by Alacrity, Chesterfield, Sandford, Somerset
Printed and bound through
s|s|media limited, Rickmansworth, Hertfordshire

Contents

Acknowledgements

MANY PEOPLE HAVE HELPED ME in the writing of this book. I am especially grateful to all the libraries, museums and archives who have opened up their holdings for me, particularly the London Library, the British Library, the Library of Lambeth Palace, the Wiener Library, the Museum of London, the Jewish Museum, the National Archive, the archives of *History Today*, the *Jewish Chronicle*, *The Times* and the Jewish Historical Society of England.

Representatives of many faiths have shared their experiences and beliefs with me, showing me their buildings, their books and their possessions.

I owe a great debt of gratitude to family, friends and colleagues for their help and encouragement, among them Professor Jack Spence, Sue Spence, Rachel Spence, Jonathan Footerman, Rabbi Dr Thomas and Mrs Renée Salamon, Valery and Chris Rees, Angus O'Neill, Claire Connick, Jill and David Leuw, Julie and David Loebell, Elizabeth Medler, Vivienne Trenner and many more, never forgetting my editor Anthony Werner, who took on the project in the beginning and saw it through to the end.

List of Illustrations

Foreword

ON THE 7TH MAY 1913, a group of suffragettes planted a bomb under the throne at St Paul's Cathedral. I was installed on that same throne as the 133rd Bishop of London – the first woman to hold the office. The *Daily Gazette* of that evening in 1913 reported,

> An enormous bomb, with a clock and battery attachment, was discovered under the Bishop's throne at the St Paul's Cathedral today...The dean conducted even-song near the Bishop's throne last evening, but neither he nor the verger then noticed the package or heard the ticking.

The relationship between London and religion has meant that the Church has never had the luxury of remaining unchanged. Wars, revolutions, famine and disease have shaped the human spirit and the way religion is represented in the capital. Through monarchs, popes, bishops and reformers, and through movements of lay people, the Spirit of God has disrupted and subverted, and caused the Church to reimagine its shape and ministry.

We know of our religious past by what others have left behind. Early maps of the city show skylines of spire and towers. Today the skyline is shaped by religion, the fire, war and now the desire to build communities in the sky – the highest being the Shard at 306 metres. But London's churches, chapels and religious buildings survive and can be seen across the city. Although a number have been lost, many are on sites of early buildings such as St Paul's Cathedral, where there has been for more than 1,400 years a Cathedral dedicated to St Paul on London's highest point. Knowing our history helps us to shape our future and to leave behind a legacy which will build resilient and coherent communities.

London today is a multi-racial and multi-faith city. Whilst some people no longer define themselves by a specific religion, many remain spiritual and maybe we are no different from those who have occupied the city throughout history. Immigration brought Christianity, Judaism – and more recently the *Windrush* brought charismatic and Pentecostal Christianity. Often it has been political, religious or economic persecution which have brought others such as Hindus and Muslims.

The post-World War Two period gave rise to more collaborative attitudes to other faiths. However, there have been more recent threats to a growing climate of tolerance, including the terrorist attacks on London, and the Brexit Referendum. Ultimately, society and the Church should have the confidence to ensure freedom of religion and belief, working in partnership. Freedom of expression, and religious and community resilience and coherence, are all vital in today's society. Otherwise we risk becoming economically, socially and culturally insecure, and afraid of 'the other'.

The Rt Revd and Rt Hon
Dame Sarah Mullally, DBE
Bishop of London

Introduction

LONDON HAS CHANGED GREATLY in the last one hundred years as the city has become the home of many different races and religions. All have found sanctuary here, some happily, some less so. But as the different tribes and communities have intermingled and expressed their beliefs, they have left their mark. But this book is not about theology or prayer, it is about people. For religion, or the lack of it, plays an important part in city life. From the earliest times, when London was a small agricultural community, overrun by the Romans and other invading peoples, she has worshipped as she wished, subject sometimes to royal command, sometimes to the will of the ordinary Londoners.

Early in her history, after the Celts vanished and the Romans left, London had only one religion, Christianity – Roman Catholicism. Within the Province of Canterbury, under the all-embracing control of the Pope, London built churches and elected bishops. But in the reign of William of Normandy another form of worship, older than Christianity, arrived in England: Judaism. The Jews of London established themselves in a small area of the city, where the community was viewed with suspicion and in 1290 Edward I banished the Jews from his kingdom.

For another 250 years London again had only one religion. Wars came and went, so did monarchs, until the civilised world's certainty about Roman Catholicism, the Pope and his dominions, was challenged by a German priest who refused to accept what few had so far dared to doubt, and the word Reformation came into English church language. In England a mighty prince saw at last a way of obtaining a long-desired divorce from his Catholic Queen and marrying his lover. He declared himself Supreme Head of the Church in England.

The sixteenth century saw the country torn apart by religious turmoil, Catholic against Protestant, family against family, until under Queen Elizabeth a fragile peace was restored, and Londoners were again permitted to worship – with discretion – as they wished.

The Stuarts believed firmly in the Divine Right of Kings – England's revolution was a political war more than a religious one. In London Charles I's execution reminded men of the frailty of even the highest of rulers, and Parliamentary rule and the Puritan ethic destroyed much of beauty and meaning in religious life. But not all men wished to worship as King or Parliament ordained. Nonconformity offered an alternative, and the Quakers, together with Baptists, Levellers and Shakers, Ranters and Sabbatarians, Muggletonians and many more, formed Dissenting groups, each with its own creed and method of worship. Under Cromwell the Jews returned and the following century John Wesley introduced Methodism.

Any religion alternative to the Anglican Protestant creed forfeited the possibility of obtaining a university degree, being called to the Bar or becoming a Member of Parliament. Finally under Queen Victoria emancipation allowed this to happen and London began to acquire the multicultural image so familiar today.

Victoria, Empress of India, ushered in a British Empire where men's eyes were opened to new religions from the dominions overseas and by the time of her death, London was a seething mass of people of many colours and creeds who worshipped God in a very different way from the comfortable English parish church style. The East End of London welcomed the Huguenots, then the Jews and by today people from Bangladesh and other Asian nations.

It is the story of these Londoners and the effect religion had upon their lives that concern this book. For religion is not only about creed and worship but about those who believe or don't, who pray or don't. Interfaith collaboration is, or should be, a feature of English life today. London has always been at the heart of the exercise of religion, the core of its history and the scene of its development. As long as she remains the capital of Great Britain it is always likely to be so.

CHAPTER I

Celts and Romans

I N ACCORDANCE WITH the principles of true history, I have simply sought to commit to writing what I have collected from common report for the instruction of posterity.'[1] So the Venerable Bede introduced his *Ecclesiastical History of the English People*, one of the earliest comprehensive accounts of religion in this country. 'Common report' since Bede's account, completed in 731 CE, has extended from historiography, archaeology and palaeography to modern methods of investigation such as carbon-dating, satellite imagery and thermography. However, Bede's account of the religion practised by his contemporaries and their ancestors, wide-ranging though it certainly was, has been far outdistanced by the huge number of different theologies and forms of worship known today in England and particularly in London.

London on Thames

This site on the north bank of the river Thames was an excellent place to build a town. Even before Julius Caesar made his first investigative visit there in 55BCE, with another invasion two years later, there must have been some small settlement there, though there is little evidence of it. In the Finsbury area, where the river Fleet – now below ground – ran towards the Thames, excavations have found traces of early civilisation. The Thames was shallower then and fordable; Rufus, Lord Noel-Buxton, tried to prove it could still be done when he attempted to walk across it at Westminster in 1952, and failed. It was a tidal river, much higher today than it was two thousand years ago, allowing boats to bring cargoes some way up river into England from the sea. The countryside around was fertile, so the inhabitants of a small settlement had access to corn and good grassland for grazing cattle. Julius Caesar mentions finding a fortified place – an *oppidum* – when he came to England.

Professor R.E.M. Wheeler, former Curator of the London Museum, was firmly of the opinion that London did not exist before the coming of the Romans. He conceded that the gravel subsoil on which London stands, was eminently suitable for a town and for a bridge across the Thames. The river, he said 'was the most constantly used of all the highways into Britain for purposes of foreign trade and immigration. But it was used as a highway rather than a mere gateway.'[2] As any incursion by Rome into neighbouring provinces was usually preceded by traders opening up lines of communication to supply the armies, it is likely that London was already a thriving port before the Emperor Claudius's arrival in 43CE.

There was probably no bridge across the river until Claudius came, when the first bridge was built, approximately where the present London Bridge now stands. On the far side lay Southwark, with two large islands in between. London was a valuable trading post, and seemed set to flourish as an important feature of Imperial Rome, until the appalling treatment of the Royal leaders of the Iceni tribe in East Anglia by the Roman governor of the province led to a violent uprising by its queen, Boudica, and her onslaught on London.

Rome's capital of Britannia, Camulodunum (Colchester), was the first to be destroyed by Boudica and her warriors, before they swept into London, which the Roman Commander-in-Chief, Suetonius, refused to defend, knowing that the impending hordes outnumbered his army. The attackers annihilated everything they could lay hands on, slaughtering men, women and children and laying waste to the town by fire. Every subsequent analysis of London's early settlement has found inches-thick layers of red ash where the early town had been consumed in the flames. Boudica and her army then went on to Verulamium (St Albans) which received the same treatment; they were finally defeated by the Roman army in the Midlands, the Queen poisoned by her own hand.

London Rebuilt

After the destruction of London, the Roman skill in building bridges, fortifications and walls, was soon put to good use, and quite quickly the small ruined agricultural settlement became a thriving town, with roads fanning out across England to the north, west and south. Even today the road names are familiar in most parts of the countryside: Watling Street to the northwest, Fosse Way to the west, Stane Street to the south. Roman technology and architectural expertise were employed to make London, rebuilt on a grid system, a centre of international trade. Situated as it was on several hills – Cornhill, Lud Hill and Tower Hill, not unlike the conquerors' home city itself – it enjoyed a commanding position above the surrounding countryside, though it never became an important military post. The rebuilding of the city after Boudica's destruction included a surrounding stone wall, two miles long, twenty feet high and about seven feet thick, enclosing an area of some 330 acres, the largest walled town in Britain, with something close to 30,000 inhabitants. Included in the reconstruction were defences, quays and workshops. New gates in the wall included those now located at Bishopsgate, Newgate and Aldgate.

By the year 100 London was the biggest town in Britain. Her population now amounted to some 45,000, including the slaves on whom a stable society depended. It was a multi-racial city; many of the wealthier citizens wore the toga and spoke Latin. When Christianity finally came to be Britain's central religion, Latin was adopted as the principal ceremonial language used by the Church, as it remained for many centuries to come. The Romans brought with them a much greater degree of literacy than the Celts had enjoyed. Indeed literacy was compulsory in the Roman army. Their homes were elaborately constructed houses, with hypocausts, gardens, mosaics and marble decoration, though little is known of how ordinary Londoners lived. London was supervised by the procurator sent from Rome, Julius Classicianus. It was a part of his duties to oversee London's financial affairs, taxation, expenditure and fiscal irregularities. When he died in 65 his wife Julia Platanus erected a great marble tomb in his honour – 'to the spirits of the departed'. Parts of it were later discovered in the stone of the Roman wall. It has now been reconstructed and is in the British Museum.

As the town grew, all the usual necessities of a thriving population, food distribution areas, workshops and granaries were constructed, together with a forum and a large basilica. This was not a church but an Imperial centre of civic government, combining administrative offices, law courts and a large market. Leadenhall market stands today on almost the same site, dating back to the early fourteenth century. London was a vital supplier of goods to the Roman army: stores, slaves and billets with a large arsenal. There was a barracks at Cripplegate, of playing-card shape, enclosing an area some 250 yards square, with a rampart, probably built in the early second century. Not far away, to the north of the present St Paul's, was a large cemetery. An amphitheatre is known to have existed on the site of the present Guildhall (where it has recently been reconstructed). In 125 widespread fire destroyed a large part of the city, but most was rebuilt, this time with a network of dykes and waterways together with a sewerage system, using some of the now underground rivers running into the Thames, the Fleet, the Westbourne, the Walbrook, Tyburn Brook and Stamford Brook.

The Religions of Roman London

There is little evidence of the old Celtic religion which played a part in the lives of early Londoners. Indeed, there are few traces of the Celts at all in the London area. A magnificent horned helmet was dredged up from the Thames at Waterloo, exhibited in the British Museum exhibition of 2015, *Celts – Art and Identity*, together with a contemporary bronze shield from Battersea. Laurence Gomme, in *The Making of London*, says, 'Celtic Londoners were tribesmen, with tribal civilisation, tribal economy and tribal methods of life.'[3] Celtic worship depended mainly on local gods and goddesses, deities of the woods and streams, with no one god in command. Small shrines and temples could be erected anywhere but very little trace is found in southern England. Peter Ackroyd, in his great book on London, ties in the Celtic religion with some of London's place names,[4] particularly those connected with water such as Holywell and Spring Street. Before the Romans took the town there must have been some attention paid to the local deities. Boudica herself was a Celt, though her short presence in London has left no evidence of worship or prayer. A few of the Celtic traditions such as the ceremony of the horned king or the Green Man, do have a resonance today, in the names of inns or districts such as Hornsey. There is a 'Green Man' carving in Westminster Abbey in the Pew Chapel, though it cannot have been of Celtic origin. The Celtic leaders, the Druids, were considered by the Romans as a possible threat through their influence over their fellow worshippers, and they were suppressed, though they have left little sign that they were ever much in evidence in London. One legend of these early times was that of Bran, the Celtic leader, who ordered that when he died his head should be cut off and buried where the White Tower of the Tower of London stands today. The name 'bran' means raven, supposedly the origin of the ravens at the Tower.

The Roman invaders usually allowed their subject states to worship in their own way, so London became a strange mixture of the old religion of the Britons, worship of the Roman gods and the interpolation of the Eastern religions that Rome admitted to her pantheon. For religion was a vital integral part of Roman life, at home in Rome itself and wherever the invaders had settled; the Emperor himself was worshipped as a God, though in Britain this did not happen until he was dead. The worship of the Emperor Claudius as a personal god was at first confined to Colchester, originally the principal city of Roman Britain, then a *provincia* of Rome. When London was rebuilt after Boudica's demolition, the cult of emperor worship was transferred there. An inscribed stone dedicated to Caesar Augustus (the Emperor's title) was found in the city, though it may have been moved during reconstruction. It bears the name of the Province of London.

The Lares and Penates, the gods of the hearth and home, found a place in the homes of Londoners, with small shrines where domestic worship could form a part of daily life, and where the gods could be petitioned for private favours in return for gifts of statuettes, jewellery or other personal possessions. Features of the Londoners' original Celtic worship were absorbed into Roman rites, including fertility cult figures and harvest festivals. The superstitions of the earlier religions melded with Roman and eastern mystic beliefs. The temples of the town, which was now big enough to be a city, could not accommodate large numbers. They were not really designed for congregations, but were guarded and managed by priests. Those erected to the eastern deities were welcomed by Londoners. These mystic deities seemed to offer a more satisfying religious need than the Roman classical gods. A belief in an afterlife, secret forms of worship to which not all were admitted and an influence on the daily life of the adherent, attracted many to offer prayers to gods and goddesses from Egypt, Persia and Asia Minor.

Religions from the East

Ralph Merrifield, sometimes referred to as 'the father of London archaeology', was the first to plot a detailed plan of Roman London. He speaks in his book *Roman London* of 'arid paganism'[5] with no future after death or comfort for the bereaved, opening the way for the warmer, more joyous features of the eastern religions imported by Rome. The temples dedicated to these more exotic deities were of simple stone construction, usually with a stone seat around the inside and a raised sanctuary in an apse at the end, as the one to Mithras showed, when excavated in Walbrook in 1957 and now reconstructed at the Bloomberg Space. There was a long narrow nave with low benches facing inwards with an outer room screened off, probably for the use of the priests. Temples to the god Mithras were usually underground, originally in a cave, and the London site would have been on the banks of the (now underground) Walbrook river. A Mithraeum existed in most garrison towns in Britain. The discovery of the temple in London included a statue of Mithras himself, and an inscription from a Roman soldier commemorating his worship of the god. The original temple dates from the second century but was later rededicated to the Roman god Bacchus.

Associated with the Mithraic cult was the ritual slaying of bulls, with links to the journey of the sun across the sky. The early Christian writer Tertullian's account of the cult describes how

> Deep in a cave, in the very camp of darkness, a crown is presented to the candidate at the point of a sword, as if in the mimicking of martyrdom, and it is placed upon his head. He gives it to the god, saying that he claims Mithras as his crown, and never crowns himself again.[6]

The Mithraic cult attracted officers from the army and wealthy traders as well as those engaged in financial and civic affairs. Only men could participate in Mithraic worship, and were expected to conform to the highest conventions of honourable and courageous behaviour.

Another temple known to have existed in London was dedicated to Cybele, the mother goddess. Her symbol was a lion on which she could cross mountains. Her cult was popular with women, who celebrated her festival in March with baptism in the blood of a bull. Cybele's priests (the Galli) castrated themselves when serving her. A bronze castration clamp was found in the Thames and is now in the Museum of London. Cybele's young lover, Attis, was also castrated. A figure, believed to be of Attis, was found in the foundations of the Bevis Marks synagogue, the first built in London in 1701, after the readmission of the Jews in 1656.

The Egyptian goddess Isis was also known to have been worshipped in a temple in London in the Tooley Street area. She and her consort Serapis, were the gods of creation and bronze statuettes of them were found on the site, with a marble statue of the god Oceanus, connected with the Mithraic cult. The goddess's devotees would scatter perfumed flowers on the roads, and celebrated her festivals with trumpets, while her sacred boat foretold a new and prosperous sailing season, wishing success and safety to all ships and sailors. Another temple dedicated to Diana may have stood at the top of Ludgate Hill, on the site later occupied by St Paul's Cathedral. William Camden gives details of finds excavated at the site as does Wren when rebuilding the Cathedral after the Fire, but no evidence of such a temple can be confirmed.

Judaism

There has been some debate as to whether there were any Jews in England before the Norman Conquest. Although it is accepted that Jews were frequently present as traders, slaves or as soldiers when the Roman armies were deployed, no tangible trace of a Jewish community has been identified. A few coins from Greece and the Levant have been found and pottery from the workshop of Vitalis, a common Jewish name, have appeared from time to time. Many recruits from Greece were known to have fought with the army but there is no reason to suppose there were Jews among them. The historian Shimon Appelbaum discussed the question at some length but came to the conclusion that although it was perfectly possible that there was a Jewish presence in England, as there was in Gaul and other Roman provinces, no definite conclusions can be drawn from this.[7]

Roman Worship

The Roman pantheon was based on the Imperial worship of Jupiter Optimus Maximus, personified by the Emperor, a symbol of Rome itself. His priests and priestesses were chosen annually from the native British tribes. They had to pay for all the trappings and celebrations of their religion. The other gods – Mars, god of war, whom the soldiers worshipped, Mercury, god of trade and commerce, communications and poetry, referred to by R.G. Collingwood as 'a genial and condescending god'[8], Hercules, the god of Rome, half human, half divine, all played a part in the huge number of small cults which grew up around the imperial religion of the conquerors. London, therefore, and much of the rest of Britain, was free to pay homage to any of the gods of Rome, of the East, or of their own home-grown Celtic religion.

In 200 Britain was divided into two: Britannia Inferior, controlled from York and Britannia Superior ruled from London. From then on the city began to decline, though it retained the title Augusta. The river levels fell during the next century, trade declined and the population shrank. By the time the Romans left in 400 it was an almost derelict city.

The Coming of Christianity

It was hardly surprising then that when a new religion arrived in Britain it needed to draw together these multiple strands of worship. What was different about Christianity was that it worshipped only one god, admitting of no other, as its mother religion, Judaism, had done. If it was adopted in England on any scale it would augur the end of both the Roman and the pagan forms of prayer. But London was declining. It was ripe for takeover by the savage barbarian tribes from North Germany and from Scandinavia.

CHAPTER II

Anglo-Saxon London

IN 284 DIOCLETIAN BECAME EMPEROR, sharing the Crown with Maximian. Predatory Saxon pirates from the German lands had been attacking the east and south-east coast (the Saxon shore) of Britain spasmodically for some years. Coming in from Gaul the invaders met defence fortifications stretching from Norfolk round the coast to Dover and westward as far as Porchester Castle at Portsmouth. The commander of *Classis Britannicus*, the British fleet, was the capable, though ruthless Carausius, who was charged with fraudulent activities concerning spoils of war and was arrested. He fled to London and declared himself Emperor. He was murdered by one of his own treasury officials, Allectus, who in turn was defeated by Constantius, made Emperor after the abdication of Diocletian and Maximian. On his deathbed in York Constantius nominated his son, Constantine I as Emperor. Constantine the Great was to bring Christianity to the Roman Empire, with his capital at Byzantium.

England in Danger

By the year 410 Rome herself was in peril. She was being attacked by Gothic hordes, led by Alaric, and summoned her armies from Britain and Gaul to assist in her defence. But Britain, too, was in danger from the Pictish forces massing on her northern border, and sent to Honorius, the Emperor in Rome for help. He sent one legion which dispatched the northern invaders. It then withdrew to Rome but was soon recalled for further assistance when the Picts came back. The third time the request met with a firm refusal. As Wheeler puts it, 'the cities of Britain can have mattered little to Honorius in the year 410.'[1]

Bede's version of events comes from the contemporary English historian Gildas in his *De Excidio et Conquestu Britanniae*, when he relates the appeal – The Groans of the British – to Flavius Aetius, the Consul General, 'To Agitius [Aetius], thrice consul: the groans of the Britons ... The barbarians drive us to the sea, the sea drives us to the barbarians; between these two means of death, we are either killed or drowned.'[2] As a result, Vortigern (king, warrior, brigand according to the different chroniclers) invited mercenaries from the Germanic tribes to help in her defence. In return he ceded Kent to the Saxons. They came to Britain under the command of the brothers Hengist and Horsa. After their victories over the Picts and Scots, they quarrelled with the English King, a battle was fought at Aylesford in Kent and Horsa was killed. The Saxons and Angles, called in to help in Britain's war with the northern tribes, turned on Vortigern and advanced on their masters to take over the green and pleasant land for themselves.

The Saxon Occupation of London

London's derelict state, though the city was never totally deserted, encouraged the Saxons to occupy the city. The wall was disintegrating, the basilica and amphitheatre in ruins. Some rebuilding was attempted using the old stone and rubble from the once splendid Roman city, but there is little evidence for the Saxons' presence. They had neither the desire nor the skill to rebuild the city. In fact the site of the larger part of London moved westward, away from the old 'square mile' area to what is now Trafalgar Square and the Strand, navigable by large ships and named accordingly. There are also traces of Saxon occupation in the Covent Garden area. This new settlement became Lundenwic (London market). Preferring the countryside to urban life the invaders spread to what are now the London suburbs. Agriculture took the place of commerce and trade.

In 448 men from the tribes of Angles and Saxons, together with Jutes and Frisians, in three warships, landed on the east coast. Bede believed they were granted land 'ostensibly to fight on behalf of the country, but their real intention was to conquer it.'[3] The Saxons – East, Middle, South and West – gave their names to the lands of Essex, Middlesex, Sussex and Wessex, the Angles to East Anglia. Their occupation of London, according to such records as exist, did not destroy the city. Some Roman British presence remained, enough for London to become the accepted centre of Christian England when Augustine came in 597 to retrieve a faith which already had some adherents in the country.

Nevertheless, Dark-Age London, as Wheeler calls it, remains a mystery. No burial sites of Saxon times have been found, few artefacts and little in the way of contemporary description. The city of Lundenwic was located further to the west. Bede's *De Temporum Ratione* – The Reckoning of Time – sheds a little light on Anglo-Saxon pagan rites and practices. He describes the names of the months and the festivals associated with them. He mentions sacrifices and worship and it is clear that most of the deities derive from ancient Germanic sources: the gods Woden (Odin of Nordic worship), Thunor (Thor), Tiw and Frig (Freya), still commemorated in our days of the week. Thunor, the god of thunder, leaves his name in a few East Anglian and south east England places, as do other gods whose names are known. But pagan worship was certainly supreme in much of England, once the Romans had left.

In 208CE Tertullian, one of the earliest Christians writing in Latin, had maintained that there were 'places among the Britons unapproached by the Romans, but subdued to Christ'[4]. Long before the arrival of St Augustine in 597, there were other allusions to the existence of Christianity in Britain. The earliest Christians may have been soldiers in the Roman army, accepted into the Church before arriving here. Some were perhaps traders from the Middle East coming to London for commercial reasons.

Christianity comes to London

The traditional view of St Augustine being the first to bring Christianity to Britain in 597 at the suggestion of Pope Gregory, does not stand up to historical examination. There were indications by early chroniclers that an active Christian presence was to be found in this country before Augustine arrived. The Roman Empire under Constantine had adopted the Christian religion by 400, and St Columba had made himself known to Ireland and to the Picts and Scots, establishing his monastery on Iona off the west coast of Scotland. The historian H.P.R. Finberg writes, 'Under his rule Iona kindled a beacon-light of Christian culture which radiated far and wide over the north.'[5]

The first known Bishop of London was Restitutus, who represented the city at the Council of Arles in 314, but nothing is known of his church. There had already been signs that London had a small Christian community. A burial ground existed in the area of Smithfield, and another near Bishopgate. It is not known if they were for Christian burials, but they did not survive in use when London later moved eastwards. Another was found beneath St Martin-in-the-Fields, closer to the Strand site, and the Anglo-Saxon custom of burying the possessions of the dead with their owners was often adopted by early Christians.

The city was now under the sovereignty of King Ethelbert of Kent, the first Christian King in Britain. He had married Bertha, the Christian daughter of the King of the Merovingians who ruled from Paris. A condition of the marriage was that she might maintain her faith, and she brought her own priest, Liudhard, with her. Ethelbert's lands stretched from the Humber in the north, west to St Albans and across most of the south of England.

Pope Gregory I sent Augustine, a Benedictine monk from Rome, on a mission to convert the English to Christianity. The Emperor Constantine was already a Christian and the Edict of Milan in 313 had permitted freedom (of any religion) to those dwelling in the Roman Empire. Augustine landed on the Isle of Thanet in Kent in 597, and met Ethelbert.

> The words and the promises you bring me are fair enough, but because they are new to us and doubtful, I cannot consent to accept them and forsake those beliefs which I and the whole English race have held for so long. But as you have come on a long pilgrimage and are anxious, I perceive, to share with us things which you believe to be true and good we do not wish to do you harm; on the contrary, we will receive you hospitably and will provide what is necessary for your support; nor do we forbid you to win all you can to your faith and religion by your preaching.[6]

With these words Ethelbert greeted the missionary and was one of the first to be converted by him. London, as the chief town of Ethelbert's kingdom, was the obvious choice for Augustine to build his church, but Pope Gregory preferred Canterbury, still within Ethelbert's realm, and there the church of St Martin's, Canterbury, was the first church in the English-speaking world and the oldest in continuous use. It had been Queen Bertha's private chapel. Augustine became the first Archbishop of Canterbury and England was obliged to accept the Christianity of Rome, its language, the Pope as its leader, and the conventions of political and theological control. Gregory wrote to the princes in Gaul to tell them that 'It has come to our ears that the English race earnestly desires to be converted to the Christian faith.'[7]

The First London Churches

In 604 Ethelbert, still determined to consider London as his capital city, built the first St Paul's Cathedral at the top of Ludgate Hill ostensibly on the site of the Roman Temple of Diana, though this has never been confirmed and no traces of a temple have been discovered. Probably built of wood, the building was destroyed by fire (as were the next three cathedrals on the site) and was rebuilt in stone. The first church in London was All Hallows by the Tower, probably the oldest church in the City, a claim made by several others. It was founded by the Abbey of Barking in 675. An arch from the Saxon church can still be seen today. In the crypt beneath is a Roman tessellated pavement, discovered in 1926.

Several other churches were known to have existed in early Saxon London, some around St Paul's itself. To the East was the church of St Augustine and to the West, adjoining the cathedral was St Gregory's, which fell with the Cathedral during the Great Fire and was never rebuilt. There was an early church of St Pancras on Cheapside, and further north, near to where

King Ethelbert's palace was supposed to lie, was a church dedicated to the
martyr St Alban which may have been a royal chapel. Perhaps the most
important church was St Peter's-upon-Cornhill, a thriving church today,
and reputed to have been built by King Lucius – the legendary King of
England, believed by Bede to have been instrumental in bringing Christianity to his kingdom – as an archiepiscopal see for London.

Shortly after Augustine's arrival in England, he was joined by another
monk from Italy, Mellitus, ordained Bishop of London, and clearly an
important member of Augustine's assembly. Writing to him in 601, the Pope
who titles himself 'servant of the servants of God', refers to Mellitus as 'My
most beloved son, Abbot Mellitus,'[8] He tells the Bishop that he is concerned
not to have heard from him as to how the mission is faring, but wishes him
to tell Augustine that he is not to destroy the pagan temples, only their
idols. These temples should be converted to Christian worship, with altars
and relics. The pagans, he feels, will be more ready to be converted if their
shrines are preserved. They should not kill animals for sacrifice but only for
food. 'Thus while some outward rejoicings are preserved, they will be more
easily able to share in inward rejoicing.'[9] He wishes Mellitus well in his
endeavours. The Bishop of London was recognised as a trustworthy priest
by his father in Rome.

Sebert, King of Essex, nephew of Ethelbert, both patrons of Mellitus,
and his uncle, died within a year of each other, leaving London still a pagan
city under the control of Sebert's sons who refused to convert. Mellitus took
refuge in Gaul. After the death of Augustine in 604, the See of Canterbury
passed to Laurence, one of Augustine's original companions on the mission.
He invited Mellitus to return to England, though not to London. He succeeded to the Archbishopric on Laurence's death in 619. Mellitus, Bishop
of London, and third Archbishop of Canterbury, is the first churchman of
whom much is known in the early years of England's adoption of Christianity. He is buried at Canterbury and was later canonised; there is a shrine
to him in Canterbury Cathedral.

The See of Canterbury fell vacant for a number of years. It was finally
awarded to Theodore of Tarsus, one of the great holders of the office. A formidable scholar and a man of exemplary faith, later canonised, Theodore
brought England's Christianity to a new height. He created Erkenwald as
the new Bishop of London, who founded an abbey at Chertsey and another
at Barking. This was in fact the site of two monasteries, for both men and
women. The sister of Erkenwald, St Ethelburga, was abbess of the convent.
Further excavations on the site showed there had been an oratory and workshops making textiles, metal works and glass, and with separate cemeteries
for the nuns and monks. The Abbey was refounded later as a Benedictine
nunnery. Described as the 'Light of London', St Erkenwald is buried in

St Paul's Cathedral, where his shrine was often visited by pilgrims. An alliterative poem written in the fourteenth century details a miracle wrought by the Saint in St Paul's, detailing how a the soul of a dead pagan in his coffin is saved by the intervention of the holy man. The first verses run:

> In London in England, not long since,
> Since Christ suffered on the Cross and established Christendom,
> There was a bishop in that town, blessed and holy,
> Saint Erkenwald as he was called.
> In that town and at that time the greatest church
> Was taken down to rebuild anew.
> For it had been heathen in Hengist's days.
> When the enemy Saxons were there.
> They beat the Britons and brought them to Wales
> And perverted all the people who dwelled in that place.
> And the realm was pagan for many rebellious years.[10]

In spite of being written three hundred years after Erkenwald's time, it seems to encapsulate in a few words the history of Anglo-Saxon London.

The seven kingdoms of England were now in disarray. Theodore himself had tried, with some success, to reconcile the warring kings. His legislation, the Councils of Churchmen he held up and down the country and his personal charisma, all combined to make him revered as one of the great Archbishops of Canterbury. He is buried at St Peter's Church in Canterbury.

CHAPTER III

The Vikings

T HE FIRST THAT THE PEOPLE of London were likely to have known about the new menace that threatened their city, was the reports of Viking raids on the Northern borders of England. The name Viking, meaning in old Norse a man from a *vik*, a creek or bay, has become synonymous with a fierce pirate from Scandinavia. The earliest Vikings had come as traders, bartering their wares for English produce, but now, apparently invincible, they had come to conquer, killing, destroying and demolishing men, buildings and countryside.

The savagery of the invaders extended further than just the slaughter of those who confronted them. In 793 they stormed Lindisfarne, destroying vast numbers of illuminated manuscripts and religious treasures. The great scholar Alcuin, living in France, considered the raids a punishment for the sins of the monastery. 'In that year,' says the *Anglo-Saxon Chronicle*, 'there were exceptional flashes of lightning and dragons were seen flying in the air. A great famine soon followed.'[1] The Jarrow Monastery, Bede's home, was looted as were several other religious houses.

The Vikings come to London

Of the Viking nations, the Danes were the people best organised to expand their kingdom by pirate raids on Britain. They first arrived on the isle of Sheppey in 835 and stepped up the number and ferocity of the raids in the following years, sometimes overwintering in Kent or in East Anglia. The first invasion of London took place in 842, described by the *Chronicle* as 'a great slaughter'. Three hundred and fifty Viking ships sailed up the Thames. The force, having previously raided Northern France, stormed London, burning much of the city. Their warships were vast in length; the one reconstructed for the Viking Exhibition at the British Museum in 2014 was thirty-five metres long.

Wessex passed to the first English king whose life, reign and achievements are fully documented, Alfred. He was the only king of England to have warranted the title of 'the Great', and a silver penny of his reign bears the inscription Alfred *rex anglorum*. London, faced with a Viking invasion, was rescued by Alfred. Fighting for his kingdom he defeated the Viking King Guthrun. Guthrun converted to Christianity and he and Alfred divided the old kingdom of Mercia between them. Alfred fortified London, more or less on the site of the old Roman city, east of the area around the Strand. This area, the old Lundenwic, not helped by several serious fires, became almost desolate as commercial life, civic control and the people of the city, moved eastwards. Alfred seems to have planned it on a grid pattern, rebuilding the old Roman walls and reconstructing the port at Billingsgate, though not all of it was completed by his death. Remembered for his foundation of the British Navy, he also designed new and more efficient warships. He appointed his son-in-law Ethelred as Governor of the city. The Danelaw, as the Danish controlled territories were called, started east of the new London, and the city became almost impregnable. When the Danes attacked again in 896, they were repulsed by the Londoners themselves.

Alfred's last years were spent in recovering the learning and culture lost in the depredations of the religious houses. He learnt Latin to be able to read the old charters and better to understand the church services. The ritual, vestments and prayers were very similar to those used in Catholic churches until very recently, with the use of candles, incense and the Eucharist. His reign, and those of his son Edward and grandson Athelstan, have been referred to as the English Renaissance, the golden age of Anglo-Saxon Art. Alfred saw the Viking invasions as the deserved vengeance of God on the English people, because of their neglect of learning and the written word, and of their Christian heritage. He inaugurated a wide programme of translation of religious works from Latin into English and tried by his own example and that of his successors to encourage his people to devote themselves to doing God's work.

Monasteries were reformed – even Bede had been dismayed by the behaviour of some of those who lived in them – and they were encouraged to become a part of the life of the neighbourhood. Local dignitaries often donated to their upkeep in return for the prayers of those within the walls. By founding new churches and monasteries, employment was given to carpenters, stone masons and builders, to scholars, calligraphers, artists and sculptors. Alfred's son Edward, together with the scholarly Bishop Duncan, carried on his father's work, as did Athelstan, Edward's son, in his turn. By the end of the tenth century England could boast a remarkable renaissance in architecture, art and scholarship, in spite of the enemy continually snapping at the door.

Alfred died in 899. The *Chronicle* called him King over all England. He was succeeded by his son Edward, the first English King of that name, but not the one known today as Edward I. Historians refer to him as Edward the Elder. He claimed London as his principal city and reinforced its defences with fortresses at Hertford, at Witham in Essex and at Buckingham. The Thames was made secure with a new fleet stationed off Sandwich, and London seemed safe from the Danes; while many parts of the country were waging intermittent war against the invaders, London remained calm. The city was able to resume its trading activities, but it was becoming increasingly the chosen centre for landsmen from the countryside who built large houses near the river, convenient for visits for commercial or civic reasons. London now became Lundenburg. It was the great commercial capital of England, though most of the official governmental and royal business was still conducted at Winchester.

The Vikings and Christianity

Alfred's conversion of his enemy Guthrum had marked a turning point in the Viking acceptance of Christianity. To achieve peace and trade with the enemy the Danes were happy to become Christian, take English wives and settle down to a peaceful existence in the new country. Like the Romans, the Vikings were prepared to accommodate the Gods of the people they conquered along with their own. Pagans in their own country, it is likely that they viewed the value of the Christian religious houses they despoiled more for the goods they could plunder than for their religious significance. However, they were perfectly content to adopt Christianity where they found it. Their paganism, like that of the Celts, centred around the gods of the countryside and the forces of nature. Thor the blacksmith, usually depicted with his hammer and his ravens, was the embodiment of strength, defending the dwarfs against the giants. The other gods represented fertility, the sea (of vital importance to the Norsemen), the produce of the land, and fire (the god Loki). The Christian interpretation of the old pagan gods had Woden as a descendant of Noah!

London was now beginning to regain its distinction as the great centre, after Canterbury, of Christianity. New churches were built within the city walls on old Roman temple sites. St Clement Danes is reputed to have been built while London was centred on the old Strand site, under Danish control. St Clement is the patron saint of mariners, which the Viking invaders were. The church, whose foundations date back to the ninth century, was rebuilt by the Normans (it was in bad repair by the time of the Great Fire of London, though not damaged by it, and was rebuilt again by Christopher Wren). Other early London churches, whose foundation goes back to Saxon times or earlier, include St Bride's in Fleet Street, founded by St Bridget from Ireland, which was certainly in use in Viking

London, and St Dunstan's-in-the-West. This was named after the eminent
churchman and scholar who was responsible for the improvement and
enlargement of the Westminster monastery, later to become the Abbey,
before the major rebuilding under the Normans. He became Bishop of
London and later Archbishop of Canterbury.

Apart from the churches, now springing up all over England, London
and its immediate surroundings were also the site of several of the great
monasteries of the south. Barking and Chertsey, founded by Erkenwald,
were the first but the Collegiate Church of St Peter at Westminster, the
future Abbey, was already in existence in St Dunstan's time as a Benedictine
monastery. The historian Alan Vince described it as 'by far the richest and
most influential monastery in the London area.'[2] The original monastery
was constructed on land by the river known as Thorney Island. Legends of
its origin are many, including the tale of the fisherman who rowed a stranger
across the river, to be confronted by a great light and a claim from his pas-
senger to be St Peter on a mission to build a church. The fisherman was
told to tell Bishop Mellitus of his adventure and his abundant catch of
salmon, a legend that has entered into Abbey history, with salmon featured
in the ancient tiles of the Chapter House floor. The discovery of a Roman
sarcophagus, now in the Abbey Museum, has suggested that the monastery
was built on a Roman temple site, but the sarcophagus has been reused and
may originally have been buried elsewhere.

There was an obligation on ministers and monasteries and those who
lived in them, to carry out pastoral duties to their neighbours in the surrounding areas. These were supplemented by the pastor of the local church,
later to fulfil the role of parish priest. The leading role in the administration
of church affairs was played by the bishops. Discussing their work, Huw
Pryce explains, in a series of essays *From the Vikings to the Normans*,

> Bishops played an essential role in ensuring the continuity of the church
> through their ordination of clergy, consecration of churches, confirmation of
> the baptized and other pastoral duties within the dioceses which formed their
> spheres of authority.[3]

Outside London, church leaders, such as abbots and bishops, often came
from noble families or even from royalty. The old tradition of the first son
inheriting the estate, the second having a military career and the third going
into the church, may well stem from social values of this time. Even if their
sons were not churchmen, aristocratic families claimed the gift of appointment to a living until very recent times.

In spite of the early persistence of the Vikings in retaining their pagan
ancestry and traditions, Christianity soon became almost universal. Those
very parish priests who had newly acquired their small churches were

assiduous in converting their Danish conquerors while the court and the aristocracy aimed at influencing the Viking leaders.

Some of the reforms of the church, under Wulfstan, Bishop of London, led to changes in society as well as in the clergy. Monogamous marriage, prohibition of incest, divorce and sex outside marriage formed a part of his insistence on strictly Christian behaviour. Payment to the church for masses for the dead and prayers for the living, was an important source of revenue. Cemeteries became a feature of the church rather than of the ancestral manor and the cult of saints and their relics encouraged pilgrimage.

The First Coronations

Athelstan, Alfred's grandson, was crowned at Kingston in 925, the first coronation of an English king. The ceremony did not have the pomp and splendour of later coronations, but together with that of his grandson, Edgar, it did inaugurate a new ritual for the monarch, when he publicly proclaimed his responsibilities to his people and his church. Edgar was anointed by Dunstan, later canonised, the distinguished prelate who was to play a vital part in the development of London and of the Church in England. Edgar's coronation derived its form from the anointing of King Solomon by Zadok the priest using words from the Old Testament, still used today, now set to music by Handel. 'And Zadok the priest took an horn of oil out of the tabernacle, and anointed Solomon. And they blew the trumpet and all the people said, God save King Solomon ... and rejoiced with great joy.'[4] Edward the Elder, Athelstan's father, had been the first king to have his queen mentioned at his consecration, but Athelstan never married so no mention of a consort was made at the crowning. It was indeed a 'crowning' for he was the first to wear a symbolic crown (rather than a helmet) and to receive the sceptre, sword and ring. The service, very similar to that still used today, asked for blessings of faithfulness from Abraham, meekness from Moses, fortitude from Joshua, humility from David and wisdom from Solomon. This religious ceremony, always performed at Westminster Abbey after the arrival of William of Normandy, was the precursor to the Establishment of the Church in England, even before England adopted a form of Christianity alternative to that of Rome. It emphasizes the semi-sacred nature of kingship and the monarch's covenant with his people, as God's was with the Israelites.

The new king, Athelstan, was a man of piety and religious conformity, with a respect for literature and art, and a determination to reform monastic life. His palace at Winchester enabled church dignitaries from all over the country to participate in affairs of state, and the bonds between Canterbury and the ruling monarch were strengthened. From that time archbishops came only from English dioceses, though they usually visited Rome to be blessed by the Pope before they took office. London's own bishop, Theodred, was a good friend of the King and died a very rich man. In his will he left considerable sums to churches in his diocese, including St Paul's, and decreed that his slaves should have their freedom.

Slavery had existed in England since Roman times. Slaves worked on the land or in the houses of the rich for no wage, but their owners were expected to feed and house them. Even the ceorls, the free peasants of Saxon England, often had one or two slaves. They were usually treated as commodities and were often a part of the stock of trading communities both for foreign buyers and for those at home. Strength for the men and beauty for the women were usually the determining factors in the price set for their purchase. The grand villas which were built for wealthy Romans and their successors usually had slave quarters incorporated into the plans, often of a high quality, though many slaves, especially in the cities, had to make do with filthy hovels.

The Danish Kings of England

In the forty years after Athelstan's death in 939 England had five kings. Most of the Danelaw had been recovered, Dunstan had crowned Edgar at Bath (after the coronation was delayed due to the King's own scandalous behaviour), and was responsible for the creation of Glastonbury Abbey under Benedictine rule. Edgar, however, (known as the Peaceful), was highly praised by the chronicler Florence of Worcester, who called him 'discreet, mild, humble, kind, liberal, merciful, powerful in arms and warlike.'[5] He gave to the Collegiate Church at Westminster considerable lands in London, covering what is now the West End. Dunstan's reformation of the monastic rule in England, with the cooperation of King Edgar, had included a wide programme of church and monastery rebuilding after the depredations of the early Vikings; he also acted as judge in church and lay disputes. His legal and ecclesiastic reforms instituted the system of tithes by which the church benefited considerably.

When the young King Ethelred 'the Unready' succeeded to the throne in 978, after the murder of his brother Edward, the country was much in need of a strong and popular monarch. It did not get one. Although Ethelred was not directly responsible for his brother's death, an atmosphere of suspicion and uncertainty was conducive to a renewal of the Danish raids on England under King Harald 'Bluetooth' who had united the Scandinavian peoples and made Christianity the national religion. The strife between Wessex and Mercia seemed over and England was getting close to becoming a single national unity. But the Vikings were not far away. In London the peaceful times seemed to be over. In earlier years the Viking invaders had established settlements on the north coast of France, and the province of Normandy had spread to include most of the ports across the channel. So when Harald's raiding parties again began threatening the towns in the south and south-west of the country they could rely on help, or certainly safe havens from their Norman cousins.

Ethelred could see only one way of dealing with the Danish invaders; he bought them off, and began the long history of the payment of Danegeld, a land tax, to Harald and his successors. The English King's weakness in military and political affairs led to continued incursions by Harald's son Swein 'Forkbeard', allied to the Norwegian king Olaf Tryggvason. In 981 a large part of London was destroyed by fire, undermining Londoners' confidence not only in their ability to defend the city from invasion, but also in their reliance on a benevolent god who would save them from such threats. In 994 Swein attacked with ninety-four ships. Unable to get the ships further upstream than the bridge, which the English soldiers were defending strongly, the attackers, according to *The Saga of St Olaf*,

> rowed up under the bridge and tied ropes round the supporting posts and rowed their ships downstream as hard as they could. The posts were dragged along the bottom until they were loosened from under the bridge ... there was a great weight of stones and weapons upon it, and the posts beneath were broken, the bridge fell with many of the men into the river; the others fled into the city or into Southwark.[6]

Swein did not succeed in taking London, but he and his Danish troops did inflict considerable damage. He was again paid off with Danegeld, and returned home to his own country.

Ethelred took two other actions to protect England from the Danes, rather than having to face them in combat. In 1001 he married Emma, the daughter of Richard, Duke of Normandy, an alliance which enabled him to keep the Danes in Normandy from invading the southern coast and also had far-reaching effects on future history when Emma's son Edward 'the Confessor' and later her grandson William, became kings of England. Thus strengthened, Ethelred, in 1002, gave the order to massacre all the Danes in his country.

Inevitably Swein returned to avenge his countrymen. It took three separate raiding parties to achieve his goal. By 1013 Swein was accepted as King of England and Ethelred fled to Normandy. On Swein's death in 1014 his son Cnut claimed the English throne. Ethelred's son Edmund 'Ironside' had lawfully succeeded after his father's death, so he and Cnut divided the country between them and when Edmund died Cnut became King of all

England. He was crowned in London at St Paul's and married Ethelred's widow, Emma, to prevent her sons from threatening his throne. Cnut was buried in Winchester which was still regarded as an important religious centre of the country. He was succeeded as King by his two sons, first by Harold 'Harefoot' and then by Harthacnut. But London came into its own as a capital city when its citizens proclaimed the end of Danish rule by choosing in 1042 Edward 'the Confessor', brought up in Normandy but of the Wessex Royal family, to be king of England, the only king ever to be canonised.

The Churches of London

Before the Norman conquest London's position within the hierarchy of the English church had always come second to Canterbury, even though Winchester was closer to the monarchy. London's bishops had counted among their number many who ranked among the greatest of churchmen, some succeeding to Canterbury or to York (that archbishopric only came into being officially in the eighth century under Egbert). St Mellitus, St Erkenwald, Theodred and St Dunstan, were among the early bishops whose learning and leadership created for London a special place in the Christian history of this country.

Another was Wulfstan who held the see between 996 and 1002. He was particularly knowledgeable on Anglo-Saxon law and concerned himself with reforming the English Church. He was dismayed at the quality of ecclesiastical administration, and his statesmanlike qualities were vital when he set himself to redraft the law codes of both Church and State. Much of his writings were in Old English, some of the last contemporary records in the vernacular before Norman-English was introduced under William I. However, Old English was used in the greatly increased output of literary works, among them Aelfric's *Catholic Homilies* and his *Lives of the Saints* – his work is often referred to as the earliest English version of parts of the Bible – and most importantly Wulfstan's own *The Sermon of the Wolf to the English* which called upon the English people to repent and ask God to save their threatened country.

London's biggest church, apart from the Abbey at Westminster, was St Paul's, twice rebuilt after fires had destroyed it, and now becoming the site for important national events, such as the coronation of King Edgar or the burial of eminent churchmen. The Abbey itself, still a monastery, acquired further importance when Edward 'the Confessor' built his own palace close by on Thorney Island beside the Thames. The small Benedictine Monastery there, which Edgar and Dunstan had founded, was rebuilt and enlarged as the West Minster (St Paul's was the East Minster). It was the first Romanesque building in London, using Norman builders. Some traces of it still remain within the Abbey. In the undercroft are some of the early remnants of the original Norman building, including the Pyx chapel, with its great door with six locks, where valuable documents were kept, and the solid Norman pillars next door in what is now the Museum. Edward died a few days after the consecration and was first buried in front of the high altar, later to be translated to a new tomb after his canonisation. The Collegiate Church of St Peter (Westminster Abbey) enjoys the distinction of being a Royal Peculiar; it is under the jurisdiction of the monarch, not a bishop or archbishop, and is governed by a Dean and Chapter. The only other Royal Peculiars in London are some of the Chapels Royal, such as that of St James Palace.

London's own churches were increasing in number. St Mildred's Bread Street, St Martin's-le-Grand, Holy Trinity Aldgate and St Mary's Clerkenwell, were all founded at about this time, though rebuilt later. As in the country outside the capital, parish government – though not by that name – was creating small communities, each with its own church, minister, and council of local landowners. Some were the personal foundations of the lord of the manor, in London as well as outside, leading to a proliferation of small churches, usually of wood, and often with small burial grounds beside them. The old church of St Pancras, however, then in Cheapside, was a stone building.

The End of Anglo-Saxon England

The issue of the rightful successor to the English throne after Edward's death is still unclear. According to some records he had promised the throne to his kinsman, William of Normandy. William had visited England not long before and claimed that he had been promised the succession. Florence of Worcester says that Harold, son of Earl Godwin, 'was elected by the leading men of all England.'[7] William of Malmesbury maintains that Harold 'seized the diadem and extorted from the nobles their consent.'[8] Harold had previously visited Normandy and apparently confirmed to William that the latter's claim was valid, only to refute this when he returned home.

Godwin, Earl of Wessex, was one of the most powerful men in England during the first half of the eleventh century. Godwin's sons, Harold and Tostig, rallied against a threat from Wales on the west country and Harold seemed a likely candidate for the throne. At this point Harald Hardrada, another claimant from Norway, invaded England and occupied York. Harold, now confirmed as King, defeated him at Stamford Bridge, always aware of an impending invasion from Normandy. On 28th September 1066 a Norman army, with Duke William at its head, landed at Pevensey Bay.

CHAPTER IV

Norman London

After Hastings

THE DEFEAT OF THE ENGLISH at Hastings was attributed by the chronicler William of Malmesbury to their dissolute behaviour and lack of respect to God.

> They wear short garments reaching to the mid-knee; they had their hair cropped, their beards shaven, their arms laden with gold bracelets, their skin adorned with punctured designs. They were accustomed to eat till they became surfeited and to drink till they were sick[1]

– a description which could well apply to some of their descendants centuries later. William's invasion of England, with the encouragement of the Pope, Alexander II, has been described by the writer David Bates as 'a triumph of co-ordinated warfare, diplomacy, organisation and propaganda.'[2]

When Harold was killed (not, it is now believed, by an arrow in the eye, but by the sword[3]) there was still, apart from Duke William, one other contender for the English throne. In London, the two Metropolitan bishops – known later as Archbishops – York and Canterbury, had proclaimed Edgar, nephew of Edward 'the Confessor', as the rightful heir. But Edgar was still very young, inexperienced in war and in politics. William of Malmesbury also believed that God was on the Normans' side, and they on his.

> They revived by their arrival the observances of religion, which were everywhere grown lifeless in England. You might see churches rise in every village and monasteries in the towns and cities, built after a style unknown before; you might behold the country flourishing with renovated rites, so that each wealthy man accounted that day lost to him, which he had neglected to signalize by some magnificent action.[3]

William, Duke of Normandy, was crowned King of England in Westminster Abbey on Christmas Day, 1066,

> swearing in the presence of the clergy and the people to protect the holy churches of God and their governors, and to rule the whole nation subject to

him with justice and kingly providence, to make and maintain just laws and
straitly to forbid every sort of rapine and all unrighteous judgments.[4]

One of William's first acts was to confirm the privileges of the City of
London. There were to be no Aldermen or Mayor of London for another
century, but there were two sheriffs and a Court of Hustings, who governed
in the King's name. William's Charter to the City, written in Anglo-Saxon,
read: William the King friendly salutes William the bishop, and Godfrey
the portreve, and all the burgesses within London, both French and English.
And I declare, that I grant you to be all law-worthy, as you were in the days
of King Edward; and I grant that every child shall be his father's heir, after
his father's days; and I will not suffer any person to do you wrong. God
keep you.

The Fortresses of London

The constant fear, well-founded, of unrest throughout the country, was the
motive force for the castle-building programme that William put in train.
Most of these Norman castles were of motte-and-bailey construction of
earth and timber, rebuilt in stone during later years. But in London, too,
the skyline was rapidly changing. Three large fortresses were constructed
in the city. Baynard's Castle was built by Ralph Baynard on the spot where
the river Fleet joined the Thames, inside the old Roman wall next to where
the church of St Andrew-by-the-Wardrobe now stands. It was later
destroyed by King John, when the then owner, Robert Fitzwaller, led the
Barons' revolt against him and is now remembered only by Castle Baynard
Ward in the City. Another large castle was Montfichet Tower at Ludgate
Hill, also a casualty of King John's fight with the barons.

  The third stronghold built in London in the eleventh century still stands
today: the White Tower at the Tower of London. Nikolaus Pevsner, the
architectural historian, describes it as 'the most important work of military
architecture in England'.[5] The work was begun early in William's reign,
under the guidance of Gundulf, Bishop of Rochester, who was a skilled
architect and worked on the improvements to Rochester Cathedral. The
White Tower, white-washed under Henry III, is the oldest part of the Tower
of London, and contains the Chapel of St John, referred to as the oldest
extant church in London, though other churches claim to be of pre-Norman
foundation. The Chapel stands today as a perfect example of Norman
design, bare and simple. It was embellished later with stained glass and
coloured decoration, but the tunnel-vaulted nave and gallery, square piers
with plain capitals and arches are among the most impressive in England.
It was used as William's private chapel.

With new churches going up across the city, and others being rebuilt, London must have appeared during these years as a huge building site. The reconstruction of Westminster Abbey, begun by Edward 'the Confessor', was proceeding. It had been consecrated shortly before Edward's death and both he and his wife Edith were buried there. A part of the Norman abbey can be seen in the pillars that support the undercroft and in the cloisters, and there are still traces of the dormitory, reredorter and refectory used by the monks.

The First Jews in London

For the first time since Christianity came to Britain, superseding paganism and the Roman gods, a new religion appeared, new at least to this country, though many centuries old. This was Judaism, mother religion of Christianity. From Rouen, the capital of the Duchy of Normandy, the first Jews arrived in Britain. The grounds for believing that there were Jews in Britain before the Norman Conquest are slim. There seems to be no tangible proof that the Jews were a presence in England, no trace of a settled community, no synagogues, no indication of Jewish religious practice. Rouen had been home to a Jewish community for some time, and they had undergone considerable oppression even before the First Crusade in 1095 later decimated their numbers. These early Jewish immigrants settled in London and one or two towns outside, such as Stamford and Oxford. In London their first settlements were in Old Jewry (originally Jews Street) and in the Liberties of the Tower. The Liberty – the length of an arrow's flight from the Tower wall – allowed the Jews to live outside the confines of the city. No citizens were permitted to live within the Liberties as a protection for the Tower, but the Jews, as Royal Wards, under the protection of the King, might do so. Otherwise they were not permitted to own land or engage in trade. They did, however, enjoy certain privileges: they were exempt from tolls, had the freedom to travel on the King's highways and could claim sanctuary in any of the royal castles. Their only option for earning an income lay in lending money or becoming physicians. The prohibition on Christians committing usury, the lending of money at interest, led to the Jews fulfilling a vital function at court and for the Church. Few traces of this early Jewish settlement remain.

There are, however, indications of at least two possible synagogues within the medieval Jewry. Two *mikvaot* (ritual baths), usually attached to a synagogue, have been found, one in Milk Street and one in Gresham Street (formerly Catte Street). The rules for the construction and use of a *mikvah* are very precise: it must use running water from a natural spring or river, at least 120 gallons, and the bath must be big enough for the water to cover a man's body. It is often found below ground level with stone steps leading into the bathing pool. The two recently discovered conform to these rules. One has been excavated and reconstructed at the Jewish Museum of London.

There was a medieval Jewish cemetery in the parish of St Giles Without Cripplegate, convenient for the Jews living in London, but as it was the only one in England, not so easy for those elsewhere, as Jews are usually buried within hours of death. These early Jews, coming originally from Normandy, spoke Norman French as their native language. They were useful to the English Church as being knowledgeable about Hebrew, necessary for Christian scholars examining early texts. They were also willing to enter into public debates with English divines one of which, in about 1090, was between Gilbert Crispin, Abbot of Westminster, and a Jew from Mayence. It seems to have been perfectly friendly, with 'no loss of temper ... and no token of surrender or note of triumph at the end.'[6]

Domesday Book

In 1085, while at Gloucester, William set up a synod to discuss with his counsellors, many of them churchmen, the state of England. He created new bishops, among them Maurice who was appointed to London, and 'compiled a register of the rent of every estate throughout England, and made all freemen of every description take the oath of fidelity to him.'[7] The Domesday Book, as the register became known, was the most complete account of land, property, men and even livestock that this country has ever produced until the modern census was inaugurated in 1801. Only London and Winchester were excluded from it, perhaps because the purpose of Domesday was to assess the nation for the levying of taxes and neither city paid tax to the King. There was a space left under Middlesex where London could perhaps have been inserted, and Winchester was still the official capital of England. Domesday, sometimes known as the Winchester Book, is so called as its decisions were deemed 'as final as the Last Judgment'.

William I died in 1087. He had returned to Normandy to put down an uprising and was buried at the Abbey of St Etienne in Caen, his own foundation. He left to his elder son Robert the Duchy of Normandy and to his younger son William Rufus the Kingdom of England. William II inherited a country used to a King who believed strongly in the rule of law and the might of the Church. It was a feudal Kingdom, where each level of society had responsibility to that above and below it, with a prosperous city as its principal seat of government, though London was not officially recognised as the capital of England until the twelfth century. The *Anglo-Saxon Chronicle* described William I as 'a man of great wisdom and power, who surpassed in honour and in strength all those who had gone before him.'[8]

London had undergone yet another disastrous fire just before William Rufus claimed his throne. St Paul's was again almost destroyed. Bishop Maurice was in charge of the rebuilding of the cathedral, using some of the stone of William's Palatine Tower (on the site of Blackfriars) which also fell in the fire. After Bishop Maurice's death the work was continued by his successor Richard de Beaumis under the patronage of Henry I, who ordered all the stone necessary for the work to be carried up the Thames free of tolls. To offset the cost of the new church, he also granted the Bishop the rights to all fish caught in the Thames as well as tithes on any venison taken in Essex. This new St Paul's was to be greater and more magnificent than any that had gone before. It took over two hundred years to build, allowing for several other terrible fires during the construction, eventually becoming a magnificent Gothic cathedral (it had started out in Romanesque style), with the longest nave in Europe, only to fall again in an even greater fire in the seventeenth century. In 1561 lightning struck the spire, the tallest in Britain after Lincoln, and it was never rebuilt.

Living in London

About a hundred years after the second Norman king, William Rufus, came to the throne, William Fitzstephen, the chaplain and biographer of Thomas Becket, wrote *A Description of the Most Noble City of London*. It has none of the pomp and ceremony of charters, law treaties or official documents, but tells the story of the ordinary citizens, their living conditions, pastimes and behaviour and the buildings they saw around them. 'The city is blest,' he says, 'in the wholesomeness of its air, in its reverence for the Christian faith, in the strength of its bulwarks, the nature of its situation, the honour of its citizens and the chastity of its matrons.'[9] All through his description runs the presence of the Church in London. He mentions thirteen greater Conventual churches (attached to a convent or monastery) and one hundred and twenty-six Parochial churches. The large houses of the wealthy were set in beautiful gardens and outside the city were pasture lands and 'a pleasant space of flat meadows, intersected by running waters which turn revolving mill wheels with merry din'.[10]

The three principal churches, the Episcopal See of St Paul's, The Holy Trinity (the Augustine Priory at Aldgate, founded by Queen Matilda in 1130) and St Martin's (St Martin's Le Grand was an early monastic foundation), all had schools – the present St Paul's School was founded by Dean Colet in 1509 – but there were also other licensed schools whose masters, on holy days, assembled their pupils for practice in rhetoric and disputation.

They ran competitions between the schools for the best debates, in verse making and grammar, all of which seemed to be carried out with a good deal of fun, their hearers 'ready to laugh their fill, with wrinkling nose repeat the loud guffaw.'[11]

Food in London was plentiful, with shops and stalls along the river bank, public eating houses, wine and dishes of every kind. A weekly horse fair was held outside one of the city gates, with racing for young and old, livestock for sale and constant sporting contests in wrestling, fencing, jousting, archery and javelin throwing, and ice skating in winter. For the first time in its long history London initiated a life of its own, when kings and church-men took second place to the ordinary citizen.

Reform in the Church

William Rufus stood in the shadow of his great father. His barons distrusted him, not knowing whether his allegiance lay toward his Kingdom in England or his Duchy in Normandy, then ruled by his elder brother Robert. His churchmen disapproved of his feckless ways and degenerate behaviour. He has been described, by the historian Frank Barlow, as 'a coarse man, with little more than a robber's interest in the church.'[12] His father, with the capable help of Archbishop Lanfranc, had gone some way to reforming the Church in England, but his son showed little interest in ecclesiastical affairs unless he needed the intervention of a priest. Anselm, Abbot of Bec and later Archbishop of Canterbury, heard his confession at a time when he was very ill, and he promised then to marry (which he never did) and to mend his ways. Anselm was never able to form a working relationship with the King, let alone a friendship. He deplored his immoral behaviour and his refusal to let the Church govern its own affairs. According to the writer John Gillingham, 'he treated the Church as a rich corporation which needed soaking.'[13]

Both William II and the brother who succeeded him were at odds with two of the great churchmen of their time, Lanfranc and Anselm. For many years much had been found wanting in the administration of the Church. More than one pope had tried to put matters right but it was Gregory VII who came furthest in achieving reform. His principal concerns were with simony (the selling of office for pecuniary gain), the celibacy of priests and the overall power and control of the pope in Rome. Gregorian reform was only the latest of many attempts at improvement in England. Even Bede had complained of the behaviour of priests and monks and Florence of Worcester mentioned that 'Anselm had not been suffered to hold a synod nor to correct the evil practices which had grown up in all parts of England.'[14]

The depravity of William's court extended to the priesthood, though many of the contemporary complaints seem today to be comparatively trivial. William of Malmesbury, always ready to complain of modern manners, disapproved strongly of 'flowing hair, extravagant dress and the invented fashion of shoes with curved points.'[15] Anselm, at a Council at Rockingham in 1095, appealed to Rome to come to his aid in a quarrel with the King, but the Papacy, already in trouble with its own hierarchy, was of no help, and the Archbishop chose to go into exile.

London and Westminster

By the end of the eleventh century it was becoming clear that what had been originally Londinium, Lundenwic, Lundenburg and finally London, was dividing itself into two cities, as it is today: London, the trading and commercial hub of England, and Westminster, the religious, royal and governmental centre. In 1097 William began the construction of a royal palace next to the splendid Abbey created by Edward 'the Confessor'. Westminster Hall, with its hammer-beam roof – at 73 x 20 metres the largest of its kind in Europe – was the focus of a complex of buildings which served as the King's personal apartments, the seat of government and the ceremonial centre of royalty. Much of it still exists in the names of modern reconstruction: Old and New Palace Yards, St Stephens Gate and of course Westminster itself, almost a synonym for Her Majesty's Government. The Hall was the work of the King's mason, Henry Yevele and carpenter Hugh Herland.

The First Crusade

In 1095 an event occurred, far from London, which was to change the face of Christendom for all time and affected almost all the countries of Europe. Pope Urban II gave a sermon on a hill outside Clermont in France, calling on all Christians to take up the cross and banish the Saracens from the holy city of Jerusalem. He ordered that all those who set out 'must bear the sign of the Lord's cross on his front or breast. Anyone who after fulfilling his vow wishes to return must put the sign on his back between his shoulder blades.'[16] The First Crusade had begun.

The New King

Five years later William died in a hunting accident in the New Forest. Was it an accident? His brother Henry, his successor and the first Norman king to be born in England, was nearby with a body of his own men. Rumours inevitably arose, but Henry was quick to quash them by acting decisively and having himself crowned by Bishop Maurice within a few days of William's death. He was also swift to reassure the nation that the treasury was safe. His immediate problem was the imminent return of his eldest brother, and rumours arise when a monarch dies suddenly. Certainly Henry acted instantly, assuring himself of the nation's treasury held in Winchester not far away, and was crowned at Westminster by Bishop Maurice within a few days of William's death. His immediate problem was the imminent return of his eldest brother Robert from the East wishing to claim the English throne. A settlement was reached, pensioning off the Duke, and leaving Henry to face a truculent Church, more than ready for the reforms which included most vitally freedom from control by the King. Anselm's return from his self-imposed exile exacerbated the situation. He refused to do homage to the King or to recognise any Church appointments made by the crown, as Pope Gregory had ordained.

In spite of ongoing controversies with Anselm, Henry was generous to the Church, establishing abbeys and monasteries (including those of the Cistercian order from Cluny). He married the daughter of the King of Scotland, Edith, who took the name of Matilda. She had been brought up in a convent and because of that there was some doubt about her eligibility to marry. However, Henry had by now the Church on his side and Anselm officiated both at the marriage and at Matilda's coronation. She turned out to be a woman of strong character, well read and pious, and effective in keeping the King and his prelates in order.

Having put down a rising in Normandy, Henry imprisoned his brother Robert and returned to England. At a Council in Westminster in 1107 he confirmed his agreement to refrain from investing new church leaders, as Pope Gregory had wished. The vacant sees were filled, including the Bishopric of Salisbury, which went to Roger of Salisbury, a most able administrator who became responsible for putting England's financial arrangements into efficient and economic order. He oversaw the improved methods for the financing of the royal household. The Exchequer (from the chequered tablecloth like a chess board on the accounting table) was put on a formal basis.

London was still, as it always had been since Roman times, a great trading centre. Its whole existence revolved around the trade and commerce of its citizens. Even the street names indicated where separate trades came together for the greater promotion of their work: Milk Street, Bread Street, Cordwainers, Candlewick, Threadneedle, Vintry, Poultry and many more. Forming themselves into Guilds (from the Anglo-Saxon 'gild' meaning payment), in return for a tribute to the King, many had their own churches. The little church of St Margaret Patten, for instance, though now rebuilt, recalls the trade of the patten makers, pattens being the overshoes which kept their wearers out of the mud of the street. They soon developed into the trade societies, or city livery companies as they are known today. The earliest 'Worshipful Company' to have its payment to the Crown recorded (in the Pipe Roll of 1130) was that of the Weavers. The Goldsmiths followed soon after, and a 'family' structure grew up around each guild, providing social help, burial arrangements and financial assistance to members, centred around their own church.

Henry I died in 1135, his vision of an heir to the throne of England and Normandy shattered when his only legitimate son, William, was killed in the tragedy of the White Ship which went down in the Channel with the death of almost everyone on board. Distraught at the death of his son, the King, still hoping for an heir, gave his daughter Matilda in marriage, after the death of her first husband, the Holy Roman Emperor Henry V, to Geoffrey of Anjou, but she left her husband and returned home. Sent back to France, she there produced a son, the future Henry II, the first Angevin king of England.

Anarchy

With no direct male heir – England had never had a female monarch – Henry's daughter Matilda, the Angevin Countess, declared herself Queen, while at the same time Stephen of Blois, the son of Henry's sister Adela, was waiting in the wings in Boulogne, ready to claim what he considered was rightfully his, as the nearest male successor. Back in London, he was welcomed warmly by the citizens. According to William of Malmesbury,

> At his arrival the town was immediately filled with excitement and came to meet him with acclamation. Whereas it had been sadly mourning the grievous death of its protector Henry, it revelled in exultant joy as though it had recovered him in Stephen.[17]

He immediately took possession of the Winchester treasury, as his uncle had done (Stephen's brother was Henry of Blois, Bishop of Winchester) and proceeded back to London for a hastily arranged coronation in Westminster Abbey by the Archbishop of Canterbury, assisted by Roger of Salisbury. Matilda herself did not arrive in England until 1139. Her arrogance did not impress the Londoners. She continued to call herself Empress (her due from her first husband) and had little time for reassuring her capital city of her regard for their laws and traditions. Bishop Henry, incidentally, was a very rich man and a great patron of the arts. The renowned Winchester Bible of 1160, one of the finest illuminated books of the twelfth century and now in Winchester Cathedral, which was left unfinished when Henry of Blois died, owes much to his interests and taste.

Stephen was held prisoner after the battle of Lincoln in 1141 but Matilda still refused to grant London its wish to abide by the laws of Edward 'the Confessor'. 'She with a grim look,' says a contemporary chronicle, 'her forehead wrinkled into a frown, every trace of a women's gentleness removed from her face, blazed into unbearable fury.'[18] The rest of the country had divided loyalties and England found itself almost at once embroiled in a civil war. The 'Anarchy' lasted for fifteen years. Matilda was never crowned Queen, though large parts of baronial England regarded her as such. After an attempt to take London, thwarted by Stephen's Queen (also Matilda) and the Londoners themselves, the Empress retired from the fray. She was imprisoned at Oxford from where she broke out in disguise, using the frozen river Isis as an escape route. At a Council at Winchester, Matilda was elected Queen but without the agreement of London. She was known as 'The Lady of England'. The papal legate (now Bishop Henry) addressed those present, 'We have despatched messengers for the Londoners who, from the importance of their city in England are almost nobles, as it were, to meet us on this business; and have sent them a safe-conduct; and we trust they will not delay their arrival.'[19] The Londoners duly appeared and after much debate confirmed their loyalty to Stephen, not Matilda. The meeting broke up in disorder.

King Stephen

In 1154 Matilda, unable to win over the hearts of most of her English subjects and aware that her young son Henry would be the ideal answer to England's search for a sovereign, returned to her dominion of Anjou, leaving the way clear for the young Henry, when the time was right, to claim his throne. Stephen lived for only another year before England welcomed her first Angevin king.

The hundred or so years before he came to the throne were described by Frank Barlow as 'perhaps one of the most religious periods of all time.'[20] He describes the style of worship of contemporary Englishmen who previously had stood to pray with their arms outstretched. Now they worshipped on their knees, supplicants, as were feudal vassals to their lords. 'Christ was no longer portrayed,' he explains, 'as the triumphant God, eyes open, serene, without pain. Instead he became the dying and suffering Lord, a piteous creature.' [21] With the Angevins, later usually known as the Plantagenets, came a confrontation between king and church, such as England had not known before.

CHAPTER V

The Angevin Dynasty

T HE EMPRESS MATILDA'S SON, Henry of Anjou, was declared 'the
lawful heir and claimant to the Kingdom of England' and greeted,
according to the *Gesta Stephani*, with acclamation because it was
rumoured that he had brought with him 'a countless quantity of treasure'.
Although Stephen would have preferred his son Eustace to succeed to the
English throne, Archbishop Theobald refused to crown him as heir apparent
on instructions from Rome. But Eustace died while plundering the Abbey
of Bury St Edmunds, wreaking, according to the chroniclers, 'God's
vengeance on his succession'.

Henry (known until he became King as Henry FitzEmpress) was the
only possible heir, now married to one of the richest and most powerful
women in Europe, Eleanor of Aquitaine. He landed in England in 1153
with 3,000 soldiers, the future possessor of England as well as of Anjou,
Brittany, Poitou, Aquitaine, Maine and Gascony, more than any other ruler
in Europe including the King of France.

On the advice of Archbishop Theobald, Stephen now welcomed
him warmly; the chronicler Henry of Huntingdon became quite lyrical –
'O what boundless joy! What a blessed day!' he wrote.[1] Stephen died within
a year of Henry's arrival and the young heir took his place at the head of
the country, the first undisputed king to do so since the Conquest.

England's First Angevin

Henry was a man of constant activity, riding about his kingdom, though
he spent much time out of it, always on the move. He had been born in Le
Mans, married in Poitiers, died at Chignon, and was buried at Fontevrault.
Highly sexed and amoral, he considered himself immune from the disapproval of the Church. However, it was to his advantage to be able to
count on the support of his leading churchmen.

The Turbulent Priest

Some thirty years before, a child had been born to a Norman family in their comfortable house in Cheapside, who was to become Archbishop of Canterbury, a martyr and a saint; his confrontation with the King led to his own death. Thomas Becket's relationship with Henry II started when he was appointed Chancellor. He had had a good education, first at Merton Priory, then in London at a grammar school, followed by some years in Paris. He obtained a position as clerk with Archbishop Theobald, who entrusted him with several important missions abroad and to the Vatican. He was appointed Archdeacon of Canterbury, and Theobald recommended him to the King as Lord Chancellor.

Henry's friendship with Thomas Becket was a close one. They rode out and hunted together, sharing their leisure hours. Thomas's years as Chancellor brought him even closer to the heart of politics, and Henry felt he could rely absolutely on Becket's discretion and support. He appointed him Archbishop of Canterbury on the death of Theobald in 1161.

A strong objection to the appointment came from Gilbert Foliot, Bishop of London. Perhaps he wanted the post for himself; he certainly remained Becket's enemy to the end. He felt him to be extravagant and worldly – when the Archbishop was received in France in exile the French were staggered by the magnificence of his household.

Henry's relationship with the Church in England was one of master and servant. He assumed all rights over the choice of higher clergy and refused any foreign power, especially the Papacy, to interfere. He claimed custody over vacant sees, even to the point of confiscating the income from them. In 1164 the Constitutions of Clarendon were drawn up to restore the powers and rights of the Church as had been in force under Henry I. But in fact the King went considerably further than his grandfather had done. Churchmen could not counter the King's ruling by an appeal to Rome nor could they leave England. Church revenues were paid over to him when a see fell vacant and the secular court had in many cases the prerogative of a ruling even when church matters were in dispute. Many of the clergy had been in the habit of pleading trial by church courts on criminal charges and were dealt with leniently, but now they were to appear before secular courts with the resulting due punishment. 'Benefit of clergy' no longer applied. The bishops, confronted almost by a *fait accompli*, protested vehemently. This assumption of royalty over church was to cost the King dear when his choice of Archbishop turned upon him later.

As it was Thomas capitulated and forced the agreement to the Constitutions by the higher clergy. Just as quickly he changed his mind and refused to adopt them. Unused to having his decrees questioned, Henry found himself at odds with the man whom he had counted as his friend and closest ally. He had Thomas charged with contempt of court. With the churchmen in turmoil as to whether to follow their Archbishop or their King, Henry appealed to Rome. Thomas fled to France.

It was becoming the custom in England, as it had been in France, for the son and heir to the kingdom to be crowned during his father's lifetime. Henry had four sons, the eldest, Henry the Younger, was to rule over England and Normandy, Geoffrey (of Anjou) was to have Brittany, and Richard, Poitou and his mother's Duchy of Aquitaine. This left little for the youngest John, his father's favourite, inevitably nicknamed 'Lackland'. Henry the Younger, known as the Young King, was crowned future King of England at Westminster Abbey in 1170, but his father refused to allow Archbishop Thomas to perform the ceremony; instead the Archbishop of York was called upon to do so. However, Henry did meet Thomas again in France and suggested he should return to England.

Bishop Foliot's antipathy continued to enrage the Archbishop, who duly excommunicated him along with others of his mind, and the Bishop retreated to Rome. He had only reached Rouen when messengers from the Pope announced his absolution and he returned. But his hatred of Becket did not change, and he was one of those who joined in the coronation of the Young King Henry by the Archbishop of York. When the Pope heard of it he excommunicated him with other bishops who supported York, adding to King Henry's fury against his former friend and ally.

Back home, Thomas's attitude to the state of the Church and Henry's attempted control of it, again provoked a storm. Henry's fury boiled over. William of Newburgh, usually a defender of the King, gave a graphic account of the event. 'On the heat of an outburst of rage he lost control of himself and spewed out crazed words from the fullness of a seething heart.'[2] The scene in Canterbury Cathedral in December 1170 is now an unforgettable part of English history. Henry's four knights overheard the King's outburst, rushed to England and finding Thomas in his own sanctuary killed him on the spot. Thomas the Martyr was canonised and the cathedral became the focus of pilgrimage. T.S. Eliot's play, *Murder in the Cathedral*, sums up perfectly the crux of the quarrel between King and Archbishop. In the play, at the moment of death, Thomas says:

> It is not in time that my death shall be known;
> It is out of time that my decision is taken
> If you call that decision
> To which my whole being gives entire consent.
> I give my life
> To the law of God above the law of Man.[3]

Henry was horrified at what had happened. He was forbidden by the Pope to enter a church, wore a hair shirt and had himself whipped by the monks of Canterbury. Miracles were reported at the martyr's tomb. But in one sense England benefited by the removal of the objector to the Constitutions of Clarendon. They were confirmed with two exceptions: the clergy were permitted to appeal to Rome, and those who transgressed could be tried by the courts of the Church.

The Templars

In 1118 a new order of soldier monks was established as a support arm of the Crusaders. The Knights of the Order of the Hospital of St John of Jerusalem, or Hospitallers, were formed to help the sick and wounded in the Holy Land during the first Crusade. The Hospitallers eventually made their home in Malta, being later known as the Knights of Malta. Some came to London and settled in Clerkenwell.

The Templars, long-time rivals of the Hospitallers, arrived a few years later and Henry II welcomed them to London, granting them accommodation at Baynards Castle. With their original home in Jerusalem in mind, they built a round church in their headquarters at the top of Chancery Lane, moving in 1184 to land by the river where they built another round church, similar to the Church of the Holy Sepulchre in Jerusalem. The church, in the grounds of what is still known as The Temple, is one of the oldest and most beautiful in London. It survived the Great Fire but was badly damaged in World War II.

Pope Innocent III declared the Templars exempt from local taxes, which enabled them to provide a secure place for the King's Treasury. They became an important part of London's banking establishment. Their rich estates, in England and abroad, their connections with the great houses of Europe, and London's reputation as a centre of commerce, gave them a unique place in the world of finance. In 1307 the Templars were suppressed by Pope Clement V, who disapproved of a religious body having financial dealings. They were accused of heresy and many, particularly in France, were executed. Some amalgamated with the Hospitallers and the lawyers of London took over their holdings by the river, dividing the buildings into the Inner and Middle Temples; the Temple Church remains as their place of worship. It is one of the few remaining round churches in this country and the only one in London.

Monasticism in London

Fitzstephen wrote of thirteen conventual churches in London. Of these many exist today only in street names. Others are part ruins, subsumed into other churches or hospitals. Some have vanished altogether, destroyed by fire or war. Towards the end of the twelfth and beginning of the thirteenth centuries, however, monasticism played a considerable part in London's religious affiliations. From the great monastic houses, founded on the continent, came the mendicant friars including the Carmelites, or White Friars, the Dominicans, Black Friars and the Franciscans, Grey Friars. The Premonstratensians, founded by St Norbert and known as the White Canons, were formed from ordained priests. The Canons were not monks as such; they did not live in a closed order, but spent their lives outside the monasteries, visiting the sick, educating the young and working for the benefit of those around them. The mendicant friars were a familiar sight in the streets of London, spending most of their days on the move, wherever they were needed, bringing the word of God to the people.

The Dominicans built a large priory in Holborn, later moving to a site at Ludgate, where Montfichet Castle had stood and where Blackfriars Bridge now stretches across the river. Theirs was a more intellectual way of life, concentrating on scholarly philosophy and rigorous argument, determined to root out heresy wherever they found it. They were later much involved in the Spanish Inquisition, obtaining from the Pope the consent to use torture when it proved necessary.

The Carmelites also had a large house to the east of the Temple. There is still a Carmelite Convent and church in Notting Hill. The order was re-founded in London in the nineteenth century by a converted Jew, Hermann Cohen, who had been a pupil of Liszt until he became a Christian and gave up his musical career.

The Franciscans built a large conventual church in the parish of St Nicholas in the Shambles (the old butchers' area) at Newgate. This later became Christ's Hospital, a school for both boys and girls, still wearing the familiar yellow stockings and dark blue coats. It later moved to Horsham.

Another large monastic foundation was St Augustine's Priory, sometimes abbreviated to Austin Friars, situated near Threadneedle Street, also of a high intellectual standing, some of whose students went on to the University at Oxford, founded under Henry II who had forbidden English students from studying at the French universities. Merton Priory, where Thomas Becket had been educated, was under the Augustinian rule, and its church at Holy Trinity, Aldgate, was an influential leader in church affairs. It had been founded by Empress Matilda with a reputation for learning.

The Franciscans preferred preaching out of doors rather than in a church; some acted as confessors to royalty and the nobility. The Gilbertian Order was founded by an Englishman, St Gilbert of Sempringham, as an order for women, based on the rule of the Cistercians. The Gilbertines wore black with a white hood and *scapular*, so that if God looked down at them it would seem that they wore a white cross on a black background. They had a house in London on the corner of Old Jewry, in the parish of St Mary Colechurch.

Some of the great London hospitals were founded by the monastic houses of this time. St Bartholomew's remains one of the oldest hospitals in Europe, certainly the oldest in continuous use. It was founded in 1123 by a courtier of Henry I, Rahere, whose tomb is still in the church. Originally both a hospital and a priory, it was on the site mentioned by Fitzstephen as the place of the horse fair. A charter for the fair was granted to Rahere to fund the Priory of St Bartholomew, and from 1133 to 1855 it took place each year on 24th August within the precincts of the Priory at West Smithfield, outside Aldersgate. It was much enjoyed by the apprentices of the city, and is commemorated by a play of that name by Ben Jonson. The fair continued, after the Dissolution, within the Liberty of the parish of St Bartholomew-the-Great. According to Fitzstephen, it was 'a region abounding in filthy water and mud, with an area above the waterline set aside for gibbets.'[4] The duties of the hospital involved prayer, spiritual advice and even social welfare as well as medicine; it was closely linked to the church beside it.

St Thomas's Hospital, named after Thomas Becket, was probably founded not long after his death by the Augustinians, at first on the southern end of London Bridge. In the lee of the Tower, St Katherine's Hospital was endowed by Matilda 'for the care of the poor and the sick'. It was also a leper hospital. There were several of these, usually in the fields outside the city, and staffed by nuns: St Giles in the Fields, St Thomas of Acre (possibly in the house in Cheapside where Thomas Becket was born), and the New Hospital of St Mary at Bishopsgate.

Queen Eleanor

Henry's marriage to the widow of the King of France brought him some joy and a good deal of grief. She bore him eight children, three daughters and five sons. Beautiful, intelligent and ruthless, with a love of music, troubadours and courtly love, Eleanor had gone on the Second Crusade with her first husband, and was not content to play a minor part in the affairs of England. She had inherited the vast rich lands of Aquitaine and although she had probably been in love with Henry, the handsome young Count of Anjou (later King of England) when she left her French husband for him, she was prepared to support her sons against him if the need arose.

His mistress, Rosamund Clifford, was claiming much of his time and Eleanor was not one to take second place. She and her four sons felt that the future of the Angevin dynasty was now at stake.

Richard I

The young King Henry had married the daughter of the French King, Louis VII, and was prepared to invoke French help in a conspiracy against his father. But he died in 1183, followed by his brother Geoffrey in 1186. The throne of England passed to Eleanor's favourite, Richard.

Later centuries have viewed Richard as, by turns, a valiant knight, a cruel fighter, a plunderer of other people's money, a talented troubadour or a homosexual tyrant. He was all of these. Of his ten year reign he spent only six months in England and never learned to speak the language. His driving force was undoubtedly his attempt to rescue the Holy Land from Saladin. Caring little for the English people, he preferred like his father to spend his time in Aquitaine, inherited from his mother, Poitou, entrusted to him by his father, or in any of the other provinces owned by the Angevin dynasty.

Richard's coronation on 3rd September 1189 should have been the most splendid event England had ever seen. All the greatest figures of the time were present – bishops, lords, barons, knights – parading through Westminster Abbey in full ceremonial robes and regalia. Archbishop Baldwin performed the anointing and the investiture, with Richard promising to keep his coronation oath. They adjourned to Westminster Palace for the coronation banquet.

No women were admitted to the Abbey for the ceremony and no Jews, according to the chronicler Matthew Paris because of their magic arts. The Jews of England had been relatively unmolested during the reign of Richard's father, Henry II. He had found them useful as moneylenders and it was in his interests and those of his court to allow them to live in peace. To show their welcome to Richard – and perhaps in the hope that their business arrangements would continue to flourish – they dressed themselves in their finery on the day of the coronation and set off to the Abbey bearing handsome gifts. It is clear that those Jews who came to London from any distance would not have known about the proclamation forbidding them entrance because it had only been issued the previous day. So they made their way in good time to the Abbey doors. The pressure from the crowds swarming forward to get a glimpse of their new King forced them on until they found themselves within the confines of the Abbey. The doorkeepers pounced at once, declaring that the Jews were disobeying the King and flung them outside, where the crowd attacked them as traitors, beating them half to death. Some did die, many were badly injured, and word got out that this was all on the orders of the King, which gave free rein to a violent mob totally out of control.

Riots in London

The news of the riot spread quickly. It is nearly three miles from the Abbey to Cheapside, the southern border of the Jewry. The raging mob, no doubt joined by others as they went, reached the Jewish homes by mid-afternoon and the disturbances raged all night. In his history of Jews in England – the earliest such account – D'Blossiers Tovey describes how 'the masses, believing they were acting in the King's interests, were breaking into Jewish homes, murdering every Jew they could find, and then, for good measure, burning their houses to the ground.'[5] Most of London's Jewry was destroyed by fire and many Jews were butchered.

The King at his coronation banquet was told what was happening and sent a deputation to put an end to the violence, but the mob were too strong and the King's men had to retreat. Richard did act by hanging three of the worst offenders (one was hanged for robbing a Christian house during the uproar and the other two for allowing a Christian house to be burned during the fire). The Jewish community itself paid for the disturbance by underwriting a large part of the costs of Richard's Crusade.

The Exchequer of the Jews

A part of the Royal Exchequer at Westminster was now devoted to the express purpose of ensuring that records were kept of who owed money to the Jews, the amount borrowed and details of repayments. This minute examination arose partly as a result of the massacre at York in 1190, after which all the documents recording financial borrowings were burnt in the nave of the Minster. The new Exchequer was composed of two Jews, two Christians, two scribes and an official from the Royal Exchequer. Precise records were kept. These documents were in the form of chirographs, duplicated notes written on a single sheet of parchment, which was then torn in two with a jagged edge, each partner in the arrangement retaining one half. Matching up the two halves in the event of a dispute prevented forgery.

The huge sum raised for Richard in London involved the city in what amounted to a popular rising, when William Fitzosbert, known as Long-beard, claimed that the ordinary citizens were paying for what should have been the responsibility of the rich who could have afforded it. He stirred up the citizens to a near riot, and when Hubert Walter, the Archbishop of

Canterbury and the King's regent, arrested him, Fitzosbert killed his guards and took refuge in the church of St Mary-le-Bow. Surrounded by soldiers the church was torched, and he was dragged out and hanged. After his death miracles were reported and he was venerated as a martyr. He is considered to be London's first demagogue.

King John

The early years of John's reign were spent fighting for his possessions in Normandy, but once Normandy was lost to Philip II, King of France, he turned to England, spending more time there than most of his ancestors had done. The King found himself immediately in conflict with the Church when Pope Innocent III appointed Stephen Langton to Canterbury when Walter died. When John protested and began to confiscate church property, England was first put under an Interdict, meaning that no priest could conduct services, oaths were suspect and church financial dealings were virtually suspended; finally John was excommunicated. However, worried about a possible invasion from France and signs of disturbance from the Church at home, he made his peace with the Pope and England became a papal fief, paying taxes to her overlord in Rome as an annual tribute.

In 1210, the King, ever short of money and anxious to find it where he could, issued an edict against the Jews. The Bristol Tallage, as it was known, was a review of the wealth of the Jews throughout the kingdom, with a tax to be paid according to the results of the survey. Any Jew who refused to admit details of his finances was imprisoned, with supervisors in every town to make sure the King's orders were carried out. By this means some 60,000 marks were raised for the royal treasury, and many Jews, not just in Bristol, remained in prison until the debts were paid. The London Jews, among the wealthiest, were sent to the Tower.

Magna Carta

John's relationship with his barons had always been a difficult one. As W.L. Warren put it in his fine biography of King John, 'He chose to keep his barons in line by fear not affection.'[6] He was not above executing sons if their fathers disputed his orders, and used the fact that they owed him money (he was of course the overlord of the Jews – their money was his money) to achieve his aims. To the King a bond, a promise or a concession meant nothing. Trust was not a feature of John's personality. There seems to have been no reason for him not to go down in history as Bad King John.

In 1863 a remarkable document was discovered in the French royal archives. It is known today as 'The Unknown Charter of Liberties' and may have been an early draft of the Magna Carta. It appears to be a personal decree from King John, promising justice, fair inheritance, arrangements for the heir and family of a deceased, no conscription to the army except in England, Normandy and Brittany, forestry laws and several other clauses of the Great Charter. It included a copy of Henry I's Coronation Charter.

After a brief but bloody war in France John returned to confrontation at home. He had been defeated by the French King and the Pope. Now he had to face the barons. They confronted him in London at the Temple Church with King Henry I's original charter of liberties of 1100 and were prepared for a full-scale rebellion if he refused to come to terms. It was mainly the northern barons who were most militant in their opposition to the King, but London too was well to the fore in demanding action. Robert Fitzwalter of Baynards Castle was a lead player in the dispute. Warren describes him as 'altogether disreputable and mischievous'[7].

John prevaricated, vowed to take the Cross on Crusade and sent delegates seeking the opinion of the Pope. They returned with instructions for the barons to rein in their more truculent leaders, but they were tired of waiting. With FitzWalter at the head of their 'army of God' they were ready to face the King. What had started off as a rebellion by certain of the barons – not all by any means – was turning into a civil war. The 'army' struck out for London and was admitted to the City. This was not a disciplined trained army. It may have been composed mainly of men of property, wealth and standing but it was in reality little more than a well-born rabble. The Jewry was virtually destroyed. According to the historian John Stow 'they brake into the Jews' houses, searched their coffers to fill their own purses, and after with great diligence, repaired the walls and gates of the city with stones taken from the Jews' broken houses.'[8] Tombstones from the Jewish cemetery at Cripplegate were found some miles away in the time of James I.

Negotiations for a truce started under the valuable direction of Stephen Langton and on 15th June 1215 both sides met 'in the meadow that is called Runnymede' beside the Thames near Windsor. Very little actually happened on that day; the barons produced an outline draft, the Articles of the Barons, but a few days later the King put his seal to this, a binding agreement to issue the Charter and the Barons swore fealty to their King. This put into effect a system of law, most of which has protected Englishmen's rights and liberties to this day, though much has changed. Thirteen copies of the Great Charter were produced, of which four remain. The only indication at Runnymede today of what transpired is the monument erected in the field by the American Bar Association in 1957. The terms of the Charter were incorporated into the American Declaration of Independence, and a sketch of it appears on the doors of the Supreme Court Building in Washington D.C.

However Magna Carta was a charter for the barons, nobility and freemen, not for the common man. He had to wait for the Petition of Right in the seventeenth century when Lord Chief Justice Coke had it rewritten for his own time. Of the four original copies, two are now in the British Library, one each at Lincoln and Salisbury Cathedrals. The Library united the four for the first time on the 800th Anniversary of the signing in 2015. Warren prints the Charter in full.[9] Like the earlier 'Unknown Charter' the sixty-one clauses cover Church and State, inheritance, debts, family law, the rights of knights and freemen, and of Jews, courts and inquests, the right of trial by peers, forestry laws, as well such lesser matters as fish-traps and measures of wine and ale. The Charter was originally one piece of writing; it was later divided up into Clauses. One clause states that no-one shall be arrested or imprisoned upon the appeal of a woman for the death of anyone except her husband. Clause 13 assures London of all its ancient liberties and free custom 'as well by land as by water'. The following year another version was issued for the accession of Henry III and in 1217 the forest clauses were removed to a Forest Charter. The Charter was written in Latin but had to be translated for the Barons who spoke Norman French.

Magna Carta has come to represent the Englishman's rights and privileges for all times. In his *History of England* Keith Feiling puts it succinctly, 'Its real essence lay in the ideal of the governing class of 1215, barons and knights and freeholders, who had served a long apprenticeship in Henry II's law.'[10] The success of its achievement is due to the moderates on both sides, who managed to subdue the wilder elements to finally bring it about.

John's Last Days

No sooner had the Charter been signed than John wrote to the Pope, his overlord, asking for it to be annulled. The Pope was sympathetic and declared the Charter void. The Papal Bull described it as 'illegal, unjust, harmful to royal rights and shameful to the English people.' The country was by now in a state of revolution. In London, where the rebels were in command, the exchequer and court sittings were virtually abandoned, for no-one could sign documents but the King, and he was busy subduing the countryside outside the city. The barons in their turn also sought help from outside the kingdom. They invited Louis, son of Philip Augustus of France, to become their King. In 1216 he landed in Suffolk with an army and made for London, occupying the Tower. The King withdrew to Winchester and Louis was excommunicated. London was placed under an Interdict on the express command of the Pope, Innocent III. He wrote to King Philip to 'give no help or favour' to the barons who opposed the English King. A similar letter was sent to the Duke of Burgundy, Philip's son, to the bishops of England and to the prelates of France.

The whole sorry situation was solved by the death of the King. Very ill with dysentery, his baggage train with all his possessions lost in the almost impassable causeway at Wisbech, John died at Newark on 18th October 1216, leaving his son Henry, aged nine, to rule over his kingdom.

CHAPTER VI

The First Plantagenets

THE FIRST OF THE ANGEVINS to use the name Plantagenet was Geoffrey of Anjou, the husband of the Empress Matilda, supposedly from the sprig of *planta genista*, the broom, which he wore in his hat. Although the nickname should strictly cover all the kings of England from Henry II to Richard III, it is usually applied to Henry III and his direct descendants. From an old legend that an ancient Angevin King had married the daughter of Satan, they were known as 'The Devil's Brood'.

The Fourth Lateran Council

In the same year that Magna Carta was signed, Pope Innocent III summoned the Fourth Lateran Council, to discuss the state of the Western Christian Church and how it should be administered. There were seventy-one clauses confirmed by those who attended, among them Stephen Langton from England. They ranged from 'clerical gluttony and drunkenness' to 'physicians of the body to advise patients to call physicians of the soul'. The majority of the decisions were concerned with the efficient administration of the Church and her workers, ecclesiastical law, and the behaviour of clerics and their parishioners. Among them were compulsory annual confession and communion, that no see should be left vacant for more than three months, and insistence on the records of diocese and church being meticulously kept.

Henry III

The boy prince, on his father's death, was hastily crowned in Gloucester Cathedral by those who had care of him, using as a crown, it is said, a gold bracelet belonging to his mother. Henry was crowned again in Westminster Abbey in 1220. The rebuilding of the Abbey and the reconstruction of Edward the Confessor's tomb were to be his life's work. As a young man he was generally considered handsome and intelligent. Maurice Powicke, the historian, mentions that he had 'a kind of innocence which remained in him throughout his life even when he was at his worst'.[1] In 1236 he married Eleanor of Provence, the sister of the French king. She was thirteen years old, and was to bring to England many of her relatives from France and Savoy, making her very unpopular, particularly in London.

The Provisions of Oxford

Reforms of the Church at the Lateran Council were not the only changes that affected England, and particularly London, during Henry's reign. The Provisions of Oxford set out rules for the English monarch with a new form of government, with a Privy Council to advise the king and oversee the administration. There were to be three parliaments a year with checks and balances to oversee the 'common wants' of the kingdom, and of the King. Previous monarchs had been accustomed to journeying around the country dealing with law and justice, quarrels and disputes, wherever they were encountered. Now London became not only the capital of England and the foremost city for trade and commerce, but the stable centre of the King's rule.

The *Domus Conversorum*

In 1232 Henry founded a house for converted Jews at the north end of New Street (later Chancery Lane) next to the building occupied by the Templars when they came to London. It was on the site of a former synagogue though this first London *Domus Conversorum* later moved down the street to where the Public Record Office stood until it went to Kew. The King ordered that

> all converted Jews who had abandoned the blindness of Judaism should come to be under a rule of honest living and enjoy a home and a safe refuge and sufficient sustenance of life without servile labour or the profits of usury.[2]

They were to receive an income from St Dunstan's-in-the-West, close by, for their upkeep. Several Jewish houses were sold by royal decree and the profits devoted to the *Domus*. A single man or woman, a married couple or a whole family could be housed there, though children had the right to choose whether to accompany their parents or return to their community. Some converts came to London from other parts of Britain and some from abroad. The wardenship of the house was by royal appointment, and the King took an interest in the individual converts, giving gifts of clothes to the women and children.

Naturally all residents had to be baptised to confirm their serious intent, some taking the name of Henry after their royal benefactor. Nearly all gave up their Jewish names, calling themselves after the apostles or by the names of the English magnates who sponsored them. The names of about forty residents in the house are known in the first years of the foundation and this had doubled by the time of the Expulsion in 1290.

The Provisions of Westminster

A year after the Council at Oxford another was held at Westminster. The original Provisions were enlarged and reinforced. This was partly to improve administration and for tax and inheritance measures to be confirmed. The royal courts were more efficiently run and some of the King's more autocratic ideas were abandoned. Once again the barons were growing restless. They felt that in spite of these new measures they were being bypassed on the one hand by royal command and on the other by too much power being granted to underlings. Reforms of local administration were wearing away old feudal ways and the new system of government was threatening ancient inherited power. The King was too close to the Papacy and his expenditure forced him to call on the barons for help.

This time, however, they had a leader. Henry's sister, also Eleanor, had married a Frenchman who was heir to the Earldom of Leicester. Simon de Montfort had come to England, speaking very little English, to claim his estates. He had no patience with the King, viewing him as incompetent and treacherous as well as extravagant. London's part in the forthcoming confrontation was vital. Having supported the barons through the earlier war, the City now had a democratic mayor. The citizens gathered to hear ranting preachers at St Paul's Cross, the outdoor forum in front of the cathedral. The three years agreed duration of the Provisions came to an end, while Henry waited. He then approached the Pope who annulled the Provisions. The barons agreed a temporary truce, but de Montfort did not. He was short of support in the country in his coming battle with the King, so he turned to London. He was welcomed too by the Cinque Ports, and south-east England was de Montfort country.

The Jewry

London was unhappy. It had shown its animosity to Queen Eleanor when she arrived with her foreign relatives, and that mistrust extended to other strangers in the city. Just as the Jews had been classed as easterners at the time of the Crusades and were treated with suspicion and violence so Londoners viewed their home-grown Jews with doubt and fear. They were rich and foreign and in 1239 the Jewry was attacked by the order of Geoffrey the Templar. Matthew Paris sympathised. 'At length after great suffering, these wretched Jews, in order to enjoy life and tranquillity, to their own ruin and confusion paid to the King a third part of all their money, debts as well as chattels.'³ A few years later, with little respite from either violence or penury, Elias the Arch Presbyter of the Jews begged to leave England, but was told, 'Whither would you fly, wretched beings? The French King hates you and has condemned you to perpetual banishment.'⁴ The French had expelled the majority of their Jews in 1182. Henry's borrowings, with little hope of repayment, were milking the Jewish community dry. The writer Robert Stacey, discussing the situation of the Jews at this time, says, 'By 1258 this enormously wealthy community was financially ruined and spiritually demoralised.'⁵ Some converted to Christianity, including the Arch Presbyter.

Archbishop Boniface

It was not just the Jews of London that were suffering. The Pope had expressed a wish that Canterbury should have his own nominee as its next Archbishop. Henry, ever anxious to agree, supported Boniface of Savoy for the See, in spite of some disagreement shown by the canons of Canterbury Cathedral. The new incumbent was no scholar nor had he an attractive personality. Matthew Paris called him 'deficient in morals and knowledge', but he was nevertheless elected. He spent much of the time abroad – he was from Savoy and related to Queen Eleanor – but on an early visit to London he insisted on a visitation (usually the prerogative of the local Bishop). He lodged in the house of the Bishop of Chichester, not at Lambeth, and told his servants to take what they needed from the markets, to the anger of the tradesmen. He proposed visiting the Chapter of St Paul's, but was opposed by the canons who appealed to the Pope, whereupon the new Archbishop excommunicated the Dean and several of the clergy.

The real scandal occurred when he visited the monks of St Bartholomew's. He was prepared for trouble, wearing a suit of armour under his robes. He was met by the sub-Prior and a splendid procession from the monastery. All the monks and many of his own men crowded into the little church. The sub-Prior explained that 'the good Bishop of London' had visited recently and they did not need another visitation. The short-tempered Archbishop rushed at the unfortunate canon, and attacked with fists flying. 'Thus it becomes me to deal with you English traitors', he shouted, asking for a sword. He tore off the rich clasp of the monk's cloak (which was lost in the melée). This violent onslaught dragged off his own robe, showing the armour beneath. The horrified monks, assaulted by the Archbishop's men, tried to protect their leader, but the poor old man was badly injured.

A deputation went to the Bishop of London, but were told to go to the King. He refused to see them, and Boniface fled by boat to tell his story to the Queen, his kinswoman. He went to Rome to plead his defence and thought it wise to remain abroad for some time. On his return he seemed calmer and less disputatious, but managed to annoy Henry by defending his ecclesiastical privileges against the King's right to interfere.

London against the King

Henry's son Edward was by now old enough to be a factor in the King's household, the support he needed when the confrontation with de Montfort finally developed into open warfare. Henry, attempting to win over the Londoners, had strengthened the Tower defences, and it was here that he took refuge with his family when it seemed likely that he would be faced with considerable personal danger in the streets. London was by now not just a capital city, a principal source of revenue and a vital trading centre – it had developed a political entity of its own. For almost the first time the people of London, ranking below the freemen and the barons, were finding their voice. The commons supported Simon de Montfort, though they had not yet formed a council or 'house' of the commons. They did have a marshal and a constable and De Montfort knew he could call on them if it came to an armed struggle. He was obliged to agree to a truce and to the arbitration of the French King. Louis came down in favour of Henry who once again repudiated the Provisions.

Westminster Abbey

However, England's new parliamentary reforms did not last long. The barons quarrelled among themselves and refused to admit the 'lower orders' to a say in government. Prince Edward escaped from his confinement and led an army against de Montfort. At the battle of Evesham the barons' leader was killed. Matthew Paris describes his death: 'Thus ended the labours of that noble man, Earl Simon, who gave up not only his property but also his person to defend the poor from oppression and for the mainte-nance of justice and the rights of the kingdom.'[6] Henry annulled the arrangements already made, though parliament still stood as the govern-ment of England. For that his reign will always be remembered. He died in 1272 having ruled for fifty-six years, the longest reign since the Normans came to England.

Henry did not live to see the climax of his great reconstruction of the Abbey at Westminster. He began on a new Lady Chapel, laying the foundation stone himself and rebuilt the old church, as John Stow put it, 'to make it more comely'. His obsession with St Edward 'the Confessor', whose influence on his life and character were immense, led him to the erection of a splendid new shrine to protect the saint's remains. These were translated there, installed behind the high altar. He employed the best craftsmen to build the memorial, with a special fund devoted to the work. Powicke says, 'The spirit of Henry III lingers in the Chapter House in Westminster Abbey, in the ambulatory about the high altar, in the choir and the transepts of our most famous church.'[7]

Westminster was not the only church building to be improved and enlarged, for this was a time of great architectural innovation. The old simple Norman designs had been superseded by the Gothic style. A new cathedral was built at New Sarum in Salisbury (the tower was not added until the fourteenth century) and a new retrochoir was added to Winchester, while in London the great Gothic cathedral of St Paul's was again enlarged. It was beginning to acquire the unfortunate reputation of being a centre of commercial affairs, chatter and disreputable adventures within the great nave.

Edward I

The new King was an imposing figure. Known as Longshanks from his great stature and bearing, he commanded attention with charismatic control. He inherited from his father a strong mistrust of the citizens of London. Henry had taken up arms against them and treated them with contempt and dislike. He favoured Westminster over the city, and his son showed the Londoners the same ill will. On coming to the throne he immediately revoked their liberties and dismissed many of their leaders, putting in his own men. The promise in earlier years of a self-governing city state came to nought as the two cities by the Thames (Westminster did not acquire city status until 1965 with the creation of Greater London) came into conflict with each other. The King had control of Westminster, the seat of government and of his own internal affairs, but he retained the Tower, much enlarged and strengthened, and the Abbot of Westminster was in overall charge. The Royal Palace adjoined the political centre.

A serious fire damaged the Palace in 1298, when it was being warmed to greet the King. It spread to the Abbey and the domestic quarters were badly burned. Five years later the monks themselves were accused of a notorious burglary in the Treasure House, when much of the King's treasure disappeared from the crypt. An inventory was ordered by the King who was in Scotland. Some of the pieces were found in the monks' quarters, and the whole population of the monastery was sent to the Tower. Some of the perpetrators were hanged, and the King moved the treasure into the Tower for safe keeping.

But it was London which had the money, not Westminster, and a strongly independent outlook. The King could not afford to neglect his trading and commercial centre. The guilds in the city controlled the working face of the capital. Their leaders called themselves barons and the aldermen had the power to vote in whoever they wished. The townsmen paid taxes to the City and had to take an oath to be able to call themselves citizens. The first freemen of the city had been created in 1237 with special privileges, including the right to be drunk and disorderly without fear of arrest, to drive sheep over London Bridge and in the unlikely event of being sentenced to death, to be hanged with a silken rope.

London's main source of income came from wool and grain, with the Thames as its main highway to the sea. It had its own seal, with the figure of St Paul on one side and that of Thomas Becket on the other. By the time Edward became King the City had put in place a series of regulations to improve the health, comfort and safety of its citizens. More houses were being built of stone, thatched roofs were forbidden and a system of pure water was piped through the city, with the main outlet – the Great Conduit – in Cheapside. Some attempt was made, not very successfully, to prevent debris and filth being thrown into the rivers. Walbrook, a particularly unpleasant open sewer, was eventually closed over. John Stow describes it as being 'arched over with brick and paved with stone equal with the ground where through it passed, and is now in most places built upon, that no man may by the eye discern it.'[8] The Fleet, too, smelled appalling; the Carmelite monks, in their home nearby, complained to the King. He left it to the Londoners to rectify the problem, but little could be done. Each ward had a public privy and the one at Ludgate was particularly nasty. It was an offence to kill or hurt the kites which helped to deal with some of the detritus left behind after the refuse carts had done their work.

The Legal System

King Edward was one of the greatest administrators of the English legal system the country has ever had. As Winston Churchill put it,

> The reign is memorable. Not for the erection of great new landmarks, but because the beneficial tendencies of the three preceding reigns were extracted from error and confusion and organised and consolidated in a permanent structure.[9]

The Statute of the Jews

In 1275, not long after he came to the throne, Edward passed the Statute of the Jews. They, like their Christian neighbours, were now forbidden to lend money at interest. Their sole means of earning a living was taken away. They could still farm land and take up craft work, but few Jews were agriculturalists and the guilds had control of all other manual labour, refusing to permit Jews to join. Other restrictions included

> Every Jewish male aged seven years and over must wear a badge in the form of two tablets of yellow cloth six fingers long and three fingers wide on their upper garment ... they may converse freely with Christians, although on no account whatsoever shall they live among them.[10]

Some Jews were forced into crime such as coin clipping or even robbery.

Rumours about the Jews were flying round London as they always had. A child was found murdered in St Paul's Churchyard. His wounds appeared to formulate Hebrew lettering, so the Jews were blamed and forced to pay £40,000 'in compensation', though no-one was charged. There were stories about Jewish conspiracies – that the Jews planned to set the city ablaze with Greek fire (a secret weapon of war used by Byzantine Greeks, probably phosphorus), that they were preparing false keys and building underground routes to 'betray the gates'. Three years after the passing of the Statute, 690 Jews from all over the country were imprisoned in the Tower of London. Of these 293 were hanged.

If Jews were to be deprived of their right to lend money, who was to take their place? The financial situation of the Church in England was appalling. Most churches, cathedrals and monasteries were impoverished, some to the extent of offering their buildings for sale, or allowing them to fall into a terrible state, borrowing far beyond their ability to repay. The Jewish community offered to buy some of the buildings outright, asking for the purchase to include the normal feudal rights, such as guardianship of minors, the marriage of wards and the right to award church livings. The bishops were horrified, arguing that 'it was an act of the King's grace that they were allowed to remain in England, and that it was outrageous that they should make such demands'.[11] As a result the Jews were forbidden to own property or receive rents.

There were of course Christian moneylenders. William Cade, a Fleming from St Omer, was one of the richest men in Europe. He lent to the English and French royal families as well as to monasteries and the aristocracy. Both Henry II and John had borrowed heavily from him. The Italian Lombards were also encroaching on what had been a Jewish prerogative in London.

The disapproval of the Church of such usurious dealings could be circumvented by disguising the arrangements as contributions towards costs, especially those of the crusades, though papal excommunication was always a possibility.

Gradually the London Jews were being usurped in their business affairs by the Flemings and the Italians. With a large part of their capital already gone they had to confine their lending to farmers, small holders and traders, especially in the countryside. They were becoming a burden. The principal synagogue in the Jewry was forced to be abandoned, because the chanting disturbed the friars worshipping next door (they took over the synagogue to extend their own building). Pope Honorius IV ordered sermons urging the conversion of the Jews. Jewish women were forced to wear the yellow badge and no Christian servants could be employed by them.

The Expulsion of the Jews

On July 18th 1290, an Act of the King in Parliament ordered all Jews to leave the country. The date was a holy one in the Jewish calendar, the Ninth of the month of Av, when many disasters had overtaken the Jewish people, including the fall of the Temple in 70 CE and in 1190 the massacre of the Jews at Clifford's Tower in York. The Order for the banishment of all Jews from the kingdom on pain of death was sent to the Constable of the Tower, where many Jews had taken shelter during the rioting, and to all Sheriffs. They were allowed to take their moveable assets with them. They could sell their properties but the monies accrued went to the Crown (the Jews were still the property of the King) with details kept meticulously by the Exchequer. The fact that the expulsion was an Order of the King in Council was important, as it meant, in 1655 when the Jews sought to come back, that there was nothing on the Statute Book to prevent them from returning. The Order has never been revoked, and very recently an Israeli writer has called attention to this, arguing that should it ever come to it, the Jews could still technically be forbidden from residing in the United Kingdom.

Once the Edict of Expulsion came into force, the Jewish community was given until 1st November to be gone. They were not to be ill-treated or suffer any harm. They were to restore all pledges to their debtors and the Cinque Ports were warned by the King that

> if and when these Jews arrive at the ports, along with their wives and children and chattels, to embark on their passage overseas, they shall have a safe and speedy passage, and safe conduct at their own expense. Any poor Jew shall be spared the cost of their fare and the others shall be charged moderately in accordance with their ability to pay.[12]

One ship's captain, whose Jewish travellers were wealthy, moored in the Thames estuary at low tide and persuaded his passengers to leave the ship for a rest. When the tide came in and the ship refloated, he set sail leaving them behind. All were drowned. He was later tried for murder and hanged. Several other deaths at sea were reported. Those Jews who reached France were banished by the French king, though some, speaking French, were able to merge in with the populace in the cities. Others went to Holland, Belgium or Spain to meet up with fellow Jews.

The Church in the Early Fourteenth Century

Rome was exercising considerable control over London, and powerful Archbishops of Canterbury were not afraid to dictate to the King or to interfere in state affairs. John Peckham in particular, a Franciscan, stepped in to mediate between Edward and the Welsh leaders, warning him of excommunication if he disobeyed the Church in any particular, and insisted on church courts ruling over any matter concerning clerics or bishops. A very large number of priests, bishops, friars, monks and nuns, as well as lay brothers – probably about 20,000 out of a population of some three million – were claiming the income and benefits of a clerical life, while both the King and the Pope expected a large part of their resources to come from the same source.

A vast organisation was needed to regulate and care for such a number and from the Pope in Rome to the humblest clerk, each had his place in the hierarchy and knew that place. The parish priest's relationship with his parishioners was clear cut, though he did not always play his part. He was supposed to ensure that they attended Mass on Sundays, knew the Lord's Prayer, the Creed and the Hail Mary by heart and taught them to their children. They should come regularly to Confession, and marry, baptise their children and be buried according to the conventions of the Catholic Church.

The rules for the behaviour of the clergy were laid down in the *Constitutiones* of Robert Grosseteste, Bishop of Lincoln. He insisted that every priest should know the Seven Deadly Sins, the Seven Sacraments and the Ten Commandments, not always easy for some of the poor, semi-literate churchmen. As to his behaviour, he should not frequent taverns, indulge in gambling nor visit plays. He should not allow a woman in his house whose presence might cause suspicion. The visitations which the bishops were supposed to carry out were hardly regular enough to ensure that the clergy under their jurisdiction were in fact behaving in a fit and proper manner.

Attending a church service was much less comfortable than it is today. Although the worshipper might have been just as familiar with the prayers, he would have found, especially in the smaller churches, no seats, no pulpit and no music. Some churches had stone benches around the walls, later giving place to wood, but few had permanent seating before the Reformation. Larger churches did have a pulpit, sometimes two, one on the left for the preacher and one on the right, the lectern for the reading. But Catholic church services paid less attention to sermons than did the Protestants to come. Many of the country clergy were very ignorant except for the basics of their calling, but at least they could read and write. Nevertheless the church was the centre of parish life, used not only for the worship of God, but for harvest suppers, baptism and death, marriage and betrothal, inquests, payment of rent and many other regular commitments by the parishioners.

After Peckham the new Archbishop of Canterbury was Robert Winchelsey, a scholar and a politician, who preferred Rome to the English Church. He was a stern and unforgiving man. It was rumoured that he so berated one erring Abbott that the poor man had a heart attack on the spot. When they refused to pay taxes to the Crown, Edward declared the clergy outlaws.

A New King

In 1307 Edward I died on his way to continue the war in Scotland. He was succeeded by a very different ruler. Even though he had a particularly strong and vigorous predecessor to follow, the second Edward fell far short of the requirements needed to reign over a nation like England. His greatest failing was his inability to choose his advisers wisely. His close and undoubtedly homosexual relationship with Piers Gaveston, the handsome young companion he had known since childhood, became a public scandal.

The young King's lack of attention to public affairs, amounting to the neglect of his kingdom, involved him in a confrontation with some of his leading magnates. Determined not to let the country deteriorate any further, they formed themselves into the Lords Ordainers, eight earls, seven bishops and six barons, who met the King at Westminster in 1311. They insisted that he get rid of his present councillors – with Gaveston particularly in mind – and come back to his Parliament for advice and command. Gaveston was exiled. When he returned to the country after a short time he was captured and executed.

Having lost Scotland to Robert Bruce at Bannockburn, Edward was now in danger of losing England. After Gaveston left England, the King married Isabella, the 'she-wolf of France', daughter of the French king; she was only six years old, and according to Stow was nicknamed 'the Little' for that reason. As she was being escorted down river so many people swarmed on

to the Bridge to see her that 'nine people were crowded to death.' Because
of his association with Gaveston, the King and Queen became estranged.
Edward replaced Gaveston in his affections with Hugh Despenser and the
barons were incensed. Their leader, Roger Mortimer, became the queen's
lover, provoking yet another royal scandal. After a short exile they returned
to England, where Despenser was captured, appallingly tortured and killed.
Parliament now faced the same problem as was later posed by Richard II
and Charles I: how to dispose of a legitimate King anointed in the name of
God. Edward had to abdicate. He agreed, provided his son (now fourteen
years old) could rule in his place. He retired to Berkeley Castle where he
was later murdered.

Famine and Plague

In 1315 the Great Famine struck Britain. The harvest throughout Europe
had been very poor after torrential rain for several months and stocks of
food were low. So bad was the quality of the soil that England stopped growing grapes except for the vineyards in monastery gardens. On one occasion
the King visited St Albans but there was no bread to give him. Edward's
extravagances and the wars in Wales and Scotland had demoralised the
nation. A contemporary poem *On the Evil Times of Edward II* summed it up:

> When God saw that the world was so over proud,
> He sent a dearth on earth, and made it full hard.
> A bushel of wheat was at four shillings or more,
> Of which men might have had a quarter before....
> And then they turned pale who had laughed so loud,
> And they became all docile who before were so proud.[13]

The Black Death

In the fourteenth century England experienced wars, royal indiscretions,
parliamentary revolutions, even famine, but nothing had such an effect on
the country as did the ravages of the Black Death. Winston Churchill wrote,
'This affliction, added to all the severities of the Middle Ages, was more
than the human spirit could endure. The Church, smitten like the rest in
body, was wounded grievously in spiritual power.'[14]

The disease started in China, racing through Asia and North Africa to
Europe. The first cases appeared in London in 1348. Bubonic plague is
carried on the fleas of black rats, though this was not discovered until 1908.
The rats came in on the ships up the Thames, and wherever they sought
refuge the fleas found human hosts, not difficult in times of poor personal

and public hygiene. It was known as the Great Pestilence and recovery was rare; some 40,000 Londoners died, perhaps half the population. Excavations in the city have discovered a mass grave near the Tower, with bodies buried five deep, the children squashed into the spaces between the adults. In 2013 excavations in the Smithfield area for the Crossrail project found another such grave beneath Charterhouse Square.

John Stow had noted that 'churchyards were not sufficient to bury the dead, but men were forced to choose out certain fields for burials.'[15] One such burial place, known as No Man's Land, was chosen as a cemetery, north of Smithfield (originally Smooth Field), with a chapel and a garden. It was first called Pardon Churchyard, and twenty years later, Sir Walter Manny rented land close by in Spital Croft, a part of St Bartholomew's Hospital, and built a Carthusian Priory on the site – The Charterhouse.

CHAPTER VII

The Later Middle Ages

The Church in Doubt

IN TIMES OF DISASTER men turn to God. War, famine and pestilence had greatly disturbed the people of London. Their confidence was shaken and their belief in the certainty of the Catholic Church was beginning to show signs of crumbling. The Pope in Rome, the centre of all things spiritual and the one sure rock around which life in every aspect surely revolved, was himself in turmoil. Italy was in disarray, with political unrest and papal control diminishing – no place for the Christian Church to call home.

In 1307 Pope Clement V removed the Papal Court to Avignon; the 'Babylonish captivity' had begun. The English treasury was a prime target for the Pope and his advisers, much resented by the King and barons in London. Added to this was the fact that England was now at war with France, a war that was to last for more than a hundred years, and it certainly seemed to the English that the Holy Father was residing in the enemy's camp. Many of the problems between Pope and King came down to money. Edward III resented papal claims on what he regarded as his own financial property. He was supported by the insularity of his people who resented the presence of those sent from Avignon by a French pope who couldn't even speak their language.

The Young King

When Edward died in 1377 he was succeeded by a boy of ten. Richard II was crowned at Westminster by Archbishop Sudbury – the boy was so tired by the end of the day he had to be carried home on the shoulders of his tutor. The reins of government lay in the hands of John of Gaunt, Duke of Lancaster. One of the wealthiest and most powerful men in the kingdom, he lived when in London at the Savoy Palace on the banks of the Thames, built by Peter of Savoy, a forebear of Gaunt's wife, Blanche of Lancaster.

William of Ockham

The trembling of Catholicism in England was down to individual misgivings, but so far no association of heretical thinkers had appeared, though it was shortly to come. Nor at this stage did it touch the lower ranks of society. It was intellectual doubt that stirred men of the Church. One of the earliest renegades was William of Ockham. Born in Surrey, William joined the Franciscans as a young man, probably in Southwark. Ockham's teachings, controversial as they were, were deemed heretical by the Papal Court and he was summoned to Avignon to defend himself, where he had to confront a formidable panel of churchmen and theologians though he was never convicted of heresy. Fearing further condemnation, he fled to Italy and was excommunicated by the 'other' Pope, John XXII. Ockham declared John a heretic.

Although William of Ockham's life and teachings had little bearing on London or England's practical religious belief, he was one of the first to question the worldly command of the Papacy. He is perhaps best remembered for his statement known as 'Ockham's Razor', the principle of economy of thought, that all things theological should be stated as simply as possible, that entities should not be multiplied unnecessarily.

John Wyclif and the Lollards

Another Oxford scholar who had a much greater influence on Londoners than Ockham was John Wyclif. His unorthodox views, particularly on the relationship between the Pope and the priesthood, resulted in his being called to London in 1377 from his home in Oxford by Simon Sudbury, the Archbishop of Canterbury, to defend himself. Wyclif was supported by John of Gaunt and appeared at St Paul's to answer charges. A large crowd of Londoners gathered outside, ready to vent their anger on the unpopular Lancaster and the meeting ended in confusion, avoiding an outright riot; but the Pope, Gregory XI, did not let the matter drop. He issued a series of bulls against Wyclif, deeming his views heretical and ordering Sudbury to imprison him until he should come to Rome to answer the charges. He wrote that Wyclif had

> burst forth in such execrable and abominable folly that he does not fear to maintain dogmatically in such kingdom and publicly to preach, or rather to vomit forth from the poisonous confines of his own breast some propositions and conclusions which threaten to subvert and weaken the condition of the entire church.[1]

The charges referred to Wyclif's view of the Pope's right of excommunication, his opinions on the King's claim to Papal revenues and the abuses committed by members of the church.

However, Wyclif's views were becoming more unorthodox. He denied the doctrine of transubstantiation, by which the substance of the bread and wine in the Eucharist becomes Christ's presence, that is, his body and blood. His radical views were accepted by a band of followers who took the name Lollards (the word in Flemish meaning mumbler), and soon grew to include many townsfolk, some lower members of the clergy and a few of the nobility. The Lollard Tower is the oldest part of Lambeth Palace, used as a prison for the Lollards in the early fifteenth century. Wyclif was accused of heresy when he pronounced his view that the Papacy had no Biblical foundation and, like the Protestant reformers to come, he believed in the efficacy of preaching the Scriptures as the true word of God. 'England belongs to no Pope,' he said, 'The Pope is but a man, subject to sin, but Christ is the Lord of Lords, and this Kingdom is to be held directly and solely of Christ alone.'[2]

The smell of heresy was getting stronger. Wyclif is often regarded as the herald of the Reformation. However, he is perhaps known as much for being responsible for the first English translation of the Bible. Wyclif himself probably had little hand in the work, though he had always felt that the Bible should be accessible to all men, few of whom had much knowledge of Latin. Nicholas of Hereford is believed to have translated most of the Old Testament. He had been a colleague of Wyclif's at Oxford and his views had also got him into trouble with the orthodox church leaders. He was an important figure in the Lollard movement; this first English version is often referred to as the Lollard Bible.

Rebellion in London

The outbreak of rioting in London in 1382, which has come to be known as the Peasants' Revolt, was partly due to the levy of a tax which in our own time has had a similar outcome – the Poll Tax. But the rebels were set on finding Archbishop Sudbury, whom they saw as the source of all their ills. He was not only the leading churchman of the nation, but was also, as Thomas Becket had been before him and Thomas More afterwards, the chancellor of England; he was accused of taking money from the poor to feed the rich.

Sudbury had earlier imprisoned, on more than one occasion, John Ball, a chaplain and leader of the rebels, a demagogue whose socialistic leanings and anti-clerical stance put him at odds with those in authority. Sudbury termed him an 'obdurate excommunicate'. He had preached to the rebels at Blackheath and encouraged them to move on to London. There is a monument to the rebels in the square at West Smithfield. On Tower Green Archbishop Sudbury was summarily executed and his head hung from London Bridge.

Archbishop Sudbury was succeeded by William Courtenay who summoned a synod at Blackfriars in 1382 to deal with Wyclif and his followers. Known as the Earthquake Council because of the tremors that occurred while it was meeting, it condemned the Lollards as heretical, though Wyclif was not mentioned by name. The conclusions of the Council were published and Wyclif was forbidden to preach. By now he was ill and frail and partly paralysed. He died in Lutterworth 1384 and was buried in the churchyard there. On the instructions of Pope Martin V his body was exhumed in 1428, burned and the ashes scattered. He left behind a legacy of independence of church doctrine, of freedom to worship according to an interpretation of religion other than that ordained by the Pope, which was taken up first by the Reformation and later by the Nonconformists and their followers. Wyclif's reputation stands on his undoubted integrity and conviction.

The Rebirth of the English Language

The feelings of unease, of change and uncertainty that had to some extent been behind the Peasants' Revolt, were symptomatic of life in England in the later Middle Ages. The ravages of the Black Death brought home the fragility of existence, and the old positive support of church, state and society were no longer reliable. Were there really questions to be asked about belief and God's purpose concerning man and his estate? It seemed so. For it was not only religious thinkers who were questioning these matters. The English language was maturing in its power of expression; reading the Bible in the vernacular, or in the majority of cases having it read, brought a new perspective to everyday life. Why should men have bothered to learn to read when there was little to attract them to books? Latin was for priests, not for the likes of farmers or fishermen. Even the majesty of the law was becoming more accessible. English was being used in London's administration. In 1356 the Sheriff's Courts switched to using English, and in 1362 Parliament passed the Statute of Pleading, because the people, as the Act put it, 'have no knowledge or understanding of that which is said for them or against them by their Serjeants and other pleaders'. Law French had been in use ever since the Conquest, but henceforth all documents were to be produced in English.

When William Langland's *Vision of Piers Plowman* appeared it seemed as if a new light had shone out for the English. A book about the countryside and the city, about churchmen and tradespeople, about the life and death of ordinary folk, was revolutionary. The full title of the poem was *The Vision of William concerning Piers the Plowman*. It was revised several times and is an allegory not unlike Bunyan's *Pilgrim's Progress*, except that the characters range from kings and knights, with their ladies, down to working people, merchants and farmers. Langland's pictures of ordinary Londoners were vivid and recognisable:

> Beggars and blackguards went busily about
> With their bellies and bags all brimming with bread,
> Feigning sick for food and fighting in the ale-house...
> Cissy the sempstress sat on a bench,
> Robin the rabbit-catcher and his wife with him,
> Tim the tinker and two of his apprentices,
> Hickey the hackney-man and Hodge the huckster,
> Clarice of Cock's Lane and the clerk of the parish,
> Parson Peter Proudie and his Peronella,
> Davy the ditcher and a dozen others.[3]

Greater even than Langland and certainly better known was Geoffrey Chaucer, the 'Father of English literature'. Born in London about 1343, he served in the royal household as an administrator. His *Troilus and Criseyde* appeared in the early 1380s and several manuscript editions still exist, so its popularity before the invention of printing must have been considerable. *The Canterbury Tales*, which were never finished, comprise the collection of stories told by those on pilgrimage to Canterbury Cathedral to the shrine of Thomas Becket. The *Tales* are remarkable for their broad humour, their descriptions of the assorted company on the road and their earthy English verse, so unlike the dry Latin religious works that were almost the only books that Englishmen, if they could read at all, could access.

Richard's Final Years

The King's relationship with his advisers now began to deteriorate. He, like several of his predecessors, did not choose his friends wisely; his imagination did not enable him to foresee the results of his extravagance or his inability to fulfil his promises. The Merciless Parliament led to the Lords Appellants, a group of dissatisfied lords, including the Duke of Gloucester and the Earls of Warwick and Arundel, removing from office some of Richard's closest supporters. For a whole year the monarchy was in abeyance, with no-one in command of the nation.

Like Edward II, Richard chose for a close intimate an effeminate young man, the Earl of Oxford, without the wisdom or experience that he desperately needed. Deep-seated changes were made to the court. It was in 1396 that the Statute of *Praemunire* was passed, claiming England's freedom from Papal control over finances and church appointments, an enactment which was to have considerable bearing on moves towards the supremacy of the monarch at the time of the Reformation.

The King's attitude to his advisers now began to border on the insane. Most were either banished like Henry Bolingbroke (now Duke of Hereford) or murdered like his uncle, the Duke of Gloucester. The Pope threatened excommunication on any who impeded Richard's right to rule. When Richard went to Ireland in 1399, Bolingbroke saw his chance and returned to England, reclaimed the Duchy of Lancaster from the King, who had appropriated it, and set in train the dethronement of the monarch. Henry's only rival to the throne was his cousin, the seven-year-old Earl of March. Both were descended from Edward III's sons, John of Gaunt and Lionel. Richard agreed to abdicate and was imprisoned in the Tower; Bolingbroke succeeded to the throne as Henry IV. Richard remained in the Tower until he was removed to Pontefract Castle where he died in mysterious circumstances a few weeks later.

The First Lancastrian

Henry Bolingbroke assumed the Crown as Henry IV, considered by many, especially the French, to have usurped the throne. Speaking at the time of his claim to the throne he said,

> In the name of God, I, Henry of Lancaster, challenge this realm and the Crown, with all the dependencies and appurtenances that relate to it, being a blood descendant of King Henry III and sent by God in his grace because of this right, with the assistance of my kin and my friends to recover it, when this realm was on the point of being ruined through poor government and lawlessness.[4]

He was invested at Westminster and anointed, it was said, with sacred oil given to Thomas Becket by the Virgin Mary. He sat, perhaps the first monarch to do so, on the Stone of Scone, won from Scotland by Edward I, the Hammer of the Scots. The French medieval historian Jean Froissart gives a vivid picture of the coronation.

> The King had put on a short doublet of cloth-of-gold in the German style. He was mounted on a white charger and wore the blue Garter on his left leg. He rode through the City of London and was escorted to Westminster by a great number of nobles with their men, wearing their various liveries and badges, and all the burgesses, Lombards and merchants of London, and all the grand masters of the guilds, each guild decked out with its particular emblems. Six thousand horses were in the procession ... white and red wine flowed from nine fountains in Cheapside.[5]

London could certainly put on a show.

However, if Henry had hoped to bring to his kingdom a peaceful co-existence of lords and commoners, a quiet religious demeanour in all parts of the realm and the end of rebellion in its furthest regions, he was to be sadly disappointed. Parliament was now established as a permanent effective force, controlling the finances of both the King and the nation, and repealing much of the legislation passed under Richard, together with the conviction of several of his advisers for crimes against the people. As far as the Church was concerned, one immediate source of controversy was the situation regarding the Schism. Henry was anxious to try to resolve the problem of now three popes, with the Italian incumbent, Innocent VII, on the brink of death. However, if England was to be taken seriously as a player in the papal stakes, she had to deal with the continued threat of heresy at home.

For the Lollards had not gone away. In 1395 the Twelve Conclusions of the Lollards were pinned to the door of St Paul's Cathedral. The text was in Middle English and the twelve tenets covered the State of the Church, the Priesthood, Clerical Celibacy, Transubstantiation, Exorcisms and Hallowings, Clerics in Secular Offerings, Prayers for the Dead, Pilgrimages, Confession, War, Battle and Crusades, Female Vows of Continence and Abortion, and Arts and Crafts; a fairly comprehensive assessment of the Christian Life. The document was in simple, plainspoken language, with a few Latin phrases thrown in, but it dealt firmly with transgression by clerics ('the priesthood of Rome is made with signs, rites and bishops' blessings, and that is of little virtue'), women ('the which be fickle and imperfect in kind') and soldiers ('taught to love and to have mercy on his enemies and not to slay them'). It ends with a prayer for reform, 'We pray God of his endless goodness reform our Church, all out of joint, to the perfections of the first beginning, Amen).'[6] It was a brave and public step to take.

Six years later Archbishop Arundel and his Council at Canterbury acted against anyone preaching without a licence. If arrested and found guilty of heresy he could be burned at the stake. *De Heretico Comburendo*, the first law to allow burning as a punishment, was not a very efficient statute, little publicised and with considerable doubt as to the precise offence incurred. Some such heretics confessed and then reoffended.

Little attention was paid to the death of the insignificant ordinary folk, but the execution of a Member of Parliament, sitting for the shire of Hereford, was far more important. Sir John Oldcastle took royal service in Scotland and coming from the west of England, where Lollardy was spreading widely, was certainly aware of such heretical activity as he moved into prominence in national as well as local affairs. He married as his second wife, Joan, granddaughter and heir to Lord Cobham who had played an important part in the governments of both Richard II and Henry IV.

Oldcastle took the title Cobham in the name of his wife and was a prime participant in diplomatic moves between France and England. He was already suspected of being associated with the Lollards and through them with their counterparts in Bohemia, the Hussites.

Oldcastle was challenged by Archbishop Arundel and tried for his dissenting views. At his trial he broke out into a long angry speech, reviling the Papacy and the Church in England. He finished, 'Those who judge me and wish to condemn me are deceiving you all, and will lead you and themselves to Hell; for that reason you should beware of them.'[7] He was saved from execution because of his standing in state affairs and sent to the Tower. He later escaped with the help of friends and plotted revenge against the King (by now Henry V), was betrayed and only just escaped capture. A wanted man on the run, he was eventually taken and burnt at the stake in 1417. John Oldcastle is believed to be the origin of Falstaff in Shakespeare's plays. At the end of Henry IV Part II, Chorus says, referring to Falstaff, 'For Oldcastle died a martyr and this is not the man.'

The ideals of Lollardy continued for another hundred years or more, until the Reformation. There were now two Lollard Towers in London. In old St Paul's the southern of the two towers on the west end of the cathedral was known as Lollards Tower, the prison of the Bishop of London. Stow says it was used as a bishop's prison 'for such as were detected for opinions in religion, contrary to the faith of the church.'[8] The Lollard Tower (still in existence) at Lambeth Palace was originally known as Chichele's Tower, after Archbishop Chichele who built it as a water-tower.

Henry IV died at the age of forty-six. He had been told by a fortune teller that he would die in Jerusalem and had tried to form an assembly to go on Crusade, with no success. In fact he died at Westminster Palace in the Jerusalem Chamber.

The Field of Agincourt

Henry V was born in 1387 in Monmouth and had attended his father's coronation, aged twelve, sitting on his father's right hand, as Harry, Prince of Wales, Duke of Cornwall, Earl of Chester. He sat with a new sword in his hand without a point, as a sign of peace, not a good omen for a King who was to achieve his greatest fame for his exploits in war. As had become common practice since Edward I's time, prayers were always offered up for success in battle. The clergy preached sermons and processions took place throughout the land, a confirmation of the link between God and the monarch. 'God for Harry, England and St George' was not an invention of Shakespeare. It was the common prayer in many churches at a time when war was a praiseworthy pursuit for a nation which felt itself chosen by God to carry out his wishes. According to Thomas Walsingham in the *St Albans Chronicle*, Henry decreed at St Paul's, soon after his own coronation, that 'the feast of St George the Martyr should be honoured in future as a double festival in that church'.[9] After Agincourt the feast was promoted from 'lesser double' to 'greater double'.

Without Shakespeare it is doubtful whether Henry V would have passed into history as one of England's greatest monarchs. He was certainly a great soldier, courageous, determined and a noble leader of men. But he was ruthless and could be cruel. However, he was undoubtedly a man of God, genuinely pious, having endowed three monasteries, the Carthusian at Sheen, the Bridgettine Order at Syon and a third, the Celestine, which never succeeded in England. His concern for reform of the Church did not find him in sympathy with the Lollards, but he was anxious to preserve England's right to independence from Papal control of appointments.

At the Council of Constance in 1417 the two contenders for the Papacy, Gregory XII and John XXIII both resigned and the third claimant, Benedict XIII was excommunicated, leaving the way clear for the election of Martin V, strongly supported by the English representatives under Bishop Beaufort. Henry Beaufort, sometimes called the Cardinal of England, was an illegitimate son of John of Gaunt. He announced the victory at Agincourt in St Paul's Cathedral, urging the King to attribute it to God not himself. He was appointed Cardinal by Martin V and continued to play an important part in the diplomatic affairs of the country.

Henry died of dysentery in France at the age of thirty-five after reigning for less than ten years. After the funeral procession through northern France he was buried in Westminster Abbey. Walsingham was effusive in his praise, writing that he was a man of sincere piety, sparing and discreet in word, astute in counsel, wise in judgment, modest in his looks but magnificent in action … a devoted servant of God.

CHAPTER VIII

York and Lancaster

The New Young King

ONCE AGAIN ENGLAND was under the rule of a child-king. Henry VI was just nine months old when his father died, never having seen his baby son. The control of the nation now lay in the hands of the Duke of Gloucester and the Duke of Bedford, the late King's brothers, together with Henry Beaufort, the Archbishop of Canterbury, Bishop Henry Chichele and the Chancellor Thomas Langley, Bishop of Durham. The young prince grew up in a scholarly and religious atmosphere, speaking perfect French and English, with an extensive knowledge of Latin. His tutor and governor was Richard Beauchamp, Earl of Warwick.

The King of France died a short time after Henry V, and his son Charles VII was crowned at Rheims, with the help of Joan of Arc. Not long afterwards the new King of England was hastily given an English coronation in Westminster Abbey at the age of eight, and proceeded to claim his French throne as arranged by the Treaty of Troyes. He paid his only visit to France to be crowned by Bishop Beaufort, as he had been in London. The French coronation took place in Notre Dame amid considerable disturbance by the Paris crowds, and shortly after his arrival the Maid of Orleans was tried and burned to death. Henry returned to England as soon as he could and was welcomed back to London with thanksgiving services in Westminster and St Paul's.

The Foundation of Eton

In London Henry was beginning to shake off the shackles of his uncles' control. His two great passions were the church and education. In 1440 he founded Eton College, near his favourite home at Windsor. A pious devotion to the Church was behind his desire to found first of all a school and then a college at Cambridge University. Scholars at King's were admitted only after attending Eton for at least two years. The College was unique in that it was free from the control of the University, though it had to conform to academic conventions as well as convocations, processions and some other trappings of university life. An academic and Carthusian who knew the King well – he wrote the first biography of Henry VI – was John Blacman. He praised him for his religious attention, for his generosity to educational pursuits and for his virtuous life. 'He was a simple man, without any crook of craft or untruth, as is plain to all. With none did he deal craftily, nor ever would say an untrue word to any, but framed his speech always to speak truth.'[1] Henry paid much attention to the running of Eton College, including the welfare of the scholars and the priests who were in charge of their welfare. 'I would rather have them somewhat weak in music than defective in knowledge of the Scriptures.'[2]

Eton may have been a royal foundation for the sons of gentlemen, but the citizens of London were anxious to provide a good education for theirs, too. Thanks to John Colet, Dean of St Paul's, a school was founded in 1509 as St Paul's School. It was established for

> 353 poor men's children, to be taught free in the same school, appointing a master, a surmaster and a chaplain, with sufficient stipends to endure forever, and committed the oversight thereof to the mercers in London, because he himself was son of Henry Colet, mercer, Mayor of London.[3]

The Rise of the House of York

The King by now was already unfit to rule and there was no obvious heir. When he heard about England's loss of almost all her lands in France, he lost his reason and declined into a catatonic state, unable to recall who or where he was. The precise nature of his mental illness is difficult to assess. His complete recovery eighteen months later precludes some sort of brain disease, and the often quoted 'catatonic schizophrenia' is also unlikely as he later regained his full faculties. Certainly some form of clinical depression must be the answer; the King was always subject to fits of melancholia and social withdrawal, and certainly his grandfather, Charles VI of France, was mentally ill. Henry did suffer from hallucinations and his religious devotions often verged on the psychotic, but other considerations such as close inter-marriage within the family and the burden of kingship from a very early age may have taken their toll. England received another shock regarding her royal family when Queen Margaret gave birth to a son. She had been married for more than eight years and it was never expected that she would have a child. Henry, when shown the baby, seemed unaware of his son, but the circumstance totally altered the future status of the English throne.

The King's Recovery

Totally unexpectedly the King recovered his wits at Christmas 1454, recognised those about him, including his baby son, and seemed quite unaware of having been ill. Although Richard of York had been made Protector during the King's illness, Queen Margaret, an ambitious and forceful woman, had tried to assume control. The Lancastrians now seemed secure as England's commanders, but the Yorkists were not prepared to go quietly. When negotiations for a peaceful solution were abandoned after a conference at Leicester, both sides resorted to armed conflict. The first battle in what has come to be known as the War of the Roses took place at St Albans, resulting in the death of several leading Lancastrians. The King, slightly wounded, was taken by the Yorkists.

The Duke, together with the King as his prisoner, travelled to London, where Henry again ceremonially received his crown from Richard, confirming the Yorkists' loyalty to the King. Londoners' suspicions of the Lancastrian King crystallised when, in 1456, there were riots in the City, led by mercers' apprentices, against the Lombards. The London merchants resented the fact that King Henry had chosen Italians, rather than English merchants, from whom to borrow money. The rioters were savagely punished by the King's choice of investigator, the Duke of Exeter. Exeter had a reputation for violence. The rack at the Tower of London, where he was Constable, was called 'the Duke of Exeter's daughter'. Exeter's decision to send the apprentices to the gallows did nothing to endear King Henry to the merchants.

In 1457 Henry held a Council at Westminster at which the Lollard heresy again came to the fore. Reginald Pecock, Bishop of Chichester but resident in London, had read widely in the literature of the Lollards in order, he said, to be able to refute their doctrines. Aware of the attention paid by Wyclif's followers to the written word, he claimed to have debated with them to expose the fallacies of their theology. However, the King was informed of Pecock's involvement with Lollard thinking and was asked to pass on to the Archbishop of Canterbury a request for an investigation. At St Paul's Cross Pecock signed a statement revoking his heresies and burnt his books. He was deprived of his See on the grounds that his appointment was invalid as he had been a heretic at the time. He was the only bishop to lose his See before the Reformation. He was probably indicted so that the King could be seen to be upholding the Church at a time when he and the Lancastrian cause needed support.

A Yorkist King

By now Henry was again losing control both of himself and of his country. The Queen was in real command. She charged the Yorkist leaders with treachery and they decided to put their case to the King. They swore loyalty to Henry but coming south from their strongholds in the north were met at Northampton with a Lancastrian army. The battle lasted half an hour and Henry was captured by the Yorkist force and taken to London. Richard of York went straight to Westminster where the chronicler Vitellius noted, 'his sword born upright before him, he took the King's place, claiming it for his right and in heritance and said he would keep it to live and die.'[4] He also reverted to his dynastic name of Plantagenet, indicating his intention to claim the throne. The action was not welcomed by his own allies. They had sworn their loyalty to Henry and were not prepared to deny their oath. Richard made himself at home at Westminster and finally accepted the King's agreement that he should accede to the throne after Henry's death.

The next armed confrontation took place at Wakefield, where the Duke of York was killed. His head was hung on the gates of the city of York, wearing a paper crown. The York army, much depleted, its leader gone, came south to meet the Queen and the Lancastrians at the second battle of St Albans. Richard's son, Edward Earl of March, defeated another wing of Margaret's army at Mortimer's Cross, on the Welsh border and proceeded to London, accompanied by the Earl of Warwick.

They were welcomed by the Londoners, Henry was declared unfit to rule and March was crowned King Edward IV. According to Vitellius, the people congregated in St John's Field and were asked 'whether the said Henry was worthy to reign still, and the people cried, "Nay, Nay". And then they were asked if they would have the Earl of March to be their King, and they said "Yea, Yea".' Edward was careful to abide by all the conventions of a properly appointed king. He attended Evensong at St Paul's before his coronation the following day. His first task was to quell the disorders arising from the weak government of his predecessor. London was glad to have a strong personality in control of the capital. The City was anxious to restore its trading traditions and its system of self-government.

The young King of England was a very eligible catch for any of Europe's princesses. Several were proposed as a future queen: the daughters of the houses of Burgundy, of France and of Scotland. It was while the Earl of Warwick was in France, negotiating a French marriage, that Edward showed he was his own man. He secretly married Elizabeth Woodville, daughter of Lord Rivers and widow of Sir John Grey. According to the chronicle of John Warkworth, though there is now some doubt about the author, the

Earl of Warwick was 'greatly displeased'. Elizabeth is described by the contemporary chronicler Edward Halle as

> a woman more of formal countenance than of excellent beauty, but yet of such beauty and favour that with her sober demeanour, lovely looking and feminine smiling (neither too wanton nor too humble), beside her tongue so eloquent and her wit so pregnant, she was able to ravish the mind of a mean person, while she allured and made subject to her the heart of so great a king.[5]

With her she brought a vast crowd of relatives from the Rivers and Woodville families who were to prove a considerable nuisance to Edward and his control of the country.

Another rising in Yorkshire necessitated the King's presence, but as Sir John Paston wrote to his brother, 'Some say that the king should come again to London, and that in haste ... the Lords Clarence and Warwick will essay to land in England every day, as folks fear.'[6] Warwick and Clarence landed in the west country in September 1470 and declared their support for Henry. They gathered allies as they crossed southern England and Edward was forced eastwards to East Anglia, from where he took ship to the Low Countries.

As soon as he was gone, the ex-King Henry was released from the Tower by the mayor and Bishop Wayneflete, the Lord Chancellor. He was proclaimed King at St Paul's Cross and taken to the Bishop of London's palace, accompanied by Warwick. Edward and his younger brother Richard were attainted.

The Final Battles

Edward's queen Elizabeth had sought sanctuary at Westminster while the King was abroad, and there in November 1470 as Edward Halle writes,

> In great penury, forsaken by all her friends, she was delivered of a fair son called Edward, which was with small pomp, like a poor man's child, christened and baptised, the godfathers being the Abbot and Prior of Westminster, and the godmother the Lady Scrope.[7]

The young prince came sadly into the world and was to leave it in similar fashion.

Edward came back to England in March 1471 and landed at Ravenspur in Yorkshire. He moved on, gathering support as he went. He reached London on Maundy Thursday to find the city still perplexed as to where its allegiance lay. The people finally settled on Edward, having debated the pros and cons of the two sides.

They considered that King Henry was such an innocent person, as of himself was not most apt to moderate and govern the public wealth of this realm. And on the other side, King Edward, by no other men's document, but only by his own policy and wit, was wont to order the realm and govern the kingdom.[8]

Edward duly called the Londoners together and thanked them warmly.

The nearest that the fighting in the long-drawn out War of the Roses came to London was the battle of Barnet in 1471. Henry, now a poor figure of a King, was taken by Warwick's brother, George Nevill, Archbishop of York, through the streets to gather together the remnants of the Lancastrian side. It was useless; Edward took the city peacefully. Bertram Wolffe, in his life of Henry VI, describes how Henry greeted Edward warmly, saying, 'Cousin of York, you are very welcome. I hold my life to be in no danger in your hands.'[9]

Edward left London on the eve of Easter Sunday, taking Henry with him, northwards as far as Barnet. Sunday dawned in heavy mist, confusing the two sides. Halle describes the fighting, 'If the battle were fierce and deadly before, now it was crueller, more bloody, more fervent and fiery, and yet they had fought from morning almost to noon, without any part getting advantage of other.'[10] Warwick was killed, as was his brother, Lord Montague, as well as over a thousand fighting men. Warwick's body was taken in an open coffin to St Paul's and then to Bisham Abbey. Edward returned with Henry to London. Three kings were on Barnet field that day, Henry VI, Edward IV and the future Richard III; it was the turning point of the whole long bloody war.

The Arrival of the Printed Book

In 1476 there returned to London a man who had more influence on the city, and indeed on the whole world, than any king, nobleman or bishop. William Caxton had been a Mercers Company apprentice and had spent some years in the Low Countries where the mercers did much business. In 1451 Johannes Gutenberg in Mainz had produced the first Bible printed in movable type, a revolution in book production, which was to have an immense effect on the minds of men in succeeding centuries. Caxton went to Cologne – Germany still maintained the greatest command of printing skills – where he bought a press and returned to Bruges. His first book was *The Recuyell of the Histories of Troy*, which he had himself translated from the French, the first book printed in English. This was followed while he was still in Bruges by *The Game and Play of Chess*.

In 1476 Caxton came back to London and took a shop in the shelter of Westminster Abbey, The Red Pale. This was an excellent site, being close to the Palace, Parliament and the homes of leading members of the nobility.

King Edward was himself a considerable book collector, with 'a preference for showy and lavishly illuminated volumes',[11] mostly in French rather than Latin. Caxton boasted of his royal patronage, with two books dedicated to the King. After a few small leaflets, the first book printed in England was Chaucer's *The Canterbury Tales*. Only twelve copies of the first edition still exist, two are in the British Library.

The invention of printing brought to the ordinary man, if he could read, a vast array of books, ranging from translations of the Bible to manuals on arts and crafts, books on travel, history and religion, encouraging political ideas and intellectual pursuits. The IPEX Exhibition of 1963 commemorated the invention of printing with a magnificent display of more than 400 books that have influenced men over the centuries. Entitled *Printing and the Mind of Man*, it included volumes ranging from Gutenberg's Bible of 1455 to Hitler's *Mein Kampf*. In his introduction, Denis Hay says, 'The world of books had been transformed and it is impossible to exaggerate the rapidity of the transformation.'[12] The invention of printing was to dominate religion, politics, military strategy and many other fields to the present day.

CHAPTER IX

The Coming of
the Tudors

An Uncrowned King

N O SOONER HAD THE YORKISTS returned to London than Henry VI died in the Tower, probably murdered. His had been a sad life, a man more suited to the Church than to the monarchy, weak in mind and body, never able to control his family or his country.

Edward IV, sure of his hold on London and with two young princes waiting, was in full command. As his biographer Charles Ross put it, 'He was able to reduce the level of violence and oppression. He managed to combine this with the avoidance of expensive foreign wars, a low level of taxation and the encouragement of English commerce.'[1] However, after so many years of armed conflict at home and abroad, it was hardly surprising that soldiers roamed the city streets, pillaging and violently abusing the townsfolk, with little fear of retribution.

Edward IV died in 1483 aged forty-one. His death was somewhat mysterious – no firm reason has been given by his contemporaries, though it is known that he was subject to considerable over-indulgence. Some chroniclers talk of an 'unknown disease' and hint of poison, one mentioning that 'in food and drink he was most immoderate'. During his last illness he was able to change his will and to discuss the future of England with his councillors. He lay in state in Westminster Palace and was then taken into the Abbey, later to be buried in his chapel of St George at Windsor.

The new King Edward, aged twelve, was brought down to London from Ludlow in the care of his Rivers relations, but at Stony Stratford the party was met by Richard of Gloucester who took charge of his nephew. They came into the city 'the king riding in blue velvet and the Duke of Gloucester in black cloth like a mourner'[2]. Edward stayed at the palace of the Bishop of London, but his mother, Queen Elizabeth, well aware of the dangers that threatened her young family, took sanctuary, together with the King's brother Richard aged seven, in Westminster Abbey. The idea of sanctuary in England dates back to the Saxon kings, and most churches offered safety to those who had committed a crime or were in need of protection. Royal seekers after a safe house were often accommodated in great comfort. Elizabeth brought with her into the Abbey so many attendants and so much furniture, that a hole had to be knocked down in the abbey wall to get it all in. She trusted no-one, but when Thomas Bouchier, the Cardinal Archbishop of Canterbury came to her and assured her that Gloucester meant no harm, she surrendered to him her younger son to be reunited with his brother the King. Both princes were accommodated in the Tower, scene of the recent deaths of Clarence and Henry VI. They could hardly have enjoyed the thought. As Shakespeare has the young Richard say, 'I shall not sleep in quiet at the Tower.'[3] There the two princes remained, never to be seen again. In 1674 the bones of two young children were found bricked up in a wall of the Tower, but they have not been conclusively attributed to the princes.

The Last Plantagenet

Richard Duke of Gloucester, self-proclaimed Protector of King Edward V, delayed the coronation of his young charge – he was in fact never crowned. At a meeting of his Council at the Tower to discuss the coronation, Richard lost his temper with Lord Hastings, his brother Edward's closest ally. Sir Thomas More's account of the affair is graphic.

> As in a great anger he clapped his fist upon the board a great rap. At which token given, one cried 'Treason' without the chamber. Therewith a door clapped and come there rushing men in harness, as many as the chamber might hold. And anon the Protector said to the Lord Hastings, 'I arrest thee traitor'.[4]

Hastings was taken outside and immediately executed on Tower Green.

At St Paul's Cross a sermon by Friar Ralph Shaa, brother of the Lord Mayor of London, stated that the King and his brother were illegitimate, with no legal claim to the throne. This relied on Edward IV's marriage to Elizabeth Woodville taking place after he had been contracted to marry the daughter of the King of France. In fact the marriage took place before the Earl of Warwick had concluded his negotiations with the French princess.

English Church Practice

The English Church at this time was still under the control and protection of the Pope in Rome. Local laws could supersede Catholic canon law where custom dictated. The Province of Canterbury ordained what went on within its boundaries and this included London. But the Diocese of Sarum

(Salisbury) was often the model for local church conventions. Church courts had considerable say in how wills were drawn up and how inheritance was ordered.

Secular courts had jurisdiction over most matters concerning crime even when these related to the clergy. The Convocations of Canterbury and York did not claim to be independent of papal authority, but they did have a certain freedom to amend them when they considered it necessary. Bishops and archbishops at their ordination took an oath of allegiance to the Apostolic See.

Kings and Popes were often still at odds when it came to appointments and to financial affairs. The Pope could move a bishop from diocese to diocese, but the King reserved the right to appoint the higher clergy, though he usually sought the agreement of the Pope. There were considerable restraints on the conduct of bishops. They had no control over collegiate foundations or royal chapels, nor could they visit a Cluniac or Cistercian monastery.

The fundamental unit of the Church in England was the parish. The local parish council was responsible for the nave, where the worshippers sat, while the priest looked after the chancel where he officiated. In London there were more than a hundred parishes, each with its church and at least one cleric. Some were closely linked to the guilds.

The higher clerics, particularly the Archbishops of Canterbury, were often involved in the politics of the nation, particularly the Exchequer, some becoming Chancellor, closest advisor to the King. John Morton, Cardinal Archbishop appointed by Edward IV, was responsible for tax-gathering. His methods gave rise to the expression 'Morton's Fork', whereby he ordered that a poor man was obviously thrifty and could therefore afford to pay taxes, while a rich man had more than enough to do the same. Morton was a strong opponent of Richard III, and as mentor to Thomas More probably encouraged the latter's view of the King in his *History of Richard III*, often regarded as the source for Tudor propaganda.

Henry VII, the first Tudor to claim the throne, traced his ancestry back through his father, Edmund Tudor, Earl of Richmond, son of Owen Tudor, second husband of Queen Catherine, widow of Henry V. His mother, Margaret Beaufort, was a direct descendant of John of Gaunt's third marriage to Katherine Swynford. It was perhaps a tenuous claim, but with the two young princes gone, and Richard's only son predeceasing him, there were no nearer contestants.

Richard's death at Bosworth Field, his crown traditionally languishing in a gorse bush, threw the succession into dispute. But Henry Tudor, brought up in Wales and then in Brittany, was at the battle in the thick of the fighting, and claimed the throne there and then. Shakespeare's picture

seems to have been generally accurate. Henry did indeed end the York/
Lancaster battle and join the white rose to the red 'in fair conjunction'. After
the battle, Henry rode straight for London. He was crowned in Westminster
Abbey.

> Here I present Henry, true and rightful and undoubted inheritor by the laws
> of God and man to the crown and royal dignity of England ... will ye, Sirs, at
> this time give your wills and assents to the same consecration, enunciation and
> coronation?[5]

They did so warmly.

The Growth of London

In the previous fifty years London had matured. Its population is estimated
at between 50,000 to 75,000. It was, by the beginning of the sixteenth
century, a large sophisticated city, sure of its situation in Europe, anxious
for peace in the streets and a firm hand to rule over it. It was the centre
of a settled Parliament, held regularly in Westminster, its companion city.
It had an established legal system governed by the King's Bench and the
Bench of Common Pleas, and its lawyers operated from the four principal
Inns of Court. The honour of being appointed King's (or Queen's) Counsel
was not introduced until Sir Francis Bacon became the first to hold the office
at the end of the sixteenth century. The integrity of England's legal system
was jealously guarded and was the envy of many richer nations across the
Channel.

London, however, was still a merchant city, though its trading economy
was gradually dividing into two: the small craftsmen in their own workshops
– leather workers, tailors, shoemakers etc. – and the more professional
investors, lawyers, businessmen and commercial entrepreneurs. Londoners
were by now more literate, more independent in mind and spirit, less willing
to accept at face value what they were told by their priests, their overlords
and their King. Import and export trade was growing. The city was
becoming cosmopolitan, even if its citizens were on the whole not too keen
on the idea.

The Predominance of London

London was now recognised as one of the foremost cities of Europe. Its
position, as Julius Caesar had found, commanded a navigable river, it was
an international port, well serviced and efficient. Around it was agricultural
land, producing corn and cloth, its two staples, and self-supporting as far
as food was concerned, with good transport by road and water. Its native

industries enjoyed a valuable export trade and its markets were well run and, by the standards of the time, honest. Blackwell Hall, situated near the Guildhall, was the centre of the cloth trade, Leadenhall was the meat and poultry market and the Stocks Market, on the site of the present Mansion House, was where livestock was sold.

Foreign visitors compared London favourably with their own systems of record keeping and supreme justice. The King kept his court close by and was present there for much of the time. The City was well defended by the constantly repaired old Roman wall, drawbridges at both ends of the bridge, and the great bridge itself, lined with shops and houses along its length, continued as it had always done, to be a symbol of London's independence. The early medieval churches formed the city's skyline – the 'dreaming spires' of London compared with any in Europe. The spire of the great gothic cathedral of St Paul's was nearly 500 feet high, the tallest in the world. Other fine buildings added to the pride of the Londoners: the Tower, Guildhall, now extended and refurbished to welcome the Lord Mayor's annual banquet, the Customs House (built by John Churchman on 'Wool Quay' to levy the customs dues on exported wool) and the halls of the Livery Companies; many of the original halls occupied the same sites as their modern equivalents. The City was now overcrowded and spreading out into the countryside. The road between London and Westminster was an easily negotiable thoroughfare between the King's palace and his capital City.

Henry VII rebuilt Baynard's Castle and started work on the Lady Chapel in Westminster Abbey. It was to be a memorial to Henry VI, whose canonisation was requested from the Pope. However, Julius II demanded such a huge sum for this that the new King, never one to spend money unnecessarily, decided instead to build a magnificent chapel at Westminster to house his remains. Together with the Abbot, John Islip, and with the encouragement of his chaplain, a young cleric by the name of Thomas Wolsey, Henry arranged for the old Lady Chapel to be demolished, and the foundation stone for the new one was laid in 1503.

Henry's mother, Margaret Beaufort, contributed to the cost of the superb new chapel. Nikolaus Pevsner writes, 'technically it is a tour de force'[6]. The fan vaulting of the high ceiling, the huge stained glass windows (sadly destroyed by the Puritan fervour of 1641), one hundred and seven figures of saints lining the walls, the towering arches leading to the side chapels, all combine to make the Henry VII Chapel one of London's greatest monuments. Both Margaret and Henry died in 1509, before the Chapel was complete, but their tombs, the work of the Italian Torrigiano, who worked with Michelangelo, are 'the noblest and most humane of the Abbey's monuments.'[7]

Princess Katherine

On 20th September 1486 a son was born to Queen Elizabeth of York. For one who was destined never to reign, he had a greater influence on England's destiny than almost any other royal child. Prince Arthur, named after Britain's most romantic hero, was created Prince of Wales and invested with the Order of the Bath. In 1497 he was betrothed to the Princess Katherine of Aragon, daughter of Ferdinand and Isabella of Spain, when he was eleven and she was twelve. According to Halle, her father

> would never make full conclusion of the matrimony to be had between Prince Arthur and the lady Katherine his daughter nor send her into England as long as this earl lived [referring to the impostor Warbeck who had claimed to be related to the Warwicks]. For he imagined that as long as any Earl of Warwick lived that England should never be cleansed or purged of Civil War.[8]

Katherine arrived in England in 1501 and she and Arthur were married a few weeks later in St Paul's Cathedral. She was attended by her new brother-in-law Prince Henry. Arthur died at Ludlow Castle in 1502, at the age of fifteen, apparently from the 'sweating sickness', a form of pestilence that was sweeping Britain. He was buried in Worcester Cathedral. The sixteen-year-old widow, who maintained she was still a virgin, in spite of Arthur's remarks to the contrary, was left alone, later to influence the fortunes of England's religious affiliation.

The New Lollards

Since the death of Wyclif, heresy had to a large extent died down, at least in London. Those who pursued their determination to differ from established church doctrine did not have the intellectual strength of Wyclif and his supporters. They met in secret but there were signs that their numbers were growing. True reform of the Catholic Church needed to come from the top. Without the collaboration of kings and bishops nothing of importance, as Wyclif had found, was going to happen.

Henry himself frequently proclaimed his allegiance to the Pope, but the Borgia Pope Alexander VI was notoriously unreliable as friend or enemy. The King carefully maintained diplomatic relations with Rome while keeping England as independent as he could, a necessary precaution as things turned out. His second son, Henry, growing up in the shadow of his brother Arthur's probable succession, received little in the way of training in statecraft or government affairs. His movements were closely restricted – he was still only twelve. His father, in close touch with his widowed daughter-in-law's parents, and now himself a widower, made some overtures about marrying Katherine himself. However, it was considered more appropriate that the young widow should be handed over to her brother-in-law. For Katherine to marry her deceased husband's brother, assuming the marriage was legitimate and consummated, a dispensation from the Pope was needed. The authorities took Arthur's word rather than Katherine's about the consummation; what Pope Alexander's view might be was a different matter. In any case the young couple had to wait another two years before Henry was old enough to marry.

Economy

Henry VII is remembered particularly for his astute command of England's finances. His control of taxation, customs levies and the expansion of trade, gave the nation an economic stability, rare in Europe at the time. He has been known, justifiably, as a great man of business. He levied payments from the Church when bishops moved from See to See, used his powers over criminals with money to dun them for legal decisions and fined the nobility for minor transgressions. His own expenditure was meagre to the point of parsimony; he loved even the feel of money. In his biography of Henry, *The Winter King*, Thomas Penn describes it: 'These were the actions, not of a miser, but of a sophisticated financial mind; a king with a complex, all-consuming obsession with the control, influence and power that money represented, both at home and abroad.'[9]

The Death of the King

The Pope took his time in coming to a decision about the validity of Katherine's first marriage; the actual requirement was a 'diriment dispensation from the impediment of public honesty' – a nullifying declaration that the marriage was illegal due to consanguinity. However the dispensation did finally arrive. King Henry, not often seen in public, now seemed hardly to appear at all. He had suffered a bad bout of tuberculosis in 1506 which recurred two years later. He remained at Richmond Palace (Henry had formerly been the Earl of Richmond and the manor of Sheen had been changed to that of Richmond), very ill and refusing to enter into any diplomatic discussions.

The sweating sickness had again broken out in London but it by-passed the royal homes and the King seemed to improve. He was occupied with the forthcoming marriage of his daughter Mary, betrothed to Charles of Castile. In the event the marriage never took place and the young princess married the King of France – her brother Henry was still a bridegroom in waiting. Around the King by this time two great diplomatic figures hovered

– Thomas Wolsey and Thomas More, both great dignitaries who could always be found at the centre of church and temporal power.

At the beginning of 1509 the King's health deteriorated. It was clear that there would have to be changes at the top. Prince Henry was a different man from his father – more worldly and less pious, inexperienced in kingship and without a domestic establishment to offer a stable environment and set an example. His father had moved for a time to the smaller hunting lodge at Hanworth but now he returned to Richmond, seeing no-one. The Princess Katherine visited occasionally but she was being kept in straightened circumstances, no-one caring for her wellbeing or for her future. Henry died on 11th April, 1509 to be buried beside his wife in the magnificent chapel in Westminster Abbey that he had created.

Once the funeral was over the new King, seventeen years old, went to Greenwich, the royal palace rebuilt by his father as Placentia, where he had been born, and a few weeks later he married Katherine in a quiet ceremony at the Franciscan chapel there.

CHAPTER X

Reformation

The Succession

THE EIGHTH HENRY seemed to possess every feature of a great leader of men. After his father's miserly control of the nation's economy, a valuable asset for its commercial standing, but not to the liking of its fun-loving populace, Henry began spending his inherited fortune on keeping his people happy. He appeared to have every talent that could possibly be bestowed on a king. Handsome, athletic, with a considerable intellect, he loved music and poetry, spoke several languages and liked to debate theology and politics. The fact that he was cruel, egotistic, without compassion and oversexed, was to emerge slowly as his reign proceeded. Henry was sure that his pretty Spanish wife, helped by his own mighty sexual prowess, would very soon provide a son to succeed him. The Queen bore him a succession of children, but after some ten years of marriage no such prince had arrived.

England did not break from the Catholic Church just because Henry VIII desperately wanted a son and needed a divorce from Katherine. In the six years between 1510 and 1516 when the only surviving child was born, she gave birth to four sons and a daughter, none of whom survived infancy. The one healthy living baby was Mary and England had never had a reigning woman on the throne. Several more pregnancies followed, but no babies survived.

Thomas Wolsey

The King relied heavily on his leading churchman. From a modest background – his father was a butcher – Thomas Wolsey was an astute farsighted young man, who could see that the only way he could prosper was in the Church. He studied at Oxford becoming Dean of Magdalen College. After several livings he became a chaplain to Henry VII and then his son's Almoner, a post close to the King and his household. He rose rapidly up the ecclesiastical and political ladders, due mainly to his own ambition and to his brilliant administrative ability, graduating to Dean of York, Bishop of Norwich and then to Archbishop of York, the second highest clerical post in the land. He made himself indispensable to the King, undertaking many of the royal duties that Henry himself found tedious. He received the cardinal's red hat a year later and many of his contemporaries considered that he had his eye on the Papacy, though for a foreigner, especially an Englishman, to succeed a long line of Italian popes was hardly likely. His control of the financial affairs of King and country put him in a strong position to dictate events in England and he was unpopular with large sections of the community, particularly in London where his extravagance on his own behalf and his parsimony concerning the City put him in disfavour with the nobility and the people alike.

Wolsey had a fine home, York Place, the London home of the Archbishops, near to the palace at Westminster. He had greatly extended it until it was one of the largest buildings in London. A serious fire in 1512 severely damaged the palace buildings. They were not rebuilt, and Henry moved for a while into Lambeth Palace, but after his quarrel with Wolsey he took over York Place, which was later to become Whitehall. Westminster Palace was kept only for national and parliamentary affairs; Henry was the last monarch to live there.

Many in the Church, too, disliked the Cardinal's control over them. Polydore Vergil, the Italian humanist scholar, recounts a meeting Wolsey had with the monks of London.

> He reproved them for many things – that they lived a life very different from that which they had professed in the beginning; that they did not employ themselves in literature and virtuous activities, but addressed themselves with quite remarkable zeal to acquiring wealth. Consequently he asserted that it was his business to correct these abuses, lest their religion should be utterly ruined.[1]

The fact that it was true hardly helped.

London City

London especially had welcomed a change of fortune when Henry VII died. From a serious commercial centre, admired by other nations for her civic pride, efficiency and integrity, as well as for her great buildings, sacred and secular, it was turning towards a more joyful, exhilarating way of life. It was the centre of the printing trade, a home of the great humanist Erasmus and of the artist Holbein, a place of pilgrimage for those seeking intellectual fulfilment, ruled over by a King who enjoyed life to the full. The magnificent ceremonial attending Katherine's wedding to Arthur had shown the world what London could do. The city was still in thrall to the only English church, the Church of Rome. Its beautiful churches, the great palaces on the banks of the Thames which mostly belonged to the Church dignitaries, Bishops of Exeter and Ely, Durham and Norwich (still honoured today in the names of the streets), the grand panoply of royal events, all this was due to London's affiliation to the Catholic religion.

The capital city enjoyed other advantages which gave it the lead in a move towards reform. The people were now more literate, and for the increasing numbers who could read there was no shortage of choice. Wynken de Worde, who had worked with Caxton, set up his own press beside St Paul's at the sign of Our Lady of Pity, printing more secular books to reach a new public. The network of narrow streets around the Cathedral – St Paul's Churchyard, Paternoster Row and Ave Maria Lane – remained the centre of the book trade, even after the Great Fire, until Hitler's bombs forced the booksellers out.

Even the English language was changing. Standard English, at least in the towns and cities, was the norm, though dialects remained, especially in London – Cockney was originally a misshapen egg, a cock's egg, and by the end of the sixteenth century a person born within the sound of Bow Bells (the church of St Mary-le-Bow). With the encouragement of the King, the humanists of Renaissance Europe were coming to London. Many Italian scholars came; some, such as Dominic Mancini, left accounts of their visit. Some were diplomatic tourists from the courts of Italian noblemen or from the Papal court. Polydore Vergil's *Anglia Historica* remains a valuable reference for later historians.

The great names associated with English humanism – Erasmus, Thomas More and John Colet among them – were no ivory tower philosophers. More was fully engaged in legal and political life, Colet, as Dean of St Paul's, was an educationalist, and Erasmus, a man of the world, believed that a healthy body, even an over-indulged one, was essential to a healthy mind. With a King on the throne who enjoyed the company of such great thinkers, it is hardly surprising that London was ready to receive new concepts concerning religious practice.

The Later Lollards

After the death of John Oldcastle in 1417, heresy went underground. There were few prosecutions. Most proceedings were taken against small numbers, particularly of women, who were usually accused of witchcraft and burnt. The guilds were warned against allowing their members to participate in gatherings that might be considered to conspire against accepted doctrine. Possession of English language religious books was deemed heretical or even treacherous. Evidence put before a court debated whether the contents of the books conformed to Catholic doctrine. One stated that the submission of worshippers to a bishop's control was invalid, that the monastic orders were useless, that churches should be simple and undecorated and that preaching was preferable to singing. The books were burned along with their owners. Some chaplains were also arrested and a law was passed forbidding anyone to employ such men. The Church itself, especially the monastic orders, was falling into disrepute. In discussing the Reformation, the historian A.G. Dickens remarks on the general dislike of the monasteries, 'When Wolsey was hated, inevitably some measure of that hatred became directed against Rome.'[2]

In 1521 Henry himself published a book, *Assertio Septem Sacramentorum* (Defence of the Seven Sacraments), which defended the sacramental nature of religion. It is believed to have been partly written by Wolsey and was dedicated to Pope Leo X. In return the Pope granted Henry the title of Defender of the Faith (the title was revoked after Henry's break with the Catholic Church but reinstated later by Parliament). It still appears on the English coinage – usually as F.D. – *Fidei Defensor.*

What was becoming clearer by now was the strong anticlericalism that was spreading through the city. Wolsey, a Cardinal, was a notorious spender; Henry, who was by now mistrustful of his leading statesman, was warned by the Archbishop of Canterbury, William Warham, that the Cardinal was dipping recklessly into his treasury. Henry told him to reprimand Wolsey and this he did in no uncertain terms. The two had long been enemies, and Wolsey felt that Canterbury should have been his. He was taking first steps on the slippery slope which finally led to his downfall. When he tried to levy a tax to defend the nation against the French he was asked by the Londoners, who provided most of the ready funds, that if not abandoned it should at least be reduced. However, according to Polydore Vergil,

> the boorish-spirited man was immediately transported with rage and replied 'I would rather my tongue were to be cut out than speak with the King concerning the reduction of any part of the total, contrary to what has already been debated, decided and granted by the nobles in Parliament'.[3]

It had not.

This internal bickering between the highest churchmen in the land was not a good sign for the future of the Catholic Church in England. In fact England boasted some of the greatest clergy in her history at a time when the Church was falling into disrepute: John Fisher, Stephen Gardiner, Thomas Cranmer and Nicholas Ridley, were all men of learning who held high office and suffered for their faith. Fisher was later canonised.

The Divorce

From the very beginning of the debate about ending his marriage, Henry had played the innocence card. He announced that he feared that his marriage had been illegal from the start, and that he was 'greatly troubled' by the thought of committing a mortal sin by marrying his deceased brother's wife. He did not explain why he had waited for nearly twenty years before coming to this conclusion. The problem revolved around whether Arthur had had intercourse with his bride. He said he had, she said no, and no one could prove it. If Katherine was right then there was no previous marriage, Henry was free to marry her, did so and could not, according to the Catholic Church, divorce her. If Arthur was right and it had been a 'proper' marriage then Henry was prohibited, according to the Bible, from marrying her, his marriage was invalid and he could marry whom he wished though he himself had more than once said that Katherine came to him as a virgin. There were two Biblical references which bore on the case. First, both Leviticus 20:21 and Leviticus 18:16, stipulated that 'if a man shall take his brother's wife, it is an unclean thing; he hath uncovered his brother's nakedness; they shall be childless'. Henry took this as his guiding instruction. Clearly, a daughter didn't count.

However, according to Deuteronomy 25:5, in a case where no son is born of the marriage, the brother is encouraged to take on his brother's widow, to provide a family – a levirate marriage. Any child of the new marriage would succeed to the dead man's estate. In Jewish law the man may relinquish his obligation by symbolically removing a shoe as was done in the Book of Ruth. Henry found the Leviticus passage more appropriate to his needs.

There were other complications. First of all it was clear to everyone that Henry's motive for a divorce was less a matter of his conscience than of his passion for Anne Boleyn. Even Katherine was aware of her husband's roving eye. Anne was young and beautiful; some believed she was married to Harry Percy, the Duke of Norfolk's son, but Wolsey warned him off. Anne had no doubts about her future – it was to be Queen of England. Henry's divorce was essential. Queen Katherine was losing her looks and could no longer produce the longed-for son. But she was still popular, in London especially. Edward Halle comments at length on the situation. 'The common people being ignorant of the truth, and especially women, favoured the queen.'[4] Wolsey, who had originated the plan for the divorce, now began to back away. He had in mind that the King, if he did divorce Katherine, should marry the sister of the French King, only to find that Henry had cast his eye in quite a different direction.

Aware of the talk, Henry summoned a council in London at Bridewell Palace, near Blackfriars. Erected under Wolsey's supervision, Bridewell had been built as one of Henry's latest London homes, consisting of two brick-built courtyards, with the royal lodgings in three storeys around the inner courtyard. There was a long gallery which connected the inner court with Blackfriars. When in residence the Queen used the gallery frequently, from which she could be seen from the street. She was reprimanded for 'smiling too much' at the people, as she passed to and fro.

The meeting was attended by Wolsey as Papal Legate and Cardinal Campeggio, sent by the Pope to hear the case. Henry explained that he felt he had brought nothing but good times to his people in his twenty years on the throne, but that he must be sure of his successor. In spite of the birth of the princess Mary

> it hath been told us by divers great clerks that she is not our lawful daughter nor her mother our lawful wife, but that we live together abominably and detestably in open adultery. These doings do daily and hourly trouble my conscience. Katherine is a woman of most gentleness, of most humility and buxomness, of all good qualities, appertaining to nobility – she is without comparison.[5]

He reminded the council of the trouble she had encountered marrying him when a dispensation had to be obtained from the Pope, a situation which now had to be amended by another Pope.

Wolsey protested that he had not been party to any doubt about the validity of the marriage. It was pointed out that the divorce, or rather annulment, would make Mary a bastard, and that such a long time had elapsed since the marriage took place that it had become 'honest'. To Henry's dismay a decision was postponed and Campeggio returned to Rome. Henry was anxious that the matter should be resolved in England and turned on Wolsey who had failed him in his 'great matter'. He was sent to Esher and then to his diocese of York, to lead a more modest existence. He apparently thought that his position in York demanded an even more luxurious lifestyle, and wrote to the King to ask for more suitable vestments. The King remarked on his insolence, 'Is there still arrogance in this fellow who is so obviously ruined?'[6] He was finally summoned to London, accused of treason, but he died on the way at Leicester.

Wolsey was replaced as Chancellor by Sir Thomas More, Henry's old friend, with whom he had had many talks while they walked together in More's garden in Chelsea. Geoffrey Elton, the eminent historian of the Tudors, said he was 'far and away the ablest minister left after Wolsey's fall.'[7] The King had had enough of churchmen; he wanted a lawyer as his head of state. More was a friend of Erasmus and Colet, of wide learning and steadfastness of mind. It was Robert Whittington, the grammarian, who described him as 'a man for all seasons'. He accepted the Chancellorship on condition he was not involved in the divorce, of which he disapproved.

Katherine wanted the Pope in Rome to resolve the problem. In 1527 her nephew, the Emperor Charles V, had led troops into Italy and sacked Rome, leaving the Pope, Clement VII, virtually a prisoner in the Castel Sant'Angelo. Clement refused to undo what his predecessor, Julius II, had put in place. Henry tried another tack. The dispensation given for the marriage, he said, was invalid, but this carried no weight, so the King turned next to another source of Biblical authority, the Jews of Italy. There were no Jews in England or Spain (at least none who could admit their Judaism), so after combing the universities of England and France for a precedent to confirm his belief in the Leviticus pronouncement, Henry went back to the original sources.

As with many debates on Biblical scholarship opinions were divided. Some scholars said the Latin translation of the original Hebrew sources was at fault, others that the Levirate marriage circumstance depended on the original marriage being consummated, which according to Katherine, hers had not. Others were of the opinion that 'the law of Deuteronomy has never been kept since the fall of Jerusalem, and that it is not intended to be kept.'[8]

The Pope issued a Bull forbidding all discussion of Henry's divorce. In Italy all parties were dragging their feet, while in England a letter to the Pope from some of the leading clerics and nobles declared openly for Henry. The King, who had composed the letter, was now making it clear that he would not bow to a superior command in another country. John Scarisbrick, Henry's biographer, calls the letter 'perhaps the most impressive piece uttered in Tudor England.'[9]

Henry had by now realised that he was not going to win over the Pope in the matter of his divorce. He must rely on his own efforts without the help of the Roman church. But there was one source of help to which he could turn – Parliament. In 1529 for the first time for six years he summoned both houses to put before them his idea of the relationship between monarch and clergy which was to change England's religious affiliation for all time.

To the House of Commons the King proposed three bills: that fees taken by the church for burials and court decisions should be limited; that clerics should be denied the opportunity of holding more than one living or to act as absentee priests; and that church courts should be investigated as to the extent of their activities.

After Wolsey's departure, Henry had acquired a new right-hand man. He knew that Thomas More would not support his anti-papal stance, but Thomas Cromwell would. Cromwell, of poor background, had risen, through his own capability, ambition and determination, to a dominance at court unprecedented outside the Church. He was a considerable linguist, had trained in the law and had a seat in Parliament. Without ostentation or obvious influence he was familiar with every leading player in politics and the court.

Henry, backed up by Cromwell, decided he must confront the Pope with all the forces at his command. He sent his envoys back to Rome with instructions to tell the Pope that the case must be heard in England, as Englishmen, including the King, were not subject to the rule of a foreign power. The Archbishop of Canterbury must hear the case with the Bishops of London and Lincoln. If he was denied an English hearing he would put the problem to a General Council, an unheard of step for a layman to take. His agents scoured the Vatican library for material to support their case but could find nothing. What they did proclaim was that the King was 'absolute emperor and pope in his kingdom'. He was 'supreme' and was free to take whatever action he wished.

In 1532 Henry declared himself 'Supreme Head of the Church in England – as far as the Law of Christ allows'. A.G. Dickens felt 'he always meant to be master in his own house rather than the junior partner and paymaster of some international conspiracy'.[10] He was still a staunch Catholic. Edward Halle described Henry's decision 'by the which the Pope with all his College of Cardinals with all their pardons and indulgences were utterly abolished out of this realm, God be everlastingly praised therefore.'[11] The following year Henry and Anne Boleyn (now pregnant) were secretly married, and Thomas Cranmer, the new Archbishop of Canterbury, declared the King's marriage to Katherine invalid.

England's Church

The state of the Church in England in the early years of the sixteenth century was pitiful. The lower orders, in the everyday care of their parishes, were very short of the respect which should have been their due. Churches were falling into disrepair, partly because the money which should have been used for their restoration was finding its way into the pockets of their leaders, while the parish priests were often penniless. Those charged with the spiritual health of the nation were often ignorant, neglectful or even criminal. The higher clergy were ostentatiously wealthy, spending large sums on themselves and their dwellings, while ignoring most of the Ten Commandments.

Worst of all were the monastic orders, living in splendid but dilapidated buildings, holding on to vast estates, many of which were run down and inefficiently managed. The very secrecy of the 'closed' orders of monks and nuns served to spread the rumours of over-indulgence, venality and selfish exploitation. The Church was very rich, in contrast to those from whom it took its tithes, its payments for arranging births and deaths and its court decisions. The corruption of these courts added to the suspicion and mistrust which attached to much of the relationship between Church and laity. Simony (the selling of church offices), absentee priests and clergy who held several parishes were rife throughout England. It is easy to speculate whether Henry's divorce was the force behind England's slide toward Protestantism, or whether it was an irrelevance in the battle for Reformation. Dickens believed that

> English Catholicism, despite its gilded decorations, was an old unseaworthy and ill-commanded galleon scarcely able to continue its voyage without the new seamen and shipwrights produced (but far too late) by the Counter-Reformation.[12]

Perhaps the divorce should be seen as just a small reef in a very rocky ocean.

Martin Luther

Martin Luther was born in 1483 and after studying at the University of Wittenberg joined the Augustinian Friars. He became aware of the corruption of the Church at Rome (what the historian Patrick Collinson called 'The Las Vegas of its day')[13] on a visit there in 1510. He found widespread laxity in the Church, from the Pope down, especially the sale of indulgences – remission of sin on payment of money intended to pay for the restoration of St Peter's – as well as simony and the reprehensible behaviour of the clergy. For many the vows of chastity, poverty and obedience seemed almost unknown. Luther's beliefs contradicted the long held Catholic idea of salvation through good deeds; he trusted in faith alone to be saved.

In 1517 at Wittenberg in the Rhineland Luther posted on the Cathedral doors his 95 Articles of Faith. The Theses stated succinctly the principles of the Christian faith, covering church laws ('Canon Law applies only to the living, not the dead'), the behaviour of the clergy ('the priest must not threaten those dying with the penalty of purgatory') and many about indulgences ('a Christian who gives to the poor or lends to those in need is doing better in God's eyes than one who "buys" forgiveness'). The Theses were very quickly printed and disseminated throughout Europe. In 1521, at a Diet (Council) held in the same city, the Pope excommunicated Luther.

England's Reformation

Until Martin Luther's name came to represent the first true reform of the Church, heretical beliefs were relatively minor attempts to differ from orthodox theology and practice. Jan Hus, John Wyclif, the Waldensians, the Cathars, all had raised their heads above the parapet but the ramparts stood firm. Luther's action at Worms may have sparked a revolution that had worldwide repercussions, but his writings were not the only ones to keep the printing presses turning. Two matters were vital to reforming the Church. The first was the insistence by the early reformers on preaching, being heard by the people. It was a procedure to be followed later by John Wesley. The other was to have the Bible available in the vernacular so that people could understand their faith. Wyclif in England had produced an English version but it was far from adequate for daily use, and it was in any case mostly read in secret and attracted a heavy penalty for anyone caught reading it. It did, however, pave the way for a much more readable Bible.

William Tyndale

Tyndale read theology at Oxford and was much influenced by Erasmus's Greek translation of the New Testament. John Foxe, the martyrologist, described him as learned and well-practised in God's matters. He preached in the West of England – Lollard country – and was in fact accused of heresy, though never convicted. He came to London where the Bishop, Cuthbert Tunstall, refused to help him, though he did preach at St Dunstan-in-the-West in Fleet Street, an early church, friendly to Reform and in the following century the benefice of John Donne. Tyndale then travelled to Cologne where he worked on his translation into English of the New Testament. Before the printing was finished he was betrayed to the authorities and escaped to Worms. The final printing of the English New Testament was finished in 1529 and smuggled to safety down the Rhine.

In England Bishop Tunstall proscribed the book and preached a sermon at St Paul's while copies of the book were being burned. William Warham, Archbishop of Canterbury, instructed his bishops to buy up all the copies they could to burn them. This first English New Testament used many phrases later 'borrowed' by the King James Version; Tyndale's language was simple and easy to understand rather than literary or scholarly. He introduced several new words into the English language, including in Leviticus, when recounting the story of the two goats, one sacrificed at the altar, the other allowed to escape into the wilderness, where it died. Hence 'scapegoat' to describe one who takes the sins of the world on his shoulders. He went on to learn Hebrew, knowledge of which was growing in England, and translated the first five Books of Moses, the Pentateuch, into English from the Hebrew, using such phrases, now so familiar, as 'God said, Let there be light, and there was light.' He had to start the work all over again when he was shipwrecked on his way back to Germany and lost his papers.

Sir Thomas More, always violently opposed to any taint of heresy, spoke against Tyndale in his *Dialogue Concerning Heresy*. The bitter debate between the two men continued in two further books by More, who became increasingly heated, and Tyndale refused King Henry's offer, via Cromwell, of a safe conduct back to England. He worked on the earlier books of the Old Testament, living by now in Antwerp, before being again betrayed by a young Englishman he had helped. He was arrested and imprisoned before being tried in Brussels and found guilty. He was graciously allowed to be strangled before being burned at the stake. In 1537 all his translations of the Bible were put together and the first complete Bible in English was printed. It was known as Matthew's Bible – Tyndale's name could not appear so the name of the apostle was used instead. Tyndale was a forerunner of great writers who used the English language to its full extent. The Tyndale scholar, David Daniell, used the phrase, 'Without Tyndale, no Shakespeare'.

The Reformation in London

London was at the fore of the anticlericalism which had flooded into English life. Most of London's splendid buildings belonged to the Church. Early maps of the city show a skyline of spires and towers and battlemented parapets of grey stone. Crosses adorned every street and relics every church and each shone with candles burning for the dead as well as for the living – workplaces for innumerable priests, nuns, clerics and laymen who crowded into the little chapels and the central naves, always open for worship and prayer.

The vast number of clergy in London was in itself a cause for concern. There were more than one hundred parishes in the city and thirty-nine monastic foundations, each with its own staff, as well as innumerable chantry priests, chaplains, clerical lawyers, foreign diplomats in orders and visiting churchmen from out of town, some on church business, many more there for personal reasons. Not all had a true vocation. Susan Brigden's history, *London and the Reformation*, makes the point that the priesthood provided a way to wealth, to constant employment, to social advancement which no lay office could bring, especially for the low-born. Some were men of intellect, who could find no other career, others were virtually illiterate.

However, not all men of the cloth were to be despised. Reform was acknowledged as essential by many obedient Catholics, some of whom were humanists, men of learning. Colet spoke with Thomas More about the true way for the devout Christian, perhaps not always the orthodox way. They and Erasmus were using the Bible to direct their lives. Some of Colet's sermons were almost heretical in tone, leading to his eventual exclusion from the pulpit of St Paul's by Bishop Fitzjames.

The citizens of London, especially the guildsmen, were ready for improvement, for reform, but not for revolution. In London there was to be no St Bartholomew's Day massacre, no war on the streets. Instead the new ideas spread downwards, to the common folk who were glad to read their beloved Bible in their own language and to listen to the new ideas, simply and attractively argued. The Head of their Church was there in London with them, not far away in Rome. Priests were men like any other and no more deserving of respect. They too must obey the King. The Act of Supremacy of 1534 made that clear.

The Act of Supremacy

The first Act of Supremacy to be passed in England asserted Henry's leadership of the Church and the superiority of civil over religious laws. It confirmed the monarch's secession from Rome and ushered in the Divine Right of Kings in the following century. The wording of the Act makes it clear that apart from excluding all 'errors, heresies and other enormities and abuses heretofore used', it is in *Anglicans Ecclesia* that spiritual authority lay, with the King and his successors, 'any usage, foreign land, foreign authority, prescription or anything or things to the contrary notwithstanding.'

Other statutes passed by Henry's parliament of 1534 withdrew payments to Rome and gave to the King the right to nominate bishops as well as the overall responsibility for clerical legislation. Also included was the right of the monarch to carry out visitations, used to legitimise the dissolution of the monasteries. Henry's own abilities and theological scholarship set him up as an able and thorough administrator of the new laws, not necessarily the case with his successors.

Both John Fisher, Bishop of Rochester and now a cardinal, and Thomas More refused to acknowledge the Act of Supremacy. After imprisonment in the Tower, when both refused to sign the Act, both were executed. More's position as Chancellor, his old friendship with the King and the acknow-ledged respect of scholars across Europe, made the execution even more shocking. Halle commented, 'I cannot tell whether I should call him a foolish wise man or a wise foolish man, for undoubtedly he, beside his learning had a great wit'.[14] At the scaffold he is believed to have told the executioner 'Help me up – I will find my own way down.'

CHAPTER XI

Monasteries and Martyrs

M OST OF ENGLAND'S MONASTERIES at the time of the break
with Rome were not in a good state. The majority were poorly
run, corrupt and wealthy beyond the dreams of those who
sought their help for sanctuary or spiritual guidance. Many young men and
women took vows they hardly understood and from which they could not
escape.

The King and Thomas Cromwell desperately needed money and turned
to those who had the most, the monastic orders. Henry's right as Supreme
Head to supervise and control church property of all kinds provided the
answer. By now Cromwell was Vicar General. He set in motion a series of
investigations into the corruption, self-seeking and misappropriation
of funds, of which most of the monastic houses were undoubtedly guilty.
In London alone there were some thirty-seven abbeys, monasteries, priories,
convents, friaries, preceptories and chantries with at least thirty more in the
surrounding countryside. About one quarter of the area of London was
made up of monastery lands. From the Thames northwards were the White
Friars, the Black Friars, the Temple, the Abbey lands of Westminster, with
Priories at Aldgate, Clerkenwell, Charterhouse, Bethlehem, the Austin
Friars, Spitalfields and Shoreditch. Further out were the great abbeys of
Barking, Merton, Ealing and Bermondsey, with smaller houses everywhere
between.

London had a reputation for disliking its churchmen, not just men
like Wolsey who commanded great estates while forcing up taxes, but the
ordinary clerk, the bishop and the men and women in holy orders. Now
that these ordinary Londoners had access to religious books in their own
language – thanks to the invention of printing there were plenty of them –
they no longer had to rely on what their priests told them. They were now
in the habit of thinking for themselves, as the peasants, the guilds and the
Lollards had shown, even at the risk of retribution.

A young man named Simon Fish had incurred Wolsey's wrath by
performing in a satirical play which featured the Cardinal unfavourably.
He was duly banished from the realm but returned to London, smuggling

in with him some of the banned books being printed on the continent. Aware of Wolsey's spies he left again for Antwerp where he wrote and published his *Supplication for the Beggars*, which denied the existence of purgatory and blamed the clergy as 'parasites', responsible for the decay of the English Church. He was condemned as a heretic but died before being tried. Fish was one of the early humanists to come from a modest rather than an academic or a clerical background. Gradually more men (and some women) were prepared to speak out. Known as 'the brethren' these anti-clerical protagonists, like the King, remained believing Catholics. As in any other secret society they helped each other, offering sanctuary, financial help and religious support to their fellows.

Protestantism

It was not until 1529 that the word Protestant was used in Germany at the diet of Speyer to describe those who protested against Emperor Charles V's attempts to crush the followers of Luther. In London the early Reformers offered no alternative religion. They were against Catholicism as led by Rome, and many queried its beliefs and worship, but no structured programme of service was suggested to replace it.

The Death of the Queen

In September 1533 Queen Anne gave birth to the child she had been bearing when she married Henry. The baby girl, named Elizabeth, was yet another disappointment to him. Now with two daughters there still seemed no prospect of the successor he so desperately wanted. He was already out of temper with Anne; she flirted with his courtiers, couldn't bear a son and was notoriously unpopular with people and court alike. Again, Cromwell came to the rescue. He drew up a formidable array of the Queen's lovers, including her own brother. After a trial of all of these and of the Queen herself, all accused of treason, they were executed at the Tower and the King was left with two young daughters and no wife. He quickly remedied this by choosing another young lady in waiting, Jane, daughter of Sir John Seymour of Wolf Hall in Wiltshire. Jane was very different from her predecessor. Modest and self-effacing as well as intelligent, she did the only thing expected of her. After a long labour, she bore a son, but to Henry's genuine grief, she died shortly after the baby, Edward, was born. It was said that the child was born by Caesarean section, but it was unlikely that any woman in the sixteenth century could survive such an operation. Henry now had three children, but in spite of marrying three times more, no further children were born to him.

The Ten Articles

In 1536, at a convocation at St Paul's, a new declaration of faith was drawn up in the form of the Ten Articles. These included only three Sacraments instead of seven: baptism, penance and the Eucharist. Omitted were the sacraments of marriage, ordination, confirmation and the last rites. Also included was an injunction against images in church, pilgrimages and the observance of some saints' days. The Mass remained a feature of Church worship. The emphasis was on the Scriptures and on good deeds. The saints were considered as examples of a good Christian life and might be called upon to intercede. Baptism was declared essential for the remission of sins, for children as well as adults.

Anabaptists

Some of the radical sects operating in Europe were sending disciples to London. Among them were the Anabaptists, of whom a certain number were tried for heresy at St Paul's. They were accused of maintaining that Christ was not a godhead, that they did not believe in the Eucharist, that children should not be baptised, and that there could be no forgiveness for sinners after they had been baptised. With Cromwell as one of the Commissioners at their trial, several were burned at the stake. The term Anabaptist was often used to indicate a heretic, regardless of his actual beliefs.

Dissolution

Cromwell's main motive for dissolving the monasteries was money. He was also aware that they were Catholic foundations which might very well be a useful support for any attempt to reinstate the Pope at the head of the English Church. He had to establish the Crown on a sound financial footing, and with the religious houses already unpopular with both people and nobility, this was the perfect answer. With his usual meticulous planning for any major programme, he started in 1535 with a large scale examination of the value of every monastery, abbey, priory, bishopric and church. The *Valor Ecclesiasticus*, an extraordinary piece of financial auditing, assessed the income of every house, allowed for necessary expenditure on pensions, overheads, charitable giving and legacies, and kept detailed notes of how it spent its money.

Starting with the smaller establishments, those with an income of less than £200 a year, of which there were some three hundred, he set in train a system of investigations by his chosen agents. Henry's earlier Statute had given him the right for this to be the prerogative of the Crown not the bishops, and those who carried it out were neither gentle nor negligent in their approach. The coming of Cromwell's men brought dismay to the men and women in the monasteries, knowing as they did that their fate lay in his hands.

The Dissolution in London

Now the movement against the monasteries moved into a higher gear. The Court of Augmentations was Cromwell's method of controlling the work. Every house destroyed by his demolition men had to be accounted for, the buildings listed, the images and treasures either sold on, with the money going to the King, or pilfered by the local populace. Vast sums of money flowed into the Treasury. The future careers of the inmates had to be assessed. Pensions were arranged for the higher clergy, some of whom left the Church altogether; some married and took on lay occupations.

At this time London lost many of her most beautiful sacred features. The reckless destruction of statues, images, paintings and glass was either the work of individuals let loose on Papist strongholds, or of those under instruction from the authorities. A visitor to London, Alessandro Magno, described St Paul's, 'It is a pitiful sight to see the beautiful marble statues of saints and other decorations there, broken and ruined because of their heresy.'[1] St Mary Patten, a guild church, lost its rood screen. All Hallows by the Tower was relatively untouched, but hid its valuable hoard of registers and documents in a lead cistern in the Tower. The Prior of St Bartholomew's was given a handsome pension when he peacefully handed over his church. The bell tower of St John of Jerusalem in Clerkenwell was blown up to provide stone for the Duke of Somerset's new house. At St Mary-le-Bow the church rooms were let out, the schoolroom 'for four shillings a year, a cellar for two shillings and two vaults under the church for fifteen shillings both.'[2] Iconoclasm was the watchword. Some of the out of town treasures were taken to London. Images were broken up to prove the falsity of the influence they were believed to exert. The houses of the Friars came down including the priories of St Helen's Bishopsgate, St Thomas Acon and St Mary Spital.

The Carthusians in particular resisted dissolution. At the Charterhouse, the Prior and six monks were executed and nine others died in prison. The house did in fact surrender to Cromwell's men and was allowed to stay for a while. Finally the Chancellor of the Court of Augmentations, Sir Edward North, claimed it as his home, destroying several of the buildings, including the church. It was valued at £642.4½. It was later bought by Thomas Sutton, said to be the wealthiest commoner in England, and was turned into a school and almshouses for eighty elderly men, a firmly Protestant foundation.

The great Abbey Church of Westminster was not immune from the wholesale devastation. On 16th January 1540 the monks met with their Abbot, William Boston, in the Chapter House, where they signed a document in which 'unanimously and of their own free will they surrendered their church and monastery to that most excellent prince, the Lord King Henry'.[3] All the Abbey's possessions – gold and silver plate, silk altar hangings, cushions, mitres, copes, candlesticks, crosses, 'the leg of St George with the foot enclosed in silver' – everything had to go. This included the office of Abbot. He was replaced by a Dean, a position taken by the last Abbot who changed his name from Boston to Benson.

St Bartholomew-the-Great retained its chancel but the long nave was pulled down, leaving only the gateway at the end, still there today. The Austin Canons at Holy Trinity, Aldgate, founded by Queen Matilda, gave up their priory as it was already desolate and failing in its religious duties.

The Bible in England

Henry's determination to rid England of any translation of the Bible into the vernacular, could not stand fast against either the multiplying of printed books or the work being done abroad on the texts available in Latin and Greek. Erasmus's translation into Greek was taken up by Luther as the basis for a German version. Both Cromwell and the King were coming round to the idea, if the Reformation was to succeed, that English was the right language for the new Church to use when encouraging its adherents to read the Scriptures. Miles Coverdale, an Augustinian monk, had gone to Germany to work on just such a translation, using Tyndale's work as his guide. He had in fact mentioned the idea to Cromwell earlier, but found it impossible to work freely in England. He joined Tyndale and in 1535 he produced the first printed English Bible, both Old and New Testaments. 'No translator,' says Arthur Dickens, 'had a better ear for the well-turned phrase and for the ring of a sentence.'[4] His version of the Psalms has retained its beauty and meaning and is much used today.

The King was asked to allow the English Bible to be used in Anglican churches around the country. He agreed and Coverdale's Bible, under the patronage of Thomas Cranmer, Archbishop of Canterbury, was ordered to be set in every place of worship; it was chained to the pulpit and a reader appointed so that all worshippers, even those who could not read, might enjoy their Scriptures. This first authorised version was known as the Great Bible, because of its size. It was replaced a few years later, under the instruction of Archbishop Matthew Parker, by the Bishop's Bible, translated not from Erasmus's Greek version, but from the original Hebrew, Aramaic and Greek.

In 1543 the King passed the Act for the Advancement of True Religion. It restricted the reading of the Bible to clerics, noblemen, the gentry and richer merchants, the majority of whom lived in London. Women below gentry rank, servants, apprentices and generally poor people were forbidden to read it. Women of the gentry and the nobility were only allowed to read it in private. The Act stated that 'malicious minds, intending to subvert the true exposition of Scripture, have taken upon them, by printed ballads, rhymes, etc., subtilly and craftily to instruct His Highness' people, and specially the youth of this his realm, untruly. For reformation whereof, His Majesty considereth it most requisite to purge his realm of all such books, ballads, rhymes, and songs, as pestiferous and noisome'.

Social Welfare at the Dissolution

As the desecration of the monasteries proceeded, Henry and Cromwell were keeping a close watch on the effect the Reformation was having on the people of London. Without the monastic establishments the social services they had been providing came to an end. What was to happen to the poor families who relied on hand outs – meals, health care, schooling – simply to stay alive? Mortality rates were high and those families who survived were usually large, replacing those children who died at birth or soon after. The priories and convents had been the only stable source of care outside the home. When the monasteries went, so did the hospitals. Simon Fish wrote, 'What remedy is there for us, the poor and the sick? Should men found more hospitals? No, the more the worse, for always the fat of the whole foundation hangs on the priests' beards.'[5]

St Bartholomew's Hospital was taken from the church and put into the care of the City once its income was removed. It was then entitled 'The House of the Poore in West Smithfield in the Suburbs of the City of London of Henry VIII's Foundation'. St Thomas's, on the south bank of the Thames, had been a part of the Augustinian Priory of St Thomas (named after Thomas Becket) belonging to Bermondsey Abbey. It too was later handed over to the City and repaired 'for the poor, impotent, lame and diseased people.' When it was rededicated it was known as the Hospital of Thomas the Apostle as Becket's canonisation had been rescinded. Coverdale's Bible was printed from premises in the grounds.

Children suffered the most by the withdrawal of medical care from the Church. According to the writer Benjamin Penny-Mason, 'the Reformation caused the single greatest change in childhood health; it had more of an effect than the Black Death, Wars of the Roses or the 100 Years War.'[6]

As the glory of the great monastic houses was destroyed, many monks, nuns, friars and clerics found themselves out of work. Some were reduced to begging in the streets, a few found positions as private pastors in the homes of the wealthy, or as school teachers, learned trades or set up shops. Those who denied the Supremacy of the King were charged with treason and condemned to death, either by hanging, burning or by the axe. Those of common status were executed at Tyburn, the nobility met their deaths on Tower Hill, and royalty, such as Anne Boleyn, within the precincts of the Tower itself. The use of the rack and other terrible instruments of torture was often an attempt to persuade the prisoner to betray his fellows, or in some cases as a bitter retribution against heresy.

The King's Marriages

Henry now had his longed-for son, a delicate boy, but no wife. He sent Cromwell to Europe to find another. Many of the princesses of the royal houses were suggested. One seemed suitable – the daughter of the Duke of Cleves. The painter Holbein, now living in England, had portrayed many royal subjects and his painting of Anne of Cleves was flattering in the extreme. She arrived in London in 1539 and Henry was horrified. The princess, to whom he was betrothed, was very plain. 'I like her not,' he said. The marriage was never consummated. Once again Henry was involved in a messy divorce, but this time it took only a few days to declare the marriage null and void, and the new queen lived out her life contentedly in the English countryside. She eventually died in Chelsea and was buried in Westminster Abbey, the only one of the wives to lie there.

Apparently undeterred by this fourth matrimonial mistake, the King tried again. He was by now gross in appearance, with leg ulcers, showing signs of a weak heart and probably the beginnings of emphysema. His fondness for extreme sports had nearly cost him his life on more than one occasion, and he had bouts of fever. Nevertheless this did not deter him from pursuing a new young wife, Catherine Howard, niece of the Duke of Norfolk. Like two of her predecessors, she was a lady-in-waiting to the Queen, but a very different woman. Scarisbrick called her 'a high-spirited minx'[7], and certainly she attracted a suite of young courtiers, to whom she never tried to hide her affection. But Henry was smitten, and seemed to recover his health and his sexual energy. He was thirty years older than his bride but as much in love as he had once been with Anne Boleyn. Three weeks after his divorce he and Catherine were married.

On that same day in 1540, Thomas Cromwell was executed. Henry had made him Earl of Essex; he had served the King well and Henry knew it. Through Cromwell's negotiating skills he had married three wives and now a fourth, he was Supreme Head of the Church in England and was one of the wealthiest monarchs in Europe. Cromwell was charged with heresy, treason and corruption among many charges, including plotting to marry the Princess Mary. Attainted without a trial, he died at the Tower after a short imprisonment. He had made many enemies from the day when as a commoner upstart he had joined the royal household and become indispensable to the King. Elton says,

> He stands out not only by his ability, nor even by his undoubted ruthlessness, but by the single-minded purpose to which he put both ability and ruthlessness. In eight years he engineered one of the few successful revolutions in English history, and he achieved this without upsetting the body politic.[8]

Death of the King

Henry now had full rights to govern England, in religion, in politics and in economy. His rule over the Church was complete, except in one respect. He took no part in the direction of worship. He could impose taxes, choose the clergy and direct church government, but he was never a priest, nor did he ever claim to be. He ruled over the Church of England, as it now was, as a royal leader not a new pope. Only by his own charismatic supremacy could this revolution have taken place.

However the King had further problems at home to worry about. Archbishop Cranmer broached him at prayer and presented him with a dissertation about Queen Catherine's misdemeanours before her marriage. These might have been admissible, though deplored, but clearly her behaviour since was no better, and adultery equalled treason. She was beheaded at the Tower, together with those found guilty with her. This time Henry waited for more than a year before marrying Catherine Parr, a sensible kindly widow who outlived Henry and made a home for his children.

Henry died in January 1547 with Archbishop Cranmer beside him. Requiem Masses were said for his soul. At Windsor, Bishop Stephen Gardiner led the funeral and the King was buried beside Jane Seymour, the mother of his only son.

A Protestant King

Yet another young child succeeded to the throne of England. Henry VIII's only son, Edward, aged nine, was not a strong lad when he inherited the throne, but he had a receptive mind. Elton describes him as 'naturally haughty and arrogant, like all the Tudors; also like all his family, he had a marked intellectual ability which an appalling schooling had turned into a precocious passion for protestant theology. The King was a cold-hearted prig.'[9] His family background was hardly conducive to a stable personality, and he was easily swayed by strong-minded advisers. His two principal counsellors were certainly that, though their achievements were neither deep nor long-lasting.

Henry had seen his Church in terms of a reformed Catholicism, not a new religion. His last address to Parliament at Christmas 1545 made it clear what he thought of the ubiquitous reception of his new English Bible:

> I am very sorry to know and hear how unreverently that most precious jewel, the word of God, is disputed, rhymed, sung and jangled in every alehouse and tavern, contrary to the true meaning and doctrine of the same; and yet I am even as much sorry that the readers of the same follow it, in doing, so faintly and coldly.[10]

Nevertheless, he left his young son to the care of thoroughgoing reformers. The Duke of Somerset, though he was now the leading power in the land, was not capable of exercising it with the strength that was needed. He repealed nearly all Henry's laws against treason and heresy, leaving Englishmen to believe how and what they wished. But gentle tolerance was not the way to achieve peace and stability at that time in the sixteenth century, although Queen Elizabeth managed it later. Archbishop Cranmer, owing everything to his late master, did his best to carry out what he considered that master had intended.

The liturgical debate was intricate; with no guidance to follow, the church leaders seemed to make it up as they went along. Their firm belief was that salvation – entry to Heaven – lay only in faith, not in a goodly life, that Christ had died to save the world and that only the chosen would live forever after their term on earth was over. Some contemporary wills subscribed to the same doctrine 'with the aid of the Blessed Virgin Mary'. Worshippers were confused. Churches were desecrated, many damaged beyond repair. Relics had disappeared. Where were men to look to sustain their faith?

The Book of Common Prayer

What was so desperately needed was what would be called today a 'manual', a book of instruction, in English, something to answer all the questions. Cranmer provided it. The Book of Common Prayer was his greatest bequest to the English people. It was really conceived in 1538 as *The Exhortation and Litany*, a prayer book for the Reformation, to be continued as an English Communion rite (communion to be given in both bread and wine) and finally in 1549 as a full Prayer Book in English to include daily offices and readings, prayers for Sundays and Holy Days, as well as special prayers for the sick, for baptism, confirmation and marriage and for most occasions of joy and sadness in English family life. Cranmer was helped by an Italian Jew, John Immanuel Tremellius, converted to Christianity, who was known as 'the King's Reader in Hebrew'.

The first edition was printed by a London printer, Edward Whitchurch, at the sign of The Well and Two Buckets. Whitchurch was an English evangelical and an experienced printer of liturgical books. He produced a magnificent title page, printed in red and black and the Preface was written by Cranmer himself. 'We have good hope,' he wrote,

> that what is here presented, and hath been by the Convocations of both Provinces with great diligence examined and approved, will be also well accepted and approved by all sober, peaceable and truly conscientious Sons of the Church of England.[11]

Cranmer's original text is very relevant today and contains many familiar phrases still in use: the words of the Ten Commandments, the Marriage Ceremony and such well-known lines as 'read, mark, learn and inwardly digest', 'Man that is born of woman hath but a short time to live' and 'all sorts and conditions of men'. In the same year the Act of Uniformity abolished the Latin Mass, and made the Prayer Book the only legal form of worship.

Music in the Reformed Church

Martin Luther's church services were often accompanied by the original Catholic music and Latin text. Both Zwingli and Calvin, with their own versions of Reform, somewhat disapproved of music in church, though Calvin did allow unaccompanied voices. Henry's request to Cranmer to supervise the new liturgy in the Church included attention to the music. The Archbishop wrote to the King,

> The song that shall be made thereunto would not be full of notes, but as near as may be for every syllable a note; so that it may be sung distinctly and devoutly ... nevertheless they that be cunning in singing can make a much more solemn note thereto.[12]

Whereas the service had always been said and sung in Latin, Cranmer now introduced an English text with plainsong tunes often composed by himself. Cathedral musicians no longer wore the tonsure.

In Edward VI's England Latin polyphony disappeared with the abandonment of the Latin Mass and the suppression of the chantries, though English composers soon began composing music for the new forms of worship in English, with settings for the Psalms, plainchant and clear and simple melodies to accompany the English text. Many parish churches possessed a small organ but some were allowed to deteriorate as choirs and the minor clergy began to disappear. Simple English musical settings took the place of the more elaborate Latin music.

London led the way in introducing the new music in churches and cathedrals, with the Chapels Royal in the forefront of change, though there appeared little instruction from the clergy about how the change was to come about. Considerable attention was paid to Psalmody, in keeping with the desire to see the Scriptures as the backbone of religion in England. In 1562 was printed *The Whole Book of Psalms Collected into English Metre by Thomas Sternhold, John Hopkins and Others*. The title continued: *Conferred with the Hebrew: set forth and allowed to be Sung in all Churches, of all the People together, before and after Morning and Evening Prayer; and also before and after Sermons; and moreover in private Houses, for their godly Solace and comfort; laying apart all ungodly Songs and Ballads, which tend only to the nourishing of Vice, and corrupting of youth.*

Protector Somerset

It was not long before Somerset's 'reign' began to cause public disapproval. He built the magnificent Somerset House in the Strand from the ruins of the priories, tearing down the adjoining buildings to make room for it. It was rebuilt in the eighteenth century to a design by Sir William Chambers. Within the Seymour family there were quarrels and disputes, and Somerset's own character was not decisive enough to weather the storms. He was, after all, not the King. Whilst both Wolsey and Cromwell were men of firm action and strength of will, they were subservient to King Henry. Edward was too young and inexperienced to control his principal minister.

Under the young King, all church properties, endorsements and chantries became the property of the Crown. The chantry clergy of the cathedrals were left virtually without employment, though the majority were pensioned off. Not all Londoners were prepared to go the whole way to accepting the new religion. The Bishop of London, Edmund Bonner, refused Parliament's instruction to preach against Catholic heretics at St Paul's, and still upheld transubstantiation. Together with Stephen Gardiner, one of Henry's old supporters, he was imprisoned in the Tower, and Somerset, quite unable to cope with an increasingly turbulent situation, was relieved of his office. He was succeeded by the Earl of Warwick, now the Duke of Northumberland. He was faced with serious financial problems, apart from the religious ones. So worrying was the situation that even further depredations of church funds could do little to help. Somerset was charged with treason and met his death on Tower Hill.

The Duke of Northumberland

Somerset's successor saw at once that his route to commanding the affairs of England lay through the King. The boy was intelligent and well read, and created a good impression at meetings of the council which he was now invited to attend. But like Wolsey, Cromwell and Somerset before him, Northumberland could not survive the accusations of attempting to rule a country of which he was not the monarch. The new leader of what Elton called the 'upstart nobility' was much preoccupied with ensuring that he personally profited from the lands and possessions of both the King and the Church. However, he did manage to improve the nation's economy and administration, though only when he could improve his own affairs on the way. Under his Protectorship more men were martyred for their beliefs than ever before. The Reformation was by now acquiring a momentum of its own. All prayer books other than Cranmer's (a revision was printed in 1552) were suppressed. Even other religious books containing too much pictorial decoration were condemned as 'papist' and duly consigned to the fire.

The introduction of the Ordinal, the book containing the rites for the ordination of deacons and priests, and the consecration of bishops, reduced the priesthood to only three ranks: bishops, priests and deacons. The clergyman was deprived of much of the sacramental character of his office; his duties were only to preach, lead services and instruct his flock. He had little more control of the divine side of his calling than a learned layman. In 1553 Cranmer introduced the Forty-two Articles (later reduced to Thirty-nine), a new statement of doctrine; the altar was replaced by a 'holy table' and any bishops who still showed doubt about the Reformation were removed from office.

The Succession

Edward's own part in the abandonment of the Catholic faith in England was by no means negligible. He was a vehement believer in Protestantism and determined to rid his country of any papist still known to exist, by torture, burning or execution. His sister Mary, an equally fanatical Catholic like her mother, had retired from court to live in the country where her religious practice was less likely to be supervised. The Act of Uniformity forbade her to use any but the Book of Common Prayer, but Somerset had given her some leeway. Under Northumberland, very nervous of his less indulgent personality, she tried to revive a previously suggested marriage to the son of the King of Portugal, or perhaps to leave England altogether, though if she did she would forfeit her right to succeed her brother on the throne.

On a visit to Greenwich in 1550 Mary was publicly rebuked by Edward for celebrating the Mass. Later she made a formal visit to London with a large following. At Whitehall she was ordered to obey the Act of Uniformity. Her cousin, the Emperor, threatened war if she was refused the Mass in private and the council gave way. This did not suit Edward but Mary continued to attend Mass in strictest privacy. It was clear that neither the King nor Northumberland could permit Mary to become Queen and return England to Catholicism. In a new will Edward declared both his sisters illegitimate and ordained that the Crown should pass to Lady Jane Grey, Northumberland's daughter-in-law, a direct descendant of Henry VIII's sister Mary by her second marriage to the Duke of Suffolk.

In 1553 Edward died at the age of sixteen. He was believed to have contracted measles and his weak constitution led to consumption. After a bad cold he was unable to survive. Four days later Lady Jane, wife of Guildford Dudley, Northumberland's son, was crowned Queen. She ruled for just nine days. In Norfolk, a strongly Catholic part of England where Mary had fled when she knew her brother was dangerously ill, proclaimed her the rightful Queen and Northumberland's attempt to thwart her failed. She was heralded as Queen on Tower Hill. However, after the Duke of Suffolk withdrew his support from his daughter, Northumberland, his son and Jane were all tried for high treason and executed. As Henry VIII's daughter Mary was welcomed to the throne, with the overriding aim of restoring England to the Catholic religion.

CHAPTER XII

The Last Tudors

A New Queen

L ONDON WAS ON HIGH ALERT. Food was short and very expensive. Orders were issued regarding the watch and who was to supervise the constables in charge. The Guilds provided 500 men to supplement the guards and the City gates were strengthened. Martial Law was declared. All this cost money and the extravagance of Protectors Somerset and Northumberland had impoverished the City. Conspiracy theories abounded, about foreigners, about Catholics and even about the late King whom it was rumoured had been poisoned. Support for Queen Jane had at first been strong in London but now everything was changing.

Surprisingly Queen Mary was welcomed by the City with huge enthusiasm, almost as if the new religion had hardly existed. England's loyalty to Henry VIII's daughter was symbolic of the patriotic fervour that superseded religious affiliation. The unpopularity of first Somerset and then Northumberland served to provide Mary with support as the true successor to the Tudor dynasty. As the first Queen to rule in England, apart from Jane's nine day rule, since the divided reign of Matilda and Stephen, she was an unknown quantity. London in particular had loved her mother Katherine, and was prepared to offer her the same affection, regardless of her Catholicism. She could, after all, now claim an undisputed succession to the throne.

Nicholas Ridley, Bishop of London and the only one to call himself Bishop of London and Westminster, in a sermon proclaiming Mary as illegitimate and likely to restore Papal control to England, was shouted down by the crowd. Londoners demonstrated in the streets, the fountains ran with wine and the church bells rang day and night. Such popularity was not to last.

Mary was proud of her Spanish ancestry and of her Catholic faith, neither of which was likely to be admired by her English subjects. Related to the most influential ruler in Europe, the Emperor Charles V, she felt herself in a strong position to rescue England from mortal sin. The situation was strengthened for Mary, though not for her country, by her proposed marriage to the future King of Spain, Philip, son of the Emperor and at the time Archduke of Burgundy.

In order to restore England to papal dominion, Mary needed to revoke her father's claim to be Supreme Head of the Church in England, but the Reformation was already too advanced to recover church possessions, monasteries and lands. As Elton says, 'The nobility, gentry and yeomanry who had invested in those lands were not prepared to disgorge them, and their self-interest saved Protestantism in England.'[1]

Suspicion of plots against the Queen's life were now rife. Even her sister, the young Elizabeth, was imprisoned in the Tower and Mary's determination to see England as a Catholic country grew daily. Those clerics who had married, as they were permitted, even encouraged, to do under the Reformation, were now deprived of their livings, though many had to be reinstated as so many vacancies left the Church without its servants. Gradually religious life was returning to the old faith. The Latin mass was heard in many parishes, though the Roman communion was still some way off. Mary's chief adviser was Cardinal Reginald Pole, a relative of the Queen and an ardent Catholic. He, like Mary, believed that the only way of rooting out the heresies of the anti-Catholic movement was by purification of fire. By 1554 new treason laws were in place (heresy was treason, a capital offence). Antipapal legislation was repealed and England's Reformation seemed to be dead in the water.

The Queen's half-sister, Elizabeth, was released to reside at Woodstock. This was the first time her allegiance to Church and State was tested. But throughout Mary's reign she was intelligent enough to keep a careful distance from all such divisive loyalties, content to bide her time quietly out of the spotlight of government.

The Spanish Marriage

Mary was not so wise. She was firmly assured of her right to rule, married or not. The wedding to the Prince of Spain took place at Winchester with due pomp and ceremony, before the bridal pair travelled to London. The Emperor gave his son the Kingdom of Naples as a wedding present. Philip was not enamoured of his new bride. He and his Spanish supporters did not appreciate English women for either their beauty or their intelligence. In fact he spent so little time in England that his duty as a husband was considered minimal. Nevertheless two months after the wedding Mary declared herself pregnant. Her doctors confirmed that she was indeed carrying a child but no child appeared, in spite of the Queen's appearance with swollen belly. When her due date passed without a birth, it was presumed that a mistake had been made in the calculation, but after another two months it was evident that she had suffered a false pregnancy.

Mary celebrated her marriage by putting in train a series of arrests and burnings which were to be her terrible legacy to England and for which she was always to be remembered. Many observant Protestants fled abroad or to Scotland where John Knox, a fervent follower of Calvin's doctrine, later found a large following. He was the founder of a new version of Protestantism, Presbyterianism, which has continued to be an intrinsic part of Scottish religious belief to this day.

The leaders of the Reformation in England, Nicholas Ridley, Hugh Latimer, even the noble Cranmer, went to the stake. The Catholic hierarchy who had been in hiding or practising their faith in secret, took their place. Parliament legalised Mary's right to the throne and abolished penalties for denial of the Supremacy, though it would not repeal the Queen's Supremacy itself nor bring back papal dominion in England. However, a few months later Parliament did just that. Cardinal Pole, as Papal legate, brought the Pope's absolution for England's secession and she became again a Catholic country. The heresy and treason laws were re-enacted and the flames took on a fiercer heat.

Martyrdom

The certainty of eternal damnation seemed a good enough excuse for the Queen and her Cardinal to save the people's souls by a widespread programme of dealing with heretics by burning. The first martyr was John Rogers. He was Vicar of St Sepulchre's, the ancient church outside Newgate, today, rebuilt after the Fire, the largest church in the City. It is believed to be the church in the rhyme 'Oranges and Lemons', the 'Bells of Old Bailey'. The bells were rung before an execution on the Newgate Prison gallows, telling the prisoner he was about to hang. The 'Execution Bell' is still in the church, which is now 'The Musicians' Church'. Rogers was also a Reader at St Paul's. He had met both Tyndale and Coverdale in Antwerp and like them was a confirmed Protestant. He married and came back to England. At St Paul's, he preached, according to Foxe, 'exhorting the people to beware of the pestilence of popery, idolatry and superstition.'[2] Bishop Bonner of London imprisoned him at Newgate and he was condemned to death. At Smithfield he begged to be allowed to speak to his wife, but was refused and was burned 'washing his hands in the flames.'[3]

For four years the fires continued to burn, some at Smithfield, some at other towns such as Oxford, where Ridley and Latimer met their deaths. Latimer's last words will always be remembered: 'Play the man, Master Ridley; we shall this day light such a candle, by God's grace, in England, as

I trust shall never be put out'. Nearly three hundred victims were killed. The English people blamed the Spaniards or the Pope but in reality it was their Queen who was the instigator of the terrible destruction. John Foxe wrote his *Book of Martyrs* recounting the whole sordid story, from the Protestant point of view, and it was later ordered to be placed in every church as a reminder of the Catholic oppression.

London's Reformation

Even apart from the burnings London was suffering terribly, from the ever recurrent plague, from appalling weather (it rained almost ceaselessly throughout the summer of 1555 when Westminster was flooded) and from the consequent poor harvests. Mortality rates were exceptionally high and children were often abandoned in the streets, either because their parents had died or because they could not afford to feed them. Without the monasteries little help was at hand to provide health care, welfare or education.

Pope Paul IV was elected to the Papacy in 1555. Mary had hoped that Cardinal Pole would be chosen but the new Pope was a firm supporter of France, and the Emperor's influence came to an end. The French King, Henry II, sided with Paul who excommunicated both Charles and his son Philip, 'King of England', much to Mary's distress. She prepared to send troops to France to support Philip in the impending war against the Pope and Henry, but Paul's response was to summon Pole to Rome to deprive him of his status as Papal Legate to England. Mary forbade him to go. In March 1557 Philip invaded France, and after early victories, which the English people were slow to praise, the battle for Calais was lost. This was a disaster for Mary. She was blamed by Philip and by her people for losing England's only land on the Continent, and never recovered from the loss.

Another pregnancy was announced, but again no child was born. The Queen fell into what would today be diagnosed as clinical depression, and was unable to ward off an illness variously described as a plague, pleurisy or an infection. She had lost the love of her husband – if indeed such love had ever existed – as well as that of the English and her only claim to her ancestors' hard-fought territory in France. She had no child and knew that her subjects disliked her and that her attempts to bring England back into Catholicism would probably die with her. She would be remembered as 'Bloody Mary', England's most unfortunate Queen.

Queen Elizabeth

On 17th November 1558 Queen Elizabeth acceded to the throne of England, a day celebrated throughout her reign as Accession Day, a day of rejoicing. Elton describes her as 'a naturally imperious, self-willed and selfish character, in the best Tudor tradition.'[4] She was twenty-five years old, young enough to be a vigorous, handsome girl with a strong, bright personality, but old enough to have experienced prison, seen her fellow countrymen burned for their faith and watched her father, brother and sister doing their best to lead their country, according to their own beliefs. Whereas Mary had taken as her guide the return of England to the Roman Church, Elizabeth's was to keep her as a united country, regardless of religion, and by so doing to establish a proud nation, her nation, whose people could work fearlessly with her to achieve their highest potential. It was to be a partnership without parallel in England's history.

Elizabeth has been called a Nicodemite, one who, like Nicodemus, the Jew who came to Jesus during the night, does not openly display his faith. She was no bigot, more of a conformist. She was prepared to fight for her country, but not for her religion. And she was not alone. Her chief advisers, William Cecil and his son Robert, William Paulet, Marquess of Winchester and Sir Francis Knollys, all believed in moderation in religious matters. It was to the Queen and the country that they owed their allegiance; she above all monarchs chose her advisers well.

The Religious Settlement

Many of the Protestants who had fled England during Mary's reign came home, often with a stronger faith, learned from Calvin. Some of them, anxious to purify the Church from Catholicism, were now known as Puritans. Elizabeth and England made their own religion: no pope, no elevation of the host, no English money spent on Catholicism abroad. But no married clergy either. The Queen's personal religious faith was almost immaterial when it came to her country's welfare. She would certainly not countenance a return to control from Rome, but she loved pomp and ceremony, colour and excitement. She showed it in her own person – a fondness for dancing and music, jewellery and fine clothes. She could not have accepted the chill and constraint of her late brother's Church or its Puritan successors. Nevertheless Elizabeth was above all a diplomat, even if a notably indecisive one. She found herself faced on the one hand by John Knox's *The First Blast of the Trumpet Against the Monstrous Regiment of Women*, and on the other by the defenders of the Old Religion. Both had their adherents in Parliament and it was Parliament which was to take over from the monarch the role of government. Free speech, freedom from arrest, and parliamentary privilege were turning that government into something more like the model we have today. This was not to say that the Queen was afraid to impose her will on its members. She was imperious in her demands, but thanks to her genius in choosing her counsellors, she managed to achieve most of what she wanted without serious confrontation. Knox was not the only one to rail against women rulers. Nicholas Heath, Archbishop of York, said in Parliament, quoting St Paul in his First Letter to Timothy, 'I do not permit a woman to teach or to assume authority over a man; she must be quiet.' Elizabeth later forgave him and he was permitted to lead his Province in peace.

In order for Elizabeth to solve the religious problems of the nation, she had to take into account not only the affiliations of her people, but of the two strongest players on the world stage, Philip of Spain and the Pope. Philip's 'Great Enterprise' was to keep England Catholic. He had after all considered himself King of England and was determined not to let 'his' country slip through his grasp. Paul IV considered Elizabeth illegitimate, but if she was to reign then he believed, at least to begin with, that she would follow her sister's lead. Elizabeth was Queen of England, France and Ireland, Defender of the Faith, etc., a somewhat dubious title which left the religious question open.

Many of the Sees were without a Bishop, even Canterbury, so Elizabeth was crowned by the Bishop of Carlisle. The hated Bonner of London refused to deny his Catholicism and eventually died in prison (Elizabeth had refused to let him kiss her hand when he knelt on her arrival in London). But she was cautious. She had seen too much horror in England in her short life, and as usual prevaricated. The religious question in the months after her accession was deliberately kept inconclusive until, just before Easter 1559, the Commons passed a Supremacy Bill, creating a Protestant English Church, with the Queen as Supreme Head. The Bill was thrown out by the Lords.

Eventually, drastically amended, Parliament passed the Act of Supremacy, with Elizabeth as Supreme Governor of the Church of England – Governor of the Church rather than Head, to avoid the charge that the monarchy was claiming divinity or usurping Christ, whom the Bible explicitly identifies as Head of the Church, a concession to a woman ruler. It became a crime to acknowledge the authority of 'any foreign prince or prelate' as treason punishable by death. This dealt with the Pope and with the King of Spain. The full title of the Act was 'An Act restoring to the Crown the ancient Jurisdiction over the State, Ecclesiastical and Spiritual, and abolishing all foreign power repugnant to the same.'

Everyone taking public office had to swear the Oath of Supremacy, ensuring the complete allegiance of all those concerned in the government of the nation. This included all Members of Parliament and those studying at university. All the Bishops (except Llandaff) were deprived of their office as were a hundred fellows at Oxford. They were replaced by those who were willing to swear. The old Prayer Book of Edward VI was recalled under the Act of Uniformity, which removed the phrase 'detestable enormities' concerning Catholics; 'altars' replaced 'tables' and clerical dress reverted to that of Protestant England.

As is the case with most compromises, no one was satisfied. The Catholics thought the new Church of England went too far, the Protestants that it did not go far enough. Many livings were vacant and some were filled by ignorant, self-serving priests. However, one person held the country together – that was the Queen. She railed against the state of the Church and annoyed those who attended service in the Chapel Royal, but like her father she kept her people together by sheer force of personality and by her determination to put the nation before herself.

Puritans and Anabaptists

Brigden says, 'The Church of England established by Queen Elizabeth aspired to contain within itself a variety of religious conviction.'[5] In an attempt to 'purify' the Church of its laxity, its 'unscriptural practices' and its corrupt habits, the new group of believers, the Puritans, gained considerable support. Those returning to England after exile brought back Calvin's ideas of the anti-Christ (the Pope), of the separation of Church and State, and an unwavering determination that only the Bible could have valid authority over men's lives. They believed that preaching was the way to achieve salvation, with images from the Bible and a personal commitment to a covenant with God. Such a disciplined religion demanded the abandonment of show and embellishment, in church services, in dress and in behaviour. Many of Elizabeth's leading counsellors were committed Puritans, avoiding the elaborate clothes of the court to wear plain dark clothes, and simple dress. Dispute over the vestments for the clergy led to considerable confrontation at Convocation. Catholic dress was too 'papist' for Elizabeth's reformed church. Some leading parliamentarians felt it should be left to the individual, others that uniformity in clerical dress was desirable. The Puritan view increased in fervour, devolving the argument about clothes into further debate over wedding rings, organs, the sign of the cross, and kneeling for communion.

The Puritan view of Church and State was that they were distinct and separate. They fought against pluralism – the holding of more than one office by the same man – and against the selling of livings, particularly to the family of the holder. They were also unhappy about the general decline of the standards of the clergy. To an Elizabethan Puritan the establishment was the enemy; all ministers of the Church should be equal. Even the bishops realised that the Church needed cleansing of its disorder.

The Queen herself disliked the Puritan ethic and was supported in this by her Archbishop of Canterbury, John Whitgift. Some Puritans had banded together to form 'separatist' organisations, believing in 'prophesyings', a form of religious classification akin to Presbyterianism. The Queen was not best pleased. She wrote to her bishops, 'these meetings caused our people, especially the vulgar sort ... to be brought to idleness and seduced in a manner schismatically divided amongst themselves into a variety of dangerous opinions.'[6]

Another separatist organisation was the Anabaptists. They had come to London at the beginning of the Reformation, but were largely persecuted or put to death. The first Anabaptist congregation had been formed in Zurich in 1525, and was soon followed by other communities in Moravia, north-west Germany and the Low Countries. Their faith was a radical interpretation of Protestantism; some introduced polygamy and most had a tendency to withdraw from the world. They refused military service or to swear oaths and concentrated on pacifism and spirituality. Many of the later variants of Christian belief, such as the Mennonites, Quakers and Plymouth Brethren can be traced back to these early Anabaptists.

In 1547 a Stranger Church was established in Britain, primarily for Italian worshippers. It had Cranmer's blessing, who insisted on Bishop Bonner attending the first sermon. The Dutch Reformed (Stranger) Church was founded at Austin Friars. It is now known as the Temple of the Lord Jesus. Anabaptist literature was brought over to London, but in 1590 the Anabaptists were ordered to leave England or join the Anglican community.

The Marprelate Tracts

The tracts issued in 1587 under the name of Martin Marprelate attacked the bishops. A satirical tirade against the leaders of the church, the seven tracts were full of puns and allusions. The first, *The Epistle – To the Terrible Priests of the Confocation House*, was 'compiled for the behoof and overthrow of the Parsons, Fyckers [vicars] and Currats [curates] that have learnt their catechisms and are past grace'.[7] The author addresses his first paragraph: To the Right Poisoned (a pun on puissant) persecuting and terrible Priests. The clergy referred to are named in full, including John Whitgift, Archbishop of Canterbury, John Bridges, Dean of Salisbury, Thomas Cooper, Bishop of Winchester and many others, mercilessly satirised and condemned as self-serving renegades.

The Jews in Tudor England

Although Edward I had banished the Jewish community from England in 1290, it is known that several had stayed on in secret, or fleeing from Spain and Portugal during the Inquisition had set up home in London, Bristol and one or two other cities. Here they could at least live with their families or friends, even if they were forbidden from worshipping openly and had to conform to Christian beliefs. A few still lived in the *Domus Conversorum* in Chancery Lane. While England was a Catholic country they had to take great care never to reveal their true religion, but for a short time under Edward VI and later under Elizabeth it is known that there were Jews living and working in the country. A Law Report tells of the evidence of a witness working in a Jewish household as a maid, who recounts in a garbled fashion how her mistress worshipped in secret. She speaks of such 'heinous practices' as a special meal at Eastertime with four white loaves (the unleavened bread of the Passover), the Sabbath on a Saturday when special clothes were worn and no work done and special food was served to the family.

One Jew, Roderigo Lopez, a Portuguese doctor, who had arrived in England in 1559, the year after Elizabeth's accession, became a physician at St Bartholomew's Hospital and acquired a practice of very distinguished patients; he was appointed Physician-in-Ordinary to the Queen herself. He was later accused of plotting to poison the Queen, found guilty and executed. Elizabeth, who called him her 'little Jew', clearly thought him innocent and remitted to his family the property taken at his attainder. In a letter to his superiors the Venetian Ambassador to Germany wrote, 'The Queen is ill; she has taken a Portuguese doctor out of prison to attend her case.'[8] This was hardly the action of someone who thought she might be poisoned!

Black People in England

Apart from a few secret Jews, no other religion is known to have existed in England by the end of the Tudor dynasty. However, there was a small number of black people in the country, some of whom may have been Muslims, though the majority, known usually as blackamoores but sometimes referred to as Africans, Ethiopians, Barbarians or Negroes, are mentioned in church records (marriages, baptism and deaths) and official documents. One, John Blanke, was known as 'the black trumpeter', serving Henry VIII and is depicted on horseback in full ceremonial robes, in the Great Tournament Roll of Westminster. His payment is recorded and he has even earned a place in the *Oxford Dictionary of Biography*. A letter from Queen Elizabeth to the Lord Mayor of London, complains of the number of blacks in England 'of which kind of persons there are already here too many'[9].

Several trading companies such as the Turkey Company and the Barbary Company were established in the sixteenth century, working out of the London docks, now much more efficient and prosperous. Trade with North Africa, particularly in sugar and fruit, was increasing and ships coming into London brought sailors and traders, many of whom were of Muslim descent. The East India Company was founded in 1585. Originally chartered as the 'Governor and Company of Merchants of London trading into the East Indies', the company rose to account for half of the world's trade, particularly in basic commodities that included cotton, silk, indigo dye, salt, saltpetre, tea and opium and was negotiating in Asia with oriental religious adherents.

Catholicism under Elizabeth

Many of Elizabeth's subjects in the north of England were still Catholic in their affiliation, and rose in revolt against their Protestant rulers in an attempt to put the Catholic Queen of the Scots on the throne of England. The leaders were the Earls of Northumberland and Westmoreland, but the rebellion fizzled out in the face of loyalty to the Queen and the dominance of the Protestants. In London anyone wishing to follow the Pope got short shrift from both church and government. Some devout Catholics went abroad, keeping in touch with their fellow-religionists at home and waited for the day when England might again become a Catholic country.

The Book of Common Prayer

The Book of Common Prayer was reissued in 1559, in a form acceptable to as many subjects as possible, with financial penalties for those of the clergy who refused to use it and for parishioners who did not attend church to hear the readings from it. Four years later Cranmer's original Forty-two Articles were published as the Thirty-Nine Articles, a declaration of the Anglican Faith, divided, as the Queen instructed, into four groups: the Catholic Articles, the Protestant and Reformed Articles, the Anglican Articles and the Miscellaneous Articles. These discussed matters of faith and creed, manner of worship in church and behaviour of the clergy, including celibacy, and personal belief, the damnation of the soul, salvation and the sacraments. The last section stated that the Bishop of Rome has no jurisdiction in England. At first the Queen refused to allow the Articles to be published but finally conceded in 1571 that the people should be aware of them. They were published in English and in Latin.

In 1570, Pope Pius V in his Bull *Regnans in Excelsis*, excommunicated 'the pretended Queen of England'. The Bull stated that she had 'oppressed the followers of the Catholic faith; instituted false preachers and ministers of impiety; abolished the sacrifice of the mass, prayers, fasts, choice of meats, celibacy, and Catholic ceremonies. She has dared to eject bishops, rectors of churches and other Catholic priests from their churches and benefices, to bestow these and other things ecclesiastical upon heretics, to abjure the authority and obedience of the Pope of Rome, and to accept her, on oath, as their only lady in matters temporal and spiritual.'[10] 'It was not possible, in future,' wrote Antonia Southern, 'to be an obedient Roman Catholic and a loyal subject of the Queen.'[11]

There were exceptions. William Byrd – 'one of the very greatest musicians that England has produced'[12] – was a practising Catholic, organist and choirmaster of Lincoln Cathedral. He was appointed a Gentleman of the Chapel Royal and joint organist there with Thomas Tallis. Here the Queen permitted the use of Latin in church choral music, and it was probably her personal protection, together with his acknowledged genius as a musician, which kept him safe. Much of his music consisted in settings to sacred texts, songs and keyboard music, as well as more contemporary songs and dances. Small wonder that Elizabeth loved his music. His later compositions were mainly for church services, particularly the Mass.

The Catholic threat to the establishment was compounded by the problem of the succession. Elizabeth's refusal to marry occupied the thoughts of her ministers and of her people. If her cousin Mary Queen of Scots, as her nearest relative, should succeed to the throne of England, she would undoubtedly insist on a Catholic regime being restored. Plots and counterplots, conspiracy theories and fears of treachery were obsessive. But the Pope's act in excommunicating the Queen had little effect on the English Catholics in the longer term. Englishmen loved their Queen more than their religion. As Rowse put it, 'The Church no longer ran the country; the country ruled the Church.'[13]

However, unlike the early years of the reign, when men were encouraged to worship – discreetly –as they wished, by the 1570s persecution of Catholics became more vigorous and more vicious. Lord Walsingham, Secretary of State, was a fervent Protestant. His system of counter-intelligence served the state well, particularly as far as Mary Queen of Scots was concerned. He was determined to protect Elizabeth from any threat from Rome, a threat which he saw personified by Mary. Catholic missionaries were prosecuted for treason, not for religious affiliation. To support the Pope, a foreign power, rather than the Queen, was reason enough to die at the stake.

In 1572 the tragedy of the St Bartholomew's Day massacre in France further reduced Catholic influence in England. The French Queen Mother,

Catherine, instigated a plot to slaughter the Huguenots of her country. Some 10,000 Protestants were cruelly killed (about 3,000 in Paris) and the terrible news only confirmed what the English believed might happen if Mary of Scotland gained the throne. Fearing an alliance between the two great Catholic powers, France and Spain, the government clamped down on English Catholics far harder than it had since Elizabeth's settlement at her accession. It now seemed unlikely that the Queen could marry either of the two Princes of France she had been considering as her husband.

St Paul's

In 1561 a terrible event struck London's principal church. During a night of heavy storms, lightning struck the spire of St Paul's. The great Gothic cathedral stood at the top of Ludgate Hill, with a commanding view over the city and beyond. On contemporary maps it clearly towers over the sky-line, with the nave the longest in Europe. A contemporary record reported the events of the night, telling of 'a marvellous great fiery lightning and immediately ensued a most terrible crack of thunder such as seldom hath been heard.'[14] The spire caught alight and the eagle and the cross at the top fell through into the south crossing beneath. The aisle caught fire and the body of the church was threatened. The Bishop of London's house was saved through the good efforts of the five hundred men who turned out to fight the blaze. Almost all the timber of the building burned away but the stone vaults and pillars survived. The spire was never restored but almost exactly one hundred years later the whole cathedral was destroyed by an even worse fire, to be rebuilt as it appears today.

Huguenot Immigration

Several Huguenot families moved to London after the Reformation where they could worship in safety, though during Mary's reign the community was dissolved. Under Elizabeth they felt free to worship as French Protes-tants though the numbers were still small. After the St Bartholomew Day Massacre many sought refuge in the Low Countries, Germany and England. The great majority were city craftsmen, weavers, glassmakers, cartographers (from Holland), artisans of all trades. Some were professional men, doctors, teachers or Protestant clerics. They could find employment in the cities, particularly London, and although most foreigners were viewed with some suspicion, these Protestant refugees (the word comes from the French *refugié*), respectable, church-going family men were made welcome. The first Huguenot Church in London was set up by a charter of Edward VI in

1550 in Threadneedle Street. In 1846 it moved to St Martins-le-Grand and in 1893 to Soho Square where it remains today.

The Armada

Philip of Spain's 'Great Enterprise' – to claim back England for the Catholic Church – came to a climax in 1588 when his Armada sailed up the English Channel. Beacons were lit along the south coast so that London would be aware that the Spanish fleet had been sighted. English naval warfare was far in advance of that of Spain, using smaller, faster ships instead of the unwieldy galleons of the Spanish forces. But bad weather played its part and once victory was assured, the hand of God was believed to be on the side of England. The Pope, Sixtus V, played little part in encouraging Spain. In fact the Venetian Ambassador to England in the year of the Armada quoted him to the Doge as saying that Elizabeth

> is a great woman; and were she only Catholic, she would be without her match and we would esteem her highly … just look how she governs; she is only a woman, only a mistress of half an island and yet she makes herself feared by Spain, by France, by the Empire, by all.[15]

Magic and Superstition

Closely associated with the devotion to religion in the Elizabethan Age was the attention paid to superstition. Sometimes the two were almost indistinguishable. The Queen's own adviser, John Dee, was a scientist, mathematician and astronomer, as well as a magician, astrologer and some said, a sorcerer. The Queen herself believed in the supernatural. She consulted with Dee on a propitious day for her coronation. Another astrologer, Simon Forman, told of his dreams about the Queen. Rowse calls him 'a forerunner of the modern psychiatrist'.[16] He interpreted the dreams as symbols of Elizabeth's life and loves, and was highly regarded by the aristocracy and even by some of the clergy. A knowledge of the heavens, the movements of the planets and the music of the spheres, bore heavily on the actions of men. The King of Spain consulted his astrologers on the most propitious date to launch the Armada. Doctors discussed with soothsayers on the prognosis of illnesses. Sometimes God and Fate were inextricable. The destruction of the spire of St Paul's Cathedral was put down to the hand of Providence, however that might be interpreted. The Puritan view of magic, following Calvin, was not to believe in astrology but to accept the new discoveries in astronomy; the dividing line between alchemy and chemistry too was blurred. Science and religion could happily exist side by side and superstition ran through both. For the ordinary

Englishman signs and portents were a part of life. Milk curdled, children were born deformed, streams dried up and storms felled trees – who was to say what was behind it? Shakespeare's plays are full of allusions to witchcraft and the supernatural. For the contemporary playgoer witches were a perfectly acceptable part of the play. 'These late eclipses in the sun and moon portend no good to us,' [17] says King Lear.

England's Renaissance

The word Renaissance is often applied to the country's flowering of intellect and scholarship during Elizabeth's reign. To produce a writer of Shakespeare's universal genius as well as the poetry of the court poets there had to develop that national pride which the Queen engendered, as well as peace at home and a degree of religious acceptance. With the great flowering of the English language in the wake of Chaucer, the Great Bible and the Book of Common Prayer came also the music of Byrd and Tallis, the miniatures of Nicholas Hilliard and the architecture of Bess of Hardwick in the shires and Thomas Gresham's Royal Exchange in London.

Part of this outpouring of cultural achievement came from education; grammar schools and universities flourished, encouraged by the examples of John Cheke and Roger Ascham in the early instruction of Edward VI and Elizabeth. Sir Thomas Elyot's *The Gouvernor* showed how the country's leaders should shoulder their responsibilities. Richard Hooker's *Laws of Ecclesiastical Polity* did the same for the Church. Renaissance is not too strong a word for Elizabethan England's surge of intellectual power.

The End of the Tudor Age

Queen Elizabeth died at the age of seventy, still unmarried, her heir unnamed until almost her last breath. She was buried in the Henry VII Chapel at Westminster Abbey. England had undergone a sea-change in its religious affairs, started by Elizabeth's father and after several cataclysmic upsets between Catholics and Protestants. Only under Elizabeth could her subjects have come through, unscathed except for those who openly protested their beliefs against the national religion. London had lost much of her sacred beauty and was to do so again after Elizabeth's death, but the city had stuck with its monarch and her determination to achieve unity and to lead her people to prosperity; peace was her legacy to them.

CHAPTER XIII

The First Stuarts

James VI and I

I T TOOK THE NEW KING, James VI of Scotland and I of England, a month to reach his new capital, but London welcomed him warmly. After years of prevarication Elizabeth had finally assented to the son of Mary of Scotland succeeding to the throne that she had made very much her own. She died, as she had lived, in full control almost to the end. John Manningham, lawyer and diarist of the time, a witty observer, wrote 'Her majesty departed this life mildly, like a lamb, easily, like a ripe apple from the tree.'[1]

The character of the new King has been much discussed, but it is generally accepted that he was an unprepossessing humourless man, arrogant until confronted, totally without the charisma that was the great distinction of his predecessor. James was the son of his mother's second marriage to Henry Stuart, Lord Darnley. Beset by conspiracies, religious and political, doomed by her passions, which ruled her head, Mary consigned her only child's upbringing firstly to her half-brother, the Protestant Earl of Mar, then to the Earl of Bothwell. The Stuart line, which was to rule England for the next one hundred years, was descended from Henry VIII's sister Margaret Tudor, who had married James IV, King of Scotland, Mary's grandfather. Her little boy, James, had a strict Protestant upbringing, though a scholarly one. Severely disciplined and given little relaxation or affection, he soon acquired an extensive knowledge of the Scriptures and was able to dispute on abstruse theological subjects with scholars much older than himself. David Willson's biography describes him as 'a nervous, excitable, overstrung boy, and the hothouse character of his education may well have increased these tendencies.'[2] James's intellect was formidable; he was a writer of some six books and many dissertations, and once remarked that if he had not been a king he would have been a 'University man'. His collected works were published in 1616.

Queen Anne of Denmark

In 1589 James married Anne, the younger daughter of the King of
Denmark. They were to have seven children, of whom only four survived
to adulthood. Anne, brought up a Lutheran at the Danish court, converted
to Catholicism, though she was discreet, worshipping privately where she
could. She quarrelled with the King over the upbringing of their elder
son, Henry. James insisted he should have the same strict tutors he had had
himself, whereas Anne wanted access to her son which James refused. Anne
joined the King in London and they were crowned at Westminster in July
1603, the first coronation to use English instead of Latin throughout the
ceremony.

Plague

In the same year there was a severe outbreak of plague in the country, the
first year in which the Bills of Mortality were published, though it did not
reach the proportions of that of 1665. Overcrowding, inadequate fresh
water and a lack of public hygiene contributed to the contagion. Some
30,000 Londoners died. The dramatist Thomas Dekker described the
Church's difficulties in dealing with the dead. 'Amongst which worm-eaten
generation the three bald sextons of limping St Giles, St Sepulchre's and
St Olave's, ruled the roost more hotly than ever did the triumvir of Rome'.[3]
The situation was not helped by the state of many of London's buildings,
including the churches. St Paul's was on the verge of crumbling.

The Millenary Petition

On his way to London to claim his throne, the King was presented with a
Petition. Some one thousand members of the clergy signed it, so it became
known as the Millenary Petition. Most were Puritans and they set out their
requests for changes to the practice of the Church of England. Among these
were some of their old grievances, such as marriage rings, the sign of the
Cross and the use of surplices by ministers. Some still perceived the odour
of papistry about the Anglican ritual, but their demands were not unreason-
able. They did not want another split within the Church:

> We, the ministers of the gospel in this land, neither as factious men affecting a
> popular parity in the Church nor as schismatics aiming at the dissolution of the
> state ecclesiastical ... could do no less in our obedience to God, service to your
> majesty, love to his Church, than acquaint your princely Majesty with our
> particular griefs.[4]

The demands included the insistence that baptism, even emergency baptism by midwives, should not be administered by women, that the Lord's Day should not be profaned and that congregations should not bow at the name of Jesus. They insisted on preaching in all church services, no 'double-beneficing', that men should not be excommunicated for 'trifles' and finally re-iterated their desire 'not for a disorderly innovation, but a due and godly reformation.'.

James was annoyed. The presentation of the petition resulted in a conference at Hampton Court at which he made his displeasure clear. He refused most of the demands, determined that the Puritans should conform to the status quo. Ceremonial, he felt, was not a Catholic prerogative but a way to keep the worshippers more closely involved with ritual and practice. He was also indicating at the very start of his reign his belief in the Divine Right of Kings which was to bring down his son.

The Hampton Court Conference

The Conference took place in the year after James's succession. He refused to acknowledge the Puritan desire for change. He liked the Anglican Church and insisted on it remaining as it was, 'no bishops, no king'. Conformity won the day; discipline in the church was to be improved, celebrants were instructed to wear the cope and surplice and the congregation should kneel while receiving communion. The Puritan influence in the Church of England decreased, but most of those who remained agreed to its canons. These were drawn up in Convocation largely under the guidance of Richard Bancroft, Bishop of London. What it did achieve, however, has come down to posterity as one of the greatest and most loved books in the English language: the King James, or Authorised Version of the Bible. 'It had the immediate effect,' says Jeremy Paxman, 'of democratising learning and created a stock of memorised stories and sentences that became a shared currency among the English people'.[5]

The work was undertaken by fifty translators working in six groups: two at Westminster, two at Oxford and two at Cambridge. Each was allotted a portion; all those taking part were distinguished scholars, including two Professors of Hebrew, the Provost of Eton and a future Archbishop of Canterbury. They took eleven years, working together and then checking each other's work. The original texts of the Geneva Bible and the Bishops' Bible were used with Tyndale's and Coverdale's translations. They strove not so much to produce a new version as 'to make a good one better.' David Daiches, a Biblical scholar and critic himself, wrote, 'Though the translators added a more liturgical prose to Tyndale's honest clarity, they retained the basic simplicity which remains the norm of narrative prose in the Authorised Version.'[6]

The Gunpowder Plot

The Hampton Court Conference left everyone dissatisfied. The King clearly felt that he had control of neither his government nor his Church. The Puritan element in the Commons was still complaining about the influence of the papists in the national Church, gradually forming a Nonconformist congress of their own. Taking themselves very seriously, they were not easy to deal with. Manningham wrote 'A Puritan is one who loves God with all his soul, but hates his neighbour with all his heart.'[7] The Catholics were discontented with the deep-seated prejudices against them, though James, at least at the beginning of his reign, showed considerable latitude towards his ordinary Catholic subjects. However, the Protestant majority refused to accept any such toleration. James found the Jesuit missionaries treacherous in their attitude to the state, and insisted on Catholics attending Anglican Church services. He was anxious that England should unite her Catholics and her Protestants in one Church, going back, perhaps, to earlier times before the existence of the Papacy, a clearly impossible aim.

Pope Clement VIII, misled by the opinion of his envoy to England that James was ripe for conversion to the 'old religion', and aware that his Queen had already converted (to the extent that even at her coronation she would not participate in the Anglican communion), sent a delegate to oversee what was happening. Henry Prince of Wales's proposed marriage to a Spanish Infanta came to nought when Spain insisted on his conversion.

English Catholics seemed to be flourishing with their King's toleration, but it was short-lived. James insisted that anti-Catholic laws should be strengthened and enforced, and a few months later he narrowly escaped with his life when a plot to blow up the Houses of Parliament, called then the Powder Treason, was foiled. It is today the name of Guy Fawkes who is most closely linked to the conspiracy, but in fact it was Robert Catesby who was the prime mover. All the conspirators were Catholics. They had rented a cellar under the House of Lords in the days before 5th November, the day of the opening of Parliament. Here they stored the barrels of gunpowder, hoping that when the fuse was lit the King, his family and his chief ministers, with as many Protestant members as possible, would be blown to bits. If the young Prince of Wales was killed, then his sister Elizabeth would become the nominal queen and could be married off to a Catholic prince, with the resulting move of England to Catholicism. 'What a Queen I should have been,' said the Princess later. 'I had rather been with my father in the Parliament House, than wear his crown on such condition.'[8]

The plot was exposed by an anonymous letter sent to Lord Monteagle[9], warning him to stay away from Parliament that day. As a result the building was searched, and Fawkes was found on watch at the door of the cellar 'a figure in a cloak and dark hat, booted and spurred as though for flight.'[10] The huge store of gunpowder, later found to be decayed and useless, was discovered, and the conspirators, who had waited to see the explosion from the high ground of Primrose Hill in Hampstead, were all put to death.

Religious Confrontation

The religious problems of James's reign were compounded by two factors. The nobility, who took an anti-clerical stance, wished simply to be allowed to worship in their own chapels, along with their families, appointing their own candidates to their livings, undisturbed by outside influences. The other element which disturbed both King and government was the financial state of the nation. James, profligate himself, in spite of, or perhaps because of his puritanical upbringing, inherited a country on the verge of bankruptcy. The majority of the clergy earned no more than a pittance and parliament had hardly enough revenue to pay for itself. An arrangement known as the Great Contract was drawn up to tighten up the nation's expenditure but the King refused to agree to its demands for him to rein in his spending.

Richard Bancroft, Bishop of London, who was much involved with the new Bible, had managed to ensure that all ministers in the London diocese conformed to the Anglican Church as it stood at present; he was appointed Archbishop of Canterbury in November 1604, though he is believed never to have visited the See. He was an austere man, exacting from his clergy a harsh conformity, depriving of their living those who overstepped the mark. He was strongly in favour of episcopacy and had written fervently against the author of the Marprelate Tracts. In spite of James's assurance that Catholics would not be harried, Bancroft was violently opposed to the Romish Church.

Arminianism

Puritanism in England was now in danger of splitting into several different affiliations. Jacob Arminius, a Dutch theologian, was the leader of a Protestant sect which had a considerable following in England. It did not accept predestination, insisting that man's free will was the guidance by which he should live. The high church Arminians threated James over his control of his Puritan kingdom, as they were inclined to revert to the early church rather than a purely Calvinist theology, raising the possibility of a return to Catholic dogma. The Counter Reformation movement encouraged them. They did not want a return to Papal control and were supportive of James and the Anglican Church, including the bishops. They were to become a motive force under Charles I.

Stuart London

London in the early seventeenth century was not a pleasant place to live. Bad harvests had led to higher food prices and if Londoners were to eat they could not spend money on their buildings. Smaller houses, shops and workshops were allowed to decay, the streets were narrow, dirty and teemed with people: beggars, starving immigrants and paupers out of work, malnourished and often criminal. Nevertheless the city was still the hub around which the rest of the nation turned, and often the envy of foreigners visiting from abroad. Some of the vagrants, especially the children, were sent overseas to Virginia at the invitation of the American colonists, though the City livery companies were unwilling to sponsor them.

New building in London was usually at the behest of wealthy merchants or the nobility, rather than at the command of government, to prevent the City welcoming in even more people. Building regulations were put in place, ordering houses to be made of brick rather than wood, with specified height and width, and with abundant open spaces. If the rules were contravened the City fathers insisted that

> you immediately repair unto the tenements aforementioned and cause them to be demolished and pulled down unto the ground, that by this example others may learn to beware how they presumptuously offend His Majesty's laws and disobey his commandments.[11]

St Paul's

St Paul's had become more of a market place than a cathedral. The great nave was known as St Paul's Walk, where gentlemen, merchants, visitors and general riff-raff could walk about – or indeed rush up and down, though ball games were forbidden – discussing the latest news, financial affairs or food prices and buy and sell all sort of goods. Shops were crowded into the cathedral close – the London booksellers were centred there – and visitors could purchase almost anything from beer and spirits to a fine goose, from jewellery to broadsides and pamphlets, and consume the food and drink inside the building. To 'dine with Duke Humphrey' was to eat nothing, referring erroneously to Humphrey, Duke of Gloucester's tomb in the cathedral aisle (he was actually buried at St Alban's). At tables in the nave were scribes and letter-writers to help citizens with letters or legal documents. There was certainly little accommodation for worship, though St Paul's Cross outside was always well attended by those who came to hear the sermons.

Bishop John Earle in his *Microcosmography* described the inside of the cathedral as the general mint of all famous lies, which are here, like the legends of popery, first coined and stamped in the church. All inventions are emptied here, and not a few pockets ... the principal inhabitants and possessors are stale knights and captains out of service, men of long rapiers and breeches, which after all turn merchants here and traffic for news.[12]

Thomas Dekker advised a young gallant how to comport himself at St Paul's, advising him to go up the tower, and

before you come down again, I would desire you to draw your knife and grave your name (or for want of a name, the mark which you clap on your sheep) in great characters upon the leads, by a number of your brethren (both citizens and county gentlemen) and so you shall be sure to have your name lie in a coffin of lead, when yourself shall be wrapt in a winding sheet; and indeed the top of Paul's contains more names than Stow's *Chronicle*.[13]

The King had wanted for some time to improve the fabric of the cathedral, but plans had always been delayed. When William Laud became Bishop of London in 1628, the project finally began to get under way. Inigo Jones was appointed Surveyor of the King's Works and was commissioned to take charge of the restoration. He retained and restored much of the chancel and choir, and in the new 'classical' style, now much in vogue, used Portland stone to reface the old Norman nave and transepts. His work for theatrical masques and plays, in which the Queen often took part, influenced his designs for the great west front portico. This was composed of ten 56ft Corinthian pillars with a tower at each side. The restoration was held up by the Civil War, when soldiers and their horses were billeted in the building, and although the portico was left relatively undamaged by the Great Fire, Wren had it pulled down when he redesigned the west front.

Another vestige of old St Paul's was recovered later from the fire. King James had been an admirer of the poet John Donne. He created him Dean of St Paul's and an effigy of him wrapped in a shroud was rescued from the flames and replaced in the South Quire Aisle of Wren's cathedral, where it remains today. Donne had been brought up as a Catholic but converted to Anglicanism and became a priest and a distinguished preacher. His early love poems had a rich erotic beauty, but once ordained he turned to equally moving but religious poetry. One of his Divine Poems, written near the end of his life, begins:

> Since I am coming to that Holy room,
> Where, with thy quire of Saints for evermore,
> I shall be made thy music; as I come
> I tune the instrument, here at the door
> And what I must do then, think here before.[14]

The Young Princes

In 1612 Henry, Prince of Wales, died of typhoid fever at the age of eighteen. The following year his sister Elizabeth was married to Frederick, the Elector Palatine, the leading Calvinist Prince in Europe. The wedding took place in London with extraordinary extravagance, and the pair left for Germany. Her father allied himself and his country with the Protestant Union of Germany, making it very clear which way England's religious affinity lay. In spite of this, the body of Catholic Mary, Queen of Scots, James's mother, was exhumed from its resting place at Peterborough Cathedral and placed in an elaborate marble tomb in Westminster Abbey a few feet away from her cousin Elizabeth, though in a more elaborate setting. The vault was later opened to admit the body of her grandson Henry. Another occupant of the same tomb was later found to be Arabella Stuart, a possible contender to the English throne. She was descended, like James, from Henry VII, but died in prison after a forbidden marriage to William Seymour.

James's successor was now his second son Charles. He was Prince of Wales as well as Duke of York. His projected marriage to a Spanish princess revived all the old fears of England becoming a Catholic nation, but Spain too was not in favour. He was then betrothed to Henrietta Maria, sister of the French King, Louis XIII. James promised concessions to English Catholics to appease the doubting French, especially Cardinal Richlieu, but continued to reassure his own Parliament that England was still a Protestant country.

The King's Favourite

James's sexuality was always in doubt though he had fathered seven children. In 1607 he had become enamoured of a handsome young Scot, Robert Carr, who came to London as his page. He embraced him in public, uncaring as to the impression he was creating at court. Carr was given English honours, Viscount Rochester and then Earl of Somerset, which enabled him to take his seat in the House of Lords, the first Scot to do so. The two became very close, and it was felt that the King's questionable behaviour in public was unlikely to be any the less in private.

James had been interested in witchcraft and sorcery since his youth. His *Daemonologie* was written when he was thirty-three, and fulminated against witches, encouraging witch hunting, a strong pursuit in Scotland. The book begins

> The fearful abounding at this time in this country, of these detestable slaves of the Devil, the Witches or enchanters, hath moved me (beloved reader) to

dispatch in post, this following treatise of mine [...] to resolve the doubting [...] both that such assaults of Satan are most certainly practised, and that the instrument thereof merits most severely to be punished.

His superstitious fears led him to be terrified of death and all ceremonial surrounding it. He refused to attend the funerals of either his son Prince Henry or his wife Anne. He was a sick man for much of his life, though active, particularly in the hunting field, in his youth, and later investigation into the illness of George III suggested that James may have suffered from porphyria, handing the disease on to his successors.

The next favourite to absorb James's affections was more dangerous for he was passed on to his son, Charles, to influence him when he succeeded to the throne. Carr, now Earl of Somerset, was imprisoned in the Tower on suspicion of having murdered Sir Thomas Overbury and James turned to George Villiers as his new companion. He was handsome and intelligent and was quickly honoured by the King, who created him the first Duke of Buckingham. James's knowledge of the Bible led him to remember that according to Acts VI:6, St Stephen's face was 'that of an angel'. Accordingly he referred to Villiers as 'Steenie', and once again found himself facing the disapproval of the court, as he expressed his feelings publicly, paying no heed to the proprieties of his position.

Parliament

At the same time the King was in trouble with Parliament. He treated the members as servants, to do his will as he proclaimed it. He was anxious to bring together his two nations, as well as his two religions, neither of which ambitions pleased his leaders. The Puritans frowned on the King's extravagance, on his inclination towards High Church bishops and on his acceptance of Sunday entertainment, as laid out in his *Book of Sports*, published in 1617, which permitted sports and pastimes as well as drinking, after church on Sundays. To James's fury the Arminian heresy again reared its head in England. In Holland, where the controversy had begun, those who supported the Arminians were cruelly suppressed. James, ever happy to enter into religious controversy, compared their beliefs with the heresies of Pelagius, the British monk of the fourth century, who was vilified for his views on man's free will. In England many of the leading churchmen were against the original Calvinist doctrine. One of them, William Laud, a supporter of Arminianism, was created a bishop by James only at the request of Buckingham. He was eventually made Archbishop of Canterbury.

The Development of London

It was very clear that London was literally falling apart. George Buck, Member of Parliament and Master of the Revels to James, certainly thought it was time to improve one of the greatest cities in the world. He wrote a treatise on *The Third University of England* (a phrase reinvented in modern times), in which he drew up plans for a thorough expansion and improvement for the city. Among other suggestions he included a theatre at St Paul's Cross so that sermons could be better heard, a refurbishment of the steeple and bell tower and a proper market place with a piazza, somewhere in the Guildhall area. London's piazza was indeed built, but on land belonging to the Russell family, the Earls of Bedford, on the old garden site of the Westminster convent. It was again Inigo Jones who designed the layout of Covent Garden. London began to drag itself up out of the disorder and deterioration. A new piping system brought clean water into the city.

Charles and Buckingham

In 1625 Charles married the French princess, Henrietta Maria. Cardinal Richelieu, First Minister of France, asked the English King for money to fight the Huguenots. Buckingham went to France, but failed to sort matters out and the English refused to fight for a Catholic monarch against a Protestant army. Charles expelled his wife's attendants, probably at Buckingham's suggestion. A further outbreak of plague in London forced Parliament to meet in Oxford, where it refused to vote subsidies for the King and a movement was beginning to rise against Buckingham's disastrous control.

The problem of Buckingham and his influence over the King and the country was solved by a deranged lieutenant in the Navy, who had not been paid. He waylaid the Duke at Portsmouth on his way to France and stabbed him to death. After Buckingham's death the King took a more personal participation in the day-to-day running of the country. His interests in painting and sculpture laid the foundation of some of England's superb collections which were to form the basis of her pre-eminence as a patron of the arts. Charles encouraged Inigo Jones's work as architect and designer and Van Dyke's portraiture putting together the great foundations of London's galleries and museums, though much was later sold off under the Commonwealth.

The national Church was another of his concerns. A devout man, he saw his role as combining that of the servant of God with that of leader of the English people. He was aware that the Puritan ethic could become inimical to the very foundations of the state. Laud had made this clear. But the King seemed incapable of taking pre-emptive action, unaware of the looming danger.

England's Religious Affiliations

Out of the mixed conglomeration that called itself Puritan, radical sects were emerging. One, under the leadership of John Traske, believed in obedience to the laws of the Old Testament. This Judaizing Sabbatarian sect maintained the dietary laws of the Pentateuch, strict observance of the Sabbath – some viewing it as the seventh day of the week – and eating only unleavened bread during the month of Lent. No work of any kind was permitted on the Sabbath, including the lighting of fires or the cooking of hot meals.

Traske himself was arrested after he tried to convert the King. He was tortured and dragged through the streets of London. His head was branded with the letter J (for holding Jewish opinions) and while in prison he was forced to eat swine's flesh. He finally recanted, only to resume his activities when released. Traske's opinions were considered heretical, hardly surprising when he publicly referred to bishops as 'bloody butchers', and Lancelot Andrewes, Bishop of Winchester and Dean of the Chapel Royal, said in the Star Chamber, 'It is good work to make a Jew a Christian, but to make a Christian a Jew hath ever been holden a foul act and severely to be punished … he is a very Christened Jew, a Maran (Marrano), the worst Jew that is.'[15]

The Arminian controversy again came to the fore. The main issue, according to Laud, who was made Archbishop of Canterbury in 1633, lay with the creation of bishops. Their claim to continue the apostolic succession was inimical to the Puritan ethic, which believed in the direct approach of man to God, without intervention of clergy and was devoted to simplicity in all things religious. The bishops believed implicitly in the Divine Right of Kings. The historian Godfrey Davies wrote, 'A position was created in which the Puritan found that any opposition to the church was regarded as sedition at court, and any criticism of the monarch was denounced as blasphemy in the pulpit.'[16]

The enmity between England and the two Catholic nations, Spain and France, impacted severely on English Catholics. They were permitted to worship in private – a prerogative of the wealthy who could afford the recusancy fines which allowed them their religious freedom, but they were forbidden to attend English universities so their children were sent abroad to study. They could not take office nor bury their dead in parish church-yards, necessitating burial by night.

Many Londoners were prepared to inform on their Catholic neighbours. A Jesuit cell was discovered in Clerkenwell, when a house in St John's, previously thought to be empty, was seen to have provisions being brought in. The neighbours informed the authorities and the place was raided. Those inside pleaded innocence and the constables, under the orders of the

Attorney General, Sir Robert Heath, withdrew. But they kept watch, returning to the find the place empty. However, on searching the cellars they discovered 'a brick wall, newly made, which they caused to be pierced',[17] and found the Catholic conspirators hiding inside. They confessed under examination to being recusants and were convicted and imprisoned.

The situation was not helped by the presence of yet another Catholic queen consort. Inigo Jones had created for Henrietta Maria a new chapel at St James's Palace and she and her court were a constant reminder of a Catholic presence in this Protestant country. The Queen was the god-daughter of Pope Urban VIII and symbolised the hope of continental Catholics that England would return to the fold. Her banished household was replaced by Capuchin friars. They were installed at her principal palace, Denmark House (formerly Somerset House), newly remodelled at vast expense for the Queen. Here she created a Catholic stronghold, with another new chapel, again designed by Jones, dedicated to the Virgin. 'During the 1630s not only did it succeed in drawing existing Catholics, it stimulated a number of high profile conversions at Court.'[18]

A further grievance of the anti-Catholics was the arrival in London of Mary de Medici, the Queen's mother. She was installed at considerable expense in St James Palace now with its own Roman place of worship. In 1634 a papal envoy arrived at Denmark House and for the first time since England left Rome the ruling monarch received a representative of the Pope. Feelings against Catholicism and against the Queen in particular were growing. She was seen, especially by Londoners, as extravagant and licentious – her lavish masques were decried by the Puritans – and as the figurehead of a popish revival.

CHAPTER XIV

Revolution

Parliament and the King

THE FINANCIAL STATE of the nation was now critical. The King
was enforcing taxes from landowners, without the consent of
Parliament, but it was the revival and enforcement of ship money
that was to provoke the storm. In London the imposition of a writ to pay
for ships at Portsmouth was met with strong opposition, Parliament seeing
this as a forerunner to a permanent tax to fill the royal coffers.

The case of John Hampden, who refused to pay, brought matters to
a head. Hampden came from Buckinghamshire (there are still two small
hamlets of the name Hampden outside Princes Risborough and John
Hampden is buried there in an unmarked grave); the area had been a centre
of rebellion from the time when the Lollards were active in the district.
At his trial the judges found for the King, but Charles ignored the danger.
His attempts to bring Scotland into line with England's religious convictions
were met with violent dissent and an English army was enlisted under the
command of Thomas Wentworth, created Earl of Strafford.

Charles prorogued Parliament in 1629, determined to rule without a
Parliament, under his claim to Divine Right, but in the present crisis it was
recalled in 1640, the Long Parliament. Wentworth, while Lord Deputy in
Ireland, had raised a force to deal with the insurrection there, leaving that
country with an innate and eternal hatred of English rule. The subsequent
massacre of Irish Protestants by the Catholics called for action by the English
Parliament, which was nervous that if it were to raise a fighting force to
deal with the Irish situation, it could be used, under the command of
the King, for other purposes. At the end of 1641 Parliament passed, by a
small majority, and with uproar, even violence, in the House, the Grand
Remonstrance.

The Grand Remonstrance

This was revolution indeed. It covered politics, religion and social problems. The leader of the opposition to the King was John Pym, an experienced Parliamentarian and a fine orator. The Remonstrance contained 204 clauses, including the removal of the Bishops from Parliament, an indictment of Catholic believers and a claim for the House to have the right to veto appointments made by the King. It was the Catholic element which was blamed for all the problems of Church and State, though the King and Queen were not specifically named. The Bill stated that it was

> for uniting all such your loyal subjects together as join in the same fundamental truths against the Papists, by removing some oppressive and unnecessary ceremonies by which divers weak consciences have been scrupled, and seem to be divided from the rest, and for the due execution of those good laws which have been made for securing the liberty of your subjects.

A proposal for a General Synod 'of the most grave, pious, learned and judicious divines' was included in the Bill. The Westminster Assembly of Divines was duly set up. Naturally the King rejected the Remonstrance and tried to impeach Pym. There followed the event usually known as 'The Arrest of the Five Members' when Charles, with an armed guard, entered the House of Commons, the first monarch ever to do so, to seek out Pym and his colleagues, John Hampden, Denzil Holles, Sir Arthur Hesilrigge and William Strode. But they had fled to the protection of the City and the Speaker, William Lenthall, declined to reveal where they were. 'So the birds have flown', said the King.

The Religious Debate

London was, as usual, the centre of the opposition to the King. Charles, now becoming more aware of his capital city's animosity towards him, left in a hurry. He took his household with him. The City and Parliament were now in the throes of a turbulent revolt. Laud's handling of the religious debate found little support. He, like his master the King, insisted on conformity in Church affairs, at a time when dissent and controversy were leading to the founding of widely differing sects and cults, the beginnings of England's schismatical tendencies which were to grow and multiply in the years to come as Nonconformity. Laud put bishops before parishioners and placed his faith in the sacraments and in magnificent churches. He re-sited the altars at the east end of the churches, with rails around them, often impeding the congregation from either seeing or hearing the celebrant. Londoners complained of an imminent rapprochement with Catholicism.

The City denied the King a share of its wealth. Monopolies and privileges were in danger of encroachment by the royal exchequer. The anti-royalist party in Parliament was supported by the City, which organised the militia and refused the King any say in its government. London refused to hand over the five members and the trained bands, in their full red and white uniforms, turned out in defence of the citizens against the royal guard.

The Long Parliament

Parliament was gearing up to rule without the monarch. Charles had taken with him the Royal Seal so no bills could be passed without his signature. The Root and Branch Petition to abolish the episcopacy 'with all its dependencies, roots and branches' was signed by 15,000 Londoners. Many of those who attacked the bishops themselves, defended their right to exist. The Church must have its leaders. The Westminster Assembly of Divines met for the first time in 1643. Scottish representatives joined with English clerics and laymen to try to establish some form of agreement between the English Puritans and Scottish Presbyterians.

The result of the debates, stretching over many years, was to produce a Confession of Faith, the Shorter and the Larger Catechism and a handbook for the liturgy of both churches. There were many differences between them, leading at times to hotly disputed sessions. The English Congregationalists wanted a greater degree of autonomy for individual churches, while the Scottish Presbyterians opted for more strictly governed regional and national bodies. The Assembly was obliged to be answerable to Parliament for its conclusions. The members were under strict orders not to reveal their discussions (an early Official Secrets Act) and those discussions had to conform to the will of Parliament. Some 120 theologians, the majority Scottish, formed the body of the Assembly which met in Westminster Abbey, first in the Henry VII chapel and then in the Jerusalem Chamber. By 1647 it had concluded its discussions, culminating in the Westminster Confession, a statement which, though never fully accepted by the Anglican Church, remains the definitive statement of Presbyterianism.

The Outbreak of War

The upheaval which shook England in the seventeenth century has variously been called a Revolution, a Civil War and a Rebellion. It has been considered a military struggle, a social confrontation and a religious affair. It was all three. Looked at with hindsight it prevented this country from being torn apart by such radical rebellions as those suffered later by France and Russia. The middle classes, not present in those two countries to the same extent as in Britain, acted as a buffer between royalty, nobility and the lower classes in the social scale. All three nations disposed of their kings, but England, after all, had no serfs and no peasants, only workers on the land and in the towns, protected by a paternalistic system where each knew his place.

Charles saw his family – the Queen and the younger children – off at Dover to take shelter in Holland. The Queen took with her the Crown Jewels to use them to finance the King. Charles himself made for Hull, where the ordnance was stored and from where he could easily reach his family in Holland. But that city kept its gates firmly closed against him. The King moved on to York where he established his base.

The Radicals

The Book of Revelations was responsible in many ways for the beliefs of some of the more feverish sects that blossomed out of the disturbances of the mid-seventeenth century. 'And he laid hold on the dragon, that old serpent, which is the Devil, and Satan, and bound him a thousand years.'[1] When the thousand years was up, thought the Millenarians, the Apocalypse would come, the Devil would be loosed and man's destiny would unfold. Even today, in the cold computerised light of the second Millennium, many still believed that the world might come to an end; clocks might stop, governmental organisations could run out of control, life would grind to a halt. How much more credulous were those who saw a king thrown out by his Parliament, radical preachers let loose on susceptible congregations and the upheaval of the class structure they had always relied on. Puritanism was an all-embracing term for the many sects which arose at that time to find answers to such deep-seated problems. 'A description of Puritanism in social terms,' wrote Patrick Collinson, 'might be modelled on a three-legged stool, the legs consisting of ministers, magistrates and people.'[2]

The Levellers

What was common to all these sectarian groups was that they refused to conform to the Presbyterian or Puritan forms of government practised by the leaders of the Anglican Church. The anticlericalism of the previous century found its outlet in the small radical groups, usually composed of working people – agricultural workers, apprentices, masters of small businesses, some professional people, and many of them young. They were great readers of the Scriptures, loved sermons and debates, and were often family men who brought their wives and children to their meetings, encouraging the participation of all.

An all-embracing title for the many different groups of radicals of the mid-seventeenth century was the Levellers. More political than religious but symptomatic of the anti-establishment cults that were emerging, the Levellers identified themselves by their green ribbons. Many were involved during the first Civil War with the New Model Army. Here they found the discipline and comradeship they had sought in peacetime, backed by a social mobility, with links to religious preaching provided by army chaplains and itinerant preachers. Shabbily treated by Parliament, the army elected agitators to plead their cause, with each soldier paying a small subscription to attend the well-organised meetings.

The Levellers enjoyed considerable support from London's journeymen and apprentices. Even the women came out into the streets to protest for peace with *The Petition of Many Civilly Disposed Women*. They wore white ribbons in their hats and were mostly the wives of fighting men. One young woman was killed 'accidentally' when the pistol of a soldier defending Parliament went off.[3] 'Londoners provided vital support for radical causes and were one key element in creating an atmosphere of political crisis and confrontation.'[4]

The Levellers put together a draft constitution, the Agreement of the People, a social contract which basically rewrote the English system of government. Every man was to have a vote, the present Parliament was to be dissolved and the House of Commons was to be the sole arbiter and ruler of the people. There was to be complete freedom of worship, reform of the law and freedom from conscription. The Agreement contained thirty clauses and was signed by John Lilburn, William Walwyn, Thomas Prince and Richard Overton. It was discussed in a series of debates held at the church of St Mary the Virgin, Putney, known as the Putney Debates. The radicals were helped by the passing of the Act of 1650 which ended compulsory attendance at church, though it was repealed in 1657.

The Diggers

A more left-wing group of Dissenters were the Diggers. They believed that wage labour should be abolished and that all men should participate equally in the bounty of the earth. They gathered on St George's Hill near Kingston, always a centre of dissent, and tried to cultivate a plot of land. Sometimes known as True Levellers, they made it clear that this was more in the nature of a political protest than a true attempt to grab the land for the common people (it was in any case a very unfertile area). The Diggers were harassed by local landowners and were taken to court. They moved off to Cobham but here too they were forced to abandon their attempts to set up a communal settlement. Their leader was Gerrard Winstanley who later joined the Quakers.

The Ranters

The Ranters were less organised than some of the other sects, with no leaders, and because of their denial of any form of authority, were considered heretical by Church and State. Christopher Hill, the historian, says 'The name came into existence as a term of abuse'[5] and certainly their behaviour brought them into considerable disrepute. In 1650 Parliament passed The Blasphemy Act – 'An Act against several Atheistical, Blasphemous and Execrable Opinions, derogatory to the honour of God, and destructive to humane Society.' Their beliefs lay in the idea that man himself was the only authority he need obey, that God was everywhere, not just in the Church. As they considered that 'sin is a product of the imagination', it is hardly surprising that they were regarded as dangerous, added to which they often went about naked, frequented taverns, got drunk and smoked tobacco.

The Seekers

The Seekers, too, denied any form of regulation or leadership and acknow-ledged no creed. However, they did believe in toleration for all forms of worship and belief, or indeed for no belief at all. They felt that government should have no link to religion and that Protestantism, in spite of its enmity toward Roman Catholicism, had inherited from the earlier faith a corruption of true belief and was to be equally condemned. However, Seekers did, like the Quakers, accept communal worship, though this too was in silence so that personal and direct inspiration could prevail. Their champion was William Ebery, an army chaplain, who believed in universal redemption and denied the divinity of Christ. He believed that the only true right to govern lay with the army who should destroy royal control.

The Muggletonians

Among the least known and yet one of the longest surviving groups were the Muggletonians. The two men who founded the sect were both London tailors, Lodowick Muggleton and John Reeve. Although Muggleton gave his name to the group it was Reeve who was the prime mover, and again a verse from Revelations – 'I will give power to my two witnesses and they shall prophesy a thousand, two hundred and three-score days, clothed in sackcloth'[6] – drove them to believe they were the two witnesses. Their mission was to curse the unbelievers (which they did in full measure), to proclaim doomsday and to bless the chosen. On Reeve's death in 1658, Muggleton took on the leadership of the sect. Some of the ideas of the Muggletonians were fanciful in the extreme, even for the revolutionaries of the seventeenth century: the stars were only six miles up and no bigger than they looked; the Millennium would bring disaster and bloodshed; and history consisted of three Ages, those of the Father, the Son and the Holy Spirit. The first was represented by the Old Testament, the Son by the New Testament and the Holy Spirit Age, just about to begin, by a time of spiritual revival, of revelation and understanding. All three were One.

The Muggletonians held that Christ was a man, not a God and that no spirit could exist without matter. Man needed no alternative to his own godliness. They believed in predestination, as recognised by their two prophets, who could curse or bless them as they felt right. The soul died with the body, and 'there was no devil but men and women'. These believers were pacifists and apolitical, with a suspicious dislike of the medical and legal professions.

The truly surprising element of the Muggletonian philosophy is that it has lasted virtually until the present day. They were alive and well in the centuries after their founding. The historian E.P.Thompson says that at the end of the eighteenth century, 'there were still Muggletonians preaching in the fields and parks of London.'[7] An interesting chapter by William Lamont in *The World of the Muggletonians*[8] tells how a huge archive of Muggletonian material was discovered in the 1970s in the Kent home of 'the last of the Muggletonians', Philip Noakes. On Noakes's death in 1979 it was handed over – eighty-eight volumes of it – to the British Library. But today there is a comprehensive website for the Muggletonians detailing their history, beliefs and structure, though it is generally believed that they no longer exist.

Regicide

In August 1647 Charles was captured and imprisoned at Hampton Court. From here he escaped and fled to the Isle of Wight where he was more closely confined. The Presbyterians in Parliament, together with the leaders of the army, principally Oliver Cromwell and his son-in-law Henry Ireton, were now convinced that the King was not trustworthy and his word was not to be relied on. They tried negotiating with him at Newport, but he still seemed not to understand that his very life was now in danger.

In London those members of the House of Commons who supported the monarchy were driven away by Colonel Thomas Pride – Pride's Purge – and Charles was arraigned at Westminster Hall. The President of the Court was John Bradshaw (all twelve High Court judges refused to take part) who informed the prisoner that the court 'being sensible of the evils and calamities brought upon the nation and of the innocent blood which had been shed, had resolved to make inquisitions for this blood and bring him to trial and judgement.'[9] The King refused to acknowledge the court, maintaining that a man must be tried by his peers and that therefore no-one had the right to try the King. He argued his case very skilfully but he was declared guilty. The court decided that he should be executed 'as a tyrant, traitor, murderer and public enemy of the good people of this land.'[10] He was not then allowed to address the court.

Few commissioners were prepared to sign the death warrant. Eventually fifty-nine did so, including Cromwell and Ireton. On 30th January 1649 Charles Stuart was executed publicly on a platform erected outside the window of Inigo Jones's Banqueting House in Whitehall. The body was taken to Windsor where it was buried in St George's Chapel. The Society of Charles the Martyr today honours the King as a saint and remembers 30th January as St Charles's Day. The diarist, John Evelyn, a staunch royalist, made a lengthy note in his diary:

> The villainy of the rebels proceeding now so far as to try, condemn and murder our excellent King on the 30th of this month, struck me with such horror, that I kept the day of his martyrdom a fast, and would not be present at that execrable wickedness.[11]

England was now a republic.

Within a few days of the King's death there was published in London *Eikon Basilike or the Portraiture of His Sacred Majesty in His Solicitudes and Suffering*. It was believed to have been written by Charles himself while in prison at Carisbrooke Castle. Several other writers later claimed authorship and John Milton published *Eikonoklastes* to counter the success of the King's book.

Commonwealth

Even before the execution Parliament had confirmed that 'the people are, under God, the original of all just power.' The House of Lords was dissolved and the monarchy abolished. A Council of State was set up, to rule initially for one year. The new Great Seal bore the words 'the first year of freedom by God's blessing restored.'

Those Members of Parliament still in office after Pride's Purge were known as the Rump Parliament. They declared themselves the Commonwealth of England and were finally ejected by the Army under Cromwell in 1653; the Barebones Parliament (only 140 members) took their place. They too lasted only a short time before they elected Cromwell as Lord Protector.

The new Puritan democracy had high ideals: freedom of religion, listening to the voice of the people, a strong navy and a standing army, and an efficient economy. It didn't always achieve its aims, but it set out on the right path. It was certainly not popular with everyone. One commentator using the name Mercurius Civicus wrote to his friend Mercurius Rusticus,

> If therefore posterity shall ask, who broke down the bounds to those streams of blood that have stained this earth, if they ask who made liberty captive, truth criminal, rapine just, tyranny and oppression lawful ... if they ask who would have pulled the crown from the king's head, taken the government off the hinges, dissolved the monarchy, enslaved the laws and ruined their country, say, 'twas the proud, unthankful, schismatical, rebellious, bloody City of London.[12]

Puritan and Catholic

London's suspicion and hatred of anything popish was having its effect on local parishes. Catholicism became confused with superstition. Churches were purged of crucifixes, images and even funerary monuments. Inscriptions and floor brasses were torn out, stained glass windows smashed. St Stephen's Walbrook lost its glass, at Christchurch Greyfriars (Newgate Street) the organ pipes were stuffed up to stop the music and at St Lawrence Jewry a statue of St Lawrence was destroyed. The Eleanor Cross at Westcheap (Cheapside), already in bad repair, was demolished by order of Parliament, though not without a demonstration by London apprentices who tried to save it. It had marked the route between the City and Westminster, a point made by a contemporary anonymous poet:

> Undone, undone the lawyers are
> They wander about the town,
> Nor can find the way to Westminster
> Now Charing Cross is down:
> At the end of the Strand they make a stand
> Swearing they are at a loss.
> And chaffing say, that's not the way
> They must go by Charing Cross.[13]

Pieces of the cross are now in the Museum of London.

There were however a number of Catholics still living secretly in London. They could only worship in the Queen's Chapel at Somerset House or at the Embassies of Catholic nations, though these too were subject to rioting and violent attacks.

Quakers

The Society of Friends was another branch of Protestantism which came into being at this time and has achieved perhaps more than any other in gaining the respect and admiration of its own contemporaries and of generations to come. In about 1650 George Fox founded the Society known as Quakers from his commandment 'to tremble in the face of the Lord'. Fox believed that the 'inner light' could be revealed without the intervention of priest, sacrament or church ritual. Every man – and indeed woman and child – could listen to the voice within him. No sermon was needed, no religious hierarchy, no membership of a church – all were equal before God. All that was required of a Friend was to attend meetings and listen in silence until moved to speak. Quakers could belong to other groups; some had leaders, some paid for the use of their 'steeple house', some sang hymns. Quaker meeting houses were simple wooden shacks. Quaker clothes too were of plain uncoloured materials, with white muslin bonnets for the women and homespun country vestments with broad-brimmed hats for the men. They were pacifists, subscribing to a simple code of conduct to govern their lives.

William Penn, a prominent Quaker, left England for America to found Pennsylvania and establish the Quaker movement there. Many Quakers have contributed to the welfare of this country, Elizabeth Fry in prison reform, Samuel Hoare in banking, John Woolman in anti-slavery, and the Gurney and Rowntree families in commerce.

Baptists

Tracing their beginnings back to the Anabaptists of the Reformation, the Baptists – today one of the largest of the Protestant churches – built their first church at Spitalfields. They subscribe to complete immersion at Baptism and for adults only who could understand their commitment. They split into two groups: the General Baptists, Arminians, believing in redemption for all; the Particular Baptists, Calvinists who believed in particular redemption and autonomy for their church. Some went to America and later spread out to do missionary work overseas.

Fifth Monarchy Men

The theological beliefs of the Fifth Monarchy Men were, unlike some of the other radical groups of the time, closely linked to their political aspirations. They took their creed from the Book of Daniel, when Daniel interprets the dream of Nebuchadnezzar. Four great kingdoms had gone and a fifth kingdom was to arise, greater than all the others, 'a kingdom which shall never be destroyed'.[14] This last kingdom would be the kingdom on earth of 'King Jesus', and it would find its place in England. This was somewhat confusingly bound up with the Second Coming and the conquest of the 'great beast' of Revelations, represented by the number 666. Some of the leading Fifth Monarchy Men had signed Charles's death warrant, among them Major-General Thomas Harrison, who suggested the election of seventy 'saints' who would welcome the arrival of King Jesus. Only twelve were elected to the Barebones Parliament and when Cromwell became Lord Protector Harrison was accused of treason and executed. His execution was witnessed by Samuel Pepys who said that he looked as cheerful as any man could. The Hung, Drawn and Quartered Pub in Great Tower Street, near Pepys's home, bears a plaque commemorating Harrison's execution. His place as head of the Fifth Monarchists was taken by Thomas Venner. After the restoration of the monarch Venner plotted the downfall of the King in favour of the imminent arrival of King Jesus and was also hanged drawn and quartered. The Fifth Monarchy was no more.

The Return of the Jews

There had always been a few Jews remaining in Britain after the expulsion in 1290. One or two, such as Roderigo Lopez, physician to Queen Elizabeth, had reached the notice of the population at large, but the majority of English people had never encountered a Jew. Nevertheless, they were aware of the Jews of the Old Testament, often naming their children after Biblical figures, and able to quote from the Scriptures, even if they were still of the opinion that the Jews had killed Christ. Hebrew was often taught in the universities and many churches, cathedrals and editions of the Bible bore inscriptions in Hebrew.

Under Cromwell a spirit of toleration for all religions was becoming generally accepted, though the Catholics were still unacceptable to the majority. As far as the Jews were concerned there was always the possibility that if they were allowed to return, they might be ripe for conversion. The admission that such toleration should be extended to the Jews was enacted in 1648 and it was now the Jews themselves who put in progress the wish to be allowed to live openly in Britain.

Rabbi Menasseh ben Israel, a scholar and theologian of high repute, lived in Amsterdam. The English Queen Henrietta Maria had once heard him preach there. He was concerned about the treatment of the Jews in Spain and Portugal and was anxious to establish another safe refuge for them such as they had found in the Netherlands. He was of the opinion that the Messiah would only come when every nation welcomed the Jews, a declaration he proposed in his book *Spes Israelis*. If this was to happen then England could not be left out. In medieval Jewish literature England was known as 'the end of the earth'. He dedicated his book to the English Parliament.

The possibility of readmitting the Jews was discussed in Parliament and ben Israel came to England to plead his cause in 1655, just before the Jewish

New Year which was celebrated openly in London. He asked for freedom to pray and live in England and to bring prosperity to the English people, as the Jews had done, he said, in the lands where they had settled, a point that particularly attracted the Lord Protector.

A conference held to debate the subject spent much time discussing the circumstances under which such admission might be granted. It was said that Jewish worship in a Christian country was blasphemous, that the Jews might try to convert their fellow citizens, that they would probably undermine the trade of the English merchants, that they would profane the Sabbath, employ Christian servants, hold public office and print anti-Christian literature. But the most vital point that emerged from the jurists present was that there was no statutory bar at all to Jews living freely in England. Their expulsion had been by royal command and applied only to those against whom it was pronounced at the time.

A Jewish cemetery was soon established in Mile End, a synagogue built in Creechurch Lane and a Jew admitted to the Royal Exchange as a licensed broker. In 1662 Samuel Pepys paid a visit to Creechurch Lane where the Jewish festival of *Simchat Torah* (Rejoicing in the Law) was in progress. He was rather horrified at the noise and the dancing (common on that occasion), but he seems to have enjoyed himself. The Creechurch Lane synagogue was later replaced by a grander one in Bevis Marks. When Cromwell died in 1658 the Jews of London, relying on him for their continued presence, were again threatened. As the Jewish historian Cecil Roth says, 'Hardly was the breath out of his body when London merchants recommenced their intrigues.'[15] They presented *The Merchants Humble Petition and Remonstrance* to Parliament, demanding the Jews be expelled and their property seized. However with the restoration of the monarchy the right of the Jews to live and work in England was finally recognised.

The Last of the Commonwealth

Once installed as Lord Protector, Cromwell inflicted a military regime on the nation. The nation wanted a new monarch, but Cromwell refused the Crown, though he did agree to be addressed as 'Your Highness, the Lord Protector'. He died in 1658 and was given a sumptuous funeral fit indeed for a King. He named as his successor his son Richard. Far less a leader than his father, Richard lasted as Lord Protector for only a few months. He was succeeded by General George Monck. Recalled from Scotland, he consulted Parliament, restoring the House of Lords, and the army. There seemed to be only one possible contender to rule England. Charles II was invited to occupy the throne as the legitimate King.

CHAPTER XV

Restoration

The King Returns

'THE COUNTRY HAD MANAGED to get on without King, Lords and Bishops; but it could never henceforth be ruled without the willing cooperation of those whom the House of Commons repre-sented.'[1] This was the historian Christopher Hill's assessment of the state of the nation as it awaited the new King, Charles II. On his arrival London's outward face changed utterly. The Puritan conventions of dress, entertain-ment, sobriety and gravity slipped away. The King was greeted by adulatory music and verse. Edmund Waller, a Parliamentarian himself, wrote:

> But your full Majesty at once breaks forth
> In the meridian of your reign. Your worth,
> Your youth, and all the splendours of your state,
> (Wrapped up till now in clouds of adverse fate!)
> With such a flood of light invade our eyes,
> And our spread hearts with so great joy surprise.[2]

Court music was revived with a much enlarged choir at the Chapel Royal which included the young Henry Purcell. Music at St Paul's Cathedral and Westminster Abbey was reintroduced as it was into many of the churches, some rebuilding or installing a new organ. A magnificent coronation recalled the old days of royal splendour, with the young King, black-haired, handsome and athletic, smiling and waving to the crowds.

Charles had made many promises in the Declaration of Breda before he left for England; a free Parliament, the army to be paid, religious toleration for all while upholding the Anglican Church. His Chief Minister was Edward Hyde, later Lord Clarendon. His six-volume *History of the Rebellion* was the base on which much later history was written. Now ageing and overweight, his arrogance was not to the liking of either Parliament or the King, but he was anti-Catholic, disapproved of the King's dissolute behaviour and acted for the good of England not himself. Two of his grand-daughters became Queens.

Nonconformity

Charles's resolute decision to bring back the old Anglican Church resulted in much oppression for those outside it. The Clarendon Code restricted Nonconformists from holding public office and Church courts were restored. But the problem of the bishops was harder to resolve. The Presbyterians disapproved of some of the behaviour of the erstwhile bishops, wary of restoring them to their original benefices. Religion in England was by now governed in large part by the leaders of the innumerable Calvinist sects. These were mostly composed of the artisan and yeoman classes, sincere in their beliefs.

Many of the Nonconformist clergy were uncomfortable with the thought of returning to the Anglican tradition. Philip Henry, a Nonconformist minister in Shropshire, already in trouble for baptising his own children, wrote in his diary, giving the reasons why he refused to kneel at the altar rail, 'which is used in our parish church at Malpas, because it is an innovation, warranted by no law, neither divine nor human, civil nor canonical and also smells rank of Popish superstition, yea of Judaism itself.'[3]

Charles himself had little religion to speak of, though outwardly he conformed by attending church regularly. Gilbert Burnet, Bishop of Salisbury, who wrote *A History of My Own Time*, spoke of the King: 'His sense of religion was so very small that he did not so much as affect the hypocrite by prayers and sacraments, but let everyone by his negligent behaviour see how little he thought himself concerned in these matters.'[4] However, he was tolerant of all faiths, particularly Catholicism, not approved by most of his subjects. His marriage to a Portuguese Catholic, Catherine of Braganza, like those of his father and grandfather, made him the object of suspicion. He promised the Pope, Alexander VII, that he would try to abolish anti-Catholic legislation, and his brother James, his heir unless Catherine had children, favoured Catholicism.

Gradually the Puritans were fading out of public life. The bishops came back, stronger and more powerful than before, men of integrity and learning. They repaired the churches and straightened out parish life.

The Act of Uniformity

As a part of the Clarendon Code, the Act of Uniformity, passed in 1662, reintroduced many of the Church practices in use before the Civil War. All ministers of the Anglican Church, as well as schoolmasters and university professors, had to swear to use the new Prayer Book and to conform to everything in it. At the Savoy Conference of 1661, held under the chairmanship of Gilbert Sheldon, Bishop of London, there had been an attempt to produce a new Prayer Book that would please everyone, but this seemed to be impossible. The clergy present, both Puritan and Presbyterian, could not come to any 'harmony'. Finally, by the end of that year the Fifth Prayer Book, much as it is today, was finally agreed and adopted by both houses of the Convocations of Canterbury and York, and the bishops were reinstated in the House of Lords. All bishops and others holding office had to be ordained in accordance with the English Church. Nonconformity was being denied to the people of England. Many clergymen left the Anglican Church altogether or were expelled from it – the 'Great Ejection'. The Act was a part of the whole Clarendon Code, which also included the Corporation Act, requiring all civic officers to be members of the Anglican Church. It also denied Nonconformists the right to be awarded degrees at universities (an exclusion that continued until the University Reform Act of 1854). This also applied to Jews, Catholics and even atheists, as they had to swear an oath of allegiance as members of the Church of England, which in all conscience they could not do.

The Act was aimed at 'preventing the Mischiefs and Dangers that may arrive by certain persons called Quakers and others refusing to take lawful oaths.' Many were imprisoned as the consequence of their disobedience. John Evelyn visited a group of Quakers in prison, describing them as 'a new fanatical sect, of dangerous principles, who show no respect to any man, magistrate or other, and seem a melancholy, proud sort of people, and exceedingly ignorant.'[5] The Conventicle Act denied meetings of more than five people, which effectively put a stop to dissident groups, while the Five-Mile Act banned Nonconformist ministers from operating within towns or coming within five miles of their former livings, or even from teaching in schools. Philip Henry found himself restricted (by a few yards) by the Five-Mile Act and wrote in the diary, 'What miles are to be understood, reputed miles or measured miles? If measured miles, how much is a measured mile?'[6] Samuel Pepys met some of these ministers in the street, as they were being arrested by the constables. 'They go like lambs, without any resistance. I would to God they would either conform or be made more wise.'[7]

Nonconformist Literature

Two of the greatest books of English literature were written at this time, both by Nonconformists though not affiliated to any established sects. John Bunyan, a tinker from Bedford, was a dissenting preacher who had fought in the Civil War. He was imprisoned for preaching without a licence and it was while he was in prison that he wrote several books including *Grace Abounding to the Chief of Sinners, or the Brief Relation of the Exceeding Mercy of God in Christ to his Poor Servant John Bunyan*. It is an account of the tribulations he encountered while seeking a religious faith, written in simple honest terms. After being freed under the Declaration of Indulgence he was later imprisoned again, and it was during this time in Bedford Prison that he wrote *The Pilgrim's Progress, from this World to that which is to Come*. It first appeared in 1678 and is remarkable for its simplicity and beauty of language, written by an unsophisticated man of little learning. Bunyan was a great reader of the Bible and its language is clearly reflected in his work. *Pilgrim's Progress* has been translated into one hundred and eight languages and has never lost its appeal.

Another of England's greatest writers, John Milton, was a Londoner. His *Paradise Lost* was published in 1667, to be followed four years later by *Paradise Regained*. The story of the disobedience of Man and his Exclusion from Paradise because of the actions of Satan, the fallen angel, appealed to the religion-conscious men of Milton's own day as well as to succeeding generations. Unlike Bunyan, Milton was a university man. He published tracts on divorce, education and the freedom of the press, as well as some of the most beautiful lyric poetry in the English language. After the death of Charles I he was appointed Latin Secretary to the Commonwealth's Council of State. David Daiches describes *Paradise Lost*: 'Classical echoes mingle with stark English simplicities and with overtones of meaning deriving from Milton's awareness of the precise meaning of the Hebrew Bible.'[8]

The Great Plague of London

Ever since the Black Death in the fourteenth century the plague had recurred frequently in London. Every few years another outbreak killed large numbers of people living in the city in overcrowded houses and filthy streets, with little awareness of public hygiene or private health care. The pestilence of 1665 was by far the worst. It was not the pneumonic plague of earlier years, but the bubonic plague, spread by fleas living on black rats which transferred the disease to human hosts. Highly infectious, it thrived in warm damp conditions with appalling symptoms. The death toll rose disastrously once the plague hit the city. It has been estimated that some 100,000 men, women and children died in London, the hardest hit city in Britain, during the six summer months that the disease raged.

In the city there was a shortage of coffins and mass graves were dug to take the overwhelming numbers of corpses, bells ringing to urge house-holders to 'bring out your dead', many of which were left in the streets with no one to carry them away. In fact those who had to do this terrible work were often drunk to be able to cope. It was a hot summer and in early September John Evelyn wrote,

Come home, there perishing near 10,000 poor creatures weekly; however, I went all along the city and suburbs from Kent Street [in Hackney] to St James's, a dismal passage, and dangerous to see so many coffins exposed in the streets, now thin of people; the shops shut up and all in mournful silence, not knowing whose turn it might be next.[9]

The blame for the outbreak was laid by most Londoners squarely on God. He was clearly taking revenge on those who had sinned. In the days before it started a bright comet was seen in the skies, three witches were burned and the Dissenters, the Jews, the Puritans and the unholy members of the Anglican Church, all came in for their share of calumny. Many of the clergy deserted their parishes; Burnet was appalled, 'Several churches were shut up, when people were in a more than ordinary disposition to profit by good sermons.'[10] One dissenting minister, Thomas Vincent, wrote a graphic account of the plague and the fire that followed it, *God's Terrible Voice in the City*, published in 1667. He addressed it 'To all such of the City who have seen the desolation of London by the late Judgment of Plague and Fire.'[11] He blamed the 'sinners' believing that such disasters 'befall the enemies only of God's people and the wicked, while the righteous do escape.'[12] The plague turned out to be no respecter of persons.

The Jewish community of London, who had returned to England only ten years before the plague struck, numbered some four hundred souls. Their newly-appointed Haham or Rabbi, Jacob Sasportas from Amsterdam, fled, never to return. His older predecessor had died of the infection, but the Jewish physician, Josef Mendes Bravo, one of the founder members of the Synagogue, stayed with his patients, relatively few in number. The community inaugurated a society for visiting the sick – one of the first to do so – a brave move considering the fear of infection. The fact that so few Jews died of the plague has been attributed to their high standard of hygiene. But it may also be that they were a close community, seldom associating with their Christian neighbours. Those who did succumb were buried in the little Jewish cemetery in the Mile End Road, many of the graves unmarked, but with tombstones laid flat as is the custom of Spanish-Portuguese (Sephardi) Jews.

Orders were issued first by the Lord Mayor and later by the King as to the conduct of Londoners during the time of the plague. They covered public places such as streets and shops as well as private dwellings. They ordered that

> Care be taken that no unwholesome meats, stinking fish, flesh, musty corn or any other unwholesome food be exposed to sale in any shops or markets; that no swine, dogs, cats or tame pigeons be permitted to pass up and down streets, or from house to house, in places infected.[13]

There were instructions for the disposal of bodies, for 'a pest-house, huts or sheds may be erected, to be in readiness' and for searchers to examine bodies 'for the usual signs of the plague, viz. Swellings or Risings under the ears or armpits or upon the groins, blains, carbuncles or little spots, either on the breast or back, commonly called Tokens.'[14]

Houses where plague was found had to be shut up for forty days, and a red cross fixed to the door with the words 'Lord Have Mercy Upon Us' in capital letters. The public was ordered to take special care 'that not only the Monthly Fasts but that public prayers on Wednesdays and Fridays be strictly and constantly observed according to His Majesty's Proclamation.'[15] The infection was a constant fear in everyone's mind.

Some of the Dissenters were refused burial in churchyards. The Quakers took a part of Bunhill Fields off the City Road. This had been used as a cemetery from Saxon times. The land actually belonged to St Paul's Cathedral but was leased to the City of London, part of it used for artillery practice. The Honourable Artillery Company still occupies a large area to the south of the present cemetery. Bunhill, originally Bone Hill, was a useful open space to use for victims of the plague. It was first covered with a deep layer of quicklime to try to obviate the terrible stench of rotting bodies. It was walled all round and because it was never officially consecrated it could be used for Nonconformist burials. A large number of Quaker and other dissenter burials took place here. It is believed there are some 120,000 graves, with more than two thousand memorials, including those of John Bunyan, Daniel Defoe, William Blake and Susannah Wesley, mother of the founder of Methodism, John Wesley. Wesley's House and Chapel lie opposite Bunhill Fields in the City Road. The cemetery was closed for burials in 1852.

There is another Quaker cemetery not far away, in Banner Street off Bunhill Row. This land was purchased by the Society of Friends a few years before Bunhill Fields came back into use. Bombed during World War II, it has been reconstructed as a peaceful garden. The old caretaker's house is now the Quaker Meeting House. George Fox, founder of the Quaker movement, is buried here. His is the only gravestone, as in the early history of the Society gravestones were frowned on as being too close to the worldly and ostentatious customs of the Anglican Church.

The Great Fire of London

London's troubles were not over. The fire that broke out in Thomas Faryner's baker shop in Pudding Lane on the night of 2nd September 1666 was to alter London's skyline beyond recognition. It raged for four days, helped by a strong easterly wind, destroying the highly combustible contents of the warehouses along the river and the wooden houses and shops so close together in its path. Fire hooks to pull down burning thatch and wood and leather buckets of water (insufficient after the hot summer), were the only equipment available, as the people tried to escape the flames with as many of their possessions as they could grab. Pepys buried his wine and his cheese in the garden. One of the most graphic descriptions of the fire was that of Thomas Vincent.

> It was in the depth and dead of night, when most doors and fences were locked up in the city that the fire doth break forth and appear abroad, and like a mighty giant refreshed with wine, doth awake and arm itself. It quickly gathered strength, when it had made havoc of some houses, rusheth down the hill towards the bridge, crosseth Thames Street, invadeth Magnus church at the Bridge foot, and though that church was so great, yet it was not a sufficient barricado against this conqueror ... this doth smell of a Popish design, hatched in the same place where the Gunpowder Plot was conceived by His Wickedness the Pope.[16]

The disaster was reported throughout Europe. The Venetian Ambassador to France wrote home to the Doge a somewhat inaccurate account received from his agents in London who reported

> the terrible sights of persons burned to death and calcined limbs ... the old, tender children and many sick and helpless persons were all burned in their beds and served as fuel for the flames. The King's palace is not touched but is possibly reserved to be the theatre of some dire spectacle. Since the Stuarts came to the throne England has never enjoyed felicity but has suffered from incessant miseries.[17]

In fact remarkably few people died in the fire, probably no more than eight. Thomas Vincent summed it up:

> Thus fell London, that ancient City! That populous City! London, which was the Queen City of the land, and as famous as most cities in the world, none so famous for the Gospel and zealous profession of the Reformed religion.[18]

Rebuilding London

The most deeply-felt element in the tragedy of the fire, in the spiritual sense as well as the physical, was the desolation of the churches. Houses could be rebuilt quickly as and when the owners could afford it, but London had more than a hundred churches, of which eight-seven were razed to the ground. St Paul's lay in a derelict smoking ruin. Almost the only pieces saved were the inscription on the architrave, the body of one bishop and the effigy of John Donne, later replaced in the south choir aisle. The booksellers around the cathedral, aware of the approaching blaze, hid their precious books in the crypt. Included among them were the unbound sheets of Shakespeare's Third Folio edition printed in 1663. When the roof fell in all were burned, making the Third Folio much rarer today than the Second or Fourth.

Plans for the new London, drawn up by both John Evelyn and Christopher Wren on a grid system, were ignored and the building started piecemeal with no overall plans. Christopher Wren, later Sir Christopher, had been a Founder Member of the Royal Society. He was an astronomer, mathematician and scientist as well as perhaps England's greatest architect. He had already been asked to start on the work of restoring the badly worn structure of the cathedral but was pre-empted by the fire. Wren set up his office in Scotland Yard and with the help of a Committee which included the Archbishop of Canterbury, Gilbert Sheldon and the Bishop of London, Humphrey Henchman, set to work. His two assistants were Robert Hooke, Wren's long-time friend and fellow Professor at Gresham College where Wren had been Professor of Astronomy, and Edward Woodroofe, Surveyor of Westminster Abbey.

Wren was responsible for rebuilding or renovating fifty-one of the ruined churches. Each was different and respected the wishes and ideas of the parish in which it was built. But each had a font and altar, for the sacraments of baptism and communion, a high pulpit from which the preacher could be clearly seen and heard, and often a link with the original design of the building before the fire. Most were built with clear glass windows, to be replaced with stained glass as the local parishioners wished. Gradually the steeples and spires began to dominate London's skyline and as the poet John Betjeman wrote, 'His churches were light, varied and happy, and seem to reflect the kind, detached smile we see on the face of his bust in the Ashmolean Museum at Oxford.'[19]

There is no question, however, that Wren's greatest achievement was the rebuilding of St Paul's Cathedral. The majestic tower and great nave of the medieval church were replaced with a quite different but equally charismatic building. It stood at the top of Ludgate Hill, where St Paul's had always stood since the first church was founded in 604. Several designs were produced and abandoned until in 1675, nearly ten years after the disaster, the Warrant Design was accepted by the King and the Dean and Chapter. It took the form of a great dome below a tall spire topped with a gold cross. The final building differed somewhat from the plan. There is no spire and the proportions have changed. St Paul's is London's Church and her people worship there quietly on a Sunday as well as in full public panoply on special occasions.

It took thirty years before the Cathedral was finished and the poet James Wright, living at Middle Temple, wrote a long poem on the various stages of the rebuilding, of which the third part, *The Choire*, includes:

> London has now a Church! Long mist before:
> For 'tis a certain truth which all must own,
> That for the space of thirty years or more,
> The Parish had a Church, the City none.
>
> He who ascends the roof, and thence looks down,
> While all around he takes th'amazing view
> Of this unbounded, and still growing town,
> Stupendous great, and no less beauteous too,
>
> Graced with so many spires, such princely halls,
> Whole streets of wonders, readily admits,
> That such a city fits a Church like Paul's
> And such a Church such city well befits.[20]

Many of Wren's other churches were damaged or completely destroyed during the blitz on London in World War II, but of those built by Wren and virtually untouched today are St Benet Paul's Wharf, the Welsh Church in Upper Thames Street, built of brick in the Dutch style with many of its original features intact and the Stuart arms on the great west door. Another which did suffer in the blitz but is now restored, is St Michael's Paternoster Royal, in College Hill, which houses the Mission to Seamen and where Richard Whittington is buried. St Margaret's Lothbury escaped almost unscathed and was able to house some of the precious possessions of other churches damaged by German bombs. St Andrews Undershaft, which houses the tomb of John Stow, survived the fire and the blitz but was badly damaged by an IRA bomb.

Two beautiful town houses, built after the fire, still exist in Laurence Pountney Hill. The Church of St Laurence Pountney was burned in the fire and never rebuilt, but the house at No. 7 has a fine garden which was the original graveyard of the Church.

The Monument

In 1677 the pillar, known always as The Monument, 202 feet high and 202 feet west of the start of the fire, was erected. It is surmounted by a golden ball of flames. An account of the fire appears engraved in stone on the sides of the plinth, the last sentence reading: 'On the third day, when it had now altogether vanquished all human counsel and resource, at the bidding, as we may well believe, of heaven, the fatal fire stayed its course and everywhere died out'. The Latin words *Sed Furor Papisticus Qui Tamdiu Patravit Nondum Restinguitur* (but Popish frenzy, which wrought such horrors, is not yet quenched) were added to the end of the inscription on the orders of the Court of Aldermen in 1681 during the foment of the Popish Plot. They were finally excised from the stone in 1830. The final point at which the fire died out on the corner of Giltspur Street is marked by the statue of The Golden Boy of Pye Corner. The statue of the boy is of wood, covered with gold, with an inscription: 'This boy is in memory Put up for the late FIRE of LONDON Occasion'd by the Sin of Gluttony.' Below the statue another inscription reads:

> The boy at Pye Corner was erected to commemorate the staying of the great fire which beginning at Pudding Lane was ascribed to the Sin of Gluttony when not attributed to the papists as on the Monument; and the boy was made prodigiously fat to enforce the moral. He was originally built into the front of a public-house called The Fortune of War which used to occupy this site and was pulled down in 1910.

The Catholic Threat

In 1667 the Third Dutch War saw the enemy burn the English fleet and attack the Medway towns. They towed the great flagship, the *Royal Charles*, out to sea and took their prize home. In the years that followed England negotiated an alliance with France, which included the promise of a large subsidy to help in the war against Holland and a rash promise from Charles to reinstate England as a Catholic country. He had always admired the French monarchy, particularly its Catholicism; his mother was French and his beloved sister Henrietta was married to the Duc d'Orleans, brother of the French King. Always known to Charles as Minette, she kept him fully informed as to events at the French court.

In England, however, the government was not happy at this new link with a Catholic country. Already blamed, with no good reason, for both the Plague and the Fire, the papists were still the enemy. The King's brother, James, the Duke of York, heir to the throne, converted to Catholicism in 1668 and fears that the nation would follow suit grew stronger. The King was known to be sympathetic. In 1672 he issued a Declaration of Indulgence which suspended all laws against Nonconformists who were permitted openly to worship as they wished, in 'approved' places.

The Act made it very clear that the King's magnanimity did not stretch to allowing any dishonour to church or state.

> If after this our clemency and indulgence any of our subjects shall presume to abuse this liberty and shall preach seditiously, or to the derogation of the

doctrine, discipline or government of the Established Church, or shall meet in places not allowed by us, we do hereby give them warning and declare, that we will proceed against them with all imaginable severity; and we will let them see we can be as severe to punish such offenders, when so justly provoked, as we are indulgent to truly tender consciences.[21]

This freedom applied too to Roman Catholics but only in private houses. However, Parliament, prorogued at the time, met again to repeal the Declaration, and the Test Act was passed, whereby all those holding military or civil office had to swear to uphold the Church of England and to take the Oath of Supremacy. This included Roman Catholics who had to refute transubstantiation, which they could not do. The oath remained a qualification for office until the nineteenth century. The Duke of York had to resign his position as Lord High Admiral.

The Popish Plot

In 1678 Titus Oates and Israel Tonge put in train a plan to accuse English Catholics of plotting to kill the King and put his Catholic brother James on the throne. Oates was a thoroughly disreputable figure. His father was an Anabaptist minister and he himself, having been expelled from both Westminster and Merchant Taylors Schools, met the same fate at Cambridge. He converted to Catholicism, but later confessed that he did so to infiltrate 'the enemy' and get to know their secrets. J.P. Kenyon describes him:

> His personal appearance was grotesquely unprepossessing. His conversation was often bawdy and blasphemous, and on this count alone he was no fit company for small boys. But worse was to come when the authorities divined his peculiar sexual tastes.[22]

Oates associated himself with some dubious characters, but he and Tonge, a disturbed Puritan clergyman, approached an Anglican magistrate, Sir Edmund Berry Godfrey, and put their accusations to him. Godfrey was found dead five days later, a murder attributed by Oates to the Jesuits. In 1680 Oates's pension was withdrawn. He was arrested for calling the heir to the throne 'that traitor, James Duke of York'. He was accused of perjury relating to his evidence about the Plot – perjury did not warrant the death penalty. Hearing the trial was the Lord Chief Justice, Sir George Jeffreys, the 'Hanging Judge', Judge Jeffreys of the Bloody Assize, as violent in the London courts as any in the West Country. Towards the end of the trial when Oates left the court, claiming he was unwell, Jeffreys observed,

The pretended infirmity of his body made him remove out of court, but the infirmity of his depraved mind, the blackness of his soul, the baseness of his actions, ought to be looked upon with such horror and desolation as to think him unworthy any longer to tread upon the face of God's earth.[23]

Oates was found guilty and sentenced to be dragged across London at regular intervals, put in the pillory and whipped 'from Aldgate to Newgate'. He remained in prison for some years and died in obscurity, his name ever to be associated with conspiracy and false evidence.

The Succession

The heir to the throne was still the King's brother, James, Duke of York, Queen Catherine not having borne a child. England was as anti-Catholic as ever but there were no other candidates. The Duke of Monmouth was Charles's eldest illegitimate son, and his favourite child (there were thirteen in all). In 1660 Anne Hyde, daughter of Lord Clarendon, had married James. Their two daughters, Mary and Anne (both later Queens of England) were in the direct line of succession, should James be barred from the throne. Charles I's eldest daughter, also Mary, had married William of Orange, from a long line of Protestant princes. Their son William was the nearest non-Catholic to the English throne. He married his first cousin, Mary, daughter of James of York, but a Protestant like her mother. They were later to share the Crown of England together.

For some time there had been talk of excluding James from the succession in view of his acknowledged membership of the Catholic Church. In 1680 the Exclusion Bill came before Parliament.

> If the said James, Duke of York, shall at any time hereafter challenge, claim or attempt to possess or enjoy, or shall take upon him to use or exercise any dominion, power, authority or jurisdiction within the said kingdoms as King or Chief Magistrate of the same, that then he, the said James, Duke of York, for every such offence shall be deemed and adjudged guilty of high treason.[24]

Charles's determination to ensure a hereditary succession prevented the Bill from being passed.

A Catholic Monarch

Charles died in February 1685 in his Palace of Whitehall. His death was unexpected as he was only fifty-five years old and seemed to have been in good health. He suffered an apoplectic fit and died four days later. He was received into the Catholic faith on his deathbed, in secret except for the presence of his brother James and Father Huddlestone, the old priest who had helped him escape at the battle of Worcester, and who gave him extreme unction. He was buried quietly in Westminster Abbey in a vault under the Chapel of Henry VII. His successor, James II was the first Catholic to reign over England since the death of Mary Tudor.

King James II of England, VII of Scotland

John Evelyn recounts James's first speech to the Council in which he promised that

> he would endeavour to maintain the Government both in Church and State as by law established, its principle being so firm for monarchy, and the members of it showing themselves so good and loyal subjects ... that he would preserve it in all its lawful rights and liberties.[25]

However, the new King 'to the great grief of his subjects' went to mass publicly at his own house of prayer 'the doors being wide open'. He also surrounded himself with Catholic friends and supporters, who included his wife Mary of Modena (Anne Hyde had died in 1671). James had already been much involved in the government of the country during his brother's last years. He had accompanied him in many of his political and even religious activities, though worshipping as a Catholic in private. Now, however, he could attend the Roman Church in full public view and ordered his fellow Catholics to be allowed the same freedom.

Catholic England

James's attempts to bring England back to Catholicism were doomed before they began. For more than a hundred years the country had been used to a Protestant way of life, derived from a home-grown leader, not one from beyond the seas. John Spurr the historian, writing of the country after the Reformation, says,

> James had no desire to force the English into Catholicism. He genuinely believed that if they were allowed to hear the Roman Catholic message without impediment or prejudice, they would flock back to the one true church.[26]

He did his best to bring the old religion back wherever he could. He tried to insist on the Charterhouse accepting Catholic 'brothers' (as the inhabitants of the almshouses there were known) but the Master refused, maintaining that the foundation was a private institution and must obey the principles on which it was established. James had to give way.

A new Ecclesiastical Commission was set up under Judge Jeffreys to 'curb the audacity of the bishops and preachers'. The Bishop of London, Henry Compton, was suspended for refusing to punish anti-popish preachers. He had been entrusted with the education of the two princesses, Mary and Anne and was a man of considerable tolerance. He showed a very liberal attitude to Nonconformists and was anxious to reunite them with the Anglican Church. In 1687 James passed a Declaration of Indulgence, insisting on freedom of worship for all and removing all civil disabilities from non-Anglicans. He publicly stated that he wished all his subjects were Catholics.

The Seven Bishops

The clergy of the Anglican Church were required to read out the Declaration of Indulgence in public on four successive Sundays. Before the first reading seven bishops including William Sancroft, Archbishop of Canterbury, formally went to the King and refused to do so. They were arrested and sent to the Tower. Evelyn wrote,

> The action of the Bishops was universally applauded, and reconciled many adverse parties, Papists only excepted, who were now exceedingly perplexed, and violent courses were every moment expected; report was that the Protestant secular Lords and Nobility would abet the Clergy.[27]

The bishops were charged with seditious libel, were supported by other churchmen, including Nonconformists, and were acquitted when they came to trial. The links between Dissenters and Anglicans were strengthening under Archbishop Sancroft's jurisdiction; he was aware of the need to prepare the nation for an out-and-out struggle against the King, his religion and his Catholic heir.

An Heir to the Throne

The Queen, Mary of Modena, went into labour at St James's Palace and her insistence on privacy at the birth gave rise to many suspicions: that the baby had been a girl exchanged secretly for a boy; that the child had died at birth, being replaced by a baby brought in in a warming-pan; or that there had never been a full term pregnancy in the first place (Mary had suffered several miscarriages). One result of the confusion at the birth was that the Home Secretary had thence forward to be present at the birth of all royal babies in line to the throne. This was not abolished until the reign of Elizabeth II. But the Prince James Francis Edward Stuart (later known as the Old Pretender) was acknowledged by his father as his true Catholic son. The Pope was invited to be godfather.

Invasion

If James was a staunch Catholic leader of his country, William of Orange was no less a Protestant leader of his. His affiliation with England was through family and through religion, against France, against Spain and for a free and active Parliament. He was fully prepared for an invasion of England to achieve his aims.

James sent his family abroad for their own safety, but when he tried to follow, after throwing the Great Seal into the Thames, he was caught by some fishermen and brought back to London. He met church leaders who would still have been prepared to have him back under certain conditions, but many of his leading politicians and soldiers – including John Churchill – deserted him. William landed at Torbay in Devon unopposed and made his way up to the city. He was welcomed by Bishop Compton as the saviour of the English Church, and James was sent under armed guard to Rochester, then fled to France. Had he stayed and negotiated with William he might have kept his perfectly legitimate crown.

CHAPTER XVI

The End of the Stuarts

A Catholic Monarchy

MANY LOYAL ENGLISHMEN were much distressed at having to sign the Oath of Allegiance to a monarch whose right to the throne they felt was somewhat dubious, having already sworn to his predecessor. Sir John Bramston, the lawyer and politician, wrote in his *Autobiography*,

> I did think, as the circumstances of the government then were by the King leaving the kingdom as he did, without any commission or care taken for the preservation of his subjects, private men, if required upon penalties, might safely swear to the Oath of Allegiance prescribed, notwithstanding King James was living, to whom I had sworn allegiance.[1]

The departure of the last Catholic King of England was described by John Evelyn, who attended the Convention Parliament in February 1689 (it could not be a true parliamentary sitting with no monarch on the throne). The House resolved

> that King James having, by the advice of the Jesuits and other wicked persons, endeavoured to subvert the laws of Church and State and deserted the Kingdom, carrying away the seals etc., without any care for the management of the Government, had by demise abdicated himself and wholly vacated his right.[2]

The subsequent succession was therefore voted to devolve upon the 'next heir': the Prince of Orange for his life, then to the Princess, his wife, and if she died without issue to her sister Anne, now the Princess of Denmark, and she failing, to the heirs of the Prince, excluding for ever all possibility of admitting a Roman Catholic. This situation exists to the present day; no Catholic can claim the throne of England. Until 2013 no spouse of a Catholic could either, but that has now been amended to permit a Catholic consort.

In 1689 some of the country's leaders felt a Regency was preferable while King James was still alive – he might, after all, convert back to Protestantism.

But William refused either to be Regent or to rule as consort to his wife Mary, the nearest direct descendant of the Stuart line. The only answer was for William and Mary to rule as joint monarchs, assuring England a Protestant Head of State. Bishop Burnet concluded his account of James's rule as

> a weak, inactive, violent and superstitious reign of a weak unfortunate prince, who by the persuasion of a revengeful Italian lady and by the projects of a set of hot, meddling priests, was induced to make that reign, whose rise was bright and prosperous, soon set in darkness and disgrace.[3]

The Declaration of Rights

Before the new sovereigns could be installed they were required to put their signatures to the Declaration of Rights. This was to nullify all James's acts and ordinances against which the 'Glorious Revolution' had been fought. It specified an Englishman's right to a fair government and a constitutional monarchy. It became an intrinsic part of the English constitution. The thirteen clauses setting out the English way of government included the rule of Parliament above the King, forbidding the Crown to dispense or execute laws, the illegality of an established Catholic Church, the right to petition the King without fear of repercussions, banning a standing army in time of peace, free elections, Parliamentary privilege and certain rules on trials by jury, taxes and property inheritance. This was enough to produce a stable government and legitimate claimants to the throne; the King became the servant of the people.

London and the Monarchs

When William arrived in London in December of 1688 the city was ready for him. Dutch troops greeted his arrival, lining his route and were charged with the safety of the King and the Queen while in the capital. Their appearance did not please all the Londoners. John Reresby, the politician and diarist whose comments on his time spent in London give such a vivid picture of the period, said,

> The guards and other parts of the army, which both in their person and gallantry were an ornament to the town, being sent to quarter ten miles off, the streets were filled with ill-looking and ill-habited Dutch and other strangers of the Prince's army.[4]

The crowds waved orange ribbons and Catholics took care to keep indoors. In spite of his dislike of the trappings of ceremony, William was crowned beside his wife at Westminster Abbey. London was happy to have him but the more far-sighted of the Parliamentarians realised that in fact James was still a ruling monarch and might still count on an army of supporters if he wished to reclaim his throne. The Divine Right of Kings still held a place in the hearts of many leading churchmen. They had sworn an oath of allegiance to James and several, including Archbishop Sancroft, could not forget it. Known as Non-Jurors, they were not able to swear to a new King and Queen and were ready to take whatever punishment might come. William's predecessors had brought confusion and dismay to many of their subjects. The historian Hugh Trevor-Roper wrote,

> Three successive kings, Charles I, Charles II and James II, by repudiating the Anglican synthesis, threw away the chance of stabilising their monarchy on a firm ideological base. By doing so they missed the chance of creating in England a modern 'despotic monarchy' on the European model.[5]

Parliament passed the Toleration Act which allowed freedom of worship to Protestants and Dissenters, but insisted on a belief in the Trinity, so excluding Unitarians as well as Catholics. It also meant that they had to swear an Oath of Allegiance, and they were forbidden from 'locking, barring or bolting their chapel doors'. With freedom to worship as they wished, the Nonconformists were flourishing. The different branches of Dissent were often willing to associate with each other, not necessarily in prayer, but in building a united front to face the Anglican Church. They formed the Happy Union of Presbyterians and Congregationalists, but their well-meaning efforts at cooperation did not last very long.

The Catholic element in the country was on the whole not actively persecuted, but Catholics could still not be appointed to military or civic office, they could not bear arms nor own a horse worth more than five pounds. More importantly, they were barred from living in or visiting London and Westminster. Nevertheless apart from a few stone-throwing drunks there was little attempt at anti-Catholic outrage.

The Jewish Community

The London Jewish community had not had an easy time since they reappeared in the city under Cromwell in 1656. They were regarded as foreigners – they certainly looked strange, spoke an unknown tongue and hardly connected with their fellow Londoners. Their commercial activities were regarded with suspicion by the city merchants, representing a threat to their business. But in Holland, the country of their new King, Jews had been welcome. They traded with countries such as Portugal which was useful to the Dutch economy, helped to provision the army and were ready to lend money to the state without security when William needed it. They were largely responsible for financing the Revolution itself. Many English

1 Reconstruction of the Mithraeum at the Bloomberg Space in Walbrook
(Photograph by kind permission of the Bloomberg Mithras Space)

2 The remains of the original Roman Wall near the Tower of London
(Photograph by Adam Bishop)

3 Statue of Boudica, by Thomas Thorneycroft, on the Embankment
(Photograph by Robin Jones)

4 The Death of Harold from the Bayeux Tapestry

5 Medieval Jews
(From the *Jewish Encyclopaedia*, 1905)

6 The plaque commemorating the Peasants' Revolt of 1381 in West Smithfield
(Photograph by David Loebell)

The quotation from the Lollard John Ball reads, 'Things cannot go on go on well in England nor ever will until everything shall be in common when there shall be neither vassal nor Lord, and all distinctions levelled.'

7 The Charterhouse
(By kind permission of The Charterhouse. Photograph by Lawrence Watson)

8 The Temple Church
(Photograph by Rob Farrow)

9 St Bartholomew-the-Great
(Photograph by David Loebell)

10 The Font, dating from 1405, at
St Bartholomew-the-Great
(Photograph by Renée Salamon)

11 Henry
VII Chapel,
Westminster
Abbey
(By Canaletto,
photographer
unknown)

12 Bunhill
Fields
Burial
Ground, in
the City
Road
(Photograph
by the author)

13 The Golden Boy, in Giltspur Street, where the Great Fire of London ended
(Photograph by David Loebell)

14 St Paul's from Peter's Hill, the steps leading down to the river
(Photograph by David Loebell)

15 The Quaker Garden, Chequer Street, Islington
(Photograph by the author)

16 Bevis Marks
Synagogue,
the oldest in London
(Photograph by kind
permission of the
Synagogue)

17 John Wesley's House, City Road
(Photograph by the author)

18 'Am I Not a Man?'
(Used during the Campaign to abolish Slavery)

19 Abdul Karim (The Munshi)
(Royal Collection Trust. © Her Majesty Queen Elizabeth II 2018)

20 Westminster Cathedral
(Photograph by the author)

21 Regents Park Mosque
(Photograph by Christine Matthews)

22 The Hindu Temple in Neasden
(Photograph by kind permission of BAPS Shri Swaminarayan Mandir)

23 The Prayer Hall at the Sikh Temple, Shepherds Bush
(By kind permission of The Central Gurdwara (Khalsa Jatha))

24 Wat Buddhapadipa, a Thai Buddhist temple in Wimbledon.
It was the first such temple to be built in the United Kingdom.
(By kind permission of the Temple)

The inscription on the memorial reads:

This tribute is erected by the Suffragette Fellowship to commemorate the courage and perseverance of all those men and women who in the long struggle for votes for women selflessly braved derision, opposition and ostracism, many enduring physical violence and suffering

Nearby Caxton Hall was historically associated with women's suffrage meetings & deputations to Parliament

25 Memorial to the Suffragettes in Christchurch Gardens, by Edwin Russell
The inscription reads: 'This tribute is erected by the Suffragette Fellowship to commemorate the courage and perseverance of all those men and women who in the long struggle for votes for women selflessly braved derision, opposition and ostracism, many enduring physical violence and suffering.'
(Photograph by Eirian Evans)

26 The Memorial to the Conscientious Objectors in Tavistock Square.
The text reads: 'To all those who have established and are maintaining
the right to refuse to kill. Their foresight and courage give us hope.'
(Photograph by Roger Davies)

27 The Church of St Sepulchre without Newgate, the Musicians' Church
(Photograph by David Loebell)

28 The Gherkin behind the Church of St Andrew Undershaft
(Photograph by Colin Pyle)

29 St Ethelburga's, Bishopsgate,
the smallest Church in London
(Photograph by David Loebell)

30 Scrolls of the Law in the
West London Synagogue
(By kind permission of the
West London Synagogue)

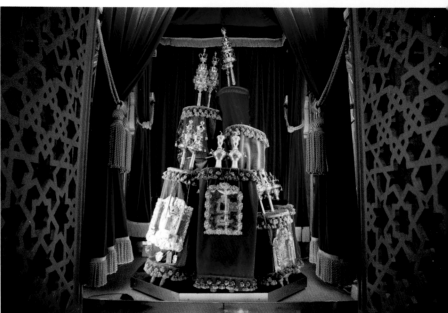

Jews were related to their coreligionists in Holland but their presence in London fell foul of the Toleration Act which insisted they should subscribe to a belief in the Trinity.

Parliament, firmly of the belief that all Jews were enormously wealthy, now brought in an Act to tax them heavily to pay for William's campaign in Ireland. In 1690 the King invaded Ireland where his predecessor had a large Catholic force. James was defeated at the Battle of the Boyne and fled to France. The Northern Ireland Unionists still celebrate the victory. William's forces were largely supported by Jewish financiers and a small Jewish community was established in Dublin.

The Jews protested vehemently at the iniquitous demands for money, insisting that about half of them were possessed of 'moderate' or 'very indifferent Estates' and the rest, as the historian David Katz puts it, 'consist partly of an industrious sort of people that assist the better sort in the management of their commerce, and partly of indigent poor people who are maintained by the rest and no way chargeable to the Parishes.'[6] They were being asked to pay the sum of £100,000 from a community of less than 600 households. As a point of law such a petition could not be presented to the House, but the Jews threatened to leave the country for Holland if the Bill was passed. It failed, but the principle of taxing a specific group of aliens in London – not all Jews had been endenizened (naturalised) – persisted. English merchants tried to ensure that custom duties on English exports by foreign (mainly Jewish) merchants were still levied but were eventually defeated.

The Expansion of London

Londoners were becoming used to moving freely about their safe, pleasant city. They met in coffee houses to carry on their business, to chat and to debate. After the Fire, London must have looked like a vast wilderness, the city expanding and being rebuilt in every direction. Commercially the Royal Exchange, originally the brainchild of Sir Thomas Gresham in Queen Elizabeth's reign, had put London's financial district on a par with Antwerp. The colonnaded interior, open to the heavens, was destroyed during the fire, but was rebuilt, only to be badly damaged by another in 1838. Today it no longer acts as a financial market but is occupied by retail outlets and restaurants.

The Royal Family

The King and Queen were perhaps the least regal of all their predecessors. Neither liked ceremony or pomp, preferring instead domesticity and a quiet life. They loved flowers and gardens, redesigned in a formal fashion, with clipped hedges, parterres and sunken gardens. But William and his wife were the sovereigns of England, and much as they would have liked to grow flowers and plan landscapes, there was business to be done. The country was being threatened on two sides. The Irish Catholics were trying to replace James on the English throne and in Europe Louis XIV had invaded the Palatinate, resulting in a war with the Grand Alliance (Austria, England, the Netherlands, Spain and some German states), known as King William's War.

The Catholics, in spite of William's victory at the Boyne, were not going to disappear. James's supporters, the Jacobites, were happy to give their blessing to his son, James Edward Stuart, the Old Pretender, when James the elder died in 1701. At that point in France he was proclaimed James III of England and VIII of Scotland, but not by his subjects at home.

Mary was proving an able administrator in her husband's absence abroad fighting in Ireland. She took over the direction of religion, with Archbishop John Tillotson, and together they managed to improve standards at court, after the debauchery of the followers of Charles II.

The Catholics in England

The fate of English Catholics during the latter years of the seventeenth century was not unlike that of the Jews in earlier times. Believed to be wealthy – and many of them were – they were asked to pay land tax at twice the normal rate. When the Queen died in 1694 and William was left to reign alone – they had no children – there was a further fear of a new Catholic uprising with the possibility of the son of James II coming to the throne. Some Catholics were arrested and accused of treason. But there was a move for legislation to prevent unjust accusations and subsequent trials. Those arrested were allowed counsel to plead for them and to call witnesses whose identity could be ascertained before the case came to court. However, no Catholic could train for the law nor could he inherit property (though this injunction was seldom put into practice).

Dissenters

Animosity towards the Papists was matched to a lesser extent by that towards the Nonconformists. When Celia Fiennes, in her journeys about the country on horseback, reached Colchester on her travels she wanted to try some oysters, but 'to gratify my curiosity to eat them on the place, I paid dear, the town full of Dissenters meetings, very full beside of Anabaptists and Quakers.'[7]

The Anglican Church was all-powerful, whether High or Low, but there seems to have been little sign of active discrimination against those Protestants who were not of its practice. William Penn, a friend of the King, had been arrested for holding a Quaker meeting in Gracechurch Street, but the jury refused to convict and were themselves imprisoned by the Judge. His forced withdrawal instigated the right of juries to be free of a Judge's influence in a court case. The prohibition on Dissenters taking civil office could be avoided by a means known as 'Occasional Conformity'. Geoffrey Holmes described it, 'They found that provided they were prepared to take the Sacrament in an Anglican Church just once in the twelve months before they stood for local election, and provided they got a certificate to that effect from the vicar, they could then take their seats as councillors, and even become aldermen and mayors, while cheerfully repairing week after week to their own meeting houses until the next Common Council election was in prospect.'[8] The Society of Friends inaugurated efficient business methods and the acceptance of fair commercial practice which led in the following century to the success of the great Quaker families such as the Frys, the Gurneys and the Cadburys.

It was eminent, too, in providing a good education for English Dissenters, who could not be awarded a degree from Oxford or Cambridge. The dissenting academies usually offered classes taught in English rather than Latin and a more modern syllabus, including science, French, history and other humanities subjects, rather than the classics, theology and natural sciences of the older universities. Christopher Hill wrote, 'When scientific invention revived in the eighteenth century, the impetus came from the Dissenting Academies and from individual craftsmen, not from the universities or the Royal Society.'[9] One of the best of the dissenting academies was that run by Charles Morton in Newington Green. Daniel Defoe was one of his students, as was Samuel Wesley the older, John's father. Morton came under suspicion for refusing to conform to the Anglican tradition and left England for America. He was in the running for President of Harvard but here too the authorities refused to admit him to such an important academic post and he took a position as pastor in Charlestown, New England. He was active in prosecuting those accused of witchcraft in Salem, Massachusetts.

The Anglicans, too, were aware of the tasks before them in not only converting waverers to their faith, but in caring for their minds and bodies when they did so. The Society for Promoting Christian Knowledge was founded in 1698 and the Society for the Propagation of the Gospel in Foreign Parts in 1701. In London some of the great English schools were founded, under the careful scrutiny of the Anglican Church. Most of the Guilds had their own schools by this time, but Charterhouse School had been established in 1611 after the old Carthusian Monastery was dissolved. Many of the charity schools were founded to afford some degree of education

to the poorest children, mostly under the direction of unemployed clergymen. The children were taught to read so that they could learn their
catechism, but frequently not to write in case they should turn out to be
independent radicals. Girls as well as boys could attend, learning to
sew and carry out simple domestic tasks, while their brothers could learn
something of a trade they might later follow as apprentices.

Death of the Queen

In 1694 Queen Mary died. 'The smallpox raged this winter about London,'
wrote Bishop Burnet, 'some thousands dying of it, which gave us great
apprehension with relation to the Queen, for she had never had it.'[10] But
she did get the infection and died a few days later. The King was distraught.
He told Burnet that 'during the whole course of their marriage he had never
known one single fault in her; there was a worth to her that nobody knew
beside himself.'[11]

The Succession

Left alone to rule what was to him a foreign nation, William grew increasingly miserable. He was by now something of an invalid, had few friends,
no family and was disliked by the majority of his subjects. The only possible
successor to the throne was Mary's sister Anne, also a staunch Protestant,
who had not liked her sister (the feeling was mutual) and like her had no
living children. She had suffered eighteen pregnancies of which only one
child survived early childhood, William, Duke of Gloucester, who died in
1701 at the age of eleven. Mary had been pleased that he was named after
her husband, but even before Anne succeeded to the throne it was clear that
upon her death there would again be a problem over the succession.

The Act of Settlement

In 1701 Parliament passed the Act which led a few years later to the Union
of England and Scotland. The Act determined that the throne, after the
death of Anne, would go to the only Protestant possible, Sophia, the Electress of Hanover. Her mother, Elizabeth of Bohemia, was the daughter of
James I and she had married Frederick, Elector Palatine of the Rhine and
King of Bohemia, thus ensuring a strong Protestant claim to the throne.
As it happened, she died before Queen Anne and it was her son George,
who became the first Hanoverian King of England and Scotland. After the
Act of Union of 1707 the two kingdoms were joined, and in 1801 Ireland
was included to become the United Kingdom of England, Scotland and

Ireland. George's claim to be King extended later to what became the Commonwealth of the United Kingdom. Included in the Act were limits on foreigners playing a part in the government of the country and on the monarch's powers regarding Parliament.

The New Queen

William III, as he was known after Mary's death, also died at Kensington Palace, in 1702, after a fall from a horse, who apparently stumbled on a mole hill, leading to the Jacobite toast to 'The little gentleman in black velvet'. There was still a strong Jacobite movement in favour of the Old Pretender, son of James II who had died the year before in France. William and Mary were still considered as having saved the country from Catholic control; Celia Fiennes wrote of them, 'whom no time can ever obliterate the memory of, their being England's deliverers in God's hands from popery and slavery which King James by the King of France's power, was involving us in.'[12]

Princess Anne of Denmark succeeded to the English throne at the age of thirty six. She had not had a very happy childhood, losing at an early age most of her close relatives, her mother, Anne Hyde, her grandmother, Henrietta Maria and her aunt Minette, as well as most of her brothers and sisters while they were still babies. When still a child she did have one friend who was destined to remain a close confidant and crony for many years. Born Sarah Jennings, she married in 1677 John Churchill, later the first Duke of Marlborough, the distinguished general, and like her husband was to play an important part in the affairs of England.

In 1683 Anne herself became engaged to be married to George, the younger brother of the King of Denmark; the marriage took place in London the same year. George was of course a Protestant, and although he was generally considered a somewhat dull personality Anne herself seems to have been very fond of him. One historian describes him unkindly:

> George's impenetrable stupidity was confirmed by his inability to express himself idiomatically in the English language after twenty years' residence, and offset only by a vast appetite, an almost unlimited capacity for hard liquor, and the fading reputation, earned before marriage, of a competent if unimaginative soldier.[13]

The new Queen was presented with a Bible 'to maintain the true Protestant religion.' Her father, King James, is reputed to have said, 'I have tried George drunk and I have tried him sober, and there is nothing in him'.[14]

Anne was a very English Queen. She had many of the qualities that her nation wanted. She was a fervent upholder of the Anglican Church, with no time or sympathy for her Catholic subjects. She disliked France, as did most Englishmen, had no pretensions to set herself on a pedestal, and even her gout and her stout figure (she had to be carried to her coronation) proclaimed her as 'one of us'. She spoke accentless English and her clothes, her household and her modest appearance were in keeping with England's notion of a good monarch.

King William's War had ended with the Treaty of Rijswick in 1697 but the issue of the Spanish Succession had preoccupied the European powers after the death in 1701 of the King of Spain, Charles II, without issue. His throne was claimed by Louis XIV for his grandson, Prince Philip of Anjou, and the French invaded the Spanish Netherlands. The idea of two great Catholic powers, France and Spain, in alliance, was anathema for the Protestant countries, especially England. An alliance between them, together with the Holy Roman Empire – the League of Augsburg – led by Prince Eugene of Savoy and the Duke of Marlborough, brought the nation to war. The great victories of Blenheim, Ramillies, Oudenaarde and Malplaquet gave to England a much needed boost to her self-confidence and to Marlborough recognition as the saviour of the nation.

Party Politics

The division of the English nation into two parliamentary parties dates from before the Glorious Revolution. The Tories' name derives from the Irish outlaws who wished to welcome James II back to his 'rightful' throne. In England, although they gave support to the Revolution, they believed in the Divine Right of Kings and a lawful royal inheritance, which was represented by the Jacobite cause. Now they represented the country gentry, resisting religious toleration and foreign ventures. The Whigs, dating from the rebel Presbyterians in Scotland during the Civil War, were the wealthy middle classes, anxious for a constitutional monarchy, excluding the Catholics from succeeding to the throne. When William became King the Whigs formed a group known as the *junto* to claim power. They were later instrumental in ensuring the throne went to George of Hanover. The two groups devolved later into the two-party system of Tories and Liberals, with the additional element of a Prime Minister and Cabinet under Sir Robert Walpole.

The strength of the Whigs was by no means acceptable to some of the High Church Tory supporters. They attacked Nonconformist meeting houses and some of the Dissenters' houses. One churchman, a fine preacher but not an especially scholarly minister, Henry Sacheverell, preached a long sermon in St Paul's Cathedral, railing against the Revolution of 1688 and what he saw as a threat to the Anglican Church. He chose the anniversary of the Gunpowder Plot for his diatribe, attributable to the Catholics. But the main burden of his address was against Nonconformists and the danger to the nation from the Whigs and from anyone who did not rigidly uphold the Church. The sermon was printed and hundreds of copies were sold. This could not be allowed to pass and Sacheverell was impeached for 'high crimes and misdemeanours'. The case caused a public outcry, leading to riots in the streets of London. Dissenters' chapels were desecrated, windows smashed and property burned. Sacheverell was found guilty but given a mild punishment. Two important results followed the trial: the Tories came to power as the High Church party, and the Riot Act came on to the Statute Book in 1714. The Act made it possible for local officials to order the dispersal of any group of more than twelve people who were 'unlawfully, riotously, and tumultuously assembled together'. Reading the Riot Act became a symbol of ordering a miscreant to stop what he was doing and behave.

Two other pieces of resulting legislation were passed after the Tories came to power. The Schism Act related to Dissenting Academies which now needed a licence from a Bishop and had to conform to the liturgy of the Church of England. It was never enforced as the Queen died on the day it was due to come into force. Four years later it was repealed. The other was the Occasional Conformity Act which rendered it illegal for a Nonconformist to take office by attending communion in an Anglican church. It too was repealed in 1719.

Anne's Last Days

In 1708 Prince George died, to the distress of his wife, though few others mourned him. However, all the obsequies of a royal death were duly observed, even to the black pins on black pincushions issued to the palace (he died at Kensington). The Tories were now in full command of the government. Anne had dismissed most of the Whigs who had served her so well: Godolphin, Sunderland (Charles Spencer) and the Earl of Oxford (Robert Harley) who had joined the Tory ranks when Anne came to the throne. She was by now a sick, lonely old woman. By Act of Parliament her successor was to be from the House of Hanover, but it was already rumoured that the embers of the Jacobite cause were glowing again. The Whigs were wholeheartedly for Hanover, but many of the great and good were biding their time to see what support the Pretender could claim. Anne kept her own counsel, though she kept in touch with her half-brother via intermediaries, trying to persuade him to change his religion, which he steadfastly refused to do.

Anne's health was precarious, though she was well enough on occasion to go out with the hunt (she had always loved horses and hunting). However her constitution was too weak to ward off any serious infection. The signing of the Peace Treaty between the Alliance and the French had been put off for some time. It was finally concluded in March 1713 much to Anne's relief. She managed to attend Parliament to confirm the Treaty, adding her own support for Hanover.

The Queen was left impoverished, partly through her own lavish expenditure, on Blenheim Palace (the nation's gift to Marlborough) and also on her financial support of a vast army of hangers-on, refugees and pensioners. Anne went to Windsor Castle, hardly able to move and in great pain. Rumours flew that she was dead, that the Pretender was on his way from France and that the Bank of England had run out of money. The mother of Prince George of Hanover, Sophia, had died early in 1714, leaving her son the heir to the English throne.

CHAPTER XVII

The Hanoverian Inheritance

The German King

BEFORE GEORGE OF HANOVER arrived in London he had been the Elector of a small German state with few links to the outside world. He was somewhat humourless, overweight and with few talents to attract him to his new English subjects. Queen Anne had refused to allow him to visit England while she was Queen, so he knew little of his kingdom and could hardly speak much English. But he was a Protestant and he was the legal heir to the throne, according to the majority of his subjects. Wary of yet another foreigner, Englishmen were nevertheless welcoming – anything was better than a Catholic monarch.

Naturalisation

To practise any religion in England, save that of the Anglican communion, was to suffer considerable discrimination, harshest of all for the Catholics, but extended to dissenters of all kinds, including Quakers and Jews. The latter, many of whom had come from overseas, found naturalisation almost impossible. It required that an Act of Parliament be passed for every application. Alternatively, denization allowed all the rights of citizenship other than political rights. It was granted by Letters Patent, as an exercise of the royal prerogative. Sophia, George's mother and before her death the heir to the throne of England, was granted naturalisation by the passing, in 1705, of the Sophia Naturalization Act. This granted English nationality to the Electress and to the Protestant 'issue of her body', allowing all her future descendants a claim to English nationality. Thus George was rightfully an English citizen when he came to claim his throne.

The woman who should have been Queen of England, George's wife Sophia Dorothea, was imprisoned in a remote castle at Ahlden in Lower Saxony. After duly producing two sons to ensure the succession in Hanover, she had had an affair with a Colonel of Dragoons, Count Königsmark. When he was found murdered in her apartments George divorced her and banished her to the fortress where she spent the rest of her days. All that England saw of a reigning woman at court was the presence of two of George's Hanoverian ladies, his mistress, Mademoiselle Schulenburg, a religious woman (in spite of her status), and Madame Kielmansegge his half-sister, also believed by many to be his mistress, though this was denied by his mother. The two were known, because of their size and shape, as The Elephant and The Maypole. The King was in no hurry to claim his throne. The Protestant succession was assured, he did not particularly like his new country and he was occupied with settling his affairs in Hanover.

The Jews in London

The number of Jews in London was greatly increased by the German Jews arriving in the wake of the new German monarch. As early as 1696 they had built a synagogue in Duke's Place, later rebuilt to a design by George Dance the Elder, and again replaced by a larger one, known as the Great Synagogue until its destruction by German bombs in World War II. The site was near the Spanish and Portuguese Synagogue in Creechurch Lane. This too was replaced in 1701 by the much larger and very splendid building in Bevis Marks. It was designed by Joseph Avis, a Quaker, who returned his fee to the synagogue, as he counted it a privilege to design 'a House of God'. Queen Anne is believed to have presented an oak beam from one of the Royal Navy's ships to be incorporated in the roof of the building. The design was based on the synagogue at Amsterdam.

The King and Politics

Once in London, the King set up his Ministry, composed mainly of the Whigs who had put him on the throne, including Earl Stanhope and Viscount Townshend, brother-in-law of Robert Walpole. The Tories' support for the Jacobite cause was stilled for the time being. They had no leader able or willing to try to re-establish James Francis Edward Stuart, the Old Pretender, as the true King, known as King James III in France. The Protestants were even more determined to keep their King George inviolate, but there were still many – Protestants as well as Catholics – who felt that the Divine Right of the Stuarts to rule England should prevail. Several went to France, Viscount Bolingbroke among them. Here he found a poorly served court in exile, with the ex-Queen Mary of Modena and her Catholic son but with no charismatic leader to revive their fortunes. James refused any advice as to how he should plan for his future.

The '15 Rebellion

Scotland, having signed the Treaty of Union in 1701, now yearned for independence, and James felt he could give it to them, as a Scottish and Catholic monarch. The Earl of Mar raised his standard at Braemar in September 1715 and marched south. His dilatoriness in taking Edinburgh, his inability to take any firm military decisions and the failure of the French to send, as promised, financial support, doomed the venture from the start. England showed little intention of favouring any Catholic threat to the throne. Parliament passed the Habeas Corpus Suspension Act giving tenants who refused to support the Jacobites the land of their landlord if he was a Jacobite. A landing in Devon of James's men under the Duke of Ormonde failed too. In Scotland, at Sheriffmuir near Stirling, a fruitless battle left both Mar's men and the English under the Duke of Argyle, without victory. The war was over almost before it began, and the chief protagonist, 'James III', had not even set foot in the country he wanted to rule.

James did then cross to Scotland, leaving France disguised as a French bishop. He was hardly a leader of men and did little to help the cause. A contemporary commentator wrote, 'When we saw the man whom they called our King, we found ourselves not at all animated by his presence, and if he was disappointed in us, we were tenfold more so in him.'[1] He reached the Earl of Mar in December 1715 and arrangements were made for him to be crowned at Scone, as James VIII of Scotland, III of England. But the coronation never took place and seeing that his goal was hopeless he returned to France a few weeks later, a lost cause.

George's son, also George, was married to Caroline of Ansbach, daughter of the Margrave of Brandenberg-Ansbach, and had been brought up after her parents died by George I's sister, Sophia Charlotte. She had refused the hand of Charles VI, the future Holy Roman Emperor, insisting on her Protestant faith. She and her husband, now the heir to the English throne, were created Prince and Princess of Wales. Caroline was the first Princess of Wales since Katherine of Aragon.

One of her ladies in waiting was Mary, Countess Cowper, who kept a detailed diary of her days at court. When the Jacobite prisoners were taken back to London after their defeat at Sheriffmuir, the Countess wrote, 'The mob insulted them terribly, carrying a warming-pan before them and saying a thousand barbarous things which some of the prisoners returned with spirit.'[2] The warming-pan reference was to the doubts expressed about the birth of the Old Pretender in France. The London mob had no sympathy with the Jacobite cause.

A clearer view of the Catholic presence in England was observed by Guy Miège, a convinced Anglican, though born in Switzerland:

If they could but keep within bounds and behave themselves peaceably they
need not fear to be molested by so gentle a Government. Nor has the Government any cause to fear them, while their Party is so inconsiderable, having lost
a great deal of ground since the fall of King James.[3]

The Georgian Church of England

This Hanoverian King – almost the first to do so – ruled over a kingdom
religiously at peace. After such a long period of dissension, England was
an indisputably Protestant nation, concentrating her energies on politics,
making money and inventing new ways to improve her standard of life.
Now firmly entrenched in stable command of England's religious sympa-
thies, the Anglican Church settled into a self-assured, if somewhat stolid
existence. As Gerald Cragg, the historian, put it, 'They equated what was
reasonable with what commended itself to common sense. Emotion
was suspect and "enthusiasm" anathema.'[4] These churchmen of George I's
reign were aware that from the court down, immorality and licentiousness
were rife, not perhaps as outrageously so as in Charles II's time, but nevertheless a trouble to their collective conscience.

In 1710 Parliament had set up a 'Commission for Building New
Churches'. It was felt that London's growing population was in need of extra
'prayer space' for the Anglican community, especially with the threat of
secession to the Nonconformists. These new churches were known as Queen
Anne Churches, though the majority were not completed for some time
after her death. Nicholas Hawksmoor was the principal architect, responsible for Christchurch Spitalfields, St George's Bloomsbury and St Anne's
Limehouse. St George's Hanover Square (Handel's church), was built by
John James. The project was funded by a tax on imported coal.

Political Developments

Gradually, the two parties, Whigs and Tories, were drawing up battle lines,
recognising their aims and structures and organising political developments
which were to coalesce into the party conventions so familiar today. Robert
Walpole, usually recognised as the first Prime Minister, ruled over a new
form of government. Although the term 'Cabinet Council' had been in
use for some years, it now acquired more precision. Those who formed it
'ministered' to the King, and George I made more formal use of this
advisory body, usually composed of like-minded members of the House of
Commons and included leading statesmen and councillors such as the Archbishop of Canterbury, the Lord Chamberlain, the First Lord of the Admiralty
and the Treasurer. The active part played by the King in party politics was

to lead to considerable friction both in Parliament and within the Royal family.

A quarrel between the Prince of Wales and the Duke of Newcastle – then Lord Chamberlain – at the christening of the Prince's son (the King had insisted on Newcastle standing as godfather) led to the King threatening his son with arrest. The Prince and his wife were banished from Kensington Palace without their children. They set up their own court at Leicester House. This was a large mansion to the north of what is now Leicester Square, built by the 2nd Earl of Leicester in about 1630. The Prince paid a rent of £500 per year, and as his 'alternative court' grew he took on Savile House next door, accessible by a covered way. After he succeeded his father as George II the house was taken by his son Frederick, Prince of Wales. The enmity between each successive monarch and his son lasted until the accession of Queen Victoria.

The Dissenting Community

The practical effect of an overwhelmingly Anglican Church in England on those who did not serve it was oppressive. Nonconformists, Catholics, Jews and even atheists were banned from holding civil office, taking a degree, being elected to Parliament or even getting legally married (until 1753 when an exception was made for Jews and Quakers). In 1718 both the Schism Act and the Occasional Conformity Act were repealed, allowing Dissenters to found their own schools and to be admitted to corporations. Cracks were beginning to appear in the hitherto solid walls of the English Church establishment. No longer was it the master of state politics. The Nonconformists were prepared to rise on behalf of the government in a national crisis – the '15 Rebellion and later the '45 – and their support was essential, whatever the Church might think. The politicians in power, particularly Walpole, were determined to keep ecclesiastical matters on an even keel. The Sacheverell affair had taught them a lesson and both sides of the religious argument had to be made to play nicely together.

The South Sea Bubble

In 1720 the passing of the South Sea Act gave the South Sea Company, incorporated in 1711, power to take over the National Debt. Investors saw a golden opportunity to put their money into what appeared an unmatchable speculation. When the crash came it brought financial chaos. Credit was at length restored, but the Riot Act was read in the House of Commons. Lord Stanhope died of a stroke while sitting in the House of Lords and, the Postmaster General committed suicide. Walpole remained in office as Whig

Leader and later, as 'Prime Minister', was granted a property at Whitehall consisting of two newly constructed terrace houses in Downing Street, though he did not take up residence until 1735.

Plots and Counterplots

The strong High Church faction, with Francis Atterbury, Bishop of Rochester, a convinced Jacobite, at its head, was a thorn in Walpole's flesh. In 1722 there was a rumour that a Jacobite plot was brewing, involving a threat to kill the King. London was put on its guard, with troops massing in Hyde Park and Catholics thrown out of the city. Habeas Corpus was suspended. The Bishop, with little evidence against him, was nevertheless banished, and Walpole came out of the whole messy business with increased respect and support.

Mlle. de Schulenburg, the King's mistress, was now the Duchess of Kendal, and the most important woman in court circles. Walpole told Countess Cowper that 'she was, in effect, as much Queen of England as ever any was.'[5] She had been granted the right to supply Ireland with coins. This patent she sold, greatly to her advantage, to the 'ironmaster' William Wood. The coins themselves were perfectly in order, as attested by Sir Robert Isaac Newton, Master of the Mint, but the Irish were suspicious that they were being fobbed off with valueless money and threatened an uprising. Their mouthpiece was the brilliant Dean Swift, and again the menace of a Catholic rebellion loomed large. No action was taken but the coins were named 'Wood's Halfpennies' and the affair rankled in Ireland for some time.

George II

When George II succeeded his father in 1727, England acquired another German monarch, who loved Hanover almost more than his new Kingdom. His other love was money and he was known to count the gold in his purse in the presence of the court. He was crowned at Westminster Abbey in October 1727, at which Handel's setting of *Zadok the Priest* was sung for the first time – it has been a part of the coronation service ever since. As his father had done, he intensely disliked his own son, Frederick Prince of Wales, but had the good fortune to have an efficient wife who could have run the country by herself. Queen Caroline and Robert Walpole made a formidable pair, recompensing England for the shortcomings of the King. George was in fact bad-tempered, lacked confidence and created in his ministers and subjects a sense of uncertainty and bewilderment. Lord Hervey, the parliamentarian and diarist, said, 'I do not believe there ever lived a man to whose temper benevolence was so absolutely a stranger.'[6]

The Evangelical Revival

The Anglican Church, apathetic and lifeless in its self-assured satisfaction, allowed the majority of its adherents to live their lives ignorant of Biblical history, theological argument and religious conventions. This state of affairs suited the clergy and the politicians, fearing to rock the boat. But there was arising a new 'enthusiastic' movement which was not content just to sit back and pray.

Meanwhile London, in spite of her eminence in the commercial world and her creative advances in art, music and science, was dirty, unhealthy and crammed with a diverse population which included a high proportion of drunks, gamblers and criminals. In spite of these her landscape was changing and spreading out widely from the confines of the city. Splendid new squares and elegant buildings were set out on land belonging to aristocratic families: the Bedfords, the Devonshires and Grosvenors, all lent their names to London thoroughfares, as did the royal family – Hanover, George, Charlotte, Prince and Princess. Miège approved: 'The Nobility and chief among the Gentry are at this time much better accommodated, in fine Squares or Streets; where they breathed good Air, and have houses built after the modern way.'[7] Not everyone approved of the expansion. Daniel Defoe commented,

> It is the disaster of London, as to the beauty of its figure, that it is thus stretched out in buildings, just at the pleasure of every builder, or undertaker of buildings, and as the convenience of the people directs, whether for trade or otherwise; and this has spread the face of it in a most straggling, confused manner, out of all shape, uncompact and unequal; neither long nor broad, round or square.[8]

Methodism

Dismayed by the pitiful state of England's established Church and those she governed, a new battalion of believers arose, prepared to fight for a more vigorous concept of religious practice. In Oxford University in 1729 Charles Wesley founded the Holy Club. He and his brother John, sons of an Anglican minister, were both ordained members of the Church of England. From their undergraduate days they led a life of strict self-discipline, ministering to the sick and visiting those in prison. They were joined by George Whitefield and founded a new dissenting faith, Methodism.

John Wesley, at its head, was a man of great presence, a brilliant organiser and a superlative orator. The newly formed community appealed to ordinary working people whose voice could at last be heard. Wesley and his fellow preachers could not take part in Anglican Church services, so they took to the open air, preaching to huge crowds wherever they could find space. George Whitefield, too, was a formidable outdoor speaker. He had founded an orphanage while in America with the Wesleys, raising funds from his audiences. In London they spoke often at Moorfields, Blackheath or Kennington with congregations of six or seven thousand.

The 'enthusiasm' frowned on by the Anglicans was allowed to run riot. Wesley recounts in his diary how after a meeting at which he preached 'I remember nothing like it for many months; a cry was heard from one end of the congregation to the other, not of grief but of overflowing joy and love.'[9] Wesley's impressions of his congregations were similar to those of one of his followers. James Lackington was an apprentice shoemaker who had taught himself to read and write and joined the Methodists, although it meant climbing out of the window of his master's house to attend a meeting. In his Memoirs he writes,

> When all are met they alternately sing and pray; and such among them as think that their *experience* (as they call it) is remarkable, stand up in their place and relate all the transactions between God, the Devil and their souls. At such seasons as this I have heard many of them declare they had just received the pardon of all their sins, while Brother such-a-one was in prayer; another would then get up and assert that he was just at that instant made perfectly free from sin; and then the Spirit is supposed to be very powerfully at work amongst them; and such a unison of fighting and groaning succeeds, that you would think they had all left their senses.[10]

Lackington later became a bookseller with a bookshop in Finsbury Square so big that a coach and four could be driven around the interior.

The practices of the Methodists were established in large part to appeal to the working people who formed the majority of the congregations: farmers, tradespeople, small businessmen and those who formed the lowest levels of society. The Anglican Church did little to attract them. There was, however, a considerable number of the nobility and middle classes who found the Methodist faith to their liking. One eminent adherent was Selina, Countess of Huntingdon. She joined the Wesleyan movement in 1746 and appointed Whitefield as her chaplain. Widowed at the age of thirty-nine, she devoted much of her life to Methodism, holding parties for her friends at which Methodist preachers addressed the guests. She is buried in Bunhill Fields.

John Wesley and his followers believed that salvation was for all and did not depend on good deeds. It could not be earned. In a little book called *What Methodists Believe,* Rupert Davies explains that Wesley was diverted 'from an intense absorption in the state of his own soul to an overwhelming urge to make known to other people what he had discovered for himself.'[11]

Charles Wesley, four years younger than his brother, is better known for the huge number of hymns he wrote, more than six thousand, many of which are still sung today, such as *Hark, the Herald Angels Sing, Love Divine all Loves Excelling,* and *Christ whose Glory fills the Skies.* He also wrote versions of the Psalms, sometimes introducing Jesus into the Old Testament text. Women played an important part in Methodist practice, speaking at meetings and participating in charitable work, though they, like any other member not ordained in the Church, could not administer the sacrament.

'Methodist' was originally a term of ridicule by the Wesleys' fellow undergraduates. The name derives from the complex system of rank and order which rules Methodist life. The overall national group is the Connexion. Then comes the District, a large area of Methodist believers; below the District is the Circuit, denoting an individual group of Methodist churches under one or more Ministers, and finally the Class, the smallest section into which the local church is divided. The Circuit is the organisation under which local activities and meetings are arranged. It appoints local Ministers and deals with minor matters of administration. Most Methodist churches renew their Covenant with God annually at a special service.

The '45

George II, always a lover of military power and splendour, personally led his forces into battle at Dettingen, in the War of the Austrian Succession, the last British monarch to do so. England had not yet officially declared war so he proudly wore the yellow Hanoverian colours. However, the fighting in Spain and Austria had nothing like as much effect on the English people as the second Jacobite uprising of 1745. Charles Edward Stuart, the Young Pretender, landed in Scotland in July 1745. The legend of a handsome, debonair young Prince may have suited Scottish folklore, but it was far from the truth. Charles was no soldier and not much of a politician. He paid little heed to his advisers and his personal behaviour left a lot to be desired. Nevertheless sweeping on in a fervour of adoration from the Scots, he took Edinburgh and turned south through England as far as Derby.

London was in shock. No Catholic threat had touched the city for many years and the news of the Young Pretender only a hundred miles away was terrifying. Parliament put a price of £30,000 on his head which prompted the Prince to reciprocate with a similar sum on the head of the 'King of Hanover'. The troops fighting in Europe were recalled.

In October the *Caledonian Mercury* published a Declaration from the self-appointed heir to the throne concerning his intentions. He promised freedom of religion and liberal laws for all his 'subjects'.

And now that we have, in His Majesty's name, given you the most ample security for your religion, properties and laws, that the Power of a British Sovereign can grant, we hereby for ourselves, as heir apparent to the Crown, ratify and confirm the same in our own name, before Almighty God, upon the faith of a Christian and the Honour of a Prince.[12]

In April 1746 the Prince met Cumberland's English force at Culloden. It was far better disciplined and equipped than his Scottish army, with nearly double the number of men, and the issue was never in doubt. Once the bloody battle was over and Charles had escaped the field, the ruthless Cumberland destroyed everything in his path. Charles, after wandering in the Highlands for some months, reached France, the last Jacobite ever to attempt to regain the throne of England. The final Catholic threat was over.

Four of the Scottish peers who fought for the Prince were taken to London to be executed at the Tower. The Governor, Lt. Gen. Adam Williamson, described the occasion, with all the gory details, in his Diary. He gave full details of the beheading. 'By the Lords' direction, the block was desired to be two feet high, and a piece of red baize to be had in it to catch their heads, and not to let them fall into the sawdust and filth of the stage.'[13]

The Huguenots in London

Those Huguenots who had fled France to find a home in London were comfortably settled, mostly in the East End of London or in Soho where they mingled with their Protestant hosts. In 1685 Louis XIV revoked the Edict of Nantes which had granted the French Protestants a degree of toleration in a Catholic country. At the mercy of the strongly Catholic French, many fled to England with their families, anxious to find a Protestant country where they would be safe, could worship as they wished and make a living, and where they could take advantage of London's world markets and commercial facilities. They were mostly craftsmen with some professional men, and together with other skilled workmen, the weavers found homes in the network of streets around Spitalfields and Whitechapel, building the houses later used by Jewish immigrant tailors, with workshops in the attic with big windows to take advantage of the light. Those windows are still there today. In spite of the Englishman's traditional suspicion of the French, these hard-working refugees enjoyed the friendship and society of the anti-Catholic Londoners, who were fully aware of the repression they had suffered in France. Their names were to reappear throughout English history. David Garrick, Walter de la Mare, Harriet Martineau and Peter Roget (of Thesaurus fame), were all direct descendants of the Huguenot refugees.

Like the Jews, the Huguenots built their own hospitals, schools and welfare organisations. The silk weavers of Spitalfields developed large workshops employing many men, women and girls, often making themselves a fortune in the process. Some of their shop signs, wooden spools of silk, can still be seen in the streets. The early Huguenot opticians (one, John Dolland, founded the firm of Dolland and Aitchison) and those who became doctors after admission to medical school, were accepted into English society. Robin Gwynn, the historian, noted, 'They contributed to a European-wide movement towards greater toleration and understanding during the eighteenth century.'[14]

There are still many traces of the Huguenot presence in the East End. Their first Church, and the only remaining one in London, the *Église Protestante Française de Londres,* was actually in Soho, and dates back to 1550. By the beginning of the eighteenth century there were twenty three. The first in the East End was Hanbury Hall, in Hanbury Street. The original Huguenot Church in Brick Lane was built in 1743. It then became a Methodist Chapel and in 1898 the Spitalfields Great Synagogue. It bears a large sundial on the south front, dated 1743 with the words *Umbra Sumus* (We Are Shadows) a reference perhaps to Plato's allegory of the cave. The building finally became a Mosque in 1976. It is a Grade II listed building. Another still flourishing synagogue, in Sandys Row off Artillery Street, was also a Huguenot church, *L'Eglise de l'Artillerie.*

The Jew Bill

The Jewish community in London was by now well settled, participating in most areas of English commercial and social life. But for those Jews who had been born abroad there was still a problem over their attaining British citizenship. Some did acquire denization by purchase of Royal Letters Patent but they still had to pay alien duties and if their children were born before it was granted they could not inherit or own property. In January 1753 Joseph Salvador, a wealthy London Jewish businessman, prominent in the Spanish and Portuguese Synagogue, put forward a proposal to allow Jews to be naturalised without taking the Holy Sacrament, and instead to swear the Oath of Allegiance. Salvador was the only Jew to be a Director of the East India Company and much respected in the City. A Bill was presented to Parliament offering naturalisation to those Jews who had lived in the country for three years, who had to bring witnesses to prove that they were indeed Jewish. It was strongly supported by leading Whig politicians, and a petition was signed by a hundred City merchants who valued the Jewish contribution to trade. The Corporation of London, however, under the Lord Mayor Sir Crisp Gascoyne, was vehemently against it. The Bill was presented in the House of Lords by Lord Halifax and passed by both Houses.

Then started the most widespread and vicious vilification of the Jews in England since the Readmission in 1656. The most extraordinary rumours spread through the land, starting with the conjecture that the whole idea was contrary to the Christian religion. The Jews, it was held, were not entitled to a settled home until they should be converted, that they were so rich that they would buy up all English land and buildings (including Westminster Abbey and the Houses of Parliament) and the Church of England would be utterly overwhelmed by this tide of Jews coming in from abroad. The trade in ham and bacon would be ruined, the governments of Spain and Portugal would take umbrage at the sanctuary given to those they had expelled. All sorts of ridiculous fears were expressed as to the future of England, once the Jews (traitors, spies, villains of every sort it appeared) were free to make their homes here. These immigrants, subjects of the Bill, were not only Jews; some were from Catholic countries and many were Huguenots. Some of the vilification did not even distinguish one group from another. One cry heard in the streets was 'No Jews, no Wooden Shoes' – a reference to the French clogs worn by the Huguenot weavers.

The government was terrified by the hornet's nest they had uncovered and hastened to repeal the Bill. A few members of the House of Lords defended the Bill though the majority were vociferously in favour of repeal. The Commons, after a bad-tempered debate, passed the Repeal Bill and it received the Royal consent. The outcry against the very moderate Bill had little to do with religious persecution; it was more of a protest against immigration, increasing naturalisation and the Englishman's instinctive mistrust of foreigners! It was to be another hundred years before a Bill was to bring the Jews – and other non-Anglican Londoners – a measure of equality.

The Prince of Wales

Frederick, Prince of Wales, according to Lord Hervey, 'had a father who abhorred him, a mother that despised him, sisters that betrayed him, a brother set up against him, and a set of servants that neglected him.'[15] It was hardly surprising that the Prince allied himself with his father's Opposition. He set up an alternative court at Leicester House, as his father had done, but together with his wife, Augusta of Saxe-Gotha, and his children, enjoyed a country home at Cliveden in Buckinghamshire. He was a patron of the arts and a keen follower of cricket, rapidly becoming a national sport. He established his own team and even occasionally went in to bat. Frederick died at Cliveden in 1751, leaving his eldest son, George, the heir to the throne at the age of thirteen.

Changing London

London, in the middle of the eighteenth century, was a strange conglomeration: a mixture of religions, mostly living in peace with one another, though ready to break out if provoked; of differing social circumstances, from the squalor depicted by Hogarth to the elegance of the aristocratic western reaches; of cultural brilliance with the music of Handel, the literary genius of Johnson, Pope and the essayists and novelists; and the art and architecture of Gainsborough, Reynolds, the Adam brothers and Hawksmoor.

Hogarth's portraits of the horrors of a gin-soaked debauched London were not exaggerated. Without the benefit of any welfare for the poor, except what the Church could offer, many Londoners were on the verge of ruin. Even if they could afford to eat, they had little recourse to even minimal social care. Illegitimate children, and many whose families could not care for them, were left on the streets, dead or alive, a pitiful sight which drove Captain Thomas Coram to build the Foundling Hospital in 1742. It was established for the 'education and maintenance of exposed and deserted young children.' To begin with the government insisted that all those who came to the Hospital should be admitted. In less than four years 14,934 children were presented. M. Dorothy George, historian of London, writes, 'The plan of wholesale reception could not survive the abuses it gave rise to.'[16] The Hospital eventually took on premises in the country, and the original site is now a Museum, offering exhibitions, contemporary art commissions, collection displays and historic archives, plus a lively programme of concerts, workshops, talks and special events, all within beautiful 18th-century interiors.

The plight of London's children struck at the heart of writers such as William Blake. His *Songs of Experience* include The Chimney Sweeper, a trade followed by the smallest children who could climb up a filthy chimney.

> A little black thing among the snow
> Crying 'weep! weep!' in notes of woe!
> 'Where are thy father and mother, say?'
> 'They are both gone up to the church to pray.'[17]

Those in debt were clapped into prison where there was little hope of release. At the Fleet Prison a system of clandestine marriages was in place, where banns were not read and the clergyman who conducted such a wedding was of dubious qualification. The Marriage Act of 1753 ruled that for a marriage to be valid it had to be performed in a church after the publication of banns or the obtaining of a licence. This did not apply in Scotland where the nearest town to England, Gretna Green, served as the destination for couples eloping to get married. Nor did it apply to Quakers or Jews.

The city suburbs were spreading. They intrigued Daniel Defoe as he rode towards London. 'From Richmond to London the river sides are full of villages, so full of beautiful buildings, charming gardens and rich habitations of gentlemen of quality that nothing in this world can imitate it.'[18] Some of the Nonconforming sects took refuge in the quieter country outside London. Amersham in Buckinghamshire had always been a centre of dissent, and a few miles away at Jordans near Chalfont, the Quakers found a peaceful home. Women played an important role in the affairs of the Friends; Mary Penistone, wife of Isaac, an eminent Quaker, wrote an account of how she visited Woodside Farm at Amersham to make the owner an offer for the house. 'In half an hour's time I had the form of the thing in my mind, what to sell, what to pull down, what to add, and cast how it would be done with the overplus money.'[19] Woodside Farm was still a working farm until very recently. It now belongs to the local community association.

George III

In October 1760 George II died, leaving his throne to his grandson, Prince of Wales, the third King George. Born and educated in England he was welcomed by people and politicians alike. His close friend, Lord Bute, was not. Young George had entrusted his friendship and his upbringing to John Stuart, 3rd Earl of Bute, though the Chief Minister, the Duke of Newcastle, was immediately aware that he would be pushed out in favour of a Scotsman.

In 1761 George married Charlotte of Mecklenburg-Strelitz, another German princess. J.H. Plumb, the historian, describes her as 'a dim, formidably ugly girl'[20], but she was interested in music, once playing with Mozart on his visit to England aged eight, and was something of any amateur botanist, taking a great interest in the gardens at Kew. The Bird of Paradise flower, *Strelitzia Regina*, was named after her. However, George was disappointed. There had been rumours that the impressionable young man had fallen in love with a young Quaker, Hannah Lightfoot, and even that he had married her and had children. The Royal Marriage Act, insisting on the Sovereign's consent to any marriage by a member of the Royal Family, was not passed until 1772, but the King could not marry outside the Church of England, and in any case Hannah had already been married off to Isaac Axford. The story has persisted but Hannah disappeared soon afterwards and there seems to be little truth in it. Augusta, George's mother, interfered intolerably in her son's marriage and the young Queen, lonely in her home at Buckingham House, was very miserable in the early years.

London Catholics

Once the furore over the Jacobite rebellion had died down, Catholics in London were left to pursue their religion in a relatively calm atmosphere. The Popery Act of 1698 had laid down stringent conditions against Catholic preaching or education, but in 1778 Parliament passed the first Catholic Relief Act which abolished the punishment of life imprisonment for priests who ran schools and offered Catholics, on swearing an oath to the King, the opportunity of purchasing and inheriting land. The oath included a promise to renounce loyalty to the Pretender and to the Pope, and to ignore such Catholic ideas as the acceptance of lawful murder of excommunicated princes. Officially they were not allowed to baptise their children into the Catholic faith, to be buried in a Church of England cemetery or to marry except under the auspices of the Anglican Church. However the authorities generally ignored all but the most flagrant transgressions. There were ways of getting round the restrictions – burial at night, a double marriage ceremony, or secret baptism.

Richard Challoner, Vicar Apostolic of London, was one of the few Roman Catholic leaders of Georgian England to be nationally and internationally respected. He had studied at the Jesuit College at Douai and arrived in London in 1728. He seemed to flourish without impediment, visiting his flock which amounted to some 25,000 London Catholics, carrying out pastoral duties and holding services in convents and private homes. He wrote many books, dissertations and articles on the Catholic faith, including *The Garden of the Soul,* published in 1740. This was a small volume of prayers for the laity, easily hidden in a pocket if necessary when attending Mass. He preached openly in the chapels of foreign Catholic embassies in London, as well as at the Ship Tavern in Holborn. This inn had offered Catholics a meeting house as long ago as Henry VIII's reign – it dates from 1549 – and although much altered is still a popular eating house.

The Anglican Church

The Church of England in the eighteenth century has had a bad press. By the middle of the century it was phlegmatic and lazy, doing little to fend off the encroachment of the lively dissenters into its congregations. The Methodists in particular were known for their missionary zeal, helped by the extensive journeys around Britain by their articulate preachers. Anglican bishops, very attentive to their political duties, frequently kept themselves beyond the reach of their poor brethren in the country parishes, which they seldom visited. They earned a great deal more than the lesser clergy and were noted for their luxurious life styles. Their behaviour was also rather dubious at times. Dr Johnson, according to James Boswell, expected the highest standard of decorum.

> A bishop has nothing to do at a tippling house. It is not indeed immoral in him to go to a tavern; neither would it be immoral in him to whip a top in Grosvenor Square; but if he did I hope the boys would fall upon him and apply the whip to him.[21]

Devoted as they were to their Church, the higher Georgian clergy were equally attentive to the government of the country, particularly the Whig administration. Edmund Gibson, Bishop of London, was fierce in his attempts to keep 'the Infidel' out of his diocese. His writings, especially his *Pastoral Letters*, were widely read. He faced the Methodist threat by warning his readers about the danger to the English Church of the intrusion of these Nonconformist ministers. He fulminated against their theological opinions and what he saw as their slanderous view of the Anglican clergy. Once again it was their 'enthusiasm' which he disliked. However, the Whig support for the Dissenters and for freedom of thought put the party at risk of alienating the established Church. Politics for churchmen were a vital part of their careers. Their presence in the House of Lords could sway the balance of power.

In spite of the Bishops' inflated standard of living, many of the lower clergy were living almost below the poverty line. They seldom saw their Bishop and often had to ride long distances (if they could afford a horse) to reach their parishioners. Parson Woodforde paid his curate £50 a year, while he himself – with a handsome private income – could enjoy a good dinner of

> some common fish, a leg of mutton and a baked pudding, the first course; and a roast duck, a meat pie, eggs and tarts the second. For supper we had a brace of partridges roasted, some cold tongue, potatoes in shells and tarts.[22]

The parson, however, did not neglect his parish duties and was generous to the less fortunate villagers.

> I took a walk to a cottage to see an old woman of eighty who belongs to Weston [his parish] and to whom I send money every year out of the charity belonging to Poor Widows of Weston. I found her spinning by the fire though she is almost blind. I gave her, to buy tobacco as she smokes, one shilling.[23]

The Enlightenment in England

The beginnings of a new way of looking at religion and faith can be traced back to such scientists and thinkers as Thomas Hobbes, Isaac Newton and John Locke. They were intrigued by the enlightened ideas of continental Europe; a view of the world as subject to order and rationality. To question the Christian faith's theology was seen by many as heretical, but those university men who felt that reason had to play a vital part in religion – the Cambridge Platonists and their friends – were respected ethical thinkers and moral philosophers. The Latitudinarian churchmen who succeeded them were rationalists, seeing perfect reason in their beliefs. They had no problem in accepting revelation and a firm conviction of God's presence as part of the natural order. Science and philosophy were perfectly compatible with faith, with a beneficent God and Man playing a central role in the Universe.

The questioning of scholars and churchmen extended into poetry and art. Alexander Pope's poem *An Essay on Man,* includes the lines:

> See then the acting and comparing powers,
> One in their Nature, which are two in ours,
> And Reason raise o'er Instinct as you can,
> In this 'tis God directs, in that 'tis Man.[24]

The scientists had more to do than think about God and Man. England was proud to be the prime mover in world-changing developments in industry, and what has come to be known as the Industrial Revolution was a part of the whole exciting expansion of mind and technology. The capital city, far larger and more populous than any other in Britain, had no mines and few factories or mills, so the dirt and smoke of the North affected the people less. But it was involved in every part of manufacture; it formed the greatest market for the import of raw materials and export of finished goods in the whole country. All roads led to London and many waterways too. The improvements in roads and canals made London far more accessible and the mill and mine owners took full advantage of them.

London was also enjoying a cultural renaissance. The theatre was flourishing, art was encouraged by the founding of the Royal Academy in 1768, with Sir Joshua Reynolds as its first President, and the new buildings springing up across the city were furnished by Chippendale and Wedgwood and the Adam brothers. The booksellers around St Paul's found ready customers. As Johnson said, 'London is nothing to some people; but to a man whose pleasure is intellectual, London is the place.'[25]

CHAPTER XVIII

Riots and Revolts

John Wilkes

WITH INDUSTRIAL AND AGRICULTURAL development in full flow, accompanied by huge fortunes being made rather than inherited, came a new concept, the liberty of the people. The English nation was more literate, more aware of its own individuality, more prepared to stand up for itself than ever before. Conversation and Debating Clubs were springing up in the major towns and newspapers flourished. The man who exemplified this emancipation and lent his name to the libertarian movement was John Wilkes. His family was 'in trade' though well-to-do and his early life was frittered away in a dissolute life-style in which he never seemed quite at home.

Wilkes was elected MP for Aylesbury and founded a newspaper which he called the *North Briton*, a pointer to the Scottish Lord Bute whose unpopularity was having a marked effect on public opinion. Wilkes' intelligent wit and verbal dexterity found an outlet in his columns for a full assault against the government and the King. Issue No. 45, which came out in 1763, denounced the King's Speech. It included the provocative comment,

> Every friend of this country must lament that a prince of so many great and amiable qualities, whom England truly reveres, can be brought to give the sanction of his sacred name to the most odious measures, and to the most unjustifiable public declarations, from a throne ever renowned for truth, honour and unsullied virtues.[1]

Wilkes was arrested and imprisoned in the Tower. He was released on the grounds that his parliamentary privilege had been infringed, but his house was searched and his papers seized. He fought back with the law behind him. He was able to establish a vital precept of English law, the rights of the individual against the state. He was also responsible for the abolition of 'general warrants', a form of official search or arrest with no specific reason for their issue. There was almost no limitation on the arresting authority, whose enemies could be arrested even having committed no crime. Loved by the mob, but pursued by the most eminent politicians, some of whom he had thought of as his friends, he left London. Plumb writes, 'Wilkes had become the idol of a savage London, seething with discontent.'[2] Wilkes' appeal to the people was almost unprecedented. Societies were formed to support the Bill of Rights and the Press became a tool which no politician could afford to ignore. It was Thomas Carlyle who first coined the phrase 'The Fourth Estate' in *The French Revolution* in 1837, though Edmund Burke is believed to have used a similar phrase much earlier.

Radical Reform

There was indeed something rotten in the state of England. The economy was in a bad way, the national debt increasing and the legal administration badly needing a considerable overhaul. Many in the established Church and among the Dissenters felt that Christian principles were fading. Politicians no longer held the respect of the nation at large. Anyone could obtain a seat in the Commons without too much difficulty, with the right friends and enough money. Lord Chesterfield wrote to his son:

> I spoke to a borough-jobber and offered five and twenty hundred pounds for a secure seat in Parliament; but he laughed at my offer and said there was no such thing as a borough to be had now, for that the rich East and West Indians had secured them all, at the rate of three thousand pounds at least.[3]

Dissent was now beginning to have a wider meaning than simply a divergence from the Church of England. The historian E.P. Thomson, in *The Making of the English Working Class*, says,

> The intellectual history of Dissent is made of collisions, schisms, mutations; and one feels often that the dormant seeds of political Radicalism lie within it, ready to germinate whenever planted in a beneficent and hopeful social context.[4]

Nonconformist Ministers like Richard Price were playing a bigger part on the world stage than simply leading a small group of independent religious believers. He set up a dissenting group at Newington Green in north London, where a Dissenting Academy was soon established. Price was a founder of the Club of Honest Whigs, which met at a London Coffee House; it included in its members Benjamin Franklin, a good friend of Price since he first visited London. Price continued to support the American Revolution, though his stance against slavery made him unpopular in some quarters. The Newington Green Meeting is still flourishing as the New Unity Church in the same red brick terrace on The Green. It is one of England's oldest

Unitarian churches, with strong ties to political radicalism for over three hundred years, and is London's oldest Nonconformist place of worship still in use.

Mary Wollstonecraft, the writer and fighter for women's rights, particularly in her *A Vindication of the Rights of Women*, was involved with Price's church. She later married the anarchist William Godwin, and their daughter, also Mary, married the poet Percy Shelley and wrote the novel *Frankenstein*. The older Mary Wollstonecraft opened a girls' school at Newington and later wrote *Thoughts on the Education of Daughters*.

The American Revolution

What in America is termed the War of Independence is usually known in this country as the American Revolution, or even by some historians as the Loss of the American Colonies. Neither England nor the Colonies were particularly well acquainted with what was happening on the other side of the Atlantic. A large number of those in America were either convicts or prostitutes or families who could not find a good life in England. The Puritans of the seventeenth century had put down roots and created homes, schools and churches in their new country and were prepared to fight to keep them. They were mostly prosperous by now, paying few taxes, with a lifestyle which if not always luxurious, was at least comfortable.

In London, however, the economy was in a perilous state. The war with France had left a yawning gap in the nation's finances, which no English taxation system could hope to fill. Why, then, should America not contribute to the Exchequer? Measures were put in place to limit migration to the west, in a vain attempt to prevent the colonists encroaching on Indian territory. Widespread smuggling to avoid duty was curtailed and as the final straw Stamp Duty was imposed on the thirteen colonies to pay at least for British troops to keep them safe from Indian incursions.

The war which broke out after the Boston tea debacle was much nearer to the hearts of English people than any European outbreak. The battlefields may have been farther away but the 'enemy' was British, with a few foreigners thrown in. In coffee houses, stately homes and cottages the debate raged. Dr Johnson spoke of the Americans with his usual asperity. 'Sir, they are a race of convicts and ought to be thankful for anything we allow them, short of hanging.'[5]

The King was an object of hate and derision for the colonists. They melted down his statue in New York and turned the metal into bullets. *A Summary View of the Rights of British America* by Thomas Jefferson, written in 1774, put into words what most of his fellow countrymen were thinking.

Our ancestors, before their emigration to America, were the free inhabitants of the British dominions in Europe, and possessed a right which nature has given to all men, of departing from the country in which chance, not choice, has placed them, of going in quest of new habitations, and of there establishing new societies, under such laws and regulations as to them shall seem most likely to promote public happiness.[6]

He was asked to draw up a Declaration of Independence which was duly presented to the new Congress of thirteen colonies held in Philadelphia and signed on 4th July 1776 by fifty-six representatives. The original title reads: *IN CONGRESS, July 4, 1776 – The unanimous Declaration of the thirteen united States of America.* It is held in the National Archive in Washington, D.C., and contains the famous declaration of rights: 'We hold these truths to be self-evident, that all men are created equal, that they are endowed by their Creator with certain unalienable Rights, that among these are Life, Liberty and the pursuit of Happiness'.

The Gordon Riots

The loss of the American colonies struck at the hearts of the English people. More recruits had had to be found for the army and it was suggested that Catholics might be enrolled, a hitherto illegal step. There were many in Ireland and Scotland who might usefully be included. To do so would need an Act of Parliament and in 1778 the Catholic Relief Act came before the House. The Act was presented by Edmund Burke and seemed certain to be passed. It allowed Catholics to take an oath which was suitable for their religion. Those taking this oath were free from the penalty of perpetual imprisonment for keeping a school. They were also enabled to inherit and purchase land. They were still forbidden to take on public office, gain a university degree, vote in elections or stand for Parliament. Nevertheless it was a step in the right direction as far as English Catholics were concerned.

Not so pleased was the English Protestant Association, a loose company of Protestants under the Presidency of Lord George Gordon, whose numbers were increasing with the threat of Catholic emancipation. Joined by their fellow thinkers in Scotland they formed a strong anti-Papist group to fight against the Bill. Many of the members were Dissenters, and petitions were signed to lobby Parliament but while the embers of discontent were smouldering it was Lord George Gordon who lit the flame.

Lord George was a Scottish peer from a very eccentric family. He was elected to Parliament at the age of twenty-two, but his unhinged mentality made him too dangerous for his fellow members of the House. Christopher Hibbert, in *King Mob*, the best account of the riots, tells of a coffee house joke that there were now 'three parties in Parliament: the Ministry, the

Opposition and Lord George Gordon.' He fought back against Burke, protesting that his Bill did not go far enough. He called it 'a mean dirty Bill, a greasy bait to draw off the attention of poor duped John Bull from the foul nest of the real grievous abominations of the evil things of this reign.'[7] Gordon maintained that regardless of his noble status, he was representing the people, a demagogue in the tradition of Jack Cade and John Wilkes, but of a very different social background.

The anti-Catholics set out their aims in *An Appeal from the Protestant Association to the People of Great Britain*, demanding the repeal of the Act. It included the ominous words,

> Should the Papists, in any future period, be possessed of power, we have reason to apprehend that the same principles would be productive of the same effects. Those principles they have never publicly disavowed; and, as Papists, cannot, with consistency, disown: therefore, as they strike at our liberties and lives, to tolerate persons professing them, is to lay the axe to the root of our dearest privileges and most sacred rights.

However, petitions from the respectable, sober middle classes were ineffectual. Some 44,000 signed the London petition (others were presented from across Britain). The Dissenters in particular were nervous of their children being taught Papist ideology in school. In 1779 John Wesley published *Popery Calmly Considered*, expressing his concerns that Catholic priests might 'undermine Holiness'.

On Friday, 2nd June 1780 members of the Association met in St George's Fields south of the river. Most of those attending were peaceful tradespeople, some carrying prayer books. They were singing hymns when Lord George arrived. He spoke to them and the procession moved off towards Westminster, led by a piper from the Scottish division. 'No popery' was the cry heard on all sides. Most of the crowd eventually dispersed, but this was only the beginning of the storm. During that night Londoners became aware of a restless party of disreputable ruffians carrying tools and weapons – pickaxes, hammers, crowbars and scythes. They waved torches and banners, making their way through the city.

They first attacked the foreign embassy chapels which had been used for Catholic worship. Sardinia's in Lincoln's Inn Fields was the first to fall. The chapel was desecrated, its contents burned. Fires were started in the neighbouring streets, the flames stirring the crowds to violence, many of them were young, excited by the frenzy. The next to go was that of the Bavarian Embassy in Golden Square. This chapel was not burned though some of its contents were smashed. It remained a Catholic chapel and is now the Roman Catholic Church of Our Lady of the Assumption and St Gregory, Warwick Street. But by now dawn was breaking and it had been a long night; the mob wandered away and it seemed that the troubles were over.

Towards the evening of the third day, the fighting broke out again, this time to the east of the City, in Moorfields. Here many Irish immigrants had settled, occupying poor run-down houses, stretching east towards Spitalfields and Whitechapel. Labour was cheap and many Irishmen were employed in the Huguenot silk factories. They had fled from the poverty and unemployment of their own country to try for a better life in London. Many were Catholics. Again the rallying cry of 'No Popery' rang out, and the Irish were ready for a fight.

The following day, a Sunday and very hot, started calmly. Like buzzing bees returning to the hive, men – and women – gathered again near Finsbury Pavement, making towards a Catholic chapel, which they destroyed. This was the signal for what amounted virtually to the annihilation of a large part of London. It was the worst riot the city has ever seen. The riots which occurred in 2011 were likened to a minor version of 1780.

By Monday night most of London seemed to be ablaze, and there was almost no attempt to control the madness. Soldiers from the Tower did eventually appear, moving around in a daze with no-one to give them orders. The poet William Cowper, known for his many hymns, including, appropriately, the lines 'God moves in mysterious ways, His wonders to perform,' wrote to his friend the Rev John Newton, who like Cowper was a hymn writer and slavery abolitionist, 'Surprise and astonishment seem at first to have struck every nerve of the police force with a palsy, and to have disarmed the Government of all its powers.'[8]

The destruction spread to Westminster and then out to the western parts of the city. In Holborn the Langdale Brewery – a Catholic business – was attacked and the ale literally ran down the streets. So voracious was the crowd in its consumption of liquor that several of the deaths were attributed to alcohol poisoning; others resulted from the alcoholic spirits setting light to the surrounding buildings before their occupants could escape.

On Tuesday, 6th June, the fifth day of the disturbances, the Riot Act was read outside the Houses of Parliament, but no-one took the slightest notice, if indeed they heard it above the din. Someone shouted 'To Newgate' and to the prison they rushed, looting and burning as they ran. Newgate was the biggest prison in Britain, dating from the thirteenth century, and a place of degradation and misery. The stone building blazed as if it were made of wood. The prisoners, men and women, most of them in chains, rushed out fearing more for their lives than desiring to escape.

One contemporary commentator, Ignatio Sancho, was a black African. Born a slave who came to England and settled down as a grocer serving the nobility, he wrote to a friend,

There is at this moment at least a hundred thousand poor, miserable ragged rabble, from twelve to sixty years of age, with blue cockades in their hats, besides half as many women and children, all parading the streets, the Bridge, the Park, ready for any and every mischief.[9]

Out of their minds with frenzy, the rabble moved towards the Bank of England, imagining perhaps that it might fall as easily as the chapels or the prisons and the prize would undoubtedly be greater. A platoon of infantry had already been sent out to the building, with heavy cannon placed in the courtyard. As soon as the first wave of rioters reached Threadneedle Street the order to fire was given. Several men were killed on the spot; the others retreated and took cover. They rallied and later tried again to force the troops back, but by now reinforcements had been summoned. This was all out warfare. Suddenly a new figure appeared on the steps of the Bank to confront the mob. It was Lord George Gordon, shouting incomprehensibly, apparently uncertain which side he was on. He was removed by the military and although the crowd tried to reach the Bank and many were killed in the attempt, the walls were never breached.

Gradually the rebellion started to die down. So did the fires, leaving ghastly black pits, still smouldering, all over London. The streets looked like a battlefield, which indeed they were. Handbills issued by the Government asked citizens not to wear the blue cockades that were the insignia of the Protestant Association.

Apart from the Great Fire, only the Blitz in World War II ever approached the destruction of the 1780 riots. Most of the escaped convicts were rounded up and put back in prison wherever there was space for them. Those rioters who were apprehended were tried in the civil courts, though many thought they should have been court martialled. Rumours flew that the whole nightmare was the result of foreign conspiracies, as several men of a 'well-dressed appearance' had been spotted in the crowd. If any fundamental reason can be found for the affair, it might be the global move towards revolution that attracted mob violence. Anti-church, anti-wealth, anti-authority feelings were sweeping across Europe and America. London had to have its own explosion – a sign of the times. Lord George only lit the fuse.

A large regiment of military guards took Gordon from his home in Welbeck Street to Whitehall and then as a prisoner to the Tower. Forty-four of the ringleaders were sentenced to death of whom twenty-one were hanged. Among them, according to Hibberd, were 'two gypsies, a West Indian slave, a demented cross-eyed beggar, three abscess-covered climbing boys, and a negro prostitute.'[10] Before any conviction could be brought against Gordon he disappeared.

Six months later a strange, unkempt figure was found in Birmingham, going by the name of Israel ben-Abraham George Gordon. He professed to be an orthodox Jew and seemed much respected as a scholar by his neighbours. Apparently he had fled to Amsterdam and then been sent back to England, taking refuge in the Birmingham house of a Jewish woman. He had long been sympathetic towards the Jewish faith. He was circumcised and started to learn Hebrew and to study Jewish law. He came down to London and joined the Hambro Synagogue in Fenchurch Street having first approached the Great Synagogue who would not have him. He was sentenced to a total of five years imprisonment.

Imprisoned at Newgate, Gordon lived as an orthodox Jew. He wore phylacteries, the small leather boxes containing Hebrew texts on vellum, worn by Jewish men at morning prayer as a reminder to keep the law. He found the necessary ten men, Polish Jews, to hold services, kept a kosher household, with Jewish bread and wine for the Friday night dinner. The Ten Commandments were painted on the wall of his cell and he entertained visitors and his fellow prisoners, Jewish and non-Jewish. Lord George died of prison fever in 1793. Against his wishes he was not buried in a Jewish cemetery, perhaps because his family would not agree. Instead he lies in an unmarked grave in the St James's Cemetery, now St James's Gardens, in Hampstead Road, near Euston Station. Work on a new railway line there may discover the spot.

Putting the Gordon Riots into perspective, Colin Haydon, in *Anti-Catholicism in Eighteenth Century England*, sees them as being 'in accordance with the old "moral economy" of pre-industrial England, intended to preserve the long established state of things'[11] – the 'have-nots' against the 'haves' perhaps. Peter Ackroyd, one of the greatest of all historians of London, wrote,

> So ended the most violent internecine period in the city's history. Like all London violence it burned brightly but quickly, the stability and reality of the city being distorted by the heat of its flames before once more settling down.[12]

The French Revolution

Now it was France's turn. England had managed to achieve, after a bloodless revolution, a reasonably constitutional monarchy. She could offer, at least to the majority of her countrymen, a good standard of living, opportunity for advancement, freedom of speech and religion. Her middle class acted as the buffer between the aristocrats and the working class. The word 'peasant' figures little in English social history. The first signs of revolution in France were welcomed by many in England; those who had fought for their liberty, such as the Dissenters, saw in France that their hopes might yet be granted. The romance of Liberty had swept through America and now came to France. William Wordsworth wrote

> What temper at the prospect did not wake
> To happiness unthought of?[13]

He, like many others, was to be sadly disillusioned.

Not everyone was bedazzled by the Utopia of freedom. Edmund Burke, in *Reflections on the French Revolution*, stood firmly on his belief in the status quo, and when the royal family of France was executed, London became fearful of more uprisings. When Fox greeted the storming of the Bastille as the greatest event in the history of the world, more sober minds recalled the destruction of Newgate Prison only ten years earlier. But reform was not the same as revolution. The terror in Paris was a lesson that London had already learned to its cost. The guillotine claimed far more victims than Lord George Gordon; England's battle was fought with words, following the precepts of the Quakers. One of the Friends was Thomas Paine who had been involved in the war in America, defending that Revolution anonymously in *Common Sense*. Back in England, he published *The Rights of Man*, replying to Burke. Mary Wollstonecraft followed it with *A Vindication of the Rights of Woman*, fighting for the education of women. She dedicated it to Talleyrand, the French revolutionary.

The new insistence on freedom not only applied to religion, politics and power, but extended into the worlds of art and architecture, literature and music. Hitherto the classical ideals of order and convention, logic and reason governed the cultural aspirations of the civilised world. Now a new perspective took its place: romanticism. Rules and precision were abandoned in favour of freedom of expression and the cult of the individual. Painters depicted storms and natural disasters, nature at her most violent. Mountains, rivers and raging seas took the place of calm landscapes and classical architecture. In poetry Romanticism found its ultimate expression in the work of William Blake, to be followed by Shelley, Keats and Byron. Blake's visionary themes connected closely with his unconventional religious beliefs. He considered himself a Dissenter, but his mysticism lent itself more to eastern philosophical belief than anything the English Church had to offer. In London he could see the horrors of the lives of the poor; his paintings and his poems illustrated the dichotomy of rich and poor, innocence and experience, industrial cities and the simplicity of the countryside. The Romantic Movement is perhaps best summed up in the words of C.M. Bowra, the classical scholar, at the beginning of *The Romantic Imagination*,

> If we wish to distinguish a single characteristic which differentiates the English Romantics from the poets of the eighteenth century, it is to be found in the

importance which they attached to the imagination and in the special view which they held of it.[14]

Revolution was not just an attempt to achieve the downfall of government control or religious tradition. It represented the opening of men's minds, the awareness of worlds they knew little of which could offer fulfilment of their dreams. Bowra wrote,

> The element of wonder which meant so much to the Romantics affected their work in a special way. In their desire to restore a lively vision of existence, they rejected the mechanistic philosophy of Locke and went far in the opposite direction, finding their metaphysics in an idealism in which the mind creates reality.[15]

The Beginnings of Empire

The East India Company was by now bringing back vast fortunes for those involved in negotiations with the native princes. It provided the only armed forces fighting there until British soldiers were sent out to support the English settlers against Indian incursions. Under Robert Clive, later the first Baron Clive of Plassey, Bengal was administered by British officials who reaped huge rewards. Despite French attempts to maintain some dominion on the subcontinent, the English were triumphant in achieving what was the beginning of the foundation of a British Empire. The Governor General, Warren Hastings, was a great administrator, but India had almost insuperable problems, deriving from extremes of wealth and poverty, from religious conflict between Hindus and Moslems, and from widely differing systems of government across the country. Added to which was the constant threat of invasion from the northern tribes of Afghans and Persians. England's command over India had a wider effect on London than simply the acquisition of a huge dominion overseas. It brought to this country new religious perceptions which were to have a lasting effect on the people of its capital city.

It was in fact the East India Company that sponsored the first known baptism of an Indian in London in 1616. The young man could read and write in English, and was christened Peter, apparently at the suggestion of the King, James I. However, the early immigrants from the East were either Lascars, sailors on the ships trading with Britain, or came to serve English families as servants or nursemaids, having been taken on when the families were working for the Company in India. Some came as emissaries from the Indian princes or as native entrepreneurs seeking to make their fortunes in London.

The earliest black people seen in England may have come as slaves or soldiers in the Roman armies. Some were taken from the early colonies

200   MITHRAS TO MORMON

established in America by the first explorers coming home, and as already mentioned a black musician appeared on the Tournament Roll of Henry VIII. By the end of the eighteenth century there were probably some three to four hundred Muslims living in London, most, particularly the sailors, in the East End, Limehouse and the Dock areas.

Deen Mahomet

One young man, whose father fought with the East India Company troops, was Deen Mahomet, a Shi'ite Muslim. Deen also went into the army, fighting against native uprisings and was part of the battalion which rescued Warren Hastings from captivity by insurgents. He resigned from the army and sailed to Ireland where he studied to improve his English and married an Irish woman, having converted to the Church of England. He was the author of the first book written by an Indian in English, *Travels of Dean Mahomet, a native of Patna in Bengal, through several parts of India, while in the service of the Honourable East India Company written by himself in a series of letters to a friend.* He moved to London and worked as a 'shampooer' in a steam bath. He then opened a coffee house in Portman Square, offering Indian specialities. Moving to Brighton, a town made fashionable by the Prince Regent's Pavilion, he started a bath-house of his own, using Indian shampoos and toiletries, claiming also to cure gout and rheumatism. He was granted a royal warrant and continued to operate as a free-lance physician until his death in 1851. Mahomet's *Travels* gives a vivid picture of contemporary Muslim life in India, though by the time he came to London he was already a practising Christian. He tells of Muslim ceremonies and practices, in excellent if slightly stilted English,

> The Mahometans are strict adherents to the tenets of their religion, which does not, by any means, consist in that enthusiastic veneration of Mahomet so generally conceived; it considers much more, as its primary object, the unity of the supreme Being, under the name of Allah. Mahomet is only regarded in a secondary point of view as the missionary of that unity, merely for destroying the idol worship, to which Arabia had continued so long in bondage.[16]

Black Communities in London

Towards the end of the eighteenth century black people in London were sufficiently numerous to have created a considerable communal life, organising life-style events such as weddings and funerals to which large numbers would congregate in friendship and celebration. Some were very poor, or still in slavery, such as the lascars or those from the slave run plantations of America. Others such as the Indian entrepreneurs and envoys of princes lived in splendid circumstances. However, there is little known about their religious life. There must have been facilities for prayer or religious services in private houses; those of the servant class or the slaves, took the religion of their masters. Those who won their freedom in England were certainly Christians. However the earliest mosques and temples did not appear until the nineteenth century when the numbers wanting to worship as their fore-fathers had done necessitated places for them to hold services according to their own traditions.

CHAPTER XIX

Empire and Dominion

Slaves in Britain

DURING THE YEARS AFTER the American War of Independence Londoners gradually became used to seeing black faces in the city. Charles Dickens, in *Barnaby Rudge*, his novel about the Gordon riots, has Gabriel Varden jokingly suggest that Miss Miggs, the servant, might be carried off by 'a black tambourine player with a great turban on'. 'Turks and Mussulmen' were to be feared by children, just as 'Boney' was later in the war with France. Little distinction was made between those from the East or from the West. Some of these black citizens had come from America as slaves, taken to England by their masters to serve in their houses. Some escaped from their miserable lives overseas and took ship to celebrate their freedom in this country, used to hard work. A few gained an education here and became, like Deen Mahomet, small-time businessmen and entrepreneurs.

Olaudah Equiano was taken as a slave to Barbados. He later wrote an account of the appalling conditions of the slave trade, particularly on the boats plying between Africa and the West Indies and America. He was taken by his master to London, converted to Christianity and was baptised at St Margaret's Westminster. He became a Methodist and bought his freedom. The Church refused his wish to return to his homeland as a missionary, but he worked to abolish the slave trade and wrote – under his new name of Gustavus Vassa – to Queen Charlotte asking for her help

> in favour of the wretched Africans; that by your Majesty's benevolent influence a period may be put to their misery; and that they be raised from the condition of brutes, to which they are at present degraded, to the rights and situation of freemen.[1]

Another literate slave who became an active abolitionist was Ottobah Cugoano. Born in present-day Ghana, he was transported as a boy to the West Indies to work on the sugar plantations. He too was taken to England where he obtained his freedom. He worked as a servant for the artists

Richard and Maria Cosway, who were prominent in London's artist community. Richard Cosway was appointed Painter to the Prince of Wales. In 1797 Cugoano published *Thoughts and Sentiments on the Evil and Wicked Traffic of the Slavery and Commerce of the Human Species*, an important book for the rapidly growing movement against the slave trade. He wanted to set up schools in Britain for African students.

The Fight for Abolition

In 1787 these intelligent freed slaves founded their own organisation to fight the trade. Called the Sons of Africa, the members wrote letters to Parliament and to the Press, spoke at public meetings and attracted the attention of influential Londoners. Granville Sharp was born into an Anglican family but apprenticed to a Quaker linen-draper, and after gaining a largely self-taught education became a freeman of the City. He was a biblical scholar and wrote several works on scriptural themes. He opposed the war in America and his evangelical interests were instrumental in his founding in 1787 the Society for the Abolition of the Slave Trade. The majority of the first Committee were Quakers, though Sharp remained a member of the Church of England. The Society was supported by John Wesley, Josiah Wedgwood the potter, Samuel Romilly, the legal reformer and other influential men of the day. Wedgwood designed the Society's seal, a kneeling African in chains above the words 'Am I not a Man and a Brother?' It was soon seen everywhere, the first publicity logo.

The Clapham Sect

The man who came to lead the abolitionist cause and whose name was ever afterwards associated with the Anti-Slavery movement was William Wilberforce. At Clapham, in south London, the Rev John Venn, Rector of Holy Trinity Church, gathered around him a strongly motivated group of evangelicals. Among them were William Wilberforce, Granville Sharp and John Thornton. Born in 1759 in Hull, William Wilberforce came to London to live with an aunt, but her evangelical leanings so frightened his mother that she took him home. He went up to Cambridge where he became friendly with William Pitt and decided on a political career. He was elected MP for Hull at the age of twenty-one, and later for Yorkshire. A meeting in Kent with Pitt and William Grenville, Pitt's cousin and a member of the government, under what was later known as Wilberforce's Oak, decided him to make the abolition of slavery his life's work.

John Thornton, said to be the richest man in Britain, was born in Clapham. His father was a director of the Bank of England and John was a devout evangelical Anglican. Most of these Claphamite families were related to each other; the Thorntons and the Wilberforces were cousins. Other families, also interrelated, were the Macaulays and the Babingtons (Thomas, the historian, took both names), James Stephen, a lawyer, married into the Wilberforce family. He was the great-grandfather of Virginia Woolf. They were known as the Clapham Sect, and rather quizzically as the Saints.

The chief preoccupation of the Clapham Sect was the abolition of the slave trade, not initially of slavery itself. The Sect was above all traditional and conservative in its attitude to society. One supporter, Hannah More, was an intelligent, educated bluestocking who founded, with her sister Patty, several schools for poor girls. She was anxious for them to learn to read, but not to write as this might give them ideas above their station. One of her books, *Thoughts on the Importance of the Manners of the Great to General Society*, published in 1788, was a treatise on the moral conduct of the great and the good towards their less fortunate brothers and sisters. She also wrote poetry, several on the subject of slavery. She was particularly concerned for the female slaves, writing

> I see, by more than Fancy's mirror shewn,
> The burning village, and the blazing town:
> See the dire victim torn from social life,
> The shrieking babe, the agonizing wife!
> She, wretch forlorn! is dragg'd by hostile hands,
> To distant tyrants sold, in distant lands!
> Transmitted miseries, and successive chains,
> The sole sad heritage her child obtains![2]

Hannah's fellow members of the Clapham Sect had similar views on the maintenance of social rank. They were self-assured, striving, not for change, but for improvement. However, they were prepared to fight fiercely to alleviate the evils in society. In 1787 they founded The Proclamation Society, or The Society for Carrying into Effect His Majesty's Proclamation against Vice and Immorality, to fight against sexual, moral and criminal misbehaviour. They were supported by the Bishop of London, Beilby Porteus, who was warmly in favour of evangelicals especially Hannah More, whom he helped with her education ideas. The Sect also established its own newspaper, *The Church Observer*, and founded other societies such as the British and Foreign Bible Society and the Church Missionary Society.

Abolition

It was Granville Sharp as much as William Wilberforce who was responsible for the movement to abolish slavery, though Wilberforce's gift of oratory brought it to parliamentary and public attention. The Quakers had already begun to speak against the idea of any man being in thrall to another, and Sharp, though not a Quaker, provided Wilberforce with the evidence and case histories he needed to put his case to Parliament. In 1786 Sharp published *A Short Sketch for the Government of Sierra Leone*. This involved a plan to set up a colony of freed slaves in Sierra Leone, known as Freetown (still the name of the capital). The country became a Crown Colony in 1808.

The history of the slave trade as far as Britain is concerned goes back to 1713 when the country was granted, at the Treaty of Utrecht, the Asiento, the right to supply slaves to the Spanish/American colonies. The South Sea Company took up this coveted prize to trade 4,800 African slaves, becoming the world's largest slave trader. The system revolved around the three-point journeys from the west coast of Africa to the West Indies and the American mainland, back to the English ports of Bristol and Liverpool, carrying cargoes, mainly of sugar, tobacco and cotton, so cruelly assembled by the Negro slaves. The slave traders, captains and owners of the ships that carried them made fortunes at the expense of the hell that was the lot of the African men, women and children. The reformers, as Dorothy Marshall the historian wrote, 'were challenging one of the greatest vested interests of the times, and challenging it not on a material but on a spiritual and moral plane.'[3]

The first Parliamentary discussion of the slave trade took place in 1788, with a speech by Charles Fox, supported by several other MPs including Edmund Burke. A Bill to examine and improve conditions aboard the slave ships was proposed and passed by the Commons but rejected by the Lords, until Pitt threatened to resign. Wilberforce's first contribution to the debate came the following year, when he made a three-hour speech arguing against the appalling conditions on the ships. The result was delayed by the anti-abolitionists, mostly involved in the trade and it was not until 1791 that Wilberforce was able to introduce a bill to abolish the slave trade, but in spite of the support of some of the most distinguished politicians of the day, it was defeated. But in 1807 a new Whig government, headed by William (now Lord) Grenville, a keen abolitionist, with Charles Fox as Foreign Secretary, passed the Bill by a large majority in both the Commons and the Lords.

Slavery

The passing of the act to abolish trading did not mean that slavery was illegal. Several cases came to court of slaves in England trying to claim their freedom, but it was the case of James Somerset that drew the attention of the world to the essential problem of emancipation. Somerset was a slave from Africa who was taken to Virginia in 1749 and bought by James

Stewart, a Scottish merchant and customs official. Stewart brought him home to London where he was baptised. The baptism of slaves was frowned on as encouraging them to associate with free men and learn ideas unsuitable for their low social status. It was also believed that conversion involved freedom in itself and it was expressly forbidden in several British colonies. Somerset ran away from Stewart's home in Holborn but was recaptured. On the order of the Lord Chief Justice, Lord Mansfield, he was granted a writ of habeas corpus and appeared before him in 1771. Mansfield referred the case to the Court of King's Bench.

In January 1772 Somerset appeared before Mansfield at Westminster Hall. The case turned on whether slavery was legal in England. After all the arguments were heard, lasting several days, the Lord Chief Justice gave his verdict. 'The state of slavery,' he said,

> is of such a nature that it is incapable of being introduced on any reasons, moral or political, but only by positive law, which preserves its force long after the reasons, occasion and time itself from whence it was created, are erased from memory. It is so odious that nothing can be suffered to support it, but positive law. Whatever inconveniences, therefore, may follow from the decision, I cannot say this case is allowed or approved of by the law of England, and therefore the black must be discharged.[4]

But slavery continued legally in Britain until 1834 when the Slavery Abolition Act was passed. All slaves in the British Empire were given their freedom. Young slaves were re-designated as 'apprentices' and slave owners were given compensation, though none was paid to the slaves.

The Prince Regent

King George had for some time suffered bouts of illness and a degree of mental instability. He blamed his disposition on the loss of his American colonies, talking incessantly and seemingly at times totally distracted. The Court moved to Kew where the royal doctors subjected their patient to a cruelly oppressive regime which involved him being brutally restrained, tied down and gagged. Behind contemporary treatment for insanity was the belief that the symptoms were the result of sin against God for which punishment was necessary. Possession by devils was at the back of it, and they had to be expelled by whatever means were necessary. Bethlehem Hospital, or Bedlam, as it later became, was the first psychiatric hospital in Europe. It was founded in the thirteenth century near Bishopsgate and moved to a new building at Moorfields in 1676. Here visitors could come to watch the lunatics – the regime was harsh and unrealistic as far as finding a cure was concerned.

At the end of 1788 the King recovered his wits and London held a service of thanksgiving for his return to health. The real reason for his illness was the onset of porphyria, which discolours the blood and urine and affects the whole nervous system. The disease is hereditary and several members of the King's widespread family suffered from it, traceable back to Mary Queen of Scots. There is no cure and the disease was not recognised in the eighteenth century. His two doctors were at odds on his prognosis. George fell ill again a few years later and was forcibly confined to his rooms. After the King made several attempts at escape, his physician, Thomas Willis had him virtually kidnapped and shut up in the palace at Kew, away from family, friends and politicians. Eventually the physicians had to be bought out, and the King was liberated. John Clarke, in his biography of the King, calls it 'one of the most disgraceful episodes in the history of royal medicine.'[5] The story was scandalous enough to be made into a play by Alan Bennett.

The troublesome Prince of Wales, now Regent during the King's illness, continued to be a thorn in the flesh of the royal family and the government. The King and Queen themselves embodied most of the middle-class virtues of Hanoverian England. They led a rather ordinary domestic life – not for nothing was he known as Farmer George – except for his numerous mistresses, but like his father and grandfather the King's relationship with his children was fraught with dislike and mistrust. It was the Prince's marriage that caused the biggest upheaval, for in 1785 he married Maria Fitzherbert, twice widowed and a Roman Catholic. The Prince eventually rejected her, though his father welcomed her into his family and provided for her for the rest of her life. The marriage was illegitimate for two reasons: because she was a Catholic and because the King's permission was not obtained.

The Prince later married, in 1795, Caroline of Brunswick, his first cousin, an unappetising woman, much disliked by all the royal family, including her husband. In 1796 she gave birth to a daughter, Charlotte, the heir to the throne. Caroline lived a dissolute life, though no worse than that of her husband, as many Englishmen believed. She was believed to have given birth to an illegitimate son, and her behaviour was the subject of a 'delicate investigation'; it was found that there was no basis for the allegations, but her visits to her daughter were restricted. She agreed to leave the country on payment of a large sum of money.

The King's Last Illness

The King's eyesight was failing, not uncommon in porphyria sufferers. The old restraints were re-imposed, but the King was clearly sinking into total insanity. His appearance was quite changed, seemingly more King Lear than King George of England, with tangled hair and a long white beard.

The Queen died in 1818, her husband unaware of her death. George died in 1820 aged eighty-one, and was buried at night in St George's Chapel, Windsor, leaving the nation he had loved to the mercies of his eldest son.

The Growth of London

By the year 1800 one million people were living in London. The first general census was held in 1801. It was taken in individual parishes, under the overall supervision of John Rickman, a statistician and Clerk to the House of Commons. The Census Act was 'an Act for taking an Account of the Population of Great Britain and of the Increase or Diminution thereof' and has been held every decade since (except for 1941 when the nation was at war). The capital was expanding westwards, with elegant town houses, shops and public buildings, creating a city whose appearance, liveliness, convenience and efficiency were the admiration of the world.

Catholic Emancipation

Rebellion in Ireland, assisted by France, to allow its citizens to vote members into the House of Commons was unsuccessful. Pitt was persuaded to allow the Irish some degree of representation in Parliament, but the Catholic majority there meant that any elected members would be bound to include a proportion of Catholics. In 1800 an Act of Union was passed between the two nations, following which a new flag for the nation was designed, incorporating the red cross of St George, the white saltire of St Andrew on a blue ground and the red saltire of St Patrick on white. Wales is not represented. The Union Jack as we know it today was born, though the narrow banding of the three flags often causes it to be flown upside down.

However, Catholic emancipation in England was quite another matter. It was the King himself who proved the sticking point. Four days before the Bill for emancipation was due to go before the House, the King heard about it for the first time. At his coronation he had been asked if he would maintain 'the laws of God, the true profession of the Gospel and the Protestant Reformed religion.' This he solemnly promised to do. How then could he now renege on his promise? That would mean that the remnant of the Stuarts would have as much right as he to rule England, Scotland and Ireland. He said no, and the country stood behind him. Pitt resigned.

Many liberal-minded Englishmen were, however, in favour of a more tolerant attitude towards the Catholic minority. James Losh, recounting in his diary in 1829 the proceedings of a public meeting he attended in Newcastle, wrote,

I admit that the English Catholics are few in number and that their religious opinions are perfectly untenable when subjected to fair enquiry, but surely these are not reasons why they should not have the rights of citizens; and I am satisfied that as soon as they are freed from all restrictions, they will mix freely and melt by degrees into the mass of society. I fear that the high church men are more alarmed at the spread of free enquiry, than at the enlargement of the papal power and the diffusion of popish doctrines![6]

The King's antagonism towards Catholicism was supported by the Irish Protestants and the Tories in Parliament. The Irish Catholics, however, had a charismatic leader in Daniel O'Connell. He stood for Parliament for County Clare in 1828, promising that if elected he would not sit until the oath requiring new members to swear as 'a member of the Church of England' was abolished. The Duke of Wellington, now Prime Minister, had to agree. In 1828 the Test Act was repealed and the following year Parliament passed the Catholic Emancipation Act.

George IV

The Prince Regent succeeded to the throne as George IV, but his wife was forbidden to attend his coronation. She tried to force her way through the locked gates of the Abbey and was cheered by the crowd who disliked the new King rather more than they liked his wife. Caroline was refused the title of Queen Consort, and returned to England to claim her rights, again greeted warmly by the people. George however decided to sue for divorce, and testimony against Caroline mounted. Parliament passed the Pains and Penalties Bill at the request of the King which aimed to dissolve his marriage. However, it was clear that unsavoury details of the King's own behaviour would certainly be put forward in evidence and the Bill was withdrawn on condition that Caroline left the country, that her name did not appear in the Royal Prayer and that she would not expect to be crowned. Princess Charlotte was married off to Prince Leopold of Saxe-Coburg-Saalfield, gave birth to a still-born son, and died herself shortly afterwards, to the distress of her father.

The Sailor King

George IV died in 1830, unloved by his family and by most of his people. Grossly fat (he had been called the Prince of Whales), lazy and dissolute, he was nevertheless a man of intelligence and considerable artistic taste. He left his mark on London by the great sweep of Regent Street, designed by John Nash, which continued northwards into Regent's Park and the Nash terraces. The architect also redesigned Buckingham House (now Palace) and his sponsor's Pavilion in Brighton.

After George's death, the throne was taken by his brother William, then Duke of Clarence, aged sixty-four. He had spent most of his life in the Navy – his language was usually that of the quarter-deck. He had little interest in affairs of state and he reigned for only seven years. His long association with the actress Dorothea Jordan produced ten illegitimate children; the only offspring of George III's fifteen children with a true right to the throne of England was the young Princess Victoria, daughter of the Duke of Kent.

Reform and the Church of England

It was still the case in 1830 that only members of the Church of England could hold public office. Parliament had been discussing political reform; now it was the Church's turn. France had dispatched her kings and when royalty could be proved unnecessary so perhaps could religion.

In 1831 John Wade published *The Extraordinary Black Book*. Its full title read: *The extraordinary black book: an exposition of the United Church of England and Ireland; civil list and crown revenues; incomes, privileges and power, of the aristocracy, privy council, diplomatic and consular establishments; law and judicial administration; representation of reform under the new ministry profits, influence and monopoly of the Bank of England and East-India Company; with strictures on the renewal of these charters; debt and funding system; salaries, fees and emoluments in courts of justice, public offices, and colonies; lists of pluralists, placement, pensioners and sinecurists; the whole corrected from the latest official returns, and presenting a complete view of the expenditure, patronage, influence and abuses of the government in church, state, law and representation.*[7]

Clearly reform was needed in all walks of life.Certainly the Church had much to answer for. The new Whig administration was radical enough literally to 'put the fear of God' into the Anglicans. The higher clergy had little time for politicians – the feeling was mutual. However, the bishops were fully aware that a full overhaul of Church practice was desperately needed, and they preferred to do it themselves rather than to have it thrust upon them. A review of the character of religion in England and particularly in London in the years before 1837 when Victoria came to the throne, makes it clear that all strands of Christian worship – the Anglican Church, the Evangelicals and those whose belief in God was weak or non-existent – were content to worship in their own way.

Whatever the faults and failures of their leaders, the majority of church-goers were peaceful, law-abiding citizens, mainly lower middle class, caring for their own families, though not always for other peoples'. The historian

E.L. Woodward maintained that 'The poor, at least in the great towns, were largely pagan, with a veneer of religious observance and much hidden superstition.'[8]

The Evangelicals contented themselves with their missionary work, spreading the Gospel at home and abroad, providing Bibles for anyone who wanted one (and many who didn't), and listening attentively to the long sermons which were so vital a part of Church services. In 1832 Lord Grey set up a Royal Commission on Ecclesiastical Revenues, which led four years later, when Grey had become Prime Minister, to a permanent commission under the guidance of the Bishop of London, Charles James Blomfield.

Blomfield was an outspoken man of commanding presence. The Archbishop of York, Vernon Harcourt, said that if he was not present 'we all sit and mend our pens and talk about the weather.'[9] John Henry Newman called him an active and open-hearted man who had been for years engaged in 'diluting the high orthodoxy of the church by the introduction of members of the Evangelical body into places of influence and trust.'[10] The Commission took upon itself a wide variety of Church matters, including pluralism, control of Church property, the power of the bishops and the appeal of Church services; it did not fear whose clerical toes were trodden on in the process.

The determination to reform the Church was all-embracing: Methodists, Presbyterians, Quakers and other Dissenters, all felt themselves a part of England's Church. Moral conduct, missionary zeal, Bible-reading, preaching and Sunday observance were common to them all. Only the Roman Catholics kept themselves apart, though they too were beginning to win the reforms they so desperately wanted.

The Oxford Movement

It was Newman himself who had the greatest influence on the Anglican Church at the time. In 1833, while still a priest in Oxford, he published the first of the *Tracts for the Times*, which were to give their name to Tractarianism and to usher in the Anglo-Catholic form of High Church worship and belief for members of the Church of England.

Its members wished to introduce some of the older traditions of the Church, and particularly its relationship with Roman Catholic prayers and services. Associated with Newman were Edward Bouverie Pusey, John Keble, after whom a new Oxford College was named in 1870, Richard Hurrell Froude and Robert Wilberforce, son of William and brother of Samuel. It was in fact Keble's sermon on National Apostasy which was to spark off an anti-liberal tradition in theology which led to Newman being accepted into the Roman Catholic Church. The deeper spirituality of the

Catholics attracted those who sought a more majestic form of service, rather than the simple worship of the Evangelicals.

The force of the Oxford Movement was in part driven by its suspicion of government interference in Church affairs. The *Tracts* continued to be published by different authors, and Newman's sermons, delivered at St Mary's Oxford, won large audiences and were widely reported. 'Newman's sermons', writes K. Theodore Hopper, 'combined the two features that make preaching great – content and style. He charmed and convinced at the same time.'[11]

The last of the *Tracts*, *Tract 90*, was written by Newman himself. It attracted the condemnation of scholars and churchmen alike, for it proclaimed the author's view that the Thirty-Nine Articles were acceptable by the Catholic view of the faith. After this he retired from university life and later established a form of Protestant monastic life. He entered the Roman Catholic Church in 1845 and was created a cardinal in 1879 by Pope Leo XIII, in recognition of his services to the Catholic Church in England. Meanwhile Father Wilfrid Faber had also converted from Anglicanism and he and several other converts joined Newman's new Oratory in Birmingham. Faber was then sent to establish the Oratory in London in May 1849. Newman was beatified in 2010 and canonisation is currently in process.

Jewish Reform

Another group of religionists were also seeking reform, though for very different reasons. The Jewish community of London consisted of two groups, the Ashkenazim (German and East European) and the Sephardim (Spanish-Portuguese), each with its own leader. A group of Sephardi Jews from the Bevis Marks Synagogue, together with a few from the Ashkenazi Great Synagogue, wanted to establish a synagogue further west, nearer their homes (orthodox Jews do not travel on the Sabbath). They also sought a sermon in English and improved decorum. Hitherto the service was conducted entirely in Hebrew with some Spanish or Yiddish.

The Chief Rabbi and the Haham (Sephardi leader) issued an ominous verdict, 'Schism has introduced its baneful influence upon us'.[12] They excommunicated the rebels, who in 1840 set up their own synagogue in the Bloomsbury area, forming the first Progressive synagogue in London, the West London Synagogue of British Jews, a title intended to bring together the two groups under the all-embracing term British. The Reform Movement, which spread rapidly through Britain, is today, with its off-shoot Liberal Judaism, the largest in the country.

Reform in Parliament

In 1832 Parliament passed the Great Reform Act, known as the Representation of the People Act. Suffrage in Britain was limited and unfair. Parliamentary seats were unevenly distributed; some men had two votes, the majority none at all. The Prime Minister, the Duke of Wellington, opposed reform, but when the Whigs came into office under Earl Grey, matters changed. Fifty-six boroughs were disenfranchised and thirty-one were limited to one M.P. Sixty-seven new constituencies were created and a greater number of small farmers and tradesmen were allowed to vote. This still meant that many working men could still not vote, and of course no women. No-one who was not prepared to swear the Oath of Allegiance as a member of the Church of England could take a seat in Parliament, however he was elected.

CHAPTER XX

Victorian London

Reform in Religion

THE ANGLICAN COMMUNITY and the Jews were not the only religious groups facing renewal. Nonconformist churches were also aware of the changing times that necessitated reform. The Baptists had come from Holland early in the seventeenth century and had established their first London church in Spitalfields. These Particular Baptists believed in Calvin's doctrine of particular redemption for the elect only, while their brethren, the General Baptists, followed the Arminian belief in redemption for all. Many English Baptists had emigrated to America where today they form an important element in that country's Christian believers. In 1813 a Union was formed to bring the groups together. Each church is self-governed, without bishops, so that all are equal, but baptism remains central to their creed. They reject infant baptism – it is for believers only, by full immersion. In 1891 the Particular Baptists and the General Baptists came together as the British Union of Baptists and in 2013 as Baptists Together. The Methodists too had sub-divided their Church into the Wesleyan, United and Primitive Methodists; each had its own system of worship and congregational structure.

Science and Belief

When the young Charles Darwin joined HMS Beagle as its on-board naturalist in 1831, he could hardly have imagined the effect that his discoveries were to have on Victorian religious belief. The voyage lasted five years during which Darwin visited parts of the world hardly known to western man, observing, collecting and exploring; he finally published the results in 1859 as *On the Origin of Species by Means of Natural Selection, or the Preservation of Favoured Races in the Struggle for Life.*

The book shook England's traditional beliefs to the core. The Bible had guided the Jews and all the Christian churches to accept that the world was 6,000 years old; that every word was historically accurate and that 'the world had been created by a sudden divine fiat and all the species of animals as well as man were ready-made.'[1] Geology, palaeontology and the study of animals, insects and plants, all played a part in disturbing the foundations of the Victorians' cosy belief in God's work of creation, as the Bible told it. Even before Darwin, Charles Lyall's *Principles of Geology* had sought to explain the creation of the material world by placing it millions of years before Noah's flood; its main thread was that to find out about the past man must look to the present and that geological remains from long ago can be understood by examining those of the present. The term evolution in relation to the development of life in all its forms was first used in Lyall's book. Following this, an anonymous work entitled *Vestiges of the Natural History of Creation* queried the sudden appearance of the world at the instigation of a Supreme Being. The author turned out to be Robert Chambers, after whom the *Chambers' Encyclopaedia* was named.

Theories of gradual evolution over a very long time, as opposed to instant creation, were simply theories, though scientifically thought through. Darwin, however, was able to add practical proof to those ideas. The Galapagos Islands, in particular, showed him how each island had thrown up differing species of finches, giant turtles and other birds and animals to suit the places where they had settled, so that the strongest and most suitable specimens outlived their fellows, the process which he named Natural Selection, the origin of the species.

What applied to the animal kingdom had to apply to man. The Church historian Alec R. Vidler said,

> The whole scheme of Christian belief, which was based on the supposition that man had all at once been created with a fully formed capacity for communion with God, a capacity that the human race had lost through the disobedience of the first human pair, was thrown into disarray.[2]

Never, since the Reformation, had the Church been dealt such a blow; and this was not a matter of affiliation or forms of worship, but of the deepest belief, belief in the Bible story as it had been accepted for nearly two thousand years.

The Oxford Debate

Seven months after *On the Origin of Species* came out the British Association for the Advancement of Science held a debate at the Oxford Museum of Natural History. The battle took place over the presentation of a paper by the American William Draper on *Darwin's Theory of Natural Selection*. The two chief protagonists were Samuel Wilberforce (often referred to as Soapy Sam) and T.E. Huxley (later known as 'Darwin's Bulldog'). Wilberforce, the Bishop of Oxford and of Winchester, was one of the most important churchmen of his generation. An outstanding speaker, he was a High Church believer, though never a Tractarian. He fought always for unity in the Church and was instrumental in improving its efficiency and its morality. As a Fellow of the Royal Society, he was eminently suitable to confront Darwin's theory and to fight it with conviction.

Huxley, more of a practical scientist, had taught natural history and palaeontology and helped to put scientific education on a practical, efficient footing. He coined the term agnostic referring to himself, though he spoke later of a 'church scientific'. He and Darwin were close friends. At the meeting the discussion ranged over the descent of man from the apes, one of Darwin's conclusions from his work. The precise wording of the confrontation between Wilberforce and Huxley is not absolutely clear – it was not recorded at the time – but according to a contemporary who was present, the Bishop

> begged to know, was it through his grandfather or his grandmother that he claimed his descent from a monkey? On this Mr Huxley slowly and deliberately arose. A slight tall figure stern and pale, very quiet and very grave, he stood before us, and spoke those tremendous words – words which no one seems sure of now, nor I think, could remember just after they were spoken, for their meaning took away our breath, though it left us in no doubt as to what it was. He was not ashamed to have a monkey for his ancestor; but he would be ashamed to be connected with a man who used great gifts to obscure the truth. No one doubted his meaning and the effect was tremendous. One lady fainted and had to be carried out.[3]

Both sides thought they had won, but the momentous debate was little noted. However there is now a commemorative plaque outside the room at the Museum where the debate took place, and a stone plinth on the lawn outside.

In 2016 modern technology discovered that the three mosaic domes of St Paul's Cathedral, designed by William Blake Richmond as what was originally believed to be the creation of the beasts, birds and fishes as God intended, were in fact what *The Times* called 'a clear acknowledgement of Darwin's theories about the survival of the fittest.'[4] They show a violent struggle between the forces of nature including a depiction of a fish with teeth 'fighting for survival', forty years after Darwin published his book.

Draper himself was much concerned with the difficulties between religious thought and scientific experiment. His book, *The History of the Conflict between Religion and Science*, was influential in the debate on Flat Earth Theory, which still has its proponents in the Flat Earth Society. Samuel

Rowbotham proposed the theory that the earth was a flat disc, using
the Bedford Level Experiment (whereby a series of poles plunged into the
Bedford River in Norfolk seemed to prove that the earth was indeed flat –
later disproved by the same method). After Rowbotham's death, Lady
Elizabeth Blount established a Universal Zetetic Society, whose objective
was 'the propagation of knowledge related to Natural Cosmogony in
confirmation of the Holy Scriptures, based on practical scientific investigation'. It was later superseded by the Flat Earth Society, still active today
with headquarters in California.

Jewish Relief Act

The emancipation of the Catholics in 1829 had encouraged the Jews to
press for a similar relaxation of restrictions on their election to Parliament.
The stumbling block, which also applied to Dissenters, was the necessity
to swear the oath as a member of the Church of England. Quakers, who
refused to swear, were permitted to affirm and could thus take their seats
once elected. Several attempts were made to take a Bill through the House
of Commons which would give the Jews the same facility. Backed by a
petition from the City of London, it finally passed a third reading but was
rejected in the Lords. The King and the Tories were vehemently against it.
Lord Holland, who supported the bill, referred to the Duke of Wellington's
speech against it as 'one of the worst and most injudicious speeches we
have yet heard from him; every word of it implied or avowed that no
relaxation of exclusive laws should ever be made but under the pressure of
necessity.'[5]

In 1835 the Sheriff's Declaration Act enabled Jews to hold the office
of Sheriff and the way seemed clear for them to take seats in the House.
Benjamin Disraeli, born a Jew though baptised at the age of twelve, had
no problem with the oath as it stood. It took until 1858, after several
attempts to clear the way to full emancipation (David Salamon, very active
in the pursuit of full emancipation, had been elected Lord Mayor of London
in 1855). Baron Lionel de Rothschild, who had been elected for the City of
London on five occasions, was then able to take the oath, his head covered,
using the words, 'so help me, Jehovah'. In 1864 the Religious Disability
Act allowed Dissenters too to become Members of Parliament. Charles
Bradlaugh, a republican and parliamentary campaigner, who founded the
National Secular Society, was elected to Parliament in 1880 but refusing
to swear on the Bible was denied his seat. He was eventually permitted to
affirm by a change in the law in 1886.

University Admission

The same problem of swearing the oath applied to the granting of a degree at British universities. There is still controversy as to which was the third university to be founded in England after Oxford and Cambridge. Durham was founded in 1832, but University College London, the first without any religious affiliation, came into being in 1827, to be followed, with King's College, as the University of London in 1848. The importance of UCL, as it is usually known today, was that students of any religion, or none, could gain a degree. In fact one of the early founders was a Jew, Sir Isaac Lyon Goldmid. The Universities Tests Act, passed in 1871, allowed Jews, Catholics and Dissenters to gain a degree at any British University.

Census of Religion

In 1851 an official Census of all Religious Worship was taken, for the first and only time. It concluded that there were '35 different religious communities or sects, 26 native and indigenous and 9 foreign.'[6] The Christian communities enumerated were Church of England and Ireland, Scottish Presbyterian (three sects), Independent or Congregationalist, Baptists (five sects), Society of Friends, Unitarians, Moravians, Wesleyan Methodists (seven sects), Calvinistic Methodists (two sects), the Sandemanians or Glasites, the New Church, and the Brethren. Foreign communities consisted of Lutherans, German Protestant Reformers, the Reformed Church of the Netherlands, and the French Protestants. Other Christian churches included were the Roman Catholics, the Greek Church, the German Catholics, the Italian Reformers, the Catholic and Apostolic Church and the Church of Latter Day Saints (the Mormons). Lastly came the Jews.

The Census was prefaced by a lengthy history of religion in Britain and the man responsible for this whole extraordinary task, together with the Registrar General, was Horace Mann. A civil servant, he wrote the report when in his twenties, and it raised considerable controversy, which is why it has never been repeated. Mann treated all religions equally and his conclusions showed that the Church of England was outstripped by other religious denominations in its members' attendance at worship.

Some of the churches revealed by the census were small, often exclusive, groups who had broken away from mainstream religious affiliation. The Glasites and the Sandemanians came from Scotland, where John Glas and his son-in-law Robert Sandeman, had inaugurated small like-minded societies who believed in a close attention to the Bible and did not wish to belong to either the Anglican or the Evangelical churches. The Brethren, who settled first in Plymouth after coming to England from Ireland, are still entirely exclusive and refuse to associate with unbelievers even in their own families.

The Great Exhibition

In the same year as the Census, though of far wider implication for Britain and the world, the Great Exhibition was opened by Queen Victoria in London. She had been on the throne for fourteen years and married to her beloved Albert of Saxe-Coburg-Gotha for eleven of them. As Prince Consort his social standing was inferior to that of his wife, but he soon found an outlet for his undoubted talents in the promotion of arts and industry, as well as the running of the royal household. This genius for administration culminated in the Great Exhibition of 1851, with its vast manifestation of British industrial, commercial and artistic achievement laid out in the huge Crystal Palace in Hyde Park. All the nation's scientific and technological invention was on show, giving for the first time an opportunity for the British working man to display what he could do. Six million visitors came to see and to wonder, many from abroad – working class families, churchmen, professional men and royalty.

The Queen wrote in her Journal, 'The Green Park and Hyde Park were one mass of closely crowded human beings, in the highest good humour and most enthusiastic.'[7] As well as the great boost given to Britain's position as the leading industrial nation in the world, the Exhibition was also much admired for its pride in England's religion. Among the exhibits was a collection of Bibles in 165 languages as well as publications from almost every religious denomination. The whole concept of the Exhibition acknowledged the hand of God as the instrument behind it. On the cover of the Exhibition catalogue was a quotation from the Psalms, 'The earth is the Lord's and all that therein is'. Special sermons were given in churches and churchmen recommended their flocks to visit, though this was sometimes accompanied by warnings against the materialism of the exhibits. Speaking of the religious aspect, Geoffrey Cantor wrote, 'Some prophetic writers saw the gathering of nations in London in the summer of 1851 as a sign of impending danger, perhaps the overthrow of Protestant England by Catholic or by secular revolutionaries.'[8]

Mormons

By the middle of the nineteenth century England was the home of more religious sects than her ancestors could ever have imagined. In 1837 the first missionaries of the Church of Jesus Christ of Latter-Day Saints, the Mormons, had arrived from America. In 1822 Joseph Smith was told by the Angel Moroni where to find God's revelation written on golden tablets. The Book of Mormon states that it

> shall establish the truth of the Bible and shall make known to all kindreds, tongues, and people, that the Lamb of God is the Son of the Eternal Father, and the Saviour of the world; and that all men must come unto him, or they cannot be saved.

The tablets had apparently been buried in Palmyra, New York, in 438 CE. Smith was arrested and later lynched. The Church turned to Brigham Young as its leader, who took it to Salt Lake City, Utah, were it made its home, 'Zion in the Wilderness'. Mormons believe in the restoration of the Church, repentance and baptism by total immersion, and have a strong missionary zeal. Their belief in polygamy caused considerable conflict and was officially abandoned in 1890, though there are still cases arising today.

The English 'Saints' set up a home in Preston, baptising their converts until they could claim some 30,000, more than the number in America. However, the mission did not last long as a great number emigrated to the United States, though Preston remained their British centre until the first temple, known as the London England Temple, was founded in 1958 in Newchapel in Surrey.

According to Malcolm R. Thorp, of the Brigham Young University, the early Mormons in England were severely treated. In Preston they were persecuted as they preached in the streets and in their meeting house, particularly by Methodists.

> An angry mob formed and surrounded the building. They then proceeded to throw stones (one of which, hurled through a window, injured a sister). The mob then attempted to beat down the door with sticks. The severity of the situation prompted Joseph Horton, a sympathetic non-Mormon, to fire a loaded gun over the heads of the angry crowd as a warning.[9]

Mormons believe that the dead can be baptised and families can continue to exist in the afterlife. This has caused considerable distress after the faith was found to be including for baptism some of the Jews who died in the Holocaust. They have agreed to delete those names, but the tracing of family records plays an important part in their activities, and their vast quantity of family records has been found to be useful to genealogists. Their London headquarters in Kensington houses many records not found elsewhere, and are now available online.

Zoroastrians

Zoroastrianism is believed to be the oldest monotheistic religion in the world. The prophet Zoroaster (Zarathustra), the first of the world's religious prophets, probably lived about 2,000 BCE, in north-east Iran. His followers were Parsis (Persians), dwelling peacefully under Cyrus the Great. By the time of the birth of Christ they were a formidable presence in the Middle East and in India. As Islam grew, so Zoroastrianism declined and its adherents were much oppressed. They accord to Zoroaster the same veneration as Muslims to Mahomed and Christians to Jesus Christ, though he is not worshipped as a God. The faith believes that God (Ahura Mazda – the Wise Lord) is the source of all good in the world while the evil comes from Anra Mainyu (the malign spirit). Eventually the good will overcome the evil.

Zoroastrianism pays much attention to death and its traditions, for death is the source of impurity. Thus anything pertaining to death, especially a corpse, is evil. Three days after death the soul is weighed in the scales of justice. If good wins, it is led across the Bridge of Judgment by a beautiful maiden; if evil wins it is led by an ugly old woman, and falls off the bridge and into hell. A corpse must be kept away and touched only by professional attendants of a low caste. (In Judaism too the priestly caste, the *Kohanim*, may not come into the presence of a dead body.) The purifying elements, fire and water, may also not touch the dead, so burial at sea, or burning, are forbidden. Traditionally the dead are offered to vultures to destroy. This tradition created difficulties for Zoroastrians in the West, who eventually turned to cremation as the answer.

A few believers came to Britain in the eighteenth century, but it was not until the middle of the nineteenth that a community was formed in London, some seeking higher education here or a knowledge of industry and commerce to take back to India. They also organised the first Indian cricket team to tour England!

In Zoroastrianism there is, as in several other religions, a formal cere- mony of confirmation to welcome a young person into the community. It involves putting on the special white garment, the *sudre*, and the *kusti*, the sword-belt of faith, when special prayers are said. It is not a missionary religion, so followers do not try to convert others. There is no known case of a white Anglo-Saxon being initiated into the faith in Britain.

The problem of establishing a house of prayer was difficult as most of the Zoroastrians in London were impoverished students, and it was not until 1929 that a Zoroastrian House was bought to provide an administrative centre as well as prayer rooms and lodgings where visitors could stay. The religion was originally a nomadic one so temples were not essential. Prayers are said in the home or in a simple prayer room, but as Zoroastrians have grown in wealth and stature they have become accustomed to building temples where they have settled. There is none so far in London. Fire is an important element in the faith, though it is not worshipped, as some seem to believe. Within the prayer room fire is kept in a sanctuary and regularly refuelled. There are no congregational prayers; each worshipper prays alone. The Zoroastrian Trust Funds of Europe is the oldest established religious voluntary organisation in the UK of South Asian origin, and Zoroastrians are recognised as one of the nine world faith communities in the UK though they are the smallest.

Muslims

In her book, *Muslims in Britain*, Sophie Gilliat-Ray takes the history of Muslims in this country as far back as Bede, but Bede's view of Islam seems confined to the Saracens fighting the Christians in the Middle East during the Crusades. He makes no reference to ever having encountered a Muslim in this country. Little direct contact between Britain and Islam can be traced here until commercial links blossomed in the nineteenth century. Certainly there were a few Turkish diplomatic associations, Lascar sailors and slaves. Queen Victoria's Muslim servant, Abdul Karim, was taken into the royal household where he enjoyed a close relationship with her, teaching her Hindustani and Urdu. She gave him the title of Munshi (teacher) – he was often called her Indian Secretary – and they had long conversations on history, philosophy and religion. He was not popular with the other servants and her advisers were wary of his influence on her. He returned to India and after her death her heir, Edward VII, destroyed his papers. A film about their relationship came out in 2017.

Other high-born Muslims did come to London either to expand their own commercial activities, on diplomatic missions or to educate their sons. Many had been working for the East India Company, but in 1833 the Company ceased trading commercially with India, leaving the subcontinent under direct British control. Missionaries hoped to evangelise the Hindus and Muslims (then known usually as Mahometans), and the British government tried to turn India away from neutrality to Christian belief. The Viceroy took practical control, but the gradual westernization of the nation resulted in mutiny against British rule. The resentment against the behaviour of the British, who knew little of the customs of the country and cared less, turned into violent uprisings across the continent. One such provocative step taken by the British was the issue of new paper cartridges greased with animal fat. The end of the cartridge had to be bitten off before it could be fired, which offended the religious sensibilities of both Muslims and Hindus. The resulting war was bitter, with many Europeans and Indians killed. In 1858 the India Act transferred the East India Company's holdings to the British government, under a Secretary of State for India, advised by a Council. In 1877 the Queen was proclaimed Empress of India, at her own wish. The last Emperor of India was George VI.

It is easy to assume that the increasing number of Muslims coming into Britain in the nineteenth century came from the same part of the Middle and Far East, spoke the same language or worshipped in a similar way. But this is far from the truth. Certainly the majority of the early arrivals had links with British colonial control, but their homes were as wide apart as Malaya (now Malaysia), the Arab peninsula, parts of Africa and the Mediterranean. They spoke a dozen different languages and many more dialects. As the British colonies grew (coloured pink on the schoolchildren's maps), so did the native Muslim population in Britain increase.

The opening up of the Suez Canal in 1869 made Arabia and Africa accessible to shipping and shortened the journey east. Britain occupied most of Egypt and East Africa, much of Malaya and the Indian subcontinent. She needed cheap labour and the Muslim nations were among those who could provide it. Once here they could settle and bring over their families. They sought wealth, comfort and education, and they found it in the cities of Scotland and the North of England, where industrialisation was at its height, and of course in London.

A myth exists that the first mosque in Britain was in Cardiff, recorded in 1860, but this seems to have been due to an error by the Register of Religious Sites. The Pan-Islamic Society from India had a branch in London as early as 1886, known as the Anjuman-I-Islam, with facilities for communal gatherings and for prayer, but the first mosque in Britain was in Liverpool, in a house taken by an Englishman, William Henry Quilliam, later known as Sheikh Abdullah Quilliam. He was brought up as a Methodist but converted to Islam after a visit to North Africa. The Liverpool Muslim Institute had prayer rooms, madrassas (schools for boys and girls), a library and museum. But for Londoners the first purpose-built mosque in south-east England was at Woking, established in 1889 as the Shah Jehan Mosque. Ten years later the mosque, now almost disused, was nearly sold, but a wealthy Indian took the case to court, arguing that it was consecrated ground akin to a church. He was able to buy and to create the Woking Muslim Mission. The first purpose-built mosque in London itself was the Fazl Mosque at Southfields, built in 1923, and the largest, the London Central Mosque in Regents Park, opened in 1977.

The majority of the Muslims in London in the second half of the nineteenth century were labourers or sailors. They lived in the poorer areas such as the East End, but the Christian missionaries were active there in their

attempts to convert them. Considerable prejudice by their white neighbours, many of them Irish or Jewish, made their lives hard. It is estimated
that by the end of the century some 10,000 Muslims lived in Britain, about
two thirds in London.

The East End

According to Peter Ackroyd, the phrase 'East End' was not invented until
the 1880s, and he suggests that this area of Flood Plain gravels goes back
some 15,000 years.[10] It has certainly been inhabited since Anglo-Saxon
times and seems always to have been that part of the city where the desti-
tute, sick and criminal elements of the population made their homes. Small
factories along the river bank produced chemicals, dyes and smelting works.
Workshops for leather and tanning, metalwork, match production and other
small industries all produced foul-smelling fumes, dirt and debris. Only
those who could afford no better would settle in such surroundings. Among
them were the immigrants, fleeing from persecution or hoping for better
times. The Huguenots had lived in the network of narrow streets off
Whitechapel High Street, to be followed by the Jews who used the silk
weavers' high windows for their tailoring sweatshops where the light was good.

Jewish Immigration

Some of London's Jewish community, unable to afford the affluent homes
in the western part of the city, had settled in the East End at the end of the
eighteenth century. But the anti-Semitism and poverty of Eastern Europe,
particularly the pogroms of Tsarist Russia, had forced many more out of the
stetls (villages) of Poland, Lithuania, Latvia and the Ukraine, to search
for a better life in the West. Their links of kinship and religion brought
thousands to London's East End. They soon established a community of
Yiddish-speaking Jewish families, many crammed into one house, eking out
a meagre living as tailors, leather and glass workers, manufacturers of
gloves, furniture and ironware, in which whole families participated in every
hour of daylight, except of course the Sabbath.

The living conditions of the immigrants in the East End left a great deal
to be desired. Public hygiene was almost non-existent and the occupants of
the slums had neither the knowledge nor the money to improve them. Lloyd
P. Gartner, in *The Jewish Immigrant in England 1870-1914*, says that the Jews
brought to the East End

> not only an extra measure of overcrowding but a seeming ignorance and indif-
> ference to sanitary requirements. Accumulated and uncollected refuse lay in

rotting piles inside and outside houses, while the interiors were often dank and malodorous from foul water closets, leaking ceilings, untrapped sinks and cracked, moist walls.[11]

The majority of these Jews were orthodox, obeying the laws of Moses in every particular, as strictly as they could, with little contact with their non-Jewish neighbours. Small synagogues sprang up on every street corner close to their homes, as Jews do not travel on the Sabbath. They were the traditional Ashkenazi Jews of Eastern Europe. It is estimated that some 20,000 Jews lived in London by the middle of the nineteenth century. They set up kosher butchers, a *mikvah* (ritual bath) and a cheder (religious school). The language taught and spoken was Yiddish. The poverty was extreme and universal, but communal relationships were unbreakable – what one family could afford, it shared with others. There was a soup kitchen set up in 1854, first in Leman Street and then in Brune Street – the fascia, engraved Soup Kitchen for the Jewish Poor (5662 –1902), is still preserved. As early as 1795 the Jewish Hospital was established in Mile End, and an Orphan Asylum in 1831. The Jews Free School had been founded in 1732, originally for orphan boys only, but a permanent site in Bell Lane, for boys and girls, opened in 1880. With the traditional respect of the Jews for education, these families determined to send their children to school whatever the cost and in whatever state the young pupils might appear. Some of the most vivid descriptions of the Jews of the East End appear in the novels of Israel Zangwill. In *The Children of the Ghetto* he speaks of those schoolchildren.

> They came in a great straggling procession recruited from every lane and by-way, big children and little children, boys in blackening corduroy, and girls in washed-out cotton; tidy children and ragged children; children in great shapeless boots gaping at the toes; sickly children, sturdy children, and diseased children; bright-eyed children and hollow-eyed children; quaint sallow foreign-looking children, and fresh-coloured English-looking children; with great pumpkin heads, with oval heads, with pear-shaped heads; with old men's faces, with cherubs' faces, with monkeys' faces.[12]

The Rothschild family were responsible for a great deal of the philanthropy in the East End, helping their fellow religionists by improving their living conditions. They formed the Four Per Cent Industrial Dwellings Company, offering modest but clean and pleasant blocks of flats. 'It is estimated that if the rentals were based on a net return of 4 per cent, excellent accommodation consisting of two rooms, a small scullery, and w.c. could be supplied at a weekly rental of five shillings per tenement.'[13] The Jewish community in the East End remained vibrant and well-maintained until the bombs of World War II almost obliterated the area. After the war it became the home of more immigrants, this time from Pakistan and Bangladesh; mosques replaced the synagogues. The Jewish presence in this ancient part of London has now almost completely disappeared.

The Salvation Army

That same urge to help those in need was the moving force behind the creation of the Salvation Army. William Booth and his wife Catherine came to London from Nottingham in 1865 and began their Christian Mission in the East End. To begin with they referred to their band of workers as 'a volunteer army', but it soon became the Salvation Army, with military uniforms, ranks and ideals. Booth was the General. They were prepared to fight a just war against ignorance, poverty and social degradation. They took their mission out of the churches into the streets, accompanied by brass bands and military music.

The movement soon spread across England and overseas, reaching out not only to those anxious to be saved, but to men and women, many of them young, who became courageously involved. These willing helpers offered food and shelter as well as spiritual renewal. Moreover, they were prepared to confront criminals, drunks and ruffians, and to give practical assistance to the socially deprived.

Booth himself was a radical – he had been influenced in his youth by the Chartists – but he had a poor education and no love for culture, the arts or philosophy. His wife, a life-long invalid, was a firm supporter of the women's rights movement. The Booths and their followers often met with ridicule verging on violence, but their relief work was much admired. They set up shelters for the poor, a match factory with good working conditions in the East End and rescue homes for women oppressed by prostitution and domestic violence. A strong Christian faith lay behind all their actions and the fact that the 'Sally Army' is still in existence today is a tribute to that faith.

Hinduism

Another religion burgeoning in London during the nineteenth century was Hinduism. Hinduism is the oldest living religion in the world. Unlike almost all others, it has no single founder, no central structure or system of government. Hindus recognise one Supreme Being (Brahman) with three primal aspects, denominated 'gods' called Brahma, Vishnu, Shiva. In this way they are in harmony with other mainstream traditions which acknowledge the One and the Three or Unity and Trinity. Myths and legends tell the story of Hindu beliefs. They are enshrined in the Vedas, the stories or hymns which form the nearest to a Bible or Koran for Hindu worshippers. They date from about 1200 BCE. One of their greatest jewels is The Bhagavad Gita, part of the Hindu epic Mahabharata. The essence of Hindu beliefs lies in truth, purity, compassion and peace. Hinduism is in fact a conglomerate religion, welcoming many different ideas and traditions, though all accept a Supreme God. As the faith spread from India to other nations and cultures, so it acquired additional forms, but within the extended religion is the essence of the soul, the life-force. It can pass from one human to another, and indeed to animals, leading to a belief in re-incarnation and to the acceptance of the animal kingdom as equally holy as that of man.

The Indians who came to London in the nineteenth century were often high-born Hindus, princes, scholars or wealthy traders, seeking – as did the Muslims – to improve their education and their commercial expertise or to investigate the western world. Among them was Sri Aurobindo, who studied at Cambridge. He was an Indian philosopher, poet and nationalist who guided a spiritual evolution and was the originator of Integral Yoga. His ashram, near Pondicherry, is still visited by thousands of westerners every year. Kathleen Raine, the poet, who visited India on several occasions, questioned whether an Indian poet could truly write poetry in the English language. She found Aurobindo's poetry lacking in the 'aura, penumbra and overtones' that is the true language of men. 'Perhaps it is precisely in his so accurate use of English words, yet without these resonances, over-tones, auras, that Sri Aurobindo fails; nor is his correct use of the English language related to any speech really used by men.'[14]

Some of the Indian immigrants brought their families and their servants. After the Queen was named Empress of India, England enjoyed a love affair with the Indian subcontinent. Victoria had a 'Durbar Room' built at Osborne House, and many wealthy homes were decorated in the 'Hindoo' style. The journey to and from India was much shorter after the Suez Canal was opened, and many young English women of good family travelled out to India to find a husband from among the lonely civil servants and junior officers. These girls were known as the Fishing Fleet[15] and some inter-married with the Indian families they found there.

In London

Like most immigrants, Indian Hindus worshipped first of all in their own homes. It was not until the 1920s that the first purpose-built Temple was founded near Earl's Court, and it is claimed today that the impressive Neasden Temple, the Shri Swaminarayan Mandir, is the first traditional Indian temple in Europe. This beautiful building is a masterpiece of traditional Hindu design and exquisite workmanship that rises serenely amid London's iconic skyline. Using 5,000 tons of Carrara marble and Indian Ambaji marble and the finest Bulgarian limestone, it was hand carved in India before being assembled in London.[16]

This huge white 'wedding-cake' of a building can accommodate thousands of worshippers. Prayers are said every day in the Mandir, with larger services at the weekends and on festivals. Hindus pray individually, led by orange-robed priests (sadhus), women and men together (there are no women priests). The temples and prayer rooms contain no seats, except for the infirm, but prayers are said standing, kneeling or sitting on the floor, the sadhus' chanting, accompanied by musical instruments. Prayers are said daily at home by each member of the family separately. The followers of Swaminarayan, who started his particular Hindu sect in 1792 at the age of eleven, are remarkable for their peaceful and loving way of life; they are vegetarians and hold the life of all living things to be sacred. There is no religious court or legal system. It is apparently unnecessary. Their founder was determined to imbue his people with the highest moral values, with compassion for all. The old Hindu customs of suttee, where a widow throws herself on her husband's funeral pyre, the killing of new-born baby girls, the caste system and other evil practices, were forbidden; education for women was introduced and charitable giving became a vital part of the faith. The language of the followers of Swaminarayan is Gujerati, spoken at home and in the temple, though naturally the second and third generation speak good English. The Neasden Temple is one of six in London, which welcomes visitors including school parties; it plays an important part in inter-faith relations.

More obvious additions to London's colourful street scene were the bands of orange-robed devotees of Krishna, waving tambourines and chanting their mantra 'Hare Krishna' as they walked along Oxford Street. Bhaktivedanta Manor, near Watford, is the UK headquarters of the Hare Krishna movement. It was donated to the movement by the Beatle George Harrison.

CHAPTER XXI

World War I

London after Victoria

WHEN THE OLD QUEEN DIED in 1901, many Englishmen felt that the country had died with her. The longest reigning monarch had represented integrity in family life, the British Empire and the British way of life, with the sovereign as Head of the Church. The Anglican Church was aware of fundamental changes in the beliefs and religious practices of the majority of its parishioners. The Commission on Ecclesiastical Discipline, set up by Prime Minister A.J. Balfour in 1904, concluded, 'The law of public worship in the Church of England is too narrow for the religious life of the present generation.'[1] It went on to recommend that change must come and come quickly. It suggested improvements to the Book of Common Prayer and inaugurated the Church Assembly to include lay members.

Political life was changing too. Women were fighting for the vote, and early socialists formed a strong group, excited by Karl Marx's writings and his daughter Eleanor's activism. London was in many areas pitifully poor and miserable. The working class movement arose from the appalling living conditions of many Londoners, particularly in the East End, now becoming a hotbed of discontent and political rebellion.

The Theosophical Society

The influence on English faith of Eastern religions led to the establishment of societies which preferred to interpret their beliefs differently from traditional church practice. One of the largest and longest-lived was the Theosophical Society. Founded in New York by Helen Blavatsky and Henry Olcott, it had a thriving branch in England, and established its headquarters near Madras in India. Blavatsky believed in full freedom of religion, whatever its source. The three Objects of the Society were to encourage the study of Comparative Religion, Science and Philosophy, to form a Universal Brotherhood without distinction of race, creed, sex or colour, and to investigate Nature's 'unexplained Laws' and the powers latent in humanity. Freedom of thought and its expression lay behind the Society's principles.

Blavatsky awaited the imminent arrival of the 'World Teacher' who would appear on earth to direct the higher evolution of mankind. The strong mystical and spiritual faith of her fellow Theosophists derived in large part from oriental influences. She was succeeded as President by Annie Besant, a Londoner, known particularly for her fight for women's suffrage. Besant adopted a young Indian boy, Jiddu Krishnamurti, whom she believed was the personification of the 'World Teacher', although he refused to accept the role. To this end the Order of the Star in the East was formed, but the Order was disbanded by Krishnamurti himself when he came to England. His teachings and religious thinking, relying on inner meditation, are still revered in many parts of the world. Besant settled in India where she became a member of the Indian National Congress. She claimed that Krishnamurti was the new Messiah, which he himself denied.

National Secular Society

Some of these societies were formed by those who wished to stand altogether clear of religion. The National Secular Society was founded in 1866. Its leader, Charles Bradlaugh, an atheist, was a political philosopher, following in the footsteps of Jeremy Bentham. Bentham's Utilitarianism was a non-religious moral philosophy, arising from the eighteenth century Enlightenment in France, and taken up by John Stuart Mill. Bentham's often quoted phrase 'The greatest happiness for the greatest number' – the touchstone for Utilitarians – was actually first coined by Francis Hutcheson in his *Inquiry into the Original of our Ideas of Beauty and Virtue*. Bentham's version was 'the greatest good to the greatest number which is the measure of right and wrong.'

Bradlaugh was instrumental in changing the oath to enable non-Christians to take their seats in Parliament, when the right to affirm passed into law. He believed in a non-religious society including the disestablishment of the Church – he was a fervent Republican – as well as the freedom of the press. With Annie Besant he published *The Fruits of Philosophy* – an early treatise on birth control, forty years before Marie Stopes's *Married Love*. Bradlaugh was the last man to be imprisoned, for his atheism, in the prison cell beneath Big Ben, though there is an urban myth that Emmeline Pankhurst occupied a cell there in 1902. The National Secular Society is still fighting for the cause of non-religious participation in politics and culture, against the BBC's excessive attention to religion, religious education in schools and the disestablishment of the Church. It was instrumental in achieving the abolition of the Blasphemy Laws in 2008.

Humanism

The British Humanist Association was formed in 1896, originally as the Union of Ethical Societies. Early Humanists were those who studied subjects such as literature and philosophy as opposed to theology. However, Humanists today hold no belief in religion, and turn instead to moral values, initiating ethical groups to exchange views and ideologies. They are committed to no political ideas, though a key value is that of the individual's right to differ from accepted laws in such matters as abortion and euthanasia. Bertrand Russell, an eminent Humanist, wrote that Man's true freedom 'lies in the determination to worship only the God created by our own love of the good, to respect only the heaven which inspires the insight of our best moments.'[2]

As well as their devotion to ethical values, Humanists are also prepared to campaign for their beliefs. They too fought for an end to the Blasphemy Laws and to compulsory religious education in schools. They were strongly represented in the Peace Movement, and supported the suffragettes. Humanists can conduct funerals – funerals have no legal status – and weddings, though these are not legally recognised.

Paganism

Strictly speaking Paganism is a theology rather than a religion. Among the most ancient of beliefs, its followers see a divine power in nature and all that surrounds it. They draw on many traditional religions and practices, such as witchcraft, Celtic tradition, Druidism and ecology. Some take their ideas from oriental religions, some from Scandinavian religious history and others from beliefs handed down from early times in rural communities. Paganism has become a part of modern life, with Pagan weddings and funerals, hospital and prison visiting and interfaith relations. In 1971 the Pagan Federation was formed to promote and explain Pagan belief.

Jehovah's Witnesses

Religious groups outside the accepted churches were growing by the end of the nineteenth century. One such was the Jehovah's Witnesses. The sect was founded by Charles Russell, an American Adventist, believing in the imminent Second Coming of Christ. He launched the magazine *Watchtower*, and soon the Witnesses had spread to many countries. Russell ordained that the world would end first in 1874 and later in 1914. This too had to be amended. Witnesses are known for their determined door-to-door evangelism and for their literal interpretation of the Bible. They reject the

Trinity and await Armageddon, when God will triumph over Satan and only the Witnesses will be saved. They do not celebrate Christmas or Easter, refuse military service and are wary of national authority. They will not agree to blood transfusions, nor take any stimulants. The term 'church' is replaced by 'Freedom Hall'. There are several in London, some in converted houses, others custom built. They own large areas of land and houses in Mill Hill in North London.

Christian Science

Another form of Christian belief to come from America was Christian Science. Mary Baker Eddy founded the Church of Christ Scientist in 1879, with herself as Chief Pastor. She based her faith on the Bible, believing that ill-heath and disease could be cured by prayer rather than medicine. Other such churches soon followed, with a strong reliance on reading the Bible and biblical texts. Each church has a Reading Room and services of healing are an important part of the Scientists' practice. Their journal, the *Christian Science Monitor*, is highly esteemed by those outside the faith, and has won several Pulitzer prizes. Mary Baker Eddy's own book, *Science and Health with Key to the Scriptures*, has sold millions of copies.

The first Christian Science services held in London took place in 1894 though there had been practitioners in Ireland some time before that. Christian Scientists, though refusing help from doctors, are not unwilling to seek help from dentists, opticians and obstetricians. There are several Christian Science churches in London, the biggest being those in Curzon Street and Kensington.

Rosicrucians

Another group of mystics whose beliefs verged on the occult were the Rosicrucians, whose emblem is the 'Rosy Cross'. Allied to the Freemasons, they were an ancient cult, their origins to be found in German folklore. Their beliefs lay in gaining a more penetrating view of the inner self which would lead to greater wisdom, a more moral and emotional maturity and eventually to a deep sense of peace. They held public lectures, met to exchange views and later set up an online bookshop. They do not claim to be a religion but welcome members of any faith. The Rosicrucian Order was re-established in the Canary Islands in 1988.

The Catholics Return to London

In 1850 Pope Pius IX issued a Bull, *Universalis Ecclesiae*, which restored to England the structure of the Catholic Church, restoring the diocesan hierarchy into four districts, London, Midland, Northern and Western. With the relaxation of many of the strictures against them by the Catholic Relief Act of 1829, thousands returned to the faith. Many came from immigrant Irish families, some were Anglicans preferring the old faith of their ancestors. 'The time has arrived,' the Bull stated, 'for restoring in England the ordinary form of ecclesiastical government as freely constituted in other nations, where no particular cause necessitates the ministry of Vicars Apostolic.'[3]

London constituted the Metropolitan Archdiocese of Westminster and the diocese of Southwark. Westminster was to have its own cathedral, this time a Catholic one. Its first Catholic Archbishop for three hundred years was Cardinal Nicholas Wiseman. A law refusing an episcopal title to anyone outside the Anglican church was passed but quickly fell into disuse.

London's Anglican community, too, was subject to change, The Union of Benefices Act was passed in 1860 to reduce the number of parishes, for the city's residential population was decreasing. The coming of the railways – and later the underground – enabled many of her workers to live outside the city. The construction work necessitated the intrusion into burial grounds and many graves had to be disturbed, their occupants re-interred in the huge City of London Cemetery near Epping Forest. It now contains nearly a million graves and anyone can be buried there regardless of religion or connection with the city. It has been designated a Grade I property by English Heritage. Some twenty-two churches were demolished over the next fifty years. Many which remained were destroyed by German bombs in the blitz on London.

Not all of England welcomed the return of the Catholics. There was no Lord George Gordon to lead a riot, but scuffles broke out across London, Catholic windows were smashed and effigies of Cardinal Wiseman and the Pope were burned in the streets. Lord Russell, the Prime Minister, wrote to the Bishop of Durham on the anniversary of the Gunpowder Plot, 'I agree with you in considering the late aggression of the Pope upon our Protestantism as insolent and insidious, and therefore I feel as indignant as you do.'[4] He asserted that the majority 'looked with contempt on the mummeries of superstition and with scorn at the laborious endeavours which Catholics are now making to confine the intellect and enslave the soul.'[5]

Westminster Cathedral

Cardinal Wiseman was succeeded in 1865 by Henry Edward Manning. From being an Anglican priest and a Tractarian – and a close friend of Newman and Wilberforce – Manning felt himself drawn to the Roman Church and was made a Cardinal and second Archbishop of Westminster. In 1884 he purchased a large plot of land in the newly developed Victoria area of London. It had originally been part of the marshy estates of Westminster Abbey, but after the Reformation it was sold off and eventually became Tothill Fields Prison. Manning did not live to see his plans for a Catholic Cathedral come to fruition, but his successor, Cardinal Herbert Vaughan bought a further stretch of land, once the prison had been demolished, and chose as his architect John Francis Bentley. The foundation stone of the new Cathedral was laid in the summer of 1895 and it was dedicated to the Most Precious Blood of our Lord Jesus Christ. The building is in early Byzantine style; according to the official booklet this was to avoid any comparison with the splendid Gothic Abbey, not far away, and because

> Byzantine churches allow for a large uncluttered space, most suitable to the Catholic liturgy, and because decoration in Byzantine churches is applied, rather than integral to the architecture and so they can be built quickly and relatively inexpensively, leaving the decoration to the resources of subsequent generations.[6]

Apart from the beauty of the building itself, with the extensive use of green granite and blood red marble (for the pillars of the nave) the interior is dominated by the huge cross, nine metres high above the sanctuary. Among the building's greatest features are the extraordinary mosaics, designed by leading modern artists and the 'Fourteen Stations of the Cross' carved in stone by Eric Gill and generally considered among his greatest works.

The first regular services were celebrated in 1903 and in the same year Edward Elgar conducted there the first London performance of his setting of Newman's *Dream of Gerontius*. At the time of its conception, when Catholicism was still suspect, the Cathedral was partially hidden by the buildings in front of it, but in 1975 a spacious piazza was constructed, opening up a view of the north front from Victoria Street.

Southwark Cathedral

Two years after Westminster Cathedral opened its doors, London gained its third cathedral, this time an Anglican one across the river at Southwark. It had formerly been the Church of St Mary Overie (over the water). Stow speaks of it as 'of old time, long before the Conquest, a house of sisters, founded by a maiden named Mary.'[7] He says it was later converted into a college of priests and then a church for Augustinian canons. For centuries it was allowed to fall into disrepair – it was renamed St Saviour's – until in 1822 restoration began, though somewhat impeded by the construction of the new London Bridge and by the suggestion of the Bridge Committee that it should be demolished. A new nave was built to a design by Arthur Blomfield, which Nikolaus Pevsner called

> a sadly uninspired copy of the Chancel in which the thirteenth century design had remained, although here and in the other medieval parts also, the restorers have relentlessly removed all those surface qualities which make a building lovable besides being respected.[8]

In fact its small size gives it an informality often lost in larger buildings, and it is dear to the hearts of the inhabitants of Southwark. It contains a memorial to Shakespeare who lived in the parish (his brother Edmund is buried there) and the Shakespeare Window has representations of some of the characters in his plays. The Cathedral is noted for its musical tradition and now that the South Bank has been developed to provide a centre for restaurants, the arts and for visitors, the building plays an important part in welcoming them to the other side of the river. In July 2017, after a terrorist attack on London Bridge, the Cathedral was damaged by the police hunting the perpetrators, but a memorial service for those killed in the attack was held there shortly afterwards.

Caring for London

London was by now an amorphous sprawling ragbag of a city. Its individuality, formerly the keystone of its character, was more of an impediment to its future development as the largest, wealthiest, most respected city in Europe. The majority of those working there went home elsewhere at the end of the day, taking with them the community spirit which had created it. Eastern London, covering Hackney, Shoreditch, Whitechapel, Stepney, south down to the river and east to the docks, was still an appalling place to live. Zangwill's novels cover that part of the region largely occupied by poverty-stricken Jews, who had at least a communal spirit and a tradition of caring for each other. Arthur Morrison, however, describes the slums around Shoreditch, which he calls The Jago, in terms which do not attempt to disguise the squalor, filth, cruelty, drunkeness and crime. In *A Child of the Jago* he says,

> The hot, heavy air lay, a rank oppression, on the contorted forms of those who made for sleep on the pavement; and in it, and through it all, there rose

from the foul earth and the grimed walls a close, mingled stink – the odour of the Jago.[9]

The churches and other religious organisations did their part to help. Many of the impoverished clergy working in the miserable parishes spent their days and nights trying to improve the lot of their parishioners. The Rev G.C. Daw, vicar of St Mary's Spital Square, was interviewed in 1895 on his work in the parish. He was asked about those who lived there now that its great days of the silk weavers were over.

> The weavers are all gone and with them the old glory of the place has departed … and factory life at the East End of London, even under the best conditions, is not what we should like it to be. You asked me what class our people belong to. We have a good number of factory hands, and of respectable artisans, but we have still more of the lower classes, such as market porters, dock labourers, costermongers and the like. Our best people dwell in the Norton Folgate part of the parish; but even there we still have a few courts. The Old Artillery Ground, however, is now quite a poor district. The streets are small, and the houses in them are nearly all let out in single rooms while the courts show a still lower order of things. Single rooms are a special feature of this part, and frequently we find a whole family huddled together in one room.[10]

The vicar goes on to talk of his parish work. He is asked about his relations with the Jewish community. He was Vice-Principal of the London Jews Society and is interested in his Jewish neighbours but adds, 'It will be a great joy to me if I am permitted to bring some of my Hebrew parishioners to a knowledge of the Lord Jesus as the true Messiah.'[11]

Not all of London was subject to the deprivation of the East End. The capital was the financial centre of the Western world and the Mecca of a flourishing tourist trade. Some four and a half million people lived there, with great buildings arising on sites formerly occupied by small workshops, modest houses and narrow courts and alleyways. New department stores, commercial offices, hotels and government buildings were appearing in the wide streets of the West End. Lyons teashops nestled between the more imposing restaurants and electric trams ran through the main streets. Visitors from the New World were sophisticated travellers, who expected modern plumbing, elegant shops and comfortable transport. By the beginning of the twentieth century Englishmen too, if they were reasonably well off, were demanding comfort, cleanliness and a healthy standard of living.

The Emancipation of Women

The fight for women's independence was already making great strides in the second half of the nineteenth century. The first woman doctor had to study in Scotland where Elizabeth Garret Anderson qualified in 1865, under the auspices of the Society of Apothecaries. Women's education was now being taken seriously, with Queen's College in Harley Street the first for women, founded in 1847 and aimed at governesses – the teaching of mathematics to girls was considered 'dangerous'. This was followed two years later by Bedford College established in London as a further education college for women.

Frances Buss, a former student of Queen's College, founded the North London Collegiate School for Girls, the first girls' school to offer girls the same educational opportunities as boys; she is believed to have been the first to use the term Headmistress. A fellow student at Queen's was Dorothea Beale, who became Principal of Cheltenham Ladies College. These two great single minded educationalists gave rise to the verse:

> Miss Buss and Miss Beale Cupid's darts do not feel.
> How different from us, Miss Beale and Miss Buss.

The first Married Women's Property Act was passed into law, enabling women to retain their own property instead of ceding it to their father or husband.

The Church was slow to follow. The first woman to take religious vows in the Church of England was Marian Rebecca Hughes. She was instrumental in reintroducing an order of nuns to the Anglican Church, the Sisters of Mercy. This was first suggested by Edward Pusey, in 1839. Marian established a convent at Oxford, the Society of the Holy and Undivided Trinity, where she became Mother Superior. However the first English woman minister, a Unitarian, was Gertrude von Petzold. Born in Prussia, she studied at Manchester College, Oxford, where she qualified in 1904. She was invited to lead the Free Christian (Unitarian) Church in Leicester. A fine speaker and a convinced suffragette, 'she argued powerfully that in the twentieth century women's right to prophesy and minister should be restored.'[12]

Votes for Women

After the election of 1906 when the Liberals came to power under Henry Campbell-Bannerman, the struggle for women's rights gained new momentum, with hunger strikes, violence and civil disobedience. Many of those in favour of women's suffrage felt that the demonstrations and protests did no good to the cause. The 'Cat and Mouse Act' allowed women prisoners to be released when they became ill, only to be rearrested when they recovered.

An interesting feature of the movement was that its supporters came from all walks of life and most religious affiliations. Many came from wealthy families like the Pankhursts, though many of their contemporaries disapproved. Jenny Churchill, Winston's mother, wrote to her sister that the suffragettes were 'too odious ... Every night they make a disturbance and shriek and rant. They damage their own cause hopelessly.'[13]

The Anglican Church found itself in a quandary. Many churchmen strongly disapproved of the suffrage movement, hardly surprising for the more violent members had burned down churches in protest and set off a bomb in Westminster Abbey which damaged the Stone of Scone. Another in St Paul's Cathedral failed to go off. Some women were able to address church audiences, though not in church buildings. The Rev C.M. Davies went in 1875 to hear a lady speaker at the Polytechnic (reserved seats cost half-a-sovereign!). She seems to have been a little overwhelming, though clearly very sincere. 'Dear precious people,' she burst forth, 'I stand here not in my own power, but, God helping me, in gratitude to Him who shed his blood that I might be washed pure and white. I would lay down my life that you may have hope.'[14]

Some well-to-do Jewish women also joined the fight. During the Service for the Day of Atonement, three women stood up in the gallery of their synagogue (they sat separately from the men) and shouted 'May God forgive Herbert Samuel and Rufus Isaacs (both Jewish members of the Cabinet) for delaying freedom to women. May God forgive them for consenting to the torture of women.' The *Jewish Chronicle* reported the fracas, commenting, 'Are there no lengths to which these quasi-demented creatures will not go?'[15]

The Catholics were more careful. They had not long gained their own emancipation and were nervous of where outright demonstration might lead them. Nevertheless the Catholic Women's Suffrage Society was founded in 1911 'to band together Catholics of both sexes, in order to secure the Parliamentary vote (for women) on the same terms as it is, or may be, granted to men.' They were supported by the Archbishop, Cardinal Vaughan, and worked closely with other churches and non-church members of the suffrage movement.

Even the eastern religions had their say. Princess Sophia Alexandra Duleep Singh, a Sikh, was the granddaughter of Maharajah Ranjit Singh, the 'Lion of the Punjab', and a goddaughter of Queen Victoria. She came to England and led a life of aristocratic luxury, while playing an active part in the development of modern India. She became involved in the fight for women's suffrage and on the death of Emmeline Pankhurst succeeded her as President of the Committee of the Suffragette Fellowship.[16]

Radicalism in London

There seems to be no clear evidence as to who first coined the phrase The Great Unrest, but it expressed neatly the state of England's working classes in the years leading up to the First World War. The Transport Workers Federation was founded in 1910 and together with the carters' and dockers' unions, its members came out solidly on strike for higher wages and better working conditions. There had been serious strikes before within living memory; perhaps the most damaging had been the dockers' strike of 1889 when starving men, desperate for their jobs, had been prepared to stop working to support their cause. The strike of the match girls two years earlier had drawn the nation's attention to the appalling conditions in which the girls were working. Annie Besant was involved in that too, writing an account of those conditions in her paper *The Link*.

By 1910, however, practical politics had changed forever. The ideologies promoted by socialists and communists drew working people into the realisation that there might perhaps be a better life if they were prepared to fight for it. To encourage them were the new Trades Unions, some Jewish in the East End, some Irish Catholic, helped by Cardinal Manning.

Russians in London

There was now a new influence affecting Londoners. Russian immigrants were coming into the capital in huge numbers to swell the already over-crowded slums of the East End. Many were Jews, fleeing the pogroms, to rejoin their relatives already here. But some were burning with the fire of revolution, ready to involve their British allies in their socialist fervour. These emigrés were not always the poor Jews from the *stetls* of Eastern Europe, but Marxist thinkers, anarchists for whom violence was their favourite weapon. Some were indeed Jews fleeing oppression, but many were literate intellectuals with no regard for any religious faith, or even contempt for it, as Marx had suggested.

The arrival in London of the anarchist movement (not all were Russian) coincided with what George Dangerfield has called *The Strange Death of Liberal England*. During the long reign of Queen Victoria and the short one of her son, England had stood steadily, sure of her place in the civilised world, containing 'a various collection of gold, stocks, Bibles, progressive thoughts and decent inhibitions.'[17] The death of Edward VII in 1910 heralded the uneasy approach of new thoughts and opinions: politics, religion, the workplace, all seemed less secure than they had been.

The Russian Social Democratic Labour Party held a conference in London in the summer of 1907. The venue was the Brotherhood Church in Southgate Road, Hackney. 'The Brotherhood' was a socialist movement which believed in the Sermon on the Mount, as Tolstoy had done, but not in Christ's divinity. It developed into a left-wing non-violent Christian association, and today has a smallholding in Stapleton, Yorkshire, which is farmed on organic and ecological principles. Among the delegates to the conference were Lenin, Trotsky, Stalin, Maxim Gorky and, from Germany, Rosa Luxemburg. Those present were Bolsheviks and Mensheviks who had seceded from the main Bolshevik alliance, and according to an observer present at the time, the majority of the Mensheviks were Jews. He added that one of the Bolsheviks 'observed in jest that the Mensheviks constituted a Jewish group while the Bolsheviks constituted a true Russian group, and therefore it wouldn't be a bad idea for us Bolsheviks to organise a pogrom in the party'.[18]

One Gentile who spoke up for the Jewish anarchist cause was Rudolf Rocker. He came to the East End of London from Germany, and learned Yiddish to be able to converse with his Jewish neighbours; he was appointed Editor of the newly founded Yiddish political journal *Arbeter Fraint*. When a revolution broke out in Russia in 1904-5, he wrote, 'It was incredible to me that people who had suffered so much in Russia, where Jews were treated as pariahs from the cradle to the grave, should retain such affectionate feeling for the country.'[19]

The Anglican Church

Meanwhile the Church of England was suffering a divisive situation arising from a new evaluation of its long held beliefs and forms of worship. What has been termed 'liberal theology' was creating a feeling of doubt in English churchgoers, not so much in their belief in God, but in the way in which the structure of that belief was put into practice. There was a dearth of new recruits to the clergy, and attendance at church was decreasing; daily prayers in upper class households, which included the servants, was almost a thing of the past, and Nonconformity was becoming a more welcome outlet for faith than the established Church. In London particularly, neighbourhood churches and all that went with them – social integration, family convention and festival celebrations – were becoming notably less important, as Londoners spent their non-working time away from the city.

Nevertheless the upper classes still went to church in top hats and pretty dresses and the socialist dream did not conflict with the religious habit of most of Britain, especially of the Nonconformists. Jeremy Paxman's witty and penetrating analysis of the Church of England got it right, maintaining that 'it is the maddening institution it is because that is how the English like their religion – pragmatic, comfortable and unobtrusive.'[20]

Among the intellectuals, the decadent world of Oscar Wilde and Aubrey Beardsley was more attractive than the Victorian ideal of religious affiliation. The historian Robert Ensor says, 'Creed sat lightly on the great majority in the middle and upper classes; the Bible lost its hold on them, and the volume of outward religious observance shrank steadily'.[21] The 'weekend' – a concept that dates back to 1639 – was a welcome part of English working life, as the five-day week became more common, with Londoners using their leisure time for entertainment. This meant that Sunday could be used for other purposes than going to church. Attractions for Sundays included the weekly meetings of the Independent Labour Party, for those with political interests. There were such distractions as the P.S.A. events (Pleasant Sunday Afternoons). These were Nonconformist chapel meetings, where families could listen to a speaker or to music. In some areas the orchestral concerts still continue; there is a small conventional amateur orchestra, operating out of the Methodist Church at Eltham Park.

The Coming of War

London's workers, and because of them most of the rest of the City, were too preoccupied with their own problems to take much heed of what was going on in other parts of the world. London was moving politically further to the left. The British Socialist Party was formed in 1911, and strikes were breaking out across the capital; the tailors of East London allied themselves with their more prosperous brothers in the West End, the railway and transport workers joined together with the miners to threaten the wellbeing of British people across the country.

In spite of the upheavals of the strikes, the suffragettes and the new politics of the East End, London (and England) seemed safe and secure from outside threat. Lloyd George declared, 'In the matter of external affairs, the sky has never been more perfectly blue.'[22]

And then came the bullet at Sarajevo. All the features that composed The Great Unrest were called into question. In the months leading up to the outbreak of war there were 937 strikes in Britain, with the likelihood of a General Strike imminent. Only one thing could prevent chaos and misery for London and it happened: war. To say that for all except possibly certain politicians and some military men, war was a surprise is to understate the case. Young men up at university, or in their first jobs, apprentices and postboys were unaware of what was to befall them. G.K. Chesterton's novel,

The Man Who was Thursday – A Nightmare, about anarchists in London, written some years before the war, is prefaced by a poem addressed to the writer and humourist Edmund Clerihew Bentley:

> A cloud was on the mind of men, and wailing went the weather,
> Yea, a sick cloud upon the soul when we were boys together.
> Science announced nonentity and art admired decay;
> The world was old and ended: but you and I were gay.[23]

1914-1918

As late as August 2nd, two days before the ultimatum to Germany expired, according to Sir Almeric Fitzroy, a distinguished civil servant, many of the members of the Cabinet felt that peace might yet be maintained. In his *Memoirs* he notes that Lord Morley (Lord President of the Council) still hoped that 'patience and diplomatic pressure at the right moment might yet avert the conflict.'[24] The Prime Minister, Herbert Asquith, told the King, 'Happily there seems to be no reason why we should be anything more than spectators.'[25] But as the hours passed hope faded. Winston Churchill, First Lord of the Admiralty at the time, wrote later,

> Once more now in the march of centuries, Old England was to stand forth in battle against the mightiest thrones and dominations. Once more in defence of the liberties of Europe and the common right must she enter upon a voyage of great toil and hazard across waters unchartered, towards coasts unknown, guided only by the stars.[26]

August 3rd was a Bank Holiday, and now aware of the looming danger, people were struggling to get home. Constance Peel, a journalist and writer, had an eye for the ridiculous. 'The King bids his chefs goodbye at Buckingham Palace, Cowes Regatta is abandoned ...'[27] The Ministry of Food issued War Cookery Recipes, including Oatmeal Rissoles, Jam Made with Saccharin and Rice Paste for Bread.

The war was not 'over by Christmas' nor by several Christmases later. All aliens over sixteen had to register at their local police station and show they were of good character and could speak English. As London was bombarded by Zeppelins and aeroplanes, people refused to take shelter but came out into the open to watch the skies. Warning systems were minimal: maroon rockets were fired when Zeppelins were seen heading towards the city, policemen on bicycles rushed around with signs reading 'Take Cover' and Boy Scouts blew bugles.

The Church of England and the War

Most churchmen were as incredulous as the rest of England when the doom-laden warnings of war came true. Their relationship with the German churches had been warm and friendly so they were appalled by the outbreak. On 2nd August British delegates to a church conference in Constance – the World Alliance for Promoting International Friendship Through the Churches – just managed to get home before the war got under way. Many were closely allied to the peace movement, but once the war started some felt their country needed their support. The Bishop of Hereford, John Percival, wrote to *The Times* after Germany's usurpation of Belgium, 'Our country had no choice but to take up the sword if honourable dealing was to have any chance of surviving in international affairs.'[28]

The Archbishop of Canterbury, Randall Davidson, supervised the prayers and forms of service for wartime use. Some were considered too violent – intended to strike the fear of God into the heart of the Kaiser – others too mild. The Bishop of London, Arthur Winnington-Ingram, was an energetic leader and an active participant in the war effort, urging Britain's fighting men on from the pulpit and even from the trenches. He was a skilled orator, recruiting volunteers and acting as chaplain to the London Rifle Brigade. He believed firmly in the cause, to fight the evil Germans, whom he hated passionately.

The Jews in the War

Other religions were less enthusiastic. Joseph Hertz served as Chief Rabbi throughout the war, though coming from Hungary he was not naturalised as British until 1915. He wrote a special prayer when war broke out, using almost Biblical terminology, 'The shout of the warrior and the roar of battle resounds to the ends of the earth because of the fury of the oppressor'. The German Jews of London had a particular problem as many of their brethren were fighting on the opposite side. Several wrote 'loyalty letters' to *The Times*. The Russian Jews were horrified at the thought of an alliance with the dreaded Tsarist regime. Londoners were suspicious of their Yiddish neighbours whose language was so nearly German. The proposition that the Jews should form their own fighting force met with considerable doubt in the government, but in 1917, following the success of the Jewish Zion Mule Corps at Gallipoli, it agreed to form a battalion of the Royal Fusiliers, known as the First Judaeans (to some the Royal Jewsiliers!). Isaac Rosenberg, the poet and artist, tried to join it but his applications seem to have been lost in red tape; he was clearly thinking of the 'Judaeans' when he wrote:

Through these pale cold days
What dark faces burn
Out of three thousand years
And their wild eyes yearn.

While underneath their brows
Like waifs their spirits grope
For the pools of Hebron again
For Lebanon's summer slope.

At least one Jewish soldier was awarded the V.C. for conspicuous bravery. Frank de Pass was Indian/Jewish by birth. There is a plaque to his memory in Victoria Embankment Gardens.

One of the first Jewish chaplains to serve in the British fighting forces was the Rev Michael Adler, 'a corpulent, red-bearded peaceable man', who travelled through the ranks in a specially commissioned car, inviting all Jewish troops to attend his Sunday services. These Services were held in all sorts of places, often in the open-air and in Y.M.C.A or Church Army huts as well as barns or ruined buildings. Adler later edited the *Jewish Book of Honour*, detailing records of all Jewish servicemen who served in the war.

Muslims' Contribution to the War

The Muslims, too, fought for their adopted country in the war. New research, commissioned by the British Muslim Heritage Centre based in Manchester, reveals that some 885,000 Muslims were recruited to fight for the Allies, over 89,000 losing their lives.

Hindus

The majority of Hindus fighting in the war came from India and served in Indian regiments, winning twelve Victoria Crosses. More than a million participated, but many were illiterate so that there is a dearth of letters home to tell their story. Many lie in France in unmarked graves, but the wounded were often sent back to Britain, usually Brighton, to recover. While they served, and in hospital, Indian soldiers were subject to a strict caste system, enforced by the British command. 'Untouchables' served as support staff. This and the fact that India lent more than a million pounds to the British treasury, was believed to militate towards independence, but it took thirty years to achieve it. Outside Brighton is a memorial to the cremation site of Hindus and Sikhs who fell in the war.

Conscientious Objectors

The treatment of those objecting to war in principle was in many cases a disgrace. Anyone who refused to fight on moral or religious grounds had to face a tribunal, often composed of military men. Many objectors were Quakers who were pacifists, and were often prepared to drive ambulances or take on other work to help the soldiers. If their applications were turned down by the tribunal and they refused military service, they had no choice other than prison. 'One outspoken tribunal councillor was heard to declare that "a man who would not help to defend his country and womankind is a coward and a cad"'.[29] If they did go to the front and disobeyed orders or refused to fight, they could be shot. At home they and their relatives were sent white feathers, a sign of cowardice, and some were abused in the streets. Many newspapers wrote contemptuous articles on the subject, and cartoons and caricatures showed the objectors as camp, limp-wristed dilettantes. Clifford Allen, the President of the No-Conscription Fellowship, told his tribunal, 'I believe in the inherent worth and sanctity of every human personality, irrespective of the nation to which a man belongs.'[30] In Tavistock Square there is a handsome slate stone monument raised to the memory of the Conscientious Objectors of the two World Wars; the inscription reads 'To all those who have established and are maintaining the right to refuse to kill. Their foresight and courage give us hope.'

The war dragged on for four long years, eating up in its voracious maw nearly a million British men and women, with even more French and Russians. The grave of the Unknown Soldier was unveiled in Westminster Abbey exactly two years after the Armistice was signed. The guard of honour was composed entirely of holders of the Victoria Cross. The Cenotaph in Whitehall commemorated Britain's loss. There are none alive today who fought in that war but one hundred years later, in 2016, the nation turned out in force to remember them.

CHAPTER XXII

Between the Wars

I gave my life for freedom – this I know:
For those who bade me fight had told me so.[1]

MANY OF THOSE RETURNING from the war felt betrayed by the military and the politicians who sent them into battle. Vera Brittain wrote, 'When the sound of victorious guns burst over London at 11am on 11th November 1918, the men and women who looked incredulously into each other's faces, did not cry jubilantly "We've won the war!"; they only said "The war is over".'[2] What had the fighting men and women come home to find? A shortage of housing, jobs and food. Many of their comrades were dead and 'the war to end all wars' must have seemed a waste of good Englishmen. The resentment against the conduct of the war was very real, and it was not the only misery that beset the nation. The influenza epidemic of 1918 killed nearly a quarter of a million people, many of them the youngsters who should have grown up to fill the vacancies left by the war dead. Lloyd George's government had to face strikes, mutiny in the army and dismay in its own ranks. Food rationing made matters worse. Viscountess Rhondda, remembering that time, wrote 'During January and February 1918 as many as a million people were standing weekly in queues in the London area alone, patiently waiting hour after hour for food which was often enough all gone before their turn came.'[3]

The welfare of the demobilising troops added to the problems. In France, at the beginning of the war, a British chaplain, Philip Clayton – known always as 'Tubby' – had set up at the transfer station at Poperinge a rest house for the weary troops. It was named Talbot House, after Lieutenant Gilbert Talbot, who had been killed, and referred to as TH, then, after the radio code of the time – T was Toc – as TocH. After the war its chapel was dismantled and taken to London where it was re-erected at All-Hallows-by-the-Tower. It later became a Trust to support ordinands for the Ministry and is still active, running visits to the original house in Poperinge, remembering Tubby Clayton and his work for the soldiers fighting in France.

Britain, however, had lost the stability of the pre-war years. Leonard

Woolf, Virginia's husband, wrote, 'By 1918 one had unconsciously accepted a perpetual public menace and darkness and had admitted into the privacy of one's mind or soul an iron fatalistic acquiescence in insecurity and barbarism.'[4]

Buddhism

One outcome of the War was to introduce another ancient religion into Britain, almost for the first time. There had been a few Buddhists in London, mainly from eastern nations, but not enough to form a community. At the outbreak of the War the whole of the Nepalese Army was placed at the disposal of the British Crown. Over 16,000 Nepalese Troops were subsequently deployed on operations on the North West Frontier and as garrison battalions in India to replace troops of the British Indian Army who had gone to fight overseas. Some one hundred thousand men enlisted in regiments of the Gurkha Brigade. They distinguished themselves particularly at Gallipoli but also in France, and on their return to England were stationed at Aldershot in Hampshire. Many were Hindus but some were Buddhists, and the town of Rushmoor, near to Aldershot, is still the home of the greatest number of Buddhists in the UK according to the most recent census. Most adhere to the school of Theravada, using the *Pali* Texts.

The first Buddhist Society was founded in 1907 with the first Buddhist Lodge in 1924. Christmas Humphreys was President. Humphreys (Christmas is a family name, but he was usually known as Toby) was a barrister whose interests extended beyond his practice. As Senior Treasury Counsel, he prosecuted in many famous cases, including those of Craig and Bentley, Ruth Ellis and Timothy Evans. He was convinced that the Earl of Oxford wrote Shakespeare's plays. He was a writer and poet, but it is as an early exponent of Buddhism that he is perhaps best known, publishing many books on the subject. His former London home is now The Zen Centre. Zen, a school of Chinese Buddhism, insists on rigorous meditation and the practice of Buddhism in personal life, with a particular emphasis on benefiting others. There are more than 150,000 Buddhists in England, believed to include Mick Jagger, Benedict Cumberbatch and Jonny Wilkinson.

The Pali texts, the basis of modern Buddhism, were translated into roman script and the Pali canon is the earliest Buddhist scripture, written in northern India about four hundred years after the Buddha died. It is referred to in Sanskrit as the Tripitaka, or 'three baskets' which include the rules of Buddhism, the writings and sayings of the Buddha, and the philosophy of Buddhist doctrine. They are all now available in English.

The most influential early work on the religion in English was *The Light of Asia* by Edwin Arnold. It was read by Charles H. Bennett, who then led the first Buddhist mission to England. He was known by his Pali name of Ananda Metteya. The difficulties of keeping to Buddhist vows in London when the mission arrived are described by Christmas Humphreys. A member of the Sangha (ordained community)

> was not allowed to sleep in a house where a woman slept; his food could only be eaten at specified hours, with nothing later than noon; he slept on a bed on the floor, to avoid breaking the precept against 'high and soft beds' ... he was not allowed to handle money so could never travel alone. But he wore at all times the bright yellow robes of the Sangha, and such a garb brought wondering crowds and ribald comment from costermongers and small boys.[5]

Bahá'is

Another small religious group which came from Iran, formerly Persia, to be represented in Britain and still has a following here was the Bahá'i faith. Their first leader, Bahaullah, took most of his adherents from the Babis of Iran, who in the nineteenth century had joined Sayyid Ali Muhammad Shirazi – the Bab – in forming a 'new' religion, believing in only one God; they also held that all mankind is united spiritually, so that every religion is joined in worshipping the one God, and all men are equal.

The Bahá'i message spread to England in 1910 where it acquired a small following, including later the potter Bernard Leach. When their leader, Shoghi Effendi died in London in 1957, the city became a place of pilgrimage for the faith; the first Bahá'i World Congress was held here in 1963. There is today a considerable number of Bahá'is in London and they are much respected for their belief in family stability, equality for women and integrity in social relations. When in 2009 Iran persecuted its Bahá'i leaders, many well-known writers and entertainers in this country expressed their disapproval in the press.

Sikhism

The ancient Sikh religion from Northern India came to London in the twentieth century, though some Sikhs had lived here earlier. A Sikh is a learner, a disciple, of the Guru. The word Guru comes from the Sanskrit word for 'heavy' or 'weighty', i.e. one who is a teacher or guide, dispelling darkness and leading to light. When a conflict of faith arose in India in the early sixteenth century between Hindus and Muslims, the first Guru, Guru Nanak, founded a new religion, designated a successor and insisted that worship needed no ritual, temple or doctrine, only an all-powerful God to whom all men must turn to achieve truth and happiness.

The faith embodies the five Ks: the Kacha, a special garment worn under outer clothing; the Kara, a steel bangle; the Kirpan, a short sword; the Kesh, long hair worn for men under a turban; and the Kangha, a comb. The Sikh community is referred to as the Panth, meaning the path or road, which represents the rule under which it lives.

In 1854, the head of the Sikh community, Maharajah Duleep Singh was banished to England, taking with him the Koh-i-Noor diamond for Queen Victoria. The son of the earlier Sikh ruler, Ranjit Singh, he was the first Sikh known to make his home in England where he lived the life of an upper-class English gentleman. He had converted to Christianity while in India but later returned to Sikhism. The first Sikh temple (Gurdwara) was built in Shepherds Bush in 1908 and the faith has spread widely to cover all walks of life, with the largest number of Sikhs living in Wembley. Clearly identified by their beards and turbans, Sikhs have undergone considerable ill treatment, particularly in recent years when they are sometimes mistaken for Muslims. Their right to wear the turban at all times has often conflicted with the professional uniform of police, firemen and other occupations, but with goodwill on both sides this problem has usually been resolved.

Political Change

Lloyd George's government was faced with more than just discontent at home. Ireland was divided into two nations after the Irish Republican Army fought bitterly against British Protestant rule, leading to the Irish Free State being formed in 1921. At home Labour was taking on the left-wing role previously held by the Liberals, encouraged by the success in 1917 of the Russian Revolution. Britain's intellectual elite welcomed the new Russia. Leonard Woolf wrote in his memoirs that 'it was a tremendous event for me and for all those whose beliefs and hopes had been moulded in the revolutionary fires of liberty, equality and fraternity.'[6]

English Jews had been excited in the same year by the signing of the Balfour Declaration: His Majesty's Government views with favour the establishment in Palestine of a national home for the Jewish people. It was to lead later to sanctuary for thousands of Jews escaping from Hitler's Europe, and to an internal war in the Holy Land, with apparently no solution.

The General Strike

In the years succeeding the end of the war, industrial unrest broke out in areas all over Britain. As discontent spread across the country, every level of society was affected and eventually the nation came out on General Strike. Cardinal Francis Bourne, Roman Catholic Archbishop of Westminster called it 'sinful'; most of the English churchmen kept their distance, though one or two offered their services to the strikers. Transport ground to a halt, food deliveries slowed, the printing presses stopped rolling, the police were unsure whose side they were on. A new newspaper, edited by Winston Churchill and called the British Gazette, was supposed to follow the government line, but the first compositors destroyed the type. *The Times* brought out a one page edition to keep the public informed of important news – its last line read, 'The Prince of Wales returned to London from Biarritz last night, travelling from Paris by air.'[7]

The strike lasted for nine days – it was the only General Strike in British history and included several acts of violence, though no deaths occurred. The 'Flying Scotsman' was derailed by the strikers, wire mesh was put over the driving cabs of buses to protect the drivers, and a two-mile long military convoy of sixteen armoured cars was used to transfer food from the docks to Hyde Park. Stanley Baldwin, the Prime Minister, was reported as saying, 'The General Strike is a challenge to Parliament and is the road to anarchy and ruin.'[8]

Nervous of public disorder, the Metropolitan Police strengthened its security arrangements. These included the construction of the smallest police station in Britain. On the south east corner of Trafalgar Square, it was fashioned from a hollowed out light fitting and could just hold two officers looking through windows across the square. There was a telephone link to Scotland Yard and its light flashed if help was needed (the light was believed to have come from HMS Victory). It is now a broom cupboard for Westminster Council's cleaning department.

Communications

One new form of communication did its best to keep the nation up to date. The British Broadcasting Company – the oldest broadcasting company in the world – had come into being in 1922 as the only broadcasting station, firstly as 2MT and then as 2LO, under the leadership of John Reith, a dour Scottish Presbyterian who disapproved of much of his company's entertainment output. The Director's Sabbatarian views were well known, and Sunday schedules were much influenced by them. Religious broadcasting was a part of BBC programming from its earliest days, though it is written into its Royal Charter that

> we must be aware of the religious sensitivity of references to, or uses of, names, images, deities, rituals, scriptures and language at the heart of the different faiths and ensure that any uses of, or verbal or visual references to them are editorially justified within generally accepted standards. Examples include the Crucifixion, Holy Communion, the Koran, the Jewish Sabbath and similar.[9]

There are warnings against 'undermining or denigrating' the religious beliefs of others. The Company – it became a public service corporation in 1926 – has never permitted any 'conversionism' such as that practised by American tele-evangelists and strives to allow all faiths to participate in its output. That first radio station was followed in the next years by several more, all controlled by the BBC, and outside broadcasting became an important feature of its programmes; the first was a performance of *The Magic Flute* from Covent Garden.

The Twenties

London after the war was not just a centre of industrial uprising, unemployment and class distinction. The city was determined to relax, to have a good time and to enjoy modern music and entertainment. The American influence was everywhere: jazz, dancing, motor cars, even a new form of language. The older generation disapproved, but London was a city for young people, who didn't care that their elders disapproved of short skirts, bobbed hair, saxophones, the 'wireless' and the 'talkies', cocktail cabinets and the Charleston.

Disapproval from the churches of the 'bright young things' was inevitable. But church attendance was again declining. A.J.P. Taylor wrote, 'Our Lord Jesus Christ became, even for many avowed Christians, merely the supreme example of a good man. This was as great a happening as any in English history since the conversion of the Anglo-Saxons to Christianity.'[10] But the established Church still had a firm hold on English hearts and minds, despite the pull of science, rationalism, atheism and secularism.

Dark Shadows

The League of Nations had been founded in 1920, without Russia or the USA, though the establishment of such a group had been suggested at the very beginning of the war. It aimed at preventing war through disarmament and collective security, with the use of arbitration to solve disputes. It had no armed force and proved useless when Germany and her allies showed the first signs of aggression toward their neighbours.

Fascism

The threat of Communism in England in the 1920s brought a reaction from the right wing of political thought, whose adherents began to form themselves into groups such as the Diehards. By 1932 those who supported the far right had established the British Union of Fascists under the leadership of Oswald Mosley.

Mosley had begun his political life as the youngest Conservative MP, but moved to join the Independent Labour Party where he was appointed minister in charge of employment. His plans, set out as the Mosley Memorandum, were turned down and he resigned to form in 1931 the New Party, which the following year became the British Union of Fascists, or BUF. He visited Mussolini in 1932 and became imbued with the Italian's fascist ideals, setting out the Party's manifesto in his The Greater Britain. Harold Nicolson was one of those who joined the New Party but left when it embraced Fascism. In his Diaries, he wrote about his friend Mosley in 1932, 'I do not think this country will ever stand for violence, and that by resorting to violence he will make himself detested by a few and ridiculed by many. He says that may be so but that he is prepared to take the risk.'[11]

In its early years the BUF was able to claim some distinguished members. The *Daily Mail* came out in favour, and it drew support from many trades and professions, including Sir Malcolm Campbell, Arthur Gillian, captain of the English cricket team, Lords Redesdale and Rothermere, Henry Williamson the writer, and most notably William Joyce, who was to broadcast as Lord Haw-Haw for the Germans during the Second World War.

On 4th October 1936 Mosley and his Fascists ('blackshirts' from their uniforms) planned to march through the East End. He had many supporters there, disgruntled Londoners, unemployed workers, right wing thugs of all sorts, against Jews, foreigners and communists. They gathered on Tower Hill, with Mosley in full Fascist regalia, peaked cap, black jacket, grey breeches, and black jackboots. Bill Fishman (later Professor Fishman) watching him arrive, saw him as a playboy aristocrat, as glamorous as ever. But the area was home to a huge Jewish community, strongly opposed to the growing threat of Fascism. Chanting 'They shall not pass' they put up barricades in Cable Street, the centre of the march. They were joined by a contingent of Irish dockers, read for a fight, be it against the blackshirts or the police. The crowd – communists, Independent Labour Party members, middle class sympathisers – numbered some 100,000. Paving stones were dug up to act as missiles, and fireworks and marbles were ready to throw under the hooves of the police horses. The Battle of Cable Street turned out to be between the East Enders and the Police. Mosley took the advice of the Commander and turned away to the empty city streets. But the following week Jewish shops and houses were viciously attacked by Mosley's men.

The Rise of the Nazis

In 1933 Adolf Hitler was elected Chancellor of Germany and a new word entered the English language – Nazism, the English version of *National-sozialismus*. Hitler had been brought up in a Benedictine monastery in his native Bavaria, where he studied the works of Martin Luther whose virulent outpourings against the Jews – when they refused to be converted – found willing acceptance in the young student. In his book *The Jews and their Lies*, written in later life, Luther had said,

> Therefore be on your guard against the Jews and know that where they have their schools there is nothing but the Devil 's nest in which self-praise, vanity, lies, blasphemy, disgracing God and man, are practised in the bitterest and most poisonous way.[12]

The manifestation of anti-Semitism in England in the thirties was very different from that springing up in Germany. Andrew Chandler, the writer and biographer, maintained that 'the established church survived in the twentieth century because there was no political revolution and no radical recasting of the British system.'[13] Eastenders could not deny that name-calling and the knocking off of hats was common on a Friday night. The worst violence was an occasional broken synagogue window or gravestone overturned. Young Jews found a few problems in being accepted at public schools or universities; golf clubs and gentlemen's West End Clubs were wary of accepting Jewish members. But English Jews were seldom subject to the sort of violence and discrimination which was sweeping through Germany.

The Nuremberg Laws of 1935 excluded Jews from citizenship of Germany, now the Third Reich. They could not marry Gentiles nor employ them at home, they were excluded from the Civil Service and the legal profession. Their books were ceremonially burned. Those Jews who realised what was happening started making plans to leave, or at least to send their children away, but many refused to believe that such an intelligent, cultured nation could ever embark on the wholesale slaughter of innocent citizens.

Catholics and the Third Reich

The Vatican was among the first to recognise Nazi Germany – many Germans were professing Catholics – but Hitler and his followers were by now anti-religious and many Catholics were persecuted and perished in the Holocaust. Nevertheless the Papacy was ill served by its leaders at such a crucial time in Europe's history.

The debate about the part played by the Pope in Hitler's rise to power goes on. Under Pius XI the traditional attitude of the Catholic Church to the Jews seemed to be changing. In 1928 he publicly condemned anti-Semitism, and when Hitler invaded Austria in 1938 he summoned Cardinal Innitzer to Rome and berated him for flying the swastika on Viennese churches. Pius believed strongly in Christianity being an Abrahamic faith which followed in the steps of the Jews. However, his silence after Kristall-nacht (the night in November 1938 when Jews and their property were smashed to pieces in an orgy of destruction) can perhaps be attributed to his ill-health and approaching death.

In England Cardinal Arthur Hinsley, Archbishop of Westminster from 1935, spoke out fearlessly against the Nazi oppression of the Jews, but unlike the European Catholic leaders, he had nothing to fear either for himself or for his flock. An article on Fascism in *The Tablet* (the British Catholic journal) commented 'There was far too much anti-Semitism among them (British Catholics) already for the Nazi attacks on the Jews to matter very much.'[14]

The Papal succession went to Pius XII, still blamed by many Jews and non-Jews for not doing more to save their co-religionists in Europe. Michael Phayer, writing on the Catholic Church and the Holocaust, refers to the Church as 'a sleeping giant'. Speaking about the diplomatic channels used, mostly ineffectually, by the Pope, he attributes the Vatican's lack of action in part to its fear of communism. 'Pope Pius XII's greatest failure, both during and after the Holocaust, lay in his attempt to use a diplomatic remedy for a moral outrage.'[15]

It took many years for the Church to recognise its failings, but in 1998 Pope John Paul II issued a document *We Remember: A Reflection on the Shoah*. The biblical word *Shoah*, meaning destruction, became the standard Hebrew term for the murder of European Jewry. *We Remember* called on Catholics to 'repent of past errors and infidelities'; the Pope was hoping that it would help to create 'a future in which the unspeakable iniquity of the Shoah will never again be possible.'

The Church of England

The Archbishop of Canterbury, Cosmo Lang, was a man of intellect and scholarship, an orator and a man of faith, but as Adrian Hastings, the Roman Catholic priest and historian, viewed him, he 'combined unctuousness with snobbery in a way that left a bad taste in many people's mouths.'[16] Lang kept in close touch with the Anglicans in Europe, including his chaplains and bishops, as well as with the Foreign Office and other diplomatic channels. In 1933 the Church of England Council on Foreign Relations was working on links with the oppressed European communities, though its chairman, the Bishop of Gloucester, took a friendly view of the Nazi power in Germany. Lang was kept closely informed about the fate of the Jews and asked Parliament to take a strong stand. At a meeting in Queen's Hall in London in June 1933 he urged those present 'to express in unequivocal terms the nation's abhorrence at the anti-Jewish persecutions in Germany.'[17]

However, the Church was much occupied with the threat of Communism; the Dean of Canterbury, Hewlett Johnson (the Red Dean) was an active Communist though never a member of the Communist Party. The English Church was naturally much concerned for the suffering of German Protestants and worried especially about the fate of Martin Niemöller, the Lutheran pastor who spoke out firmly about the actions of the Nazis and the fight between democracy and dictatorship. As news filtered through to England about concentration camps, atrocities against the Jews and other minority groups, the Church woke up to its responsibilities. One churchman who spoke up clearly and at length was George Bell, Bishop of Chichester. He wrote letters to *The Times*, and to German churches, with whom England had close links. He visited Germany to keep channels of communication open. Another was William Temple, Archbishop of York until translated to Canterbury in 1942. Unlike Lang, he was less at home in the higher reaches of society, and more familiar with the young and active, often on the left wing. He was a pastoralist who understood the problems, social, political and religious that the ordinary man had to face. He fought tirelessly against the Nazi threat, organising a letter-writing campaign against the camps. If the Church's stance against Hitler appeared weak, as Tom Lawson, writing on the Anglican church and the Holocaust, says, 'the political responsibilities of being the established Church in England seemed to proscribe more vociferous intervention.'[18]

The Quakers

The Society of Friends was one English religious group particularly noted for its aid to the Jews. From 1933 onwards it reported on conditions in Germany where there was a small but active Quaker community, and assisted those Jews coming to England, particularly by the *Kindertransport*, the trains carrying Jewish children to safety in Britain. The Quakers met the refugees at the stations, helped them with education and housing, and found them work. The Friends' Service Council set up camps for the new arrivals, providing food and shelter as well as inexpensive hostels; the Jews were forbidden to take money or valuables with them when they left. Almost all Quakers in Britain played some part in the rescue of the Jews. In 1947 the Quakers were awarded the Nobel Peace Prize, and the Quaker community is recognised by Yad Vashem, the Holocaust Museum in Jerusalem.

The Jewish Community in Britain

There is still much controversy about whether Britain did enough to rescue the Jews from the Holocaust. The Jews here were of course very aware of what was happening in Germany. Friends and family were in close contact. In *The Myth of Rescue*, William Rubinstein describes Hitler as a 'mono-maniacal psychopath' and maintains that 'No scheme of rescue of the Jews could possibly have succeeded, nor was any such proposed either by church leaders, politicians or individuals.'[19] However, many individual Jews did make it to safety in Britain; some of the distinguished figures such as Bruno Walter, Lucien Freud and Richard Tauber, were welcomed by public acclamation. Families were helped by the Central British Fund, now World Jewish Relief. The Fund was set up in 1933 to help German Jews to get to Palestine. It extended its activities to bring aid to others coming to Britain, particularly university graduates, lawyers and doctors. Children were admitted, often on the *Kindertransport*, without papers and were put in touch with families here, Jewish or non-Jewish. By 1939 nearly ten thousand children had been rescued, nearly all Jewish. An Artists Refugee Committee was formed to help German Jewish artists, under the guidance of Augustus John, Muirhead Bone and Henry Moore among others.

The People in Britain

Many British people were wary of these German Jews, indeed of Jews in general. Among the upper classes it was an instinctive reaction to foreigners and strangers in their midst. Some, like the Mitfords, gravitated towards the Fascists and Hitler. But the natural goodwill of many made them shrink from the horrors that were becoming clear. Harold Nicolson wrote to his wife Vita Sackville-West in 1938 about the Austrians,

> There is a devilish sort of humour in their cruelty ... they made the Jewish gentlemen take off all their clothes and walk on all fours on the grass. They made the old Jewish ladies get up into the trees by ladders and sit there. They then told them to chirp like birds.[20]

After more than eighty years, the debate goes on. Did English church-men and politicians know what was going on in Nazi Germany before the outbreak of World War II? Did the men in the London streets understand the enormity of Hitler's Final Solution? If so what did they do about it?

Could they have done more to rescue the persecuted Jews from the horrors of the Holocaust? Could Pope Pius XII have exercised the wealth and influence of the Vatican to help? Many millions of words have been written and spoken about the biggest crime in world history. Bits of the truth ooze out from time to time but it is fair to say that the debate about the genocide of the thirties continues to this day, even if the perpetrators and the victims have changed.

Abdication

By 1936 the established Church in England had something nearer home to worry about. King George V died in January. A.J.P. Taylor described him as 'a model of constitutional rectitude and a model of conservative respectability also in his private life.[21] He was indeed much respected, even loved, by his people, as they showed at the time of his Silver Jubilee and in the days that followed his death. But to his children he was feared and unapproachable.

As Prince of Wales, the new King (usually known then as David) had been debonair, light-hearted and very popular. In high society he was seen everywhere, dancing, drinking, escorting pretty girls – or married women – but the nation loved his visits to the working classes and his promises of better things to come. Those in his immediate circle knew about his relationship with the glamorous American divorcée, Wallis Simpson. It was no secret. The Church was wary. Harold Nicolson, early in the relationship, wrote, 'I had an uneasy feeling that Mrs Simpson, for all her good intentions, is getting him out of touch with the type of person with whom he ought to frequent.'[22] His opinion was that the upper classes minded her being an American more than the fact that she was divorced.

The established Church was threatened by the behaviour of its Head. Lang told Harold Nicolson that the King lacked religion. 'I told his mother [Queen Mary] so. I said to her, "Ma'am, the King has no religious sense ... I love the man but he must go".'[23]

The new King made it very clear to his ministers, particularly Stanley Baldwin, the Prime Minister, and to the religious leaders of his country, that he wanted both his throne and marriage to Mrs Simpson. The situation was kept under wraps. No British newspaper ventured to divulge to its readers the very serious constitutional crisis that threatened the nation. Plans were already being made for the coronation later in the year. Lang could refuse to crown a king married to a divorced woman. Several suggestions were offered to solve the situation. The King could have a morganatic marriage, whereby his new wife would not be queen. Wallis offered to go abroad and leave England for ever, but the King would not countenance any of this. The situation was well-known abroad – the American press in particular had splashed the scandal across their pages. Wallis's American nationality made her front page news in the States, but in England the press lords conspired to ignore her.

In December 1936, the cat was let out of the bag by Alfred Blunt, the Bishop of Bradford, who at his diocesan conference, speaking of the forth-coming coronation, said,

> The benefit of the King's coronation depends upon ... the faith, prayer and self-dedication of the King himself; and on that it would be improper of me to say anything except to commend him to God's grace, which he will so abun-dantly need, as we all need it – for the King is a man like ourselves – if he is to do his duty faithfully. We hope that he is aware of his need. Some of us wish that he gave more positive signs of such awareness.[24]

The secret was out and the national press seized upon it at once.

The Times leader on 11th December read,

> What seems almost incredible is that any man who was born and trained to such high responsibilities, who had clearly the capacity to undertake them, and who had in fact begun to exercise them with the complete goodwill of the nation, should sacrifice it all to a personal preference for another way of life.[25]

The Editors of some of the leading newspapers met with their pro-prietors, Lords Beaverbrook and Rothermere (*The Times*, the *Morning Post* and the *Daily Telegraph* were not invited as their discretion was not in ques-tion) to discuss the situation. The King said later when Duke of Windsor, 'The British Press kept its word, and for that I shall always be grateful.'[26] Lang and Baldwin could see no way out. The King had to abdicate if he wanted to marry Mrs Simpson. She had obtained her second divorce, she was a commoner and a foreigner. England could not accommodate such a woman at the head of its royal family. On 13th December Lang explained in a broadcast to the nation. 'It was a craving for private happiness. Strange and sad it must be that for such a motive, however strongly it pressed upon the heart, he should have disappointed hopes so high and abandoned a trust so great.'[27]

Edward VIII, the uncrowned King, was succeeded by his younger brother as George VI, a shy, awkward young man with a stutter, but with a young family, a strong sense of duty, and an equally strong faith in God and the religion of England. His brother, who took the title of Duke of Windsor, was much attracted to Hitler whom he visited on several occasions. He was removed from public sight by being made Governor of Bermuda, but many felt that England would have been in grave danger from Germany had his reign continued.

CHAPTER XXIII

World War II

'Peace for our Time'

THE LITTLE PIECE OF PAPER brandished by Neville Chamberlain on his return from Munich in September 1938 to show what he had achieved at his meeting with Hitler, has become a symbol of the uselessness of appeasement when dealing with such a tyrant. The Prime Minister's success was greeted with acclamation by the House of Commons and by most of the country. One man who stood back, and was reviled for it, was Winston Churchill.

Unlike in the First World War, this time the element of surprise was almost missing. Between the time of the Munich Agreement and the actual outbreak of hostilities a year later, the nation was aware of preparations for war: the construction of Spitfires, factories given over to munitions, the provision of gas masks and air raid sirens, and the early plans for evacuation of children. Clearly war, if not a certainty, was a strong possibility. Communications were far more efficient by 1939. Almost every family had a 'wireless set' or if they didn't they very soon bought one. Leonard Woolf wrote, 'One of the most horrible things at that time was to listen on the wireless to the speeches of Hitler, the savage and insane ravings of a vindictive underdog who suddenly saw himself to be all-powerful.'[1]

This time no-one wanted war. This was not an idealistic project for the fine young men of 1914. It was aimed at a vicious tyrant who had already annexed Czechoslovakia and Poland and would clearly not be stopped. Most of those alive today will remember where he was that hot summer Sunday when Chamberlain announced that Hitler had not replied to his ultimatum to withdraw and 'therefore we are at war with Germany'. The air raid sirens wailed (a false alarm) and the 'phoney' war lulled the nation into a sense of false security.

Moral Re-Armament

MRA was the Christian group founded by Frank Buchman, an American missionary, who believed that a strong and unswerving faith in God would cure all the world's ills, and if man lived according to a Christian ethic, without selfishness or fear, all would be well. Moral Re-Armament started as the Oxford Group, evangelical Christians (from whom later sprang Alcoholics Anonymous), much praised by laymen and churchmen alike. Buchman was very wary of the move towards re-arming by the European nations and felt that what was needed was a greater moral sense of right and wrong. In America the movement gained strength and at the outbreak of war was considered a valuable asset in the Allied cause.

In 1933 a service in St Paul's Cathedral, led by the Rev Winnington-Ingram, Bishop of London, was attended by five hundred MRA members, with more than a hundred Church of England clergy present. Germany and her allies refused to countenance the movement, suppressing its adherents. When the war started some active members claimed exemption from military service, but the government refused to allow any such step and insisted they should serve.

Jewish Emigration

By 1940 the situation regarding Jews in countries under Nazi control was critical. Those who managed to escape to England told heart-rending stories of what they and their families had had to endure. But the full horror of the gas chambers and the concentration camps was as yet not fully known. The children escaping on the *Kindertransport* were too young to understand and many of their parents clung to the hope that all would eventually be well, and refused to go.

It was necessary to have a visa to enter Britain and these were almost impossible to get. There are many stories of the Righteous Gentiles – recognised for their valour by Yad Vashem in Jerusalem – such as Frank Foley, Raoul Wallenberg, Oskar Shindler and the Japanese Consul in Lithuania, Chiure Sugihara, who did their best to help, stamping passports or sheltering Jews, in violation of Nazi orders. In England jobs for immigrants were restricted, especially for professional or entrepreneurial refugees; many intelligent, educated women went into domestic service to be able to stay.

Some refugees were interned on the Isle of Man; if they managed to enlist they were put into the Pioneer Corps, a non-combatant unit. Some later lent their knowledge of German to the Intelligence Services, or if they were scientists put their knowledge and experience to good use in helping England's war effort. British government policy restricted the number of refugees, nervous of public reaction to a flood of foreigners coming in from a country with whom it was at war.

The Church in England

Cosmo Lang, Archbishop of Canterbury, was seventy-five years old when war broke out. He had led the Anglican Church through ten years of difficulty – social unrest, the rise of fascism and abdication – and now another war. In the First World War, while Archbishop of York, he had been denounced for admiring the Kaiser, which had greatly troubled him and supposedly led to his early ageing. In 1927 the Church had inaugurated a revision of the Book of Common Prayer. The General Assembly (later the General Synod) had to submit such changes, in this case an entirely new Prayer Book, to Parliament for its acceptance. There were objections to the first draft from both Anglo-Catholics and Evangelicals, the 'right' and 'left' of the Church. However, after much debate a draft was finalised which pleased no-one. As the historian Robert Beaken put it, 'The 1927 Revised Prayer Book was unacceptable to Anglo-Catholics because it was not Catholic enough, and unacceptable to Evangelicals because it was too Catholic.'[2] Finally it was agreed by the Assembly and submitted to Parliament. The Lords duly passed it, but it was rejected by the Commons. It was modified but again rejected. Lang's predecessor at Canterbury, Randall Thomas Davidson, resigned and Cosmo Lang took his place.

In 1940 Cardinal Hinsley, head of the Catholic Church in England, founded the Sword of the Spirit. This was a democratic Catholic initiative to counter the tendency of many English Catholics to support right-wing idealism, and to further the realisation that the Church could not abstain from intervention without betraying its mission. It was mainly an organisation run by laymen and was welcomed by Catholics and Anglicans alike. On December 21st, 1940 a letter was published in *The Times* signed by Cosmo Lang, William Temple and the Moderator of the Free Churches, W.H. Armstrong, as well as the Cardinal. It began,

> The present evils in the world are due to the failure of nations and peoples to carry out the laws of God. No permanent peace is possible in Europe unless the principles of the Christian religion are made the foundation of national policy and of all social life. This involves regarding all nations as members of one family under the Fatherhood of God.[3]

The signatories accepted the Five Peace Points promulgated by Pope Pius XII in 1939: the right to life for all nations, disarmament, some new jurisdiction to guarantee such conditions, the defence of small nations, and a plea for moral guidance by the laws of God.

Once the war was under way the Church became fully engaged. Chaplains were appointed to care for the welfare of the troops under a Chaplain General (Major General), Chaplains 1st Class (Colonels) and Chaplains 2nd Class (Lt. Colonels). Church services were held regularly which anyone could attend; members of the forces came in uniform, as did those who had joined the voluntary organisations. Churches and other religious houses opened their doors to serving personnel from any nation. The story is told of one allied soldier, seeking entertainment, who wandered into the West London Synagogue on the Day of Atonement and asked, 'What sort of a show have you got here? Is it any good?' The reply was, 'It ought to be – it's been running for nearly six thousand years!'[4]

As the war wore on the Christian churches, often full, tried to adopt a more collaborative attitude to other faiths. When an Anglican church was bombed, a neighbourly Catholic one might offer temporary shelter. Jewish congregations held overflow services on the Holy Festivals in the meeting places of Christian communities. William Temple inaugurated the British Council of Churches to bring together, at such a time of distress, varying denominations in a practical joint effort. In several cities, often badly damaged by German bombs, ministers of Anglican, Evangelical, Methodist, Catholic and other faiths came together in an ecumenical sharing of prayer and comfort. The inter-faith movement of post-war England owes much of its inception to such wartime collaboration. When Cardinal Hinsley died in 1943 his funeral brought together in the Catholic Westminster Cathedral a joint congregation to mourn someone whose faith was not necessarily the same as theirs.

The Blitz

London experienced little of the war for the first year of the fighting. Church bells were ordered to be silent and rung only to signal an invasion. Once that danger was over in 1943, ringing of the bells recommenced. The battle was being fought at sea and in the air. At Dunkirk the 'little ships' had brought back home the remains of the British Expeditionary Force, to turn a defeat into a national victory. The Battle of Britain turned the skies over southern England into a new battlefield, when young men, like those who in 1914 had died in the trenches in France, flew their Spitfires into dog fights with equally young German pilots in their Messerschmitts. People rushed out of their houses to watch and young boys collected shrapnel as souvenirs. Hitler left London alone. But on 16th July 1940 he issued his Directive No. 16, the intention to invade England. German bombers had already attacked coastal towns with some success, and moved north to try to eliminate the RAF airfields around southern England. On September 7th

1940 the first bombs were dropped on London. The BBC announced on the Nine O'clock News, 'The German air force has unleashed a wave of heavy bombing raids on London, killing hundreds of civilians and injuring more.' The first targets were the East End and the docks. The Blitz had begun.

The bombing lasted for fifty-seven consecutive days and nights. Barrage balloons floated like flying elephants in the summer skies. Casualties were heavy, not only for the RAF and Civil Defence, but for all the various groups hastily assembled to defend London: the Home Guard (formerly Local Defence Volunteers), the Air Raid Precautions Wardens, the Auxiliary Fire Service, Women's Voluntary Service and the many other organisations, official and unofficial, who helped in the fight.

It was, of course, the civilian casualties who fared the worst. Bombed out of their homes, taking refuge in the Air Raid shelters or damaged churches, losing their families, sleeping on Underground train platforms, they somehow maintained a show of spirit and humour unlike anything England had known in her long history of warfare.

London

Just as London's landscape had changed out of all recognition after the Great Fire, so it did again now. Some sixteen of Sir Christopher Wren's churches were destroyed, including St Dunstan's-in-the-East, St Mildred's Bread Street, St Albans Wood Street, Christ Church Greyfriars and St Augustine's Watling Street. Churchill, now Prime Minister, ordered St Paul's to be saved at all costs, and when a bomb did land on the dome, firefighters were ready to douse the flames. One of the most significant photographs of the war was that of St Paul's Cathedral ringed by fire but standing almost untouched. Less well known is the fact that the Bevis Marks Synagogue, less than a mile away and London's oldest synagogue, was also unharmed, though the Great Synagogue beside it was razed to the ground. Lambeth Palace suffered much damage to its Chapel and to Morton's Tower. The Archbishop had to move out of his London home. Westminster Cathedral escaped serious damage, although bombs fell all around Victoria Street, including several on Victoria Station.

The human damage was far greater. Some 32,000 civilians were killed during the Blitz and 87,000 were seriously injured. Many servicemen and women returned home from active service to find their homes destroyed and their families gone. The poet Ruthven Todd wrote:

> Remember the walls of brick that forty years
> Had nursed to make a neat though shabby home;
> The impertinence of death, ignoring tears,
> That smashed the house and left untouched the Dome.

Bodies in death are not magnificent or stately,
Bones are not elegant that blast has shattered;
This sorry, stained and crumpled rag was lately
A man whose life was made of little things that mattered.[5]

Broadcasting

The BBC played a vital part during the war. It could be transmitted to occupied countries, though often had to be listened to in secret. The foreign services broadcast from Bush House in the Strand, and the French Service in particular, was used by the intelligence services to communicate with agents parachuted into occupied France. A message, for example, to the effect that 'Dora has a new pair of gloves' could be interpreted as meaning that an agent was to be dropped that night into enemy territory. Often the only source of news of the progress of the war, the BBC was welcomed into the homes of many Europeans prepared to risk raids from the Germans and the consequent severe punishment.

The first religious programmes had been broadcast in 1928, with the special Studio 3E set aside for their use. The studio's ceiling was inlaid with sun, moon and stars. It was badly damaged by the bombs that fell on Broadcasting House and did not survive the Corporation's return to London after the war. Television programmes ceased altogether.

Asians in Wartime Britain

The depression of the 1930s had hit Asian migrants hard. Jobs in Britain were given to British workers, but there was still some immigration, particularly of students and professionals from India. Working-class Indians often managed to find menial work with the help of relatives already here. As in the case of the Jews, ties of family and religion were strong, and poor, often illiterate, newcomers were prepared to work for what to white British workers was not a living wage. They could peddle cheap imported clothes, work in small restaurants or, in the dockland areas, find jobs on ships. The Indian Seamen's Welfare League helped and the Hindustani Social Club offered a place for relaxation and a minimum of education.

When war came Asian immigrants found they were needed, on the ships, in the factories, on the land, as Britons were called up for military service. Even the women, speaking little English and with no training, could find work as hospital orderlies, pushing trolleys in factories or employed as cleaners. Rozina Visram, in *Asians in Britain*, makes the point that 'to dismiss all working-class Indians as illiterate peasants is to do them an injustice'.[6] Many were educated or semi-skilled – teachers, engineers or

clerical workers – and had to find work 'beneath them'. A colour bar operated in many areas, with the usual English suspicion of foreigners, especially
while the nation was at war, even though it desperately needed workers.
Protests were sent to Parliament. Visram quotes the story of the first Indian
President of the Oxford Union, D.F. Karaka, who wrote, 'I forget that I am
a Parsee, or an Indian or anything else, and I realise that the most significant
fact about myself is that I am born dark.'[7]

The Muslim population in Britain found similar problems as Hindus and
Sikhs. There was the additional concern about Arab relations with Hitler.
At first he considered those in the Middle East as his allies in his attempt to
eliminate the Jews. The question of Palestine loomed large in their relationship, but he privately viewed Arabs as 'non-Aryan', a degenerate race.
Muslims living in Britain looked on this country as their home and were
prepared to fight on her side.

Fighting for Britain

British military forces in World War II included some two and a half million
from India, bigger than all the rest of the Empire put together. The Indian
army and air force, many as pilots, together with the women's services,
made an enormous contribution to the war effort, to say nothing of the
engineers and technical staff working at home. The Indian Comforts Fund,
working via the Red Cross, was set up from India House in London, to care
for Indian soldiers on active service and at home, and for Indian prisoners
of war, sending parcels and food.

Indian 'Bevin boys' (youngsters sent to the coal pits by Ernest Bevin
while Minister of Labour) were sent down the mines, worked on the railways
and on food production. Large sums were donated from India to the 'war
effort'. Hindus, Sikhs and Muslims fought in France and Italy, in the air
and at sea. One Indian woman, Noor Enayat Kahn, was sent into France
to work for the Resistance. She was betrayed and executed by the Germans.
Students volunteered, Indian women sewed parachutes and knitted socks.
However, there are few memorials to these fighting forces, though many
won medals for bravery.

England and the Jews

The story of Hitler's Final Solution, the Holocaust as it became known, the
Shoah to Jews, has been widely told. Gradually news was seeping through
to Britain of the railway lines to Auschwitz, of concentration camps, and
rumours – unproven until the end of the war – of gas chambers and the
wholesale slaughter and degradation of millions of Jews, men, women and

children in German-occupied territories. The British government was not very helpful. Individuals such as Archbishop Temple made speeches, approached ministers and tried to make public the inhumanity of the Nazis. It was not easy. Harold Nicolson wrote, 'Although I hate anti-Semitism, I do dislike Jews.'[8]

Most Britons preferred to concentrate on winning the war rather than rescuing a foreign, non-Christian, far away people from their appalling fate. 'Nazi anti-Semitism was as successful as it was, one may conclude, because it rang a bell in many respectable Christian hearts, British as well as German.'[9] It was not until British (and Russian and American) troops uncovered the horror that was Bergen-Belsen that the world understood what men could do to other men.

The Coming of Peace

When the war between the Allies and the German powers was declared over on 8th May (Victory in Europe Day), the great task of the religious leaders lay before them. Churchill's iconic leadership was finished and Britain had to acclimatise herself to a very different world, politically, socially and religiously. Out went some of trivial class distinctions of masters and servants, in came a social levelling-up where merit and opportunity lay open to all who could use them, or that was the theory. A wartime batman might find himself in a bank, refusing an overdraft to his commanding officer. A member of the FANYs (First Aid Nursing Yeomanry), who did such sterling nursing work during the war, could become Matron of a large hospital, with young aristocratic university men under her charge.

With William Beveridge in charge of the plans, a new society crawled slowly out of its shell: nationalising of the railways, a National Health Service, free at the point of delivery, improved education, the school leaving age raised to fifteen and more universities springing up. The welfare state was certainly not perfect, but it put an end to 'going on the panel' when visiting a doctor; unemployment was almost non-existent with so many jobs needing to be filled.

The Rebuilding of the City

London's skyline was changed forever. Yawning chasms had opened up between buildings, quickly filled with the purple spikes of rosebay willow-herb, the invasive wild flower that grows anywhere its seeds come to rest, or buddleia, the butterfly bush, growing out of cracks in old brickwork and difficult to eradicate. Rebuilding began almost at once, but as all architects know, design cannot go back. New ideas, new materials, new equipment were needed everywhere. The influence of American cities inaugurated skyscrapers, glass instead of stone, stretching upward instead of outward. Commercial enterprise had to resume quickly if the country was to get back on its feet. Banks, offices, businesses of all kinds, took the place of houses and shops, streets were widened to accommodate the increased number of cars; wherever possible churches were rebuilt or repaired, though some congregations united with others to make use of whatever was left from the desecration of the German bombs.

Swinging London

As Britain's Empire gradually receded into the distance, it took with it much of the ancient ideals of respect, the supremacy of the old and class veneration. London was moving fast. Music, art, clothes, even finance, all bowed to the exuberance of the young. New roads, communications, cultural behaviour, were exemplified by John Osborne's *Look Back in Anger* and the kitchen sink dramas of the post-war years. Marches, demonstrations and the left-wing press may have seemed startlingly new, but were in fact in the tradition of Wat Tyler, leader of the Peasants' Revolt of 1381, the Lollards and John Wilkes. Suddenly churches, mosques and synagogues seemed out of date. The elegant old world Toryism of Harold MacMillan gave way to *Private Eye* and Carnaby Street. New universities gave another meaning to 'red brick'; with the Wolfenden Report and the Lady Chatterley Trial, sex was no longer a forbidden word.

Religious Affairs

The Second Vatican Council, held in 1962, brought about an extraordinary closure of the rift between Protestants and Catholics. The first tentative suggestion of rapprochement came from Pope John XXIII, and by the time of the visit to Rome of Michael Ramsey, the one hundredth Archbishop of Canterbury, in 1966, it was possible for an ecumenical service to be held in St Paul's Basilica Outside the Walls, at which both great Christian leaders took part. As Adrian Hastings concluded, 'Here was both a deliberate example of prayer in common and a degree of mutual recognition which would have seemed unimaginable a decade earlier.'[10]

Two books were published in the early sixties which helped to jolt the Church of England out of its impending lethargy. One was the *New English Bible* which came out in 1970. Three panels were appointed for the translations of the Old Testament, the New Testament and the Apocrypha. The Chairman of the Joint Committee overseeing the immense project was Donald Coggan, Archbishop of York, who wrote in the Preface,

Apprehending, however, that sound scholarship does not necessarily carry with it a delicate sense of English style, the Committee appointed a fourth panel, of trusted literary advisers, to whom all the work of the translating panels was to be submitted for scrutiny.[11]

The other book, far more contentious, was John Robinson's *Honest to God*, published in 1963. Robinson, Bishop of Woolwich, had given evidence at the Lady Chatterley trial, and felt the time had come to speak out on the prickly subject of a modern belief in God. He used the writings of Paul Tillich, Rudolf Bultman and Dietrich Bonhoeffer – German theologians who fought for a less traditional religious acceptance of God – to expound, in plain words, his belief in the necessity of bringing faith into the twentieth century without many of the trappings that surrounded it. The publication of the book was preceded by a long article in the *Observer* by Robinson explaining something of the book's ideas.

> Man is discovering that he can manage quite happily by himself. He finds no necessity to bring God into his science, his morals, his political speeches. Only in the private world of the individual's psychological need and insecurity – in that last corner of the 'sardine-tin of life' – is room apparently left for the God who has been elbowed out of every other sphere.[12]

The book was an immediate bestseller and brought controversy which still continues today.

Scientology

In 1951 L. Ron Hubbard, an American science fiction writer, introduced his theory of dianetics, a form of psychotherapy, though not recognised by the medical profession. It encourages the individual to free himself of earlier traumas in his life by 'clearing' his mind of painful memories, thus dispelling mental problems and psychosomatic illnesses. The system was not originally considered a religion but the therapy process transformed into a form of theological belief. The cult set up churches, the first in Washington D.C. By 1957 Hubbard was living in London in Fitzroy House, formerly the home of George Bernard Shaw; the main London Church of Scientology is in Victoria Street, but its offices are still centred in Fitzrovia. Its first global headquarters were in East Grinstead, still its principal English home.

Scientology has not had a warm welcome. In 1968, Kenneth Robinson, then Minister for Health called its practices 'a potential menace to the personality and well-being of those so deluded as to become its followers'.[13] Foreign Scientologists were excluded from Britain. Retaliation came from the Scientology press who declared Robinson had 'created "death camps" to which persons (including mental patients) could be forcibly abducted and there killed or maimed with impunity.'[14] He sued for libel and won substantial damages.

Hubbard himself was a somewhat dubious character with an unaccredited doctorate and several clashes with American police forces. He spent several years on a yacht at sea, the *Sea Org*, from which he directed the movement; he claimed that the boat had to keep moving from port to port because if he was captured there could be a Nuclear War. He returned to California where he lived in hiding until his death in 1986. His system of auditing, engrams and E-meters, used in dianetic therapy, seemed too much like science fiction for the average man. However, several Hollywood stars, including Tom Cruise and John Travolta, have pledged themselves to Scientology and it is now recognised in England as a religion. It lays no claim to a particular god, religious system, or hierarchy. Its adherents can seek the truth through their own observations and investigations. There are reputed to be about 25,000 Scientologists in America, while the 2001 census in Britain showed 1,781.

Indian Independence

Another movement which was to change the face of London for ever was gaining strength. The 'jewel in the crown' of the British Empire, India, had been actively seeking independence for many years. That nation's heroes, Mahatma Gandhi, Jawaharlal Nehru and Muhammad Ali Jinnah (who had been leader of the All-India Muslim League), strove with nationalistic pride to counter the old ideas of Empire, where white men governed black. In 1919 the Government of India Act had introduced a fully self-determining English style of Parliamentary rule: two houses, suffrage for the indigenous people – though only a small number, about five million, of the wealthiest had the vote – and ministers in the provinces to deal with education, welfare and public works. However, other matters such as tax reforms, the fighting forces and the police remained the prerogative of the British.

The Indian National Congress had been formed in 1885, but after the First World War it gained momentum. Many military commanders had refused to grant a commission to Indians fighting for Britain in the war, and parliamentarians, particularly Lord Birkenhead, felt the same way about their ability to govern themselves. They feared the break-up of the British Empire.

Finally in 1947 India was partitioned into two, India under the premiership of Nehru and Pakistan with Jinnah as Prime Minister. The Marquess of Reading had been appointed Viceroy of India in 1921 but when independence was granted the office became that of Governor General. The first to hold the post after independence was Viscount Mountbatten of Burma. The partition of the sub-continent led to much rioting and disturbances between Muslims, Sikhs and Hindus and between Pakistan and India. In 1971, Bangladesh, formerly East Pakistan and East Bengal, seceded from Pakistan.

Ugandan Independence

Another part of the British Empire whose claim to independence was to have a lasting effect on London's population was Uganda. The rise to power of Idi Amin, its self-appointed leader, in 1971 after a military coup, took an appalling toll of its Asian inhabitants, many of whom had been established there for generations. Thousands upon thousands of Ugandans disappeared, among them law officers, religious leaders, writers and artists. All Ugandans who were not citizens of the country were expelled, lucky to escape with their lives; the Asians often held British passports, invariably their businesses were destroyed or taken over by the military. With no experience of commercial enterprise, the soldiers let them disintegrate, taking the spoils for themselves. The country's economy was in a disastrous state.

The majority of the Asians who had left Uganda during Amin's tyranny came to England. Most were Hindus though there were some Muslims among them. Many settled in London, often in the Wembley area, and in other big cities. With their families they quickly established small shops and businesses, frequently being granted the Post Office franchise. They spread out across the country, fulfilling the need for a 'corner shop' as the great supermarkets increasingly became a feature of English towns and cities. Like many other immigrants coming to England, they were dispossessed and glad of sanctuary. With the blessing of a good education, they were able to find success in finance, commerce, medicine and pharmacy. They brought up their children as valuable British citizens. The majority retained their religious affiliation and as the numbers grew there appeared an increasing number of temples and mosques in the city. In the East End in particular, which the Jewish community had left during the war and to which they never returned, synagogues were turned into mosques, kosher restaurants became curry bars and the high streets changed for ever.

The Caribbean

On 22nd June 1948, the MV *Empire Windrush* docked at Tilbury with the first group of 492 Jamaican immigrants. The *Windrush*, as the MV *Monte Rosa*, had been used as a cruise ship and then by Hitler's youth movement before the war. She brought servicemen on leave from Kingston answering an advertisement offering cheap passage to England for those in search of jobs. Many came intending to stay for a short while but decided to settle down, find work and raise a family. They did not know what to expect. Nor did England. One Jamaican woman, Lucile Harris, said,

> When I came to England I live in Brixton, near the market. I tell you when I came here there were hardly any buildings standing and far as you can look it bomb and burn outright through and through. My husband sorted out a place to live, before he sent for me.[15]

In 1998, an area of public open space in Brixton was renamed Windrush Square to commemorate the fiftieth anniversary of the arrival of the West Indians. Some found acceptance and friendship, others only resentment and a colour bar.

These new immigrants found greater difficulties in integrating into the community than had most others before them. They were on the whole not as well educated as the Asians and needed the unskilled jobs then being done by British people. They were happy to take on jobs in transport, cleaning and the postal industry, bringing them into day-to-day contact with their neighbours. Clashes broke out with the white community. Their presence was obvious and their lifestyle noisier and less restrained. Many single men had arrived without their families and their playground was the streets and public places. Without the help of the Caribbean community, hospitals, transport, cleaning and other services in London would certainly have ground to a halt.

London's Immigrant Communities

Within fifty years of the end of World War II London was a different place, unrecognisable from the nineteenth century capital city, teeming with churches, predominantly white citizens, restaurants serving often unappetizing English food, small individual shops and businesses. The city's appearance had changed to admit gleaming glass towers, pavemented streets and uncountable cars, buses and commercial vehicles. Many churches damaged in the Blitz had not been rebuilt, replaced by offices and huge conglomerate headquarters, for London, whatever had happened, was still a world centre of finance and commerce.

The population of London reached just over eight million in 1951 but then began to decrease until by 1991 it was about six million, after which it began again to rise and is still rising today. The huge increase of immigrants to London needed legislation to prevent outright discrimination by those already here and their operation of a colour bar both in public and privately. The first Race Relations Act came in 1965 which outlawed discrimination on the grounds of colour, race or ethnic or national origins in public places. The Race Relations Board was set up in 1966 to deal with complaints, but there was as yet no banning of such behaviour in private organisations or on domestic grounds.

The Charismatic Movement

With the influx of colourful black Christians from the West Indies a new church movement began to grow. It was in fact not new to America, but in England the tight hold of the Anglican Church had prevented much in the way of charismatic worship from taking hold. The Pentecostal movement emphasizes the influence of the Holy Spirit on the believer, as it had appeared to Christ's disciples. 'Speaking in tongues' is a feature of God's presence, giving the worshipper the opportunity to live a good Christian life. Baptism, sometimes total immersion, and a very active and dynamic attitude to prayer are essential to the faith, together with the use of music and dancing. In London, adherents to Pentecostalism are almost entirely black, holding services in small churches – tabernacles – headed by a pastor. There are also other Christian churches who encourage worshippers with music and a personal approach (the 'clap-happy' congregations); in London Holy Trinity Brompton is one such, and was the first to introduce the Alpha Course of encouragement to prayer. The Alpha Course, now known simply as Alpha, is evangelistic in its programme, introducing the basics of the Christian faith through a series of talks and discussions. It is described by its organisers as 'an opportunity to explore the meaning of life'.

The New Faces of London

By the end of the twentieth century London wore a new face. In some areas, such as Peckham, Harlesden, Southall and the Borough of Brent, white faces were fewer than black. But gradually the old English suspicion of foreigners and coloured faces was beginning to die away, helped by further legislation against discrimination and the presence in schools of increasing numbers of English-born non-white children. The huge number of different religions now practised in London introduced a glimpse of their own forms of worship to young people, most opening up their premises and their services to visitors of different faiths. All was set for change. As T.S. Eliot, condemning the bishops at the Lambeth Conference of 1930, had put it, 'Not only Youth but Middle Age is on the march; everybody is on the march; it does not matter what the destination is, the one thing contemptible is to sit still.'[16]

CHAPTER XXIV

The Millennium
and After

The Recovery of London

I T TOOK A LONG TIME for London to rebuild itself after Hitler's bombing. For many years after the war gaping holes were still evident in London streets. But gradually they were filled by the giant skyscrapers of the financial and commercial companies, vying with each other to tower above the city, higher and higher until London looked more like New York than its former ancient medieval cityscape. St Paul's was now partly obscured by the new glass and concrete and most of Wren's churches peeked out warily from their surrounding neighbours. The new constructions were much derided. A letter to *The Spectator* read,

> In our view no effort should be spared to stop this outrage to history and good taste. It is a national disgrace that St Paul's Cathedral should be desecrated by an unlet office block the result of which will be to deny to millions a beautiful setting and vista for Sir Christopher Wren's great masterpiece.[1]

The Queen as Head of the Church

In 1953 a new Queen was crowned in Westminster Abbey. Like Queen Elizabeth I and Queen Victoria before her she was young and attractive when she came to the throne, though unlike them already married. That day London, in spite of the pouring rain, welcomed the return of pageantry to the city, still grey with wartime deprivation. In the splendour of the Abbey, the young Queen swore the Coronation Oath. The Archbishop of Canterbury, Geoffrey Fisher, asked her, 'Will you to the utmost of your power maintain the Laws of God and the true profession of the Gospel? Will you to the utmost of your power maintain in the United Kingdom the Protestant Reformed Religion established by law? Will you maintain and preserve inviolably the settlement of the Church of England, and the doctrine, worship, discipline, and government thereof, as by law established in England? And will you preserve unto the Bishops and Clergy of England, and to the Churches there committed to their charge, all such rights and privileges, as by law do or shall appertain to them or any of them?' She replied, 'I promise so to do.'

There was thus no question as to the monarch's position as Head of the Church of England, in spite of the fact that the majority of her subjects were not practising Christians. However in her Coronation speech, broadcast the same night, she asked for the prayers of all her subjects, whatever their religion. Archbishop Fisher, addressing the Cambridge Union that year, said, 'The disestablishment of the Church of England would send a cold terror through the hearts of every Christian on the Continent.'[2] Prince Charles, the heir to the throne, later said on his sixtieth birthday that he would be known as Defender of Faith, making it clear that Britain's multi-cultural society was inclusive, not solely Protestant.

Nuclear Disarmament

After the two atomic bombs had dropped on Hiroshima and Nagasaki, England, as well as America and the whole of Europe, were frightened by the possibility of further nuclear war, and in 1958 the first public meeting of the Campaign for Nuclear Disarmament (CND)was held in London. This was followed by the march to Aldermaston in Berkshire, the site of the Atomic Weapons Establishment. Churchmen were to the fore in the CND, particularly Canon John Collins of St Paul's Cathedral and Monsignor Bruce Kent. Marches, demonstrations and disturbance of meetings were part of their action plans and the movement had the backing of politicians from all sides. Fear of the growth of nuclear weapons by smaller states added to the alarm.

More Bombs in London

What the city did not expect was that without any declaration of war she was to be under fire from bombs placed with the sole purpose of causing as much disruption and injury as possible. In 1969 the Protestant majority of Northern Ireland found itself at the mercy of violent political and sectarian rioting. A civil rights campaign was demanding an end to discrimination against Irish Catholics, with Ulster Protestant loyalists, aided by the largely Protestant Royal Ulster Constabulary, more than ready to defend themselves.

The Rev Ian Paisley headed the Unionists while Sinn Fein represented the Republicans. As the conflict increased the IRA widened the scope of their attacks. During the 1970s bombs were set off in London, causing some loss of life and considerable damage. Car bombs exploded at London tube and mainline stations, at Madame Tussauds, government offices, department stores, the Post Office Tower, the Tower of London and ministers' residences. Two of the worst outrages occurred in Hyde Park and Regents Park in 1982 when eight mounted soldiers on ceremonial duties were killed with their horses in two blasts.

The repercussions of the London bombings were felt across the world, and lost the Republicans much of the sympathy they might otherwise have had. Tourism in London fell sharply and Londoners found it difficult to understand that they were yet again experiencing a religious war on their home territory.

Religious Change

The modernisation of English culture in all its forms had to affect the Church too. Hastings refers to it as 'secularisation'.

> The main churches, including both Roman Catholics and Evangelicals, were now linked by what was almost a common liturgy and Eucharistic understanding, as well as by a wider sense of fellowship including a shared theological tradition and willingness to work together which would have seemed almost impossible to imagine twenty years earlier.[3]

Many churchmen fought shy of bringing their church into the new English way of life. Christenings were fewer than they had traditionally been, funerals were often humanist or even pagan, led by lay leaders, often in unconsecrated ground. The movement towards a respect for nature and a 'green' outlook on life (and death), combined with an awareness of ecological problems, was proving a force for peace in the face of a materialistic society. Marriage, too, was believed unnecessary by many young people – the word 'partner' was becoming synonymous with 'husband' or 'wife'.

One particular change brought the Church considerable internal difficulties; this was the question of sex between partners of the same orientation. Homosexuality, until 1957, was illegal between two men. The MP Henry Labouchère had been a strong opponent of homosexuality; it was his clause added to the Criminal Law Amendment Act 1885 that made it illegal. Oscar Wilde was tried for the offence ten years later. Lesbians were not constrained by the same legal prohibition, because it was said – incorrectly – that Queen Victoria did not believe sex between women was possible. In 1957 the Committee on Homosexual Offences and Prostitution in Great Britain, under the chairmanship of Lord Wolfenden, met to discuss the matter and recommended that private homosexual acts between consenting adults should no longer be illegal. The Criminal Law Amendment Act of 1967 implemented the recommendations.

The Wolfenden Report was to bring in its train considerable problems for the Church, and for many other religions which relied on the Biblical injunction, 'If a man also lie with mankind, as he lieth with a woman, both of them have committed an abomination: they shall surely be put to death; their blood shall be upon them.'[4] On several occasions since, Synod has overwhelmingly voted against accepting homosexual relationships; in 1987 it concluded that 'all Christians are called to be exemplary in all spheres of morality, including sexual morality; and that holiness of life is particularly required of Christian leaders.'[5] However, in 1991 the House of Bishops decided that the conscientious decision of those who enter into such relationships must be respected, and that the Church must 'not reject those who sincerely believe it is God's call to them'.[6]

Abolition of the Death Penalty

In 1965 Parliament passed the Murder (Abolition of Death Penalty) Act, which abolished the death penalty for murder in ᵗhis country, replacing it with a mandatory sentence of imprisonment for life. It was introduced as a Private Members Bill by the Jewish MP Sydney Silverman. The Jewish religion, while admitting the old prescription 'an eye for an eye', had always fought against capital punishment by making it too difficult to administer. The Act overlooked four other capital offences: high treason, 'piracy with violence' (piracy with intent to kill or cause grievous bodily harm), arson in royal dockyards and espionage, as well as other capital offences under military law, though these were finally proscribed in 1998 by the Human Rights Act and the Crime and Disorder Act.

Judith Maltby, writing in *The Guardian*, noted that it was the Nonconformist churches that led the movement towards abolition, but gradually the Church of England came round to support it, even though the majority of the rest of the nation wanted to keep the death penalty.[7] From time to time the question of abolition has been raised again, particularly when terrorism or threat of attack have troubled the United Kingdom, but the Church and Parliament have always fought off any attempt to bring back the death penalty.

Women in the Church

The Anglican Church was faced with another major problem at this time which had been simmering for many years: the question of admitting women to the Ministry. Quakers and some other dissenting religions had always viewed both sexes as equal when it came to leading the community in prayer, which included preaching. In 1992 General Synod passed a vote to ordain women. Because not everyone agreed to the idea, it set up the following year an official structure to enable parishes to refuse women's ministry. Congregations led by male priests could accept a Provincial Episcopal Visitor or 'flying bishop', who also rejected women as priests. This avoided a split in the Church and two other options allowed male priests to reject women's ministry. Men were allowed to leave the priesthood with appropriate financial support until they had resettled; and the Roman Catholic Church allowed married (and unmarried) Anglican priests to join its priesthood. The Archbishop of Canterbury, Robert Runcie, supported the ordination of women, and in 1994 thirty-two women were ordained as deaconesses. It took another twenty years until there could be a woman bishop. In January 2015 the Right Reverend Libby Lane was made Bishop of Stockport.

In London Dr David Hope, Bishop of London, had always opposed the idea of the ordination of women. *The Guardian* reported that most of his assistant bishops agreed with him, the one exception being the Bishop of Willesden, the Right Reverend Graham Dow. In his diocesan letter Dr Hope wrote that any parish opposed to women priests which found itself in an area administered by a bishop who has ordained or employed them, may transfer its allegiance to the Bishop of Fulham, the Rt Rev John Klyberg, who disagreed with female ordination. Some London churchmen said that they would break off all relations with a bishop who ordained women; others that they would secede to the Catholic church. Eventually even the most stringent insistence on 'men only' had to give way. The Master of the Charterhouse is now a woman, and the 'brothers' now include a 'sister' living in the almshouses.

Millennium

It is still disputed, among scholars as well as laymen, which year is the first year of a new millennium, in the current case 2000 or 2001. But as 1999 drew near the nation edged itself into a state of concern, bewilderment, even terror. The situation was referred to as the Millennium bug, or Y2K in computer-speak. For the United Kingdom was now a computerised nation. Computer programs used only the two final figures to mark the date, so that 1900 was the same as 2000. In 1997 rules were drawn up to govern both the current date when the Millennium came and the decision as to whether 2000 was a leap year. This, according to the Gregorian Calendar, was not a leap year as it was divisible by 100, but the exception to the rule was those years which could be divided by 400; so 2000 was indeed a leap year.

The Cabinet Office set up a website to help anyone concerned about what was likely to happen. The main problem lay with the roll-on effect of computer programs, especially those concerned with hospitals, banks, business and government. Apprehension as to what was coming led to fears of planes falling out of the sky, train crashes, banks closing (safes and doors were computer operated) and bombs going off without human intervention. Organisations and businesses were advised to prepare in plenty of time to override their online data.

The concept of food and fuel shortages and the disruption of transport led to families uprooting themselves to lead self-sufficient lifestyles away from the cities, and survivalist groups gave out severe warnings of the imminent end-of-the-world-as-we-know-it. In America in particular fundamentalist prophets of doom foretold apocalyptic events necessitating mass repentance, and in some cases the obligatory raising of funds to achieve salvation. Writers and preachers found readers and audiences beyond their wildest dreams and church leaders were amazed at their increased congregations.

In the event nothing happened at all. The biggest wonder was that the twenty-first century could evoke such perturbation, reminiscent of medieval ignorance and superstition. *Computer Weekly* referred to it as 'the biggest non-event of all time'.

London and the Millenium

Stuart Bell, representing the Church Commissioners, told Parliament,

> Among other things, hundreds of local congregations are making plans for activities and events under the three themes: 'a new start with God', 'a new start at home' and 'a new start for the world's poor'. Every parish in England will be encouraged to distribute millennium candles to their parishioners.[8]

There was a schools arts project called JC2000, and the Open Churches Trust encouraged every church bell in the land to be rung on New Year's Day.

The People and the Church

Perhaps the biggest problem facing the Church of England in the early years of the twenty-first century lay in the attitudes of its own parishioners. No longer were church leaders looked upon as inviolable, angels leading devils. They were mostly respected but no longer venerated. Some wore jeans and t-shirts, were called by their Christian names and introduced pop music to their services.

They were mortal men like any others, who could sin, transgress, misbehave and be called to account. Their words were available in the Press or online, anything they did or said was subject to debate. And it no longer threatened a man's immortal soul to deny the existence of God. As the authors Brown and Woodhead put it neatly, 'Deference became a thing of the past and paternalism was despised.'[9]

The reasons behind this diminution of church influence did not lie only in a general freedom from authoritarian restraint. There was an awareness, particularly in London, that Christianity was no longer all powerful. Other beliefs were competing for attention. In almost every street in the capital, living side by side, might be Jews and Catholics, Quakers and Muslims, struggling, often with complete success, to get along together. In the East End, for example, synagogues had become mosques, in Wembley former dress shops sold saris and in Borough Market almost any food could be bought, from yams and water melons, to Indian spices, Chinese rice or African coffee. London was by now truly cosmopolitan, in food, dress and religion.

The Inter Faith Movement

This widening of the boundaries encouraged the leaders of the different religions to work together to try to dispel racism and ignorance. Many opened their doors to visitors, spoke to schools to explain their beliefs and practices and even exchanged pulpits to offer a different slant on how to worship God. Religious freedom was becoming the norm with Londoners worshipping (or not) as they wished with little risk of condemnation or even disapproval.

The exception was the reaction of individuals, on the right or the left, who vented their dislike, verging sometimes on hatred and violence, by public outcry or private vilification. Defence of free speech and a free press had to be tempered with damage limitation so that the law was upheld and that the freedom of religion was maintained. In 1987 the Inter Faith Network was initiated with sixty founder organisations. Their hope lay in

> promoting greater understanding between the members of the different faith communities to which we belong and of encouraging the growth of our relationships of respect and trust and mutual enrichment in our life together.

The founders included Christians, Jews, Muslims, Sikhs, Hindus, Bahá'is, Buddhists and Jains, forming the first national interfaith structure in the world. The Jains were one of the latest eastern faiths to come to Britain, establishing a temple in Colindale, North London, in 2010.

The Network took it upon itself to meet together to discuss respect and understanding of all faiths, with local branches organising meetings to assemble their different religious bodies and improve their relationships. In the year of her Golden Jubilee the Queen stressed the importance of multi-faith and cultural rapprochement. She hosted a reception for 700 representatives of different faiths, and visited one place of worship of each of the major faiths. A Young Faith Forum welcomed eighty young people to come together to discuss their own religions and how they might integrate with those of others.

Racism in London

Nevertheless with all the goodwill in the world, London was never to escape the fearsome cloud of racism. Institutional racism reared its ugly head in such metropolitan organisations as the Police Force and Prison Service, the spread of the internet and the mobile phone enabled vicious onslaughts of religious and racial comment in spite of anti-discrimination laws and the work of the Commission for Racial Equality, formerly the Race Relations Board. Trevor Phillips, formerly its head, told *The Times* that he believed it would be impossible for a black candidate in the United Kingdom to rise to the top in politics because of institutional racism within the Labour Party. He said, 'If Barack Obama had lived here I would be very surprised if even somebody as brilliant as him would have been able to break through the institutional stranglehold that there is on power within the Labour party.'[10] Since that party's election of Jeremy Corbyn as its leader in 2015, similar accusations have been levelled against it concerning anti-Semitism.

Faith Schools

Church schools, convents, orthodox Jewish schools (Yeshivas), and Islamic schools (Madrassas) had existed in England for many years, but by the twenty-first century faith schools were becoming more popular. It had been mandatory for daily prayers to be held in all state-funded schools according to the Education Act of 1944. This was later changed to a 'collective act of worship' which had to be mainly of a Christian character. Independent schools were outside this statute and both Christian and Jewish schools could obtain state-funding. Other religious schools were included in the Labour Government provisions when they came to power in 1997, and the term 'faith schools' was used to describe them.

Many of these schools, especially the Catholic and Jewish schools, offered a very high standard of secular education, as well as studies of their own faiths. They had to follow the National Curriculum, which included a ban on teaching creationism as a scientific theory or failing to teach evolution in their science subjects. In 2016 the curriculum insisted on the teaching of a faith other than that to which the school belonged. Several religions produced teaching guides to help to explain their faith to those who had little knowledge of it.

Considerable concern was raised about the teaching methods of some religious academies. Islamic schools in some areas were found to be segregating pupils, failing to teach some subjects to girls and instructing their men and women staff separately. In London by this time many state schools had a minority of pupils for whom English was their first language, and white faces were outnumbered by black. Some faith schools were teaching in a foreign language. After inspection of some Jewish schools in London and other cities it was found that children born in this country could only speak Yiddish. In spite of strict rules on the setting up of faith schools, some were found to be unregistered and without adequate health and hygiene regulations in place.

In 1998 the Woolf Institute was set up in Cambridge under the direction of Lord Woolf. The Institute studies how 'relations between Jews, Christians and Muslims can enhance our understanding of key concepts of public life: community and identity, mutual respect, personal responsibility, and social solidarity.' In 2003 it established the Commission on Religion and Belief in Public Life. Chaired by Baroness Elizabeth Butler-Sloss, its aim is to consider the place and role of religion and belief in contemporary Britain. Its report, issued in 2015, covered such matters as faith schools, the Press and the BBC, and legal definitions of race, ethnicity and religion. It also made recommendations to ensure that all religious traditions are treated equally, that counter-terrorism legislation is enacted and that there is compliance with UK standards of gender equality and judicial independence by religious and cultural tribunals.

Same-sex Partnership

In November 2004 the United Kingdom passed the Civil Partnership Act legally recognising a union between two persons of the same sex. This could take place on any approved premises in Britain, but could not include any reading or music relating to religion. While the majority of British people approved of the step, many, particularly those with strong religious affiliations, did not. This was followed in 2013 by the Marriage (Same Sex Couples) Act. The marriage could take place in any location where a man and woman could marry, reserving the right for any religion to bar such a ceremony without contravening any discrimination legislation. The Act leaves it entirely up to the discretion of religious authorities to decide whether to carry out such a marriage. However, the Church of England does not countenance same sex marriage. As *The Guardian* stated,

Support for same-sex marriage among church members has significantly increased over the past three years despite the leadership's insistence that marriage can only be between a man and a woman, and its refusal to conduct church weddings for gay couples or allow gay priests to marry.[11]

Neither orthodox Jews nor Muslims permit same sex marriage.

CHAPTER XXV

Looking to the Future

The Establishment of the Church

THE CHANGES IN THE RELIGIOUS STRUCTURE of London have probably been greater in the twenty-first century than ever before. The Reformation had brought in Protestantism as the state religion, with the monarch as the Head of the Church. However, other religions have often taken centre stage, especially when discrimination and intolerance stole the headlines. Three future kings wait now in the wings to declare their allegiances. They may well feel that the disestablishment of the Church of England is overdue, particularly as the Royal family itself loses some of its pomp and circumstance. New generations of leaders will certainly form their own ideas as to their situation in modern religious developments. It is argued that the present Queen has provided her capital city with a solid foundation in politics, religion and social reform. She recognises that her faith, to which she is undoubtedly devoted, is not that of the majority of her people as far as active participation is concerned.

Disestablishment has been debated on and off by the clergy for centuries. In a lecture at Lambeth Palace in 2002 George Carey, then Archbishop of Canterbury, said,

> From the perspective of the Church of England, establishment helps to underwrite the commitment of a national Church to serve the entire community and to give form and substance to some of the deepest collective needs and aspirations.[1]

The Bishops still come down heavily on the side of retaining establishment, but concern about the cost of royal commitment may militate against future monarchs remaining head of the Church.

London as the Capital of the United Kingdom

London has never been a static element in Britain's religious life. It has inevitably changed over the centuries, in appearance, in culture and in ideas. It is still changing. Benedict XVI's visit to the United Kingdom in 2010 was the first state visit by a pope to the United Kingdom. The visit included the beatification of Cardinal Newman. His Holiness met the Queen and the Archbishop of Canterbury. In November 2016 Westminster won planning permission to add its first new tower in almost three hundred years, offering public access to a museum of treasures and curiosities housed in the triforium, the church's attic gallery.

Outbreaks of violence in European cities – Paris, Brussels and Berlin in recent times – have led to increased security measures in London. Armed police are becoming more evident on the streets, churches are kept locked at night and visitors' bags are searched on entry. The authorities are known to be taking more care in public places, such as restricting access to the Changing of the Guard at Buckingham Palace and increasing the police presence at football matches and entertainment. The 'enemy' is often regarded as the threat of terrorism by anti-Western elements, though the fear of individual acts of violence is equally a matter of concern. Jews are aware of increased anti-Semitism online, in universities and in anti-Israel demonstrations, while Muslims are sometimes the subject of discrimination in the workplace or on transport, and mosques have been attacked. However, the majority of Londoners go about their daily lives without too much fear of violence.

Isolated acts of terror, such as the outrages on Westminster Bridge and at Borough Market in 2017, have usually been shown to be committed by small numbers of criminals, sometimes working alone, but they do necessitate increased vigilance by the authorities. This can provoke resentment. It is perhaps the young who are most estranged from the 'authorised' religions they see about them. While still at school, they read, or more likely exchange on social media, idealistic dreams of putting the world to rights, as youngsters have always done. But the ease of flying abroad or buying dangerous materials online have altered their perspectives, and there is no-one to say 'no'. Every generation of parents has disapproved of its children's behaviour, and religion no longer has the controlling influence it once had.

There are exceptions. 'Honour killings' are abhorrent to the majority of Englishmen today, as is female genital mutilation. Religion has much to answer for. London has seen too many examples, from the fires at Smithfield to the terror of 7/7. But religion cannot be blamed for all the outrages that the capital city has undergone in its long history. The Plague, the Great

Fire of London, the Blitz and the Grenfell Tower disaster have all taken their toll, God being blamed perhaps, but not his followers. The majority of citizens live out their lives without being too much influenced by their religious affiliations. They pay little attention to the great upheavals that the Church has undergone in the last two thousand years. England is still a Christian country, in name at least. But Muslims can celebrate Ramadan, or Jews Yom Kippur, without being afraid, though fewer Christians attend Church at Christmas than do Jews at their New Year. There are more black faces in Peckham than white, and there are more spaces for worshippers in the Regent's Park mosque than in the average London parish church.

What London has gained by opening her gates to almost every religion known to man, is variety, tolerance, colour and learning. Schoolchildren teach their parents about their friends' faith. They visit strange places of worship and eat food their elders have never heard of. Sport, music, theatre and art have all played their part in bringing this about, and gradually the old fears and prejudices are beginning to disappear. They are still there but they have no proper place in London life. Modern communications have played a part; contact is immediate, which brings its own dangers. The capital city has fought hard to retain its character, its buildings and the personality of its people. Its religion is the biggest factor in achieving the distinctive nature of London. Remnants of religious constraints still linger. An orthodox Jew will not sit next to a woman on a London bus. A Sikh will not remove his turban to drive that bus. An observant Christian will not do his weekly shop on a Sunday. But all of these are free to do as they wish.

Nevertheless London's religious history has changed the face of the city out of all recognition. Districts such as the East End have sheltered different groups of immigrants – Irish, Huguenots, Jews, Bangladeshi – allowing them all to live where they liked, however mean, to worship as they wish, to dress the way they are used to. A Roman official would not recognise his town, nor would a Catholic friar, nor a Puritan Parliamentarian. But London has weathered all the storms, is still the capital of England and provides a home for any religious adherent who wants to live here.

It is hard to see what further changes in the religious life of London can lie ahead. New religions can form at any time. Perhaps in the future one all-prevalent form of faith will take over, though it seems hard to credit. Englishmen, and particularly Londoners, are too individualistic to accept such conformity. It is possible that a disregard for all forms of religion may become the norm. Richard Dawkins is quoted as saying, 'We are all atheists about most of the gods that societies have ever believed in. Some of us just go one god further.'[2] Dawkins himself has been embroiled in many often bitter discussions about belief – he is not the only one. Atheism, refusal to believe in God, and agnosticism, ignorance of God's existence, are as much a part of Londoners' faith as any religion. Today they are at liberty to say so without fear of punishment.

The Diocese of London was vacant for a time. Richard Chartres retired early in 2017 and a complex system of choosing a new bishop is now complete. In an amusing article about the problem in the *Spectator*, Ysendra Maxtone Graham wrote,

> The London profile is likely to be a nice friendly married person who knows London, not too raving Evangelical, not too raving High, who has worked in London before and has grown-up children and a few grandchildren and a dog.[3]

She was not far wrong. But the chosen candidate, in spite of fulfilling most of Graham's criteria, is a woman, the Right Reverend Dame Sarah Mullally, Bishop of Crediton. We are not informed about the dog!

Many commentators believe that religion, perhaps in a different form, is having a comeback. The quickest growing section of Jews in London is the ultra-orthodox. Many churches, particularly those with a more modern outlook, are enjoying an increase in church attendance. In spite of this it is becoming clear that it is organised religion that is going through a crisis. The charismatic churches are expanding, offering a less traditional religious experience to busy Londoners, especially the young, who are seeking something more than church services in the old style. They see religion as based on man's search for meaning in life, understanding his place in the universe. 'Mindfulness' is the key. The object is to offer a spiritual dimension to Londoners' daily lives. The Mindfulness Project delivers 'a full programme of mindfulness meditation courses, events and therapy'. Meditation has always played an important part in religious experience, particularly in the beliefs of oriental religions, and similar modern-day thought processes are providing for many what they believe to be lacking in the practical exercise in which they were brought up. Even the National Health Service is encouraging patients to use their minds to help their bodies. It suggests that 'paying more attention to the present moment – to your own thoughts and feelings, and to the world around you – can improve your mental wellbeing'.

London itself is open to all ideas on God or any other subject. As Peter Ackroyd says at the end of his book, 'London goes beyond any boundary or convention. It contains every wish or word ever spoken, every action or gesture ever made, every harsh or noble statement ever expressed. It is illimitable. It is Infinite London.'[4]

Notes

ABBREVIATIONS
A.S.C.   *Anglo-Saxon Chronicle*, Everyman Library, Dent, 1967
D.N.B.   *Oxford Dictionary of National Biography*
O.H.E.   *Oxford History of England*
O.I.H.E.   *Oxford Illustrated History of England*
Transactions *Jewish Historical Society of England Transactions*

CHAPTER 1 – CELTS AND ROMANS
 1 Bede, *Ecclesiastical History of the English People*, Oxford World Classics Edition, Oxford
    University Press, 1999, p.5
 2 Wheeler, R.E.M., *London in Roman Times*, London Museum Catalogue No. 3, Lancaster
    House, 1930, p.16
 3 Gomme, Laurence, *The Making of London*, Oxford University Press, 1912, p.43
 4 Ackroyd, Peter, *London – The Biography*, Vintage Books, 2001, pp.13-17
 5 Merrifield, Ralph, *Roman London*, Cassell, 1969, p.179
 6 Tertullian, *De Corona XV*, 3-4, Quoted in Guy de la Bédoyère, *Gods with Thunderbolts –
    Religion in Roman Britain*, Tempus, 2002, p.172
 7 Appelbaum, Shimon, 'Were there Jews in Roman Britain?' in *Jewish Historical Society of
    England Transactions*, No. 17, 1951/2
 8 Collingwood, R.G. and Myers, J.N.L., *Roman Britain and the English Settlements*, O.H.E.,
    1945, p.263

CHAPTER II – ANGLO-SAXON LONDON
 1 Wheeler, *op. cit.*, p.23
 2 Gildas, *De Excidio et Conquestu Britanniae*, 1, p.20
 3 Bede, *op. cit.*, p.27
 4 Quoted by David Streater, 'How England Became Christian', in *Crossway*, Summer,
    1995, No. 57
 5 Finberg, H.P.R., *The Formation of England, 550-1042*. Paladin, 1976, p.36
 6 Bede, *op. cit.*, p.40
 7 Finberg, *op cit.*, p.37
 8 Bede, *op. cit.*, p.56
 9 *Ibid.*, p.57
10 The original of the poem is in the British Library (Harley MS 2250), but was reprinted
    by Israel Gollancz in 1926

CHAPTER III – THE VIKINGS
 1 A.S.C., p.54
 2 Vince, Alan, *Saxon London: An Archaeological Investigation*, Seaby, 1990, p.6
 3 Pryce, Huw, 'The Christianisation of Society', in Davies, Wendy (ed.) *From the Vikings
    to the Normans,* The Short Oxford History of the British Isles, Oxford University Press,
    2003, p.142

4 I Kings, I:39
5 Forester, Thomas (ed.), *The Chronicle of Florence of Worcester,* Bohn, 1894, p.102
6 From the *Saga of St Olaf,* 13th cent., quoted by Wheeler, op.cit., p.14
7 Florence of Worcester, *op.cit.,* p.168
8 William of Malmesbury, *op.cit.,* p.225

CHAPTER IV – NORMAN LONDON
1 William of Malmesbury, *ibid.,* p.279
2 Bates, David, 'William I', in *Dictionary of National Biography*
3 William of Malmesbury, *Ibid.,* p.280
4 Florence of Worcester, *Ibid.,* p.171
5 Pevsner, Nikolaus, *The Buildings of England,* Vol. I, Penguin Books, 1957, p.185
6 Quoted in Joe Hillaby, 'The London Jewry: William I to John', *Transactions of the Jewish Historical Society of England,* Vol. XXXIII, 1992-1994, p.3
7 William of Malmesbury, p.291
8 A.S.C., p.219
9 Fitzstephen, William, *A Description of London,* translated by H.E. Butler, in F.M. Stenton, *Norman London, An Essay,* The Historical Association, 1934, p.25
10 *Ibid.,* p.27
11 *Ibid.,* p.28
12 Barlow, Frank, *The English Church 1066-1154,* Longmans, 1979, p.27
13 Gillingham, John, The Early Middle Ages 1066-1290, in *The Oxford Illustrated History of England,* Oxford University Press, 1980, p.114
14 Florence of Worcester, *op. cit.,* p.203
15 William of Malmesbury, *op. cit.,* p.337
16 Asbridge, Thomas, *The First Crusade,* Free Press, 2004, p.66
17 William of Malmesbury, *op. cit.,* p.342
18 Potter, K.R. (ed.), *Gesta Stephani,* Oxford University Press, 1976, p.4
19 *Ibid.,* p.123
20 Barlow, *op. cit.,* p.2
21 Barlow, *op.cit.,* p.3

CHAPTER V – THE ANGEVIN DYNASTY
1 Greenway, Diana (ed.), Henry, Archdeacon of Huntingdon, *Historia Anglorum,* Clarendon Press, Oxford, 1996, p.771
2 Walsh, P.G., Kennedy, M.J., *William of Newburgh – The History of English Affairs,* Aris and Phillips, 2007, Book II, p.105
3 T.S. Eliot, *Murder in the Cathedral,* Faber and Faber, 1935, p.73
4 Fitz Stephen, *op. cit.,* p.26
5 D'Bloissiers Tovey, *Anglia Judaica,* Weidenfeld & Nicolson (1738), 1999, p.16
6 Warren, W.L., *King John,* Eyre and Spottiswood, 1964, p.181
7 *Ibid.,* p.230
8 Stow, John, *A Survey of London,* The History Press, 2009, p.31
9 Warren, *Ibid.,* p.265
10 Feiling, Keith, *A History of England,* MacMillan, 1966, p.160

CHAPTER VI – THE FIRST PLANTAGENETS
1 Powicke, Maurice, *The Thirteenth Century,* O.H.E., O.U.P. 1953, p.19

2 Adler, Michael, *Jews of Medieval England,* The Jewish Historical Society of England, 1939, p.282

3 Paris, Matthew, *English History: 1235-1273*, three vols., translated by J.A. Giles, Bohn, 1852, III, p.115

4 *Ibid.,* III, p.76

5 Stacey, Robert, 'The English Jews under Henry III', in *The Jews in Medieval Britain,* ed. Patricia Skinner, The Boydell Press, 2003, p.41

6 Paris, *op. cit.,* III, p.347

7 Powicke, *op. cit.* p.224

8 Stow, *op. cit.,* p.117

9 Churchill, Winston, *A History of the English-Speaking Peoples,* Cassell, 1956, Vol. I, p.226

10 Tovey, *op. cit.,* p.110

11 Quoted in Abrahams, B.L., 'The Condition of the Jews at the Time of Their Expulsion in 1290', in *Transactions,* Vol. 2, 1894/5, p.29

12 Tovey, *op. cit.,* p.130

13 Wright, Thomas, *On the Evil Times of Edward II,* 1321

14 Churchill, *op. cit.,* Vol. l, p.278

15 Stow, *op. cit.,* p.361

CHAPTER VII – THE LATER MIDDLE AGES

1 Quoted in Stephen Lahey, *John Wyclif,* Oxford University Press, 2009, p.18

2 From John Wyclif, *On Civil Dominion,* quoted in *History Today,* May 2015, p.8

3 Quoted in Arthur Bryant, The Age of Chivalry (*The Story of England),* Collins, 1963, p.481

4 Walsingham, Thomas, The St Albans Chronicle, *The* Chronica Maiora *of Thomas Walsingham, II,* Taylor, John, Wendy R. Childs, Leslie Watkiss (eds.), Clarendon Press, Oxford, 2011, p.207

5 Froissart, Jean, *Chronicles,* Penguin Edition, 1968, p.464

6 Translated from 'The Twelve Conclusions of the Lollards', English Historical Review, 22 (1907), p.292.

7 Walsingham, *op. cit.,*p.633

8 Stow, *op. cit.,* p.313

9 Walsingham, *op. cit.* p.621

CHAPTER VIII – YORK AND LANCASTER

1 James, M.R. (ed.), *Henry VI – A Reprint of John Blacman's Memoir,* Cambridge University Press, 1919, p.26

2 *Ibid.,* p.34

3 Stow, *Ibid.,* p.111

4 Vitellius, in C.L. Kingsford (ed.), *Chronicles of London,* Clarendon Press, Oxford, 1905, p.173

5 Halle, Edward, *Chronicle; containing the History of England,* J.Johnson, 1809, p.254

6 Gairdner, James (ed.), *The Paston Letters,* Alan Sutton, 1986, No. 753

7 Halle, *op. cit.,* p.285

8 *Ibid.,* p.294

9 Wolffe, Bertram, *Henry VI,* Eyre Methuen. 1981, p.345

10 Halle, *op.cit.,* p.296

11 Ross, Charles, *Edward IV,* Eyre Methuen, 1974, p.265

12 Carter, John, Percy Muir (eds.), *Printing and the Mind of Man* catalogue, Cassell & Co., 1967, p.xxii

CHAPTER IX – THE COMING OF THE TUDORS
1 Ross, *op.cit.,* p.162
2 Vitellius, *op.cit.,* p.190
3 Shakespeare, *Richard III,* Act III, Scene 2
4 Quoted in Saint, Andrew and Darley, Gillian in *The Chronicles of London,* Weidenfeld & Nicolson, 1954
5 Field, John, *Kingdom, Power and Glory – A historical guide to Westminster Abbey.* James and James, 2008, p.66
6 Pevsner, *op. cit.,* Vol. I, p.359
7 Field, *op.cit.,* p.75
8 Halle, *op. cit.,* p.491
9 Penn, Thomas, *The Winter King – The Dawn of Tudor England,* Penguin Books, 2011, p.156

CHAPTER X – REFORMATION
1 Vergil, Polydore, *Anglia Historica,* Trans. Denys Hay, Royal Historical Society, 1950, p.259
2 Dickens, A.G., *The English Reformation,* Collins, The Fontana Library, 1970, p.65
3 Vergil, *op. cit.,* p.307
4 Halle, *op.cit.,* 754
5 *Ibid.,* p.755
6 Vergil, *op.cit.,* p.333
7 Elton, G.R., *England Under the Tudors,* Methuen & Co., 1971, p.122
8 Quoted in David. S. Katz, *The Jews in the History of England,* Clarendon Press, Oxford, 1994, p.30
9 Scarisbrick, J.J., *Henry VIII,* Penguin Books, 1971, p.340
10 Dickens, *op. cit.,* p.121
11 Halle, p.816
12 Dickens, *op. cit.,* p.155
13 Collinson, Patrick, *The Reformation,* Phoenix Books, 2005, p.45
14 Halle, p.817

CHAPTER XI – MONASTERIES AND MARTYRS
1 Magno, Alessandro, *London Journal,* in The London Journal, Vol. IX, 1983, p.142
2 Stow, *op. cit.,* p.226
3 Field, *op. cit.* p.79
4 Dickens, *op. cit.,* p.185
5 Quoted in Dickens, *ibid.,* p.146
6 Penny-Mason, Benjamin, 'The Children of the Reformation', in *Current Archaeology,* April 2015
7 Scarisbrick, *op. cit.,* p.486
8 Elton, *op. cit.,* p.159
9 *Ibid.,* p.202
10 Quoted in Scarisbrick, *op. cit.,* p.607
11 From the Preface to *The Book of Common Prayer,* 1549
12 Le Huray, Peter, *Music and the Reformation in England, 1549-1660,* Herbert Jenkins, 1967, p.7

CHAPTER XII – THE LAST TUDORS

1 Elton, *op. cit.,* p.216
2 Foxe, John, *Book of Martyrs,* ed. W.B. Forbush, Zondervan, 1967, p.209
3 *Ibid.,* p.210
4 Elton, *op. cit.* p.262
5 Brigden, Susan, *London and the Reformation,* Clarendon Press, Oxford, 1989, p.636
6 Cardwell, Edward, *Documentary Annals of the Church of England,* Oxford University Press, 1844, Vol. I, p.374
7 Black, Joseph L., *The Martin Marprelate Tracts,* Cambridge University Press, 2008.
8 *Venetian State Papers, 1594,* No. 258. Shakespeare is believed to have based Shylock in *The Merchant of Venice* on Roderigo Lopez
9 John Roche Dasent (ed.), Queen Elizabeth to the Lord Mayor, 11 July 1596, in *Acts of Privy Council of England*
10 *Regnans in Excelsis,* Excommunicating Elizabeth I of England, Pope St Pius V – 25 February 1570
11 Southern, Antonia, *House Divided – Christianity in England 1526-1829,* Academia Press, 2014, p.74
12 Squire, W. Barclay, 'Music' in *Shakespeare's England,* Oxford University Press, 1950, Vol. ii, p.27.
13 Rowse, A.L., *The England of Elizabeth – The Structure of Society,* McMillan & Co., 1951, p.391
14 Simpson, W. Sparrow, *Documents Illustrating the History of St Paul's Cathedral,* Camden Society, 1880
15 *Venetian State Papers, 1588,* No. 642, 644
16 Rowse, *op.cit.,* p.144
17 Shakespeare, *King Lear,* Act I, Scene 2

CHAPTER XIII – THE FIRST STUARTS

1 Manningham, John, *The Diary,* edited by Robert Parker Soulien, University Press of New England, 1976, p.208
2 Willson, David, *King James VI and I,* Jonathan Cape, 1956, p.25
3 Dekker, Thomas, *The Plague Pamphlets,* ed. F.P. Wilson, Clarendon Press, 1925,
4 Fuller, Thomas, *A Church History of Britain,* Oxford University Press, 1845, Vol. V, p.305
5 Paxman, Jeremy, *The English,* Penguin Books, 2007, p.112
6 Daiches, David, *A Critical History of English Literature,* Secker and Warburg, 1960, p.467
7 Manningham, *op. cit.,* p.218
8 Southern, *op. cit.,* p.110
9 This letter is now believed to be a fake.
10 Quoted in Antonia Fraser, *The Gunpowder Plot,* Weidenfeld and Nicolson, 1996, p.169
11 Acts of the Privy Council, 1618/19
12 Earle, John, *Microcosmography; or A Piece of the World Discovered,* (ed.), Philip Bliss, John Harding & White & Cochrane, 1811, p.105
13 Dekker, Thomas, *The Gull's Horn Book,* J.B. Gutch, Bristol, 1812, p.105
14 In the *Oxford Book of Seventeenth Century Verse,* chosen by H.J.C. Grierson and G. Bullough, Clarendon Press, 1934, p.147
15 Phillips, Henry E.I., 'An Early Stuart Judaizing Sect', in *Transactions,* Vol. XV, p.67
16 Davies, Godfrey, *The Early Stuarts, 1603-1660,* O.H.E., 1937, p.69
17 *Camden Miscellany,* Vol. 55, 1853

18 From a lecture 'Cultural Revolution: Palaces of the Early Stuart Kings' by Simon Thurley, at Gresham College, 8th October 2014

CHAPTER XIV – REVOLUTION
  1 Revelations, XX:2
  2 Collinson, Patrick, *English Puritanism,* Historical Association, 1983, p.26
  3 See Sara Read's 'A Women's Revolt' in *History Today,* August, 2015, p.6
  4 Lindley, Keith, *Popular Politics and Religion in Civil War London,* Scolar Press, 1997, p.404
  5 Hill, Christopher, *The World turned Upside Down,* Penguin, 1985, p.203
  6 Revelations, XI:3
  7 Thompson, E.P., *The Making of the English Working Class,* Pelican Books, 1972, p.52
  8 Hill, Christopher, Barry Reay, William Lamont, *The World of the Muggletonians,* Temple Smith, 1983
  9 Davies, *op. cit.,* p.154
  10 *Ibid.,* p.154
  11 Evelyn, John, *Diary,* Everyman Edition, 1945, Vol. I, p.245
  12 Saint, Darley, *op. cit.,* p.102
  13 Baron, Xavier (ed.), *London 1066-1914, Literary Sources and Documents,* Helm Information, 1997, Vol. I, p.386
  14 *Daniel,* II:44
  15 Roth, Cecil, *A History of the Jews in England,* Oxford University Press, 1942, p.167

CHAPTER XV – RESTORATION
  1 Hill, Christopher, *The Century of Revolution,1603-1714,* Sphere Books Ltd., 1975, p.165
  2 Quoted in C.V. Wedgwood, *Poetry and Politics under the Stuarts,* Cambridge University Press, 1961, p.126
  3 Henry, Philip, *Diary and Letters,* ed. Matthew Lee, Kegan Paul, Trench & Co., 1882, p.179
  4 Burnet, Gilbert, *A History of His Own Time,* ed. Thomas Stackhouse, Everyman Edition, J.M. Dent and Sons, 1910, p.33
  5 Evelyn, *op. cit.* Vol. I, p.319
  6 Henry, *op. cit.,* p.177
  7 Pepys, Samuel, *The Shorter Pepys,* Selected and Edited by Robert Latham, Bell & Hyman, 1985, p.413
  8 Daiches, *op. cit.,* p.438
  9 Evelyn, *op. cit.,* Vol. I, p.404
  10 Quoted in Watson Nicholson, *The Historical Sources of Defoe's 'Journal of the Plague Year',* The Stratford Co., 1919, p.59
  11 Vincent, Thomas, *God's Terrible Voice in the City,* Soli Deo Gloria Ministries, 1997 Introduction
  12 *Ibid.,* p.2
  13 National Archives, Orders for the prevention of the plague (SP29/155 f.102)
  14 *Ibid.*
  15 *Ibid.*
  16 Vincent, *op. cit.,* p.46/47
  17 Venetian State Papers, 1666, No. 77
  18 Vincent, *op. cit.,* p.57
  19 Betjeman, John, *The City of London Churches,* Pitkin Books Ltd., 1974
  20 *London 1066-1914, op.cit.,* p.552

21 Kenyon, John, *The Stuart Constitution 1603-1688*, Cambridge University Press, 1986, p.383
22 —, *The Popish Plot*, Pelican Books, 1974, p.58
23 *Ibid.*, p.289
24 —, *The Stuart Constitution*, p.388
25 Evelyn, *op. cit.*, p.212
26 Spurr, John, *The Post-Reformation: Religion, Politics and Society in Britain 1603-1714*, Pearson Longman, 2006, p.173
27 Evelyn, *op. cit.*, p.277

CHAPTER XVI – THE END OF THE STUARTS
1 Bramston, Sir John, *Autobiography*, Camden Society, 1845, p.355
2 Evelyn, *op. cit.*, p.290
3 Burnet, *op. cit.*, p.297
4 Reresby, John, *Memoirs*, Royal Historical Society, 1991, p.545
5 Trevor-Roper, Hugh, *Catholics, Anglicans and Puritans*, Secker & Warburg, 1987, p.118
6 Katz, David S., *The Jews in the History of England, 1485-1850*, Clarendon Press, 1994, p.13
7 Fiennes, Celia, *The Journeys of Celia Fiennes* (ed. Christopher Morris), The Cresset Press, 1949, p.143
8 Holmes, Geoffrey, *Religion and Party in late Stuart England*. Historical Association, 1875, p.15
9 Hill, *The Century of Revolution*, p.252
10 Burnet, *op. cit.*, p.359
11 *Ibid.*, p.360
12 Fiennes, *op. cit.*, p.294
13 Kenyon, J.P., *The Stuarts*, B.T. Batsford, 1958, p.205
14 Quoted in Hopkinson, M.R., *Anne of England*, Constable & Co., 1934, p.90

CHAPTER XVII – THE HANOVERIAN INHERITANCE
1 A True Account of the Proceedings at Perth, Written by a Rebel, J. Baker, 1716, p.20
2 Cowper, Mary, Countess, *Diary*, John Murray, 1864, p.62
3 Miège, Guy, *The Present State of Great Britain and Northern Ireland in Three Parts*, 4th Edition, 1718, p.150
4 Cragg, Gerald R., *The Church and the Age of Reason*, Penguin, 1990, p.117
5 Cowper, *op. cit.*, p.132
6 Hervey, Lord, *Memoirs of the Reign of George II*, John Murray, 1848, Vol. I, p.289
7 Miège, *op. cit.*, p.104
8 Defoe, Daniel, *A Tour Through the Whole Island of Great Britain*, Penguin Edition, 1871, p.286
9 Wesley, John, *The Journal*, Everyman Edition, 1948, Vol. I, p.343
10 Lackington, James, *Memoirs of the First Forty-Five Years of the Life of James Lackington*, 1791
11 Davies, Rupert, *What Methodists Believe*, A.R. Mowbray, 1976, p.95
12 *The Caledonian Mercury*, October 14th, 1745
13 Saint and Darley, *op. cit.*, p.140
14 Gwynn, Robin, 'England's "First Refugees"', in *History Today*, May, 1985
15 Hervey, *op. cit.*, p.298
16 George, M. Dorothy, *London Life in the Eighteenth Century*, Penguin Books, 1966, p.57
17 Blake, William, *Songs of Experience*, Oxford University Press, 1967, p.212
18 Defoe, *op. cit.*, p.174

19 Summers, W.H., *Memories of Jordans and the Chalfonts,* Headley Brothers, 1904, p.119
20 Plumb, J.H., *The Four Georges,* Fontana/Collins, 1956, p.100
21 Boswell, James, *The Life of Dr.Johnson,* Everyman Edition, 1913, Vol. II, p.369
22 Woodforde, James, *The Diary of a Country Parson, 1758-1802,* Oxford University Press, 1931, p.148
23 *Ibid.,* p.318
24 Pope, Alexander, *Essay on Man,* Epistle III, Oxford University Press, 1966, p.261
25 Boswell, *op. cit.,* Vol. II, p.268

CHAPTER XVIII – RIOTS AND REVOLTS
1 *North Briton,* No. 45, 1763
2 Plumb, J.H., *England in the Eighteenth Century,* Penguin Books, 1950, p.121
3 Chesterfield, Lord, *Letters,* Oxford University Press, World's Classics, 2008, p.361. The opening of trade with India brought many wealthy 'nabobs' over to England to 'buy' seats in Parliament.
4 Thompson, *op. cit.,* p.39
5 Boswell, *op. cit.,* Vol. 1, p.526
6 Jefferson, Thomas, *A Summary View of the rights of British America,* Clementina Rind, 1774, p.1
7 Quoted in Christopher Hibbert, *King Mob,* Longman, Green & Co., 1958, p.9/10
8 Cowper, William, *The Works 1765-1735,* Fraser & Co., 1835, p.66
9 Baron, *op. cit.,* Vol. 1, p.731
10 Hibbert, *op. cit.,* p.130
11 Haydon, Colin, *Anti-Catholicism in eighteenth Century England,* Manchester University Press, 1993. P.242
12 Ackroyd, *op. cit.,* p.492
13 Wordsworth, William, From The Prelude, *Poetry and Prose,* Rupert Hart-Davis, 1955. P.458
14. Bowra, C.M., *The Romantic Imagination,* Oxford University Press, 1950, p.1
15 *Ibid.*p.287
16 Mahomet, Deen, *the Travels of Dean Mahomet,* ed. Michael H. Fisher, University of California Press, 1997, p.69

CHAPTER XIX – EMPIRE AND DOMINION
1 Quoted in Walvin, James, *A Short History of Slavery, Penguin Books,* 2007, p.181
2 More, Hannah, *Slavery, A Poem,* T. Cadell, 1788
3 Marshall, Dorothy, *English People in the Eighteenth Century,* Longmans, Green, 1956, p.157
4 Howell's *State Trials,* Vol. 20, Cols. 1-6, 79-82, National Archives
5 Clarke, John, *The Life and Times of George III,* Weidenfeld and Nicolson, 1972, p.181
6 Losh, James, *Diaries,* The Surtees Society, 1963, Vol. II, p.79
7 Wade, John, *The Extraordinary Black Book,* E.Wilson, 1831, Title Page
8 Woodward, E.L., *The Age of Reform, 1815-1870,* O.H.E., 1949, p.483
9 Quoted in Alec R. Vidler, *The Church in an Age of Revolution,* Penguin History of the Church, Penguin Books, 1990, p.47
10 Newman, John Henry, *Apologia Pro Vita Sua,* World's Classics, Oxford University Press, 1964, p.31
11 Hopper, K. Theodore, 'The Oxford Movement', *History Today.* March 1967
12 Bernard, Philippa, *A Beacon of Light – The History of the West London Synagogue,* West London Synagogue, 2013, p.15

CHAPTER XX – VICTORIAN LONDON

1 Vidler, *op.cit.*, p.114
2 *Ibid.*, p.117
3 *MacMillan's Magazine*, October 1898
4 *The Times*, 2.3.2016
5 Kriegel, Abraham (ed.), *The Holland House Diaries, 1831-1840*, Routledge & Kegan Paul, 1977, p.236
6 British Parliamentary Papers, 1851. Census Great Britain, Report and Tables on Religious Worship in England and Wales, Irish University Press, 1970
7 Quoted in Gibbs-Smith, C. *The Great Exhibition 1851*, HMSO, 1981, May 1851
8 Cantor, Geoffrey, 'The Great Exhibition: Commerce and Christianity' in *History Today*, July 2010
9 Thorp, Malcolm R., 'Sectarian Violence in Early Victorian Britain: The Mormon Experience, 1837-1860', *Bulletin of the John Rylands University Library of Manchester*, 70, Autumn, 1988
10 Ackroyd, *op. cit.*, p.675
11 Gartner, Lloyd P., *The Jewish Immigrant in England 1870-1914*, Simon Publications, 1973, p.152
12 Zangwill, Israel, *Children of the Ghetto*, Heinemann, 1893, p.30
13 *Jewish Chronicle*, 13.3.1885
14 Raine, Kathleen, *India Seen Afar*, Green Books, 1990, p.18
15 See Anne de Courcy, *The Fishing Fleet – Husband-Hunting in the Raj*, Weidenfeld & Nicolson, 2012
16 From the Neasden Temple website: BAPS Shri Swaminarayan Mandir, Neasden

CHAPTER XXI – WORLD WAR I

1 Held at the Lambeth Palace Library
2 Russell, Bertrand, *Mysticism and Logic*, Penguin Books, 1953, p.54
3 See *Papal Encyclicals* online
4 Vidler, *op. cit.*, p.161
5 *Ibid.*, p.162
6 Langham, Mgr. Mark, *Westminster Cathedral*, (revised Patrick Rogers, 2011), p.4
7 Stow, *op. cit.*, p.342
8 Pevsner, *op. cit.*, Vol. II, p.392
9 Morison, Arthur, *A Child of the Jago*, Oxford World Classics, 2012, p.11
10 *An East End Vicar and his Work*, Tower Hamlets History Online, *www.mernick.org.uk*, 1895
11 *Ibid.*
12 Gilley, Keith, *Gertrud von Petzold*, D.N.B.
13 Quoted in Anne Sebba, *Jenny Churchill*, John Murray, 2008, p.269
14 Davies, Charles Maurice, *Unorthodox London*, Tinsley Brothers, 1875 (republished by Forgotten Books, 2002), p.182
15 *The Jewish Chronicle*, 17.10.1913
16 See Anand, Anita, Sophia: Princess, Suffragette, Revolutionary, Bloomsbury Publishing, 2015
17 Dangerfield, George, The Strange Death of Liberal England, MacGibbon & Kee, 1966, p.20
18 London Congress of the Russian Social-Democratic Labour Party (Notes of a Delegate), Foreign Languages Publishing House, Moscow, Marxist Internet Archive
19 Rocker, Rudolf, *The London Years*, Five Leaves Publications, 2005, p.93

20 Paxman, *op. cit.*, p.98
21 Ensor, Robert, *England, 1870-1914*, O.H.E., 1975, p.527
22 Bergonzi, Bernard, *Heroes' Twilight*, Constable, 1965, p.20
23 Chesterton, G.K., *The Man Who Was Thursday*, J.W. Arrowsmith, 1908
24 Fitzroy, Sir Almeric, *Memoirs*, George H. Doran, 1925, Vol. II, p.560
25 Quoted in Martin Gilbert, *The First World War*, Harper Collins, 1995, p.22
26 Churchill, Winston, *The World Crisis*, 1911-1918, Odhams Press, 1939, Vol. I, p.186
27 Peel, C.S., *How We Lived Then*, John Lane, 1929, p.16
28 *The Times*, 12.8.1914
29 *Daily Telegraph*, 3.5.2014
30 Quoted in Gilbert, *op. cit.*, p.280

CHAPTER XXII – BETWEEN THE WARS
 1 Ewer, William Norman, *Five Souls*, in *The Nation*, 3.10.1914
 2 Brittain, Vera, *Testament of Youth*, Little, Brown, 1978, p.460
 3 Rhondda, The Viscountess, *This was My World*, Macmillan, 1933, p.210
 4 Woolf, Leonard, *Downhill All The Way*, Autobiography, Vol. IV, Hogarth Press, 1967. p.9
 5 Humphreys, Christmas, *The Development of Buddhism in England*, The Buddhist Lodge, 1937, p.21
 6 Woolf, Leonard, *op. cit.*, p.207
 7 *The Times*, 5.5.1924
 8 *British Gazette*, 6.5.1926
 9 BBC Charter, Editorial Guidelines, 12.2.3.
10 Taylor, A.J.P., *English History, 1914-1945*, O.H.E., 1965, p.168
11 Nicolson, Harold, *Diaries and Letters 1930-1964*, Collins, 1980, p.41
12 Luther, Martin, *Of the Jews and their Lies*, Christian Nationalist Crusade, 1948, p.22
13 Chandler, Andrew, 'Faith in the Nation? The Church of England in the 20th Century', *History Today*, May, 1997
14 *The Tablet*, February, 1939
15 Phayer, Michael, *The Catholic Church and the Holocaust 1930-65*, Indiana University Press, 2000, p.xii
16 Hastings, Adrian, *A History of English Christianity 1920-1985*, Collin, 1986, p.251
17 Quoted in Anthony Julius, *Trials of the Diaspora: a History of Anti-Semitism in England*, Oxford University Press, 2010, p.432
18 Lawson, Tom, *The Church of England and the Holocaust*, The Boydell Press, 2006, p.34
19 Rubinstein, William D., *The Myth of Rescue*, Routledge, 1997
20 Nicolson, *op. cit.*, p.128
21 Taylor, *op. cit.*, p.398
22 *Ibid.*, p.89
23 *Ibid.*, p.108
24 *The Yorkshire Post*, 9.12.16
25 *The Times*, 11.12.36
26 Windsor, Duke of, A King's Story, Cassell, 1951, p.317
27 BBC, 13.12.36

CHAPTER XXIII – WORLD WAR II
 1 Woolf, Leonard, *op. cit.*, p.254
 2 Beaken, Robert, *Cosmo Lang, Archbishop in War and Crisis*, I.B. Tauris, 2012, p.149
 3 *The Times*, 21.12.1940

4 Bernard, *op. cit.*, p.126
5 Todd, Ruthven, 'These are Facts' in *The Terrible Rain – The War Poets 1939-45*, Eyre Methuen, 1966, p.65
6 Visram, Rozina, *Asians in Britain, 400 Years of History*, Pluto Press, 2002, p.268
7 *Ibid.*, p.275
8 Nicolson, *Diaries and Letters, 1939-45*, Collins, 1967, p.469
9 Hastings, *op. cit.*, p.377
10 *Ibid.*, p.531
11 *The New English Bible*, Oxford University Press, 1970, p.v
12 *The Observer*, 17.3.63
13 Anniversary Dinner of the National Health Service at the Guildhall, 25.7.68
14 *The Times*, 6.6.73
15 BBC British History, Windrush Arrivals, 2014
16 Eliot, T.S., 'Thoughts after Lambeth', in *Selected Essays*, Faber and Faber, 1976, p.366

CHAPTER XXIV – THE MILLENNIUM AND AFTER
1 *The Spectator*, 22.5.1964
2 *The Times*, 7.11.1953
3 Hastings, *op. cit.*, p.585
4 Leviticus 20:13 (King James Version)
5 General Synod, November 1987
6 Issues in Human Sexuality, CHP 1991
7 *The Guardian*, 19.8.11
8 Hansard – Parliamentary Business, 10.5.99
9 Brown, Andrew and Woodhead, Linda, *That Was The Church That Was*, Bloomsbury, 2016, p.16
10 *The Times*, 8.11.08
11 *The Guardian*, 29.1.16

CHAPTER XXV – LOOKING TO THE FUTURE
1 Quoted in R.M. Morris (ed.), *Church and State in 21st Century Britain*, Palgrave MacMillan, 2009, p.186
2 Dawkins, Richard, *On Militant Atheism*, TED Conference, February 2002
3 *The Spectator*, 11.2.17
4 Ackroyd, *op. cit.*, p.778

Bibliography

Abrahams, Israel, *Jewish Life in the Middle Ages,* E. Goldston, 1932
Ackroyd, Peter, *London – The Biography,* Vintage Books, 2001
— *London Under,* Chatto & Windus, 2011
Ansari, Humayun, *The Infidel Within: Muslims in Britain since 1800,* Hurst, 2004
Arnold, John H.(ed.), *The Oxford Handbook of Medieval Christianity,* Oxford University Press, 2014
Bank, J. and and Gevers, Lieve, *Church and Religion in World War II,* Bloomsbury Academic, 2016
Barlow, Frank, *The English Church1066-1154,* Longmans, 1979
Baron, Xavier (ed.), *London 1066-1914, Literary Sources and Documents*, Helm Information, 1997
Barron, Caroline, *London in the Later Middle Ages,* Oxford University Press, 2004
Beaken, Robert, *Cosmo Lang, Archbishop in War and Crisis,* J.B. Tauris, 2012
Bede, The Venerable, *Ecclesiastical History of the English People*, Oxford World Classics Edition, O.U.P., 1999
Bell, W.G., *Unknown London,* John Lane, 1909
— *The Great Plague in London,* The Bodley Head, 1951
Bernard, G., *The Late Medieval Church,* Yale University Press, 2012
Bernard, Philippa, *A Beacon of Light – the History of the West London Synagogue,* West London Synagogue, 2013
Betjeman, John, *The City of London Churches,* Pitkin Books Ltd., 1974
Black, Joseph L., *The Martin Marprelate Tracts,* Cambridge University Press, 2008
Bloom, Clive, *Violent London,* Sidgwick & Jackson, 2003
Booth, William, *In Darkest England, and the Way Out,* Salvation Army, 1890
Bowra, Maurice, *The Romantic Imagination,* Oxford University Press, 1950
Boswell, James, *The Life of Dr. Johnson,* Everyman Edition, 1913
Bramston, Sir John, *Autobiography,* Camden Society, 1845
Brigden, Susan, *London and the Reformation,* Clarendon Press, 1989
Brittain, Vera, *Testament of Youth,* Little, Brown, 1978
Brooke, Christopher and Gillian Keir, *London 800-1216; The Shaping of a City*Secker & Warburg, 1975
Brooke, Christopher and Rosalind Brooke, *Popular Religion in the Middle Ages,* Thames & Hudson, 1984
Brown, Andrew and Linda Woodhead, *That Was the Church That Was ...* Bloomsbury, 2016
Bullock, Alan, *A Study in Tyranny,* Hamlyn, 1973
Burnet, Gilbert, *A History of His Own Time,* ed. Thomas Stackhouse, Everyman Edition, J.M. Dent and Sons, 1910
Calley, Malcolm, *God's People,* Oxford University Press, 1965
Cardwell, Edward, *Documentary Annals of the Church of England,* Oxford University Press, 1844

Carey, Brycchan and Peter Kitson (eds.), *Slavery and the Cultures of Abolition*, English Association, Woodbridge, 2007
Causton, Bernard, *The Moral Blitz,* Secker & Warburg, 1941
Cheney, C.R. & Mary G. (eds.), *The Letters of Pope Innocent III,* Clarendon Press, 1967
Chesterfield, Lord, *Letters to His Son,* Oxford University Press, World's Classics, 2008
Churchill, Winston S., *The World Crisis,* Thornton Butterworth, 1923-31
— *A History of the English-Speaking People,* Cassell, 1956
Clarke, John, *The Life and Times of George III,* Weidenfeld and Nicolson, 1972
Clements, Ben, *Surveying Christian Beliefs,* Palgrave MacMillan, 2016
Collingwood, R.G. and Myers, J.N.L., *Roman Britain and the English Settlements,* O.H.E., 1945
Collinson, Patrick, *The Reformation,* Phoenix Books, 2005
Cottret, B.J., *The Huguenots in England,* Cambridge University Press, 1991
Cowper, Mary, Countess, *Diary,* John Murray, 1864
Cowper, William, *The Works, 1765-1735,* Fraser & Co., 1835
Dangerfield, George, *The Strange Death of Liberal England,* MacGibbon & Kee, 1966
D'Arblay, Fanny, *Diaries and Letters,* Routledge, 1931
Davies, Charles, *Unorthodox London,* Tinsley Brothers, 1875
Davies, Godfrey, *The Early Stuarts, 1603-1660,* O.H.E., 1937
Davies, Rupert, *What Methodists Believe,* A.R. Mowbray, 1976
— *Methodism,* Wipf and Stock, 2017
D'Bloissiers Tovey, *Anglia Judaica,* Weidenfeld & Nicolson (1738), 1999
Defoe, Daniel, *A Tour through the Whole Islands of Great Britain,* Penguin Books, 1871
Dekker, Thomas, *The Plague Pamphlets,* ed. F.P. Wilson, Clarendon Press, 1925
De la Bédoyère, Guy, *Gods with Thunderbolts – Religion in Roman Britain,* Tempus, 2002
Dickens, A.G., *The English Reformation,* Collins, The Fontana Library, 1970
Dickens, Charles, *Barnaby Rudge,* Penguin Classics, 1998
Eliot, T.S., 'Thoughts after Lambeth', in *Selected Essays*, Faber and Faber, 1976
Elton, G.R., *England Under the Tudors,* Methuen & Co., 1971
Ensor, Robert, *England 1870-1914,* O.H.E., 1975
Evelyn, John, *Diary,* Everyman Edition, 1945
Feiling, Keith, *A History of England,* MacMillan, 1966
Fiennes, Celia, *The Journeys of Celia Fiennes* (ed. Christopher Morris), The Cresset Press, 1949
Finberg, H.P.R., *The Formation of England, 550-1042,* Paladin, 1976
Fitzroy, Almeric, *Memoirs,* George H. Doran, 1925
Fitzstephen, William, *A Description of London,* translated by H.E. Butler, in F.M. Stenton, *Norman London, An Essay,* The Historical Association, 1934
Forester, Thomas (ed.), *The Chronicle of Florence of Worcester,* Bohn, 1894
Forrest, Ian, *Detection of Heresy,* Clarendon Press, 2005
Fraser, Antonia, *The Gunpowder Plot,* Weidenfeld and Nicolson, 1996
Fuller, Thomas, *A Church History of Britain*, Oxford University Press, 1845
Fryer, Peter, *Staying Power: The History of Black People in Britain,* Pluto Press, 1984
Gairdner, James (ed.), *The Paston Letters,* Alan Sutton, 1986
Garcia, Humberto, *Islam and the English Enlightenment*, John Hopkins University Press, 2011
Gartner, Lloyd P., *The Jewish Immigrant in England 1870-1914,* Simon Publications, 1973

George, Dorothy, *London Life in the Eighteenth Century*, Penguin Books, 1966
Gerzina, Gretchen, *Black England*, John Murray, 1995
Gilbert, Martin, *The First World War*, Harper Collins, 1995
Gildas, *De Excidio et Conquestu Britannica* (ed. Hugh Williams) Dodo Press, 2010
Giles, J., *Roger of Wendover's Flowers of History*, Henry Bohn, 1845
Gilley, Sheridan and W.J. Sheils (eds.), *The History of Religion in Britain*, Wiley-Blackwell, 1994
Gilliatt-Ray, S., *Muslims in Britain*, Cambridge University Press, 2010
Gillingham, John, *The Early Middle Ages 1066-1290*, O.I.H.E., Oxford University Press, 1980
Gilmour, Ian, *Riot, Risings and Revolution*, Hutchinson, 1992
Glendinning, Victoria, *Leonard Woolf, A Biography*, Simon & Schuster, 2006
Gombrich, Richard F., *How Buddhism Began*, Athlone Press, 1996
Gomme, Laurence, *The Making of London*, Clarendon Press, 1912
Greenway, Diana (ed.), Henry, Archdeacon of Huntingdon, *Historia Anglorum*, Clarendon Press, 1996
Halle, Edward, *Chronicle; containing the History of England*, J. Johnson, 1809
Hastings, Adrian, *A History of English Christianity 1920-1985*, Collins, 1986
Haydon, Colin, *Anti-Catholicism in 19th Century England*, Manchester University Press, 1993
Henig, Martin, *Religion in Roman Britain*, Batsford, 1984
Henry, Philip, *Diary and Letters* (ed. Matthew Lee), Kegan Paul, Trench & Co., 1882
Hervé, Picton, *A Short History of the Church of England*, Cambridge Scholars Publishing, 2015
Hervey, Lord, *Memoirs of the Reign of George II*, John Murray, 1848
Hibbert, Christopher, *King Mob*, World Publishing Co., 1958
Hill, Christopher, *The World turned Upside Down*, Penguin Books, 1985
— *The Century of Revolution,1603-1714*, Sphere Books Ltd., 1975
— *Society and Puritanism in Pre-Revolutionary England*, Secker & Warburg, 1964
Hill, Christopher; Reay, Barry; Lamont, William, *The World of the Muggletonians*, Temple Smith, 1983
Holinshed, Raphael, *Chronicles*, Clarendon Press, 1923
Hopkinson, M.R., *Anne of England*, Constable & Co., 1934
Humphreys, Christmas, *The Development of Buddhism in England*, The Buddhist Lodge, 1937
Inwood, S., *A History of London*, Basic Books, 1999
Jacobs, Joseph, *The Jews of Angevin England*, David Nutt, 1893
James, M.R. (ed.), *Henry VI – A Reprint of John Blacman's Memoir*, Cambridge University Press, 1919
Jenkyns, R., *Westminster Abbey*, Profile Books, 2004
Jones, Gwyn, *A History of the Vikings*, Oxford University Press, 1968
Julius, Anthony, *Trials of the Diaspora: A History of Anti-Semitism in England*, Oxford University Press, 2010
Katz, David, *The Jews in the History of England, 1485-1850*, Clarendon Press, 1994
Kenyon, John, *The Stuart Constitution 1603-1688*, Cambridge University Press, 1986
— *The Popish Plot*, Pelican Books, 1974
— *The Stuarts*, B.T. Batsford, 1958
Kent, John, *William Temple*, Cambridge University Press, 1992

Kingsford, C.L. (ed.), *Chronicles of London*, Clarendon Press, Oxford
Kriegel, Abraham (ed.), *The Holland House Diaries 1831-1840*, Routledge & Kegan Paul, 1977
Lackington, James, *Memoirs of the First Forty-five Years of the Life of James Lackington*, 1791
Lahey, Stephen, *Wyclif*, Oxford University Press, 2009
Langham, Mark, *Westminster Cathedral* (rev. Patrick Rogers), Hudson's Heritage Group, 2011
Lawson, Tom, *The Church of England and the Holocaust*, Boydell Press, 2006
Le Huray, *Music and the Reformation in England, 1549-1660*, Herbert Jenkins, 1967
Leys, M.D.R., *Catholics in England*, Longmans, 1961
Lindley, Keith, *Popular Politics and Religion in Civil War London*, Scolar Press, 1997
Liu, Tai, *Puritan London*, University of Delaware Press, 1986
Lockhart, J.G., *Cosmo Gordon Lang*, Hodder & Stoughton, 1949
Lorimer, Douglas A., *Colour, Class and the Victorians*, Leicester University Press, 1978
Losh, James, *Diaries*, The Surtees Society, 1963
Luther, Martin, *Of the Jews and Their Lies*, Christian Nationalist Crusade, 1948
Mahomet, Deen, *The Travels of Dean Mahomet*, (ed. Michael H. Fisher), University of California Press, 1997
Marshall, Dorothy, *English People in the Eighteenth Century*, Longmans, Green, 1956
Mason, Emma, *Westminster Abbey and its People*, Boydell Press, 1996
McFarlane, K.B., *Wycliffe and English Non-Conformity*, Pelican Books, 1972
Merrifield, Ralph, *Roman London*, Cassell, 1969
— *London, City of the Romans*, Batsford, 1983
Morison, Arthur, *A Child of the Jago*, Oxford World Classics, 2012
Morris, R.M. (ed.), *Church and State in 21st Century Britain*, Palgrave MacMillan, 2009
Newman, John Henry, *Fifteen Sermons Preached Before the University of Oxford*, Oxford University Press, 2006
— *Apologia Pro Vita Sua*, World's Classics, Oxford University Press, 1964
Nicolson, Harold, *Diaries and Letters, 1930-1964*, Collins, 1980
Norman, E.R., *Church and Society in England 1770-1970*, Oxford University Press, 1976
Nuttall, Geoffrey F., Chadwick, Owen (Eds.), *From Uniformity to Unity, 1662-1962*, S.P.C.K., 1962
Paris, Matthew, *English History: 1235-1273*, translated by J.A. Giles, Bohn, 1852
Parkes, James, *A History of the Jewish People*, Weidenfeld & Nicolson, 1962
— *Judaism and Christianity*, Victor Gollancz, 1948
— *The Jew in the Medieval Community*, The Soncino Press, 1938
Paxman, Jeremy, *The English*, Penguin Books, 2007
Peel, C.S., *How We Lived Then*, John Lane, 1929
Penn, Thomas, *The Winter King – The Dawn of Tudor England*, Penguin Books, 2011
Petts, David, *Christianity in Roman Britain*, Tempus, 2003
Pevsner, Nikolaus, *The Buildings of England*, Penguin Books, 1957
Phayer, Michael, *The Catholic Church and the Holocaust 1930-65*, Indiana University Press, 2000
Picard, Liza, *Elizabeth's London*, Weidenfeld & Nicolson, 2003
— *Victorian London*, Weidenfeld & Nicolson, 2005
Plumb, J.H., *The Four Georges*, Fontana/Collins, 1956
— *England in the Eighteenth Century*, Penguin Books, 1950
Pocock, John, *Diary of a London Schoolboy*, Historical Publications, 1996

Porter, Roy, *A Social History of London*, Hamish Hamilton, 1994

Porter, Stephen, (ed.), *London and the Civil War*, MacMillan, 1996

Potter, K.R. (ed.), *Gesta Stephani*, Oxford University Press, 1976

Price, Huw, 'The Christianisation of Society', in Davies, Wendy (ed.) *From the Vikings to the Normans*, The Short Oxford History of the British Isles, Oxford University Press, 2003

Raine, Kathleen, *India Seen Afar*, Green Books, 1990

Rasmussen, Steen Eiler, *London: The Unique City*, Jonathan Cape, 1937

Reresby, John, *Memoirs*, Royal Historical Society, 1991

Rhondda, Lady, *This Was My World*, MacMillan, 1933

Rocker, Rudolf, *The London Years*, Five Leaves Publications, 2005

Ross, Charles, *Edward IV*, Eyre Methuen, 1974

Roth, Cecil, *A History of the Jews in England*, Oxford University Press, 1942

Rowse, A.L., *The England of Elizabeth – The Structure of Society*, McMillan & Co., 1951

Rubinstein, William, *The Myth of Rescue*, Routledge, 1997

Rubinstein, William and Hilary, *Philosemitism: Admiration and Support in the English-Speaking World for Jews, 1840-1939*, St Martins Press, 1999

Russell, Bertrand, *Mysticism and Logic*, Penguin Books, 1953

Rupp, E. Gordon, *Religion in England*, Clarendon Press, 1986

Saint, Andrew and Gillian Darley, *Chronicles of London*, Weidenfeld and Nicolson, 1994

Saleem, Shahed, *The British Mosque, An Architectural and Social History*, English Heritage, 2017

Scarisbrick, J.J., *Henry VIII*, Penguin Books, 1971

Seed, John, *Dissenting Histories: Religious Division and the Politics of Memory*, Edinburgh University Press, 2008

Shackle, Christopher, *The Sikh Religion, Culture and Ethnicity*, Curzon, 2001

Shyllon, F.O., *Black Slaves in Britain*, Oxford University Press for the Institute of Race Relations, 1974

Simpson, W. Sparrow, *Documents Illustrating the History of St Paul's Cathedral*, Camden Society, 1880

Stenton, F.M., *Norman London, An Essay*, Published for the Historical Association by G. Bell and Sons, 1934

Stow, John, *A Survey of London*, The History Press, 2009

Summers, W.H., *Memories of Jordans and the Chalfonts*, Headley Brothers, 1904

Tacitus, *The Agricola*, Cambridge University Press, 2014

Taylor, A.J. P., *English History, 1914-1945*, O.H.E., 1965

Thomas, Keith, *Religion and the Decline of Magic*, Weidenfeld & Nicolson, 1971

Thompson, E.P., *The Making of the English Working Class*, Pelican Books, 1972

Thomson, John A.F., *The Later Lollards*, Oxford Historical Series, 1967

Thorp, Malcolm R., 'Sectarian Violence in Early Victorian Britain: The Mormon Experience, 1837-1860', *Bulletin of the John Rylands University Library of Manchester*, 70, Autumn, 1988

Tomkins, Stephen, *The Clapham Sect*, Lion Books, 2012

Trevor-Roper, Hugh, *Catholics, Anglicans and Puritans*, Secker & Warburg, 1987

Tristan, Flora, *London Journal*, George Prior, 1980

Venetian State Papers, Calendar of State Papers Venetian, 1202-1675

Vergil, Polydore, *Anglia Historica*, trans. Denys Hay, Royal Historical Society, 1950

Vidler, Alec R., *The Church in an Age of Revolution*, Penguin History of the Church, 1990

— *The Orb and the Cross,* S.P.C.K., 1945

Vince, Alan, *Saxon London: An Archaeological Investigation,* Seaby, 1990

Vincent, Thomas, *God's Terrible Voice in the City,* Soli Deo Gloria Ministries, 1997

Visram, Rozina, *Asians in Britain: 200 Years of History,* Pluto Press, 2002

Wallis, Russell, *Britain, Germany and the Road to the Holocaust,* I.B. Taurus, 2014

Walsh, P.G., Kennedy, M.J., *William of Newburgh – The History of English Affairs,* Aris and Phillips, 2007

Walsingham, Thomas, *The* Chronica Maiora *of Thomas Walsingham, II,* Taylor, John, Wendy R. Childs, Leslie Watkiss (eds.), Clarendon Press, Oxford, 2011

Walvin, James, *A Short History of Slavery,* Penguin Books, 2007

Warkworth, John, *A Chronicle of the First Thirteen years of the Reign of King Edward IV,* Camden Society, 1839

Warren, W.L., *King John,* Eyre and Spottiswood, 1964

Wesley, John, *The Journal,* Everyman Edition, 1948

Wheatley, Henry (ed.), *The Diary of Samuel Pepys,* J.M. Dent, 1968

Wheeler, R.E.M., *London and the Saxons,* London Museum, 1935

— *London in Roman Times,* London Museum Catalogue, No. 3, Lancaster House, 1920

Wilkinson, Alan, *The Church of England and the First World War,* S.P.C.K., 1978

— *Dissent or Conform,* Lutterworth Press, 2010

Winnington-Ingram, Arthur, *Fifty Years Work in London,* Longmans, 1940

Willson, David, *King James VI and I,* Jonathan Cape, 1956

Wilson, D., *Anglo-Saxon Paganism,* Routledge, 1992

Wolffe, Bertram, *Henry VI,* Eyre Methuen. 1981

Woodforde, James, *The Diary of a Country Parson, 1758-1802,* Oxford University Press, 1931

Woodward, E.L., *The Age of Reform, 1915-1870,* O.H.E., 1949

Woolf, Virginia, *Diaries* (ed. Anne Olivier Bell), Hogarth Press, 1978

Zangwill, Israel, *Children of the Ghetto,* Heinemann, 1893

Index